The Strong Arm of the Law

# The Strong Arm of the Law

## Armed and Public Order Policing

P. A. J. WADDINGTON

CLARENDON PRESS · OXFORD

1991

Oxford University Press, Walton Street, Oxford OX2 6DP
Oxford New York Toronto
Delhi Bombay Calcutta Madras Karachi
Petaling Jaya Singapore Hong Kong Tokyo
Nairobi Dar es Salaam Cape Town
Melbourne Auckland

and associated companies in
Berlin Ibadan

Oxford is a trade mark of Oxford University Press

Published in the United States
by Oxford University Press, New York

British Library Cataloguing in Publication Data
Waddington, P. A. J. (Peter A. J.)
The strong arm of the law: armed and public order policing.
1. Great Britain. Police
I. Title
363.20941
ISBN 0–19–827359–2

Library of Congress Cataloging in Publication Data
Waddington, P. A. J.
The strong arm of the law: armed and public-order policing / P. A. J. Waddington
p. cm.
Includes bibliographical references and index.
1. Police—Great Britain.   2. Firearms—Great Britain—Use in crime prevention.
3. Riot control—Great Britain.   I. Title.
HV8195.A3W33   1991      363.2'32—dc20      90–22671
ISBN 0–19–827359–2

Typeset by Pentacor PLC, High Wycombe, Bucks
Printed in Great Britain by
Biddles Ltd,
Guildford & King's Lynn

*For Bevan and Shelley*

# ACKNOWLEDGEMENTS

The research upon which this book is based was undertaken under the auspices of the Police Foundation, without whose help, support, and assistance it could not have been successfully completed.

This book addresses one of the most controversial and sensitive issues in modern policing—the use of force by what we have been traditionally proud to describe as our unarmed and non-aggressive police. The research has only been made possible by the fullest co-operation received from all ranks of the Metropolitan Police. I am, therefore, indebted to Sir Kenneth Newman, the Commissioner of the Metropolitan Police at the time the research commenced, and to Sir Peter Imbert, who was then Deputy Commissioner and has now succeeded Sir Kenneth, both of whom supported and encouraged the research from the beginning. Their willingness to grant complete access to hitherto confidential internal documentation, to allow me to interview serving police officers, and to permit my participation in training courses for armed officers and those engaged in riot control is ample testimony to their confidence in the Metropolitan Police.

I am particularly grateful to all members of the Force Firearms Unit, formerly known as D11 and now, following reorganization, known as PT17. All members of the unit welcomed me, and tolerated my inquiries with good humour and friendliness. My thanks go especially to Chief Superintendent Bob Wells for his courtesy and frankness, and also to his successor, Rick Johnson; also to Chief Inspector Mike Waldren for taking time to educate me in some of the technicalities of firearms and firearms tactics, and correcting an earlier draft of this book; and to all the instructors on the various courses in which I participated who treated me as just another trainee. I am equally grateful to my fellow trainees on those courses who treated me as one of them, despite the

fact that I would never have to face the dangers and dilemmas
that they might face.

I am equally indebted to all those involved in public-order
policing, especially those who work in the Public Order
Forward Planning Unit, New Scotland Yard, and the
instructors at the Public Order Training Centre, Hounslow.
I am particularly indebted to Commander Robinson for
allowing me such freedom, and to Chief Superintendents
Mike Shadrack, George Crawford, Ian Hurd, and Roger
Barr and Superintendent Syd McKay, for their time and
advice. I am equally grateful to Chief Inspector Peter Buck
and Inspector Peter Power for their help and assistance in
finding relevant documentary material. All the instructors at
'riot city' earned my thanks and repect, not least for
demonstrating just how many muscles can be made to ache
simultaneously! They, like their colleagues in PT17, accepted
my intrusions with good grace and humour, and for that I
am more than grateful. To the many ordinary police officers
whom I joined, huddled together behind shields, and to those
others who threw wooden blocks at me with no less force
than at anyone else, go my gratitude and the hope that they
will not face such a situation 'for real'.

Although this research concentrates upon policy and
training, it proved immensely valuable to have been allowed
to observe actual police public-order operations. I am,
therefore, most grateful to Deputy Assistant Commissioner
Douglas Cree for permitting me to observe the Gold control
room at Wood Green during the weekend following the
conviction of Winston Silcott and others for the murder of
PC Keith Blakelock. I am similarly grateful to Deputy
Assistant Commissioner Hunt for allowing me to observe
the policing operation on the occasion of a major reggae
concert on Clapham common in the summer of 1987. Most
of all, I am indebted to Assistant Commissioner Paul
Condon, who twice allowed me to observe the policing of
the Notting Hill Carnival and see anything I wished, from
the briefings for senior officers to rioting at close quarters. At
Clapham I accompanied Chief Superintendent George Crawford and at Notting Hill I twice spent two very long days
with Chief Superintendent Rod Havard. I must thank them

not only for willingly accepting the additional burden of my presence but for ensuring that I lived to tell the tale!

Writing this report has been a labour I have shared with others. I have already expressed my thanks to Mike Waldren for the technical assistance he gave me. My thanks also go to Professor Tony Smith and Peter Schofield, both of the Department of Law, and to Malcolm Hamilton and Ken Robertson, from the Department of Sociology, all at the University of Reading, and to Mollie Weatheritt, Deputy Director of the Police Foundation and Robert Reiner of the London School of Economics, for reading various sections of the manuscript and helping me translate my thoughts into English. I am particularly indebted to Peter Schofield who, as a pacificist, read this account of guns and rioting with repugnance, but was the more able, thereby, to challenge any ill-thought-out arguments. However, the prize for dedication, as well as staying power, must go to my wife, Diane, who read the entire manuscript whilst maintaining order in the Waddington household.

I would also like to thank the Police Foundation for permission to base much of the discussion in Chapters 3 and 4 and Appendix 1 on my interim report, *Arming an Unarmed Police*. I am also grateful to the Rt. Hon. Sir Leon Brittan for permission to quote from a letter written to Dr David Owen; also James Anderton, Chief Constable of the Greater Manchester Police, for permission to quote from his report of the 1981 riot in Moss Side. My thanks also go to Mike Hoare, for permission to reproduce a figure from his unpublished M.Sc. dissertation, 'The Pattern of Experience in the use of Firearms by Criminals and the Police Response'. I must thank the Policy Studies Institute for granting permission to quote a lengthy extract from volume iii of their report *Police and People in London*.

P.A.J.W.

*June 1990*

# CONTENTS

# PART I

# Police *Force*

# 1

# Introduction

The appearance of police officers openly and routinely carrying sub-machine-guns at international airports, or clad in protective clothing and carrying shields as they battle with rioters and violent pickets, has led to widespread public concern and anxiety. It seems that the traditional commitment of an unarmed police to the principle of 'minimum force' is threatened. It is feared that the British police may be abandoning their policy of 'policing by consent' in favour of an alien style of policing based upon coercion.

Yet, despite being highly controversial, these developments have gone without explanation or analysis. It is the purpose of this book to provide that analysis. But before we can begin to examine recent developments in the police use of firearms and the policing of public order, it is necessary to analyse the nature of the anxiety that these developments create. Why does the sight of a police officer carrying a sub-machine-gun or a riot-clad officer carrying a shield evoke such concern? What is it about our traditions that is threatened by these developments? A commonly heard answer to these questions is that these developments threaten the distinctive and valuable British police tradition of 'policing by consent'; however, this raises as many questions as it answers.

## 'Policing by Consent'

The extraordinary feature of routine police work is that public compliance is the norm. The police only rarely force anyone to do anything; usually they simply request, and their request is complied with. This extends even to those whom they arrest. One study of routine policing discovered that most arrests took place *within* the police station by *appoint-ment* (Waddington, 1985). Even in the case of large crowds, it is customary for a small number of unarmed, unprotected police to marshal much larger numbers.

This level of public compliance, which, though not unique, is a distinctive feature of British policing, has popularly been known as 'policing by consent'. Unlike the police of many other countries, it is often asserted, the British police do not need to be armed, nor must they present a formidable appearance, because the British public willingly complies and does not have to be coerced. In short, the British public *consent* to being policed.

Whilst this is a term which captures the extent of public compliance, it is also misleading. A much better description is that the police act with *legitimate authority*. A police officer may request that a demonstrator remain behind a crush barrier, but the demonstrator is not free to reject that request, for he[1] may find himself arrested and prosecuted if he does not do as he is told. The police may actually achieve the compliance of the public, but ultimately their task is to tell people what to do and, if they do not comply, to force them to do so. So what is it that distinguishes the police officer from the thug, who might also make people do what he tells them? What the police officer possesses, and the thug does not, is *authority*: the power he or she wields is recognized as *legitimate* by those who are subjected to it. The result is that people conform to the instructions of the police, whereas they are likely only to comply with those of a thug. The distinction between conformity and compliance is crucial to the issue of the police use of force, and deserves detailed exposition.

Wielding naked power involves the power-holder in inducing, threatening, or forcing others to bend to his will. Thus, a gunman might successfully direct traffic at a Beirut intersection, but only so long as the presence of his Kalashnikov intimidates motorists into complying. Deprived of the means of intimidation, the erstwhile gunman would be unable to secure compliance. Thus, the exercise of naked power involves the power-holder bringing pressure to bear upon others: power flows from the power-holder on to the subject.

A police officer exercising authority, for example, by directing traffic at an intersection, might achieve directly comparable results to that of the Beirut gunman, but does so by a fundamentally different process. The unarmed police officer cannot intimidate motorists into compliance, for they know that if only a few of them refuse to obey his directions, there is little, if anything, he can do. The police secure compliance, not because of the threats or inducements they can bring to bear, but because motorists accept the officer's *right* and *duty* to direct them. In other words, those who are subject to authority (in this case, motorists) believe they have a duty to obey. Thus, power is transformed into authority because it is believed to be legitimate by those subject to it.

Legitimate authority is, paradoxically, both a robust and a delicate form of power. It is robust because it is largely self-imposed by those subject to authority. Therefore, those in authority do not need continually to expend resources in inducing or compelling others to comply, so much so that authority can be exercised *in absentia*, for example, when police leave an unattended signboard announcing a diversion. Most motorists coming upon such a signboard will willingly conform, since they accept the right of the police to impose such a diversion and their obligation to obey, even though it will be for many of them an unenforceable imposition.

In so far as authority requires those who are subject to it to confer legitimacy upon those who exercise it, it may seem little different to the notion of 'policing by consent'. However, 'policing by authority' avoids the false impression given by 'policing by consent', one which is sometimes exploited by critics of the police, that compliance relies upon the police enforcing the law in accordance with popular wishes. Indeed, the opposite is true. The legitimacy of the police in Britain has been traditionally founded, not upon conformity to popular wishes, but upon impartiality. Critics may dispute the actual impartiality of the police, pointing to how they have consistently supported the *status quo* (Brogden *et al.*, 1988), but this is to miss the point. Whether valid or not, the British police have *claimed* to be impartial and that claim has been widely *accepted*, albeit 'grudgingly' amongst the lowest strata in society (Miller, 1977).

Whilst the notions of 'policing by consent' and 'policing by

authority' differ fundamentally over the issue of popularity
and impartiality, they overlap in two crucial respects: the
non-threatening character of the British police and the
revocability of legitimacy. Together, these pose the fundamental dilemma of police use of force.

## Policing with Acceptable Authority

Because the claim to legitimate authority has been so widely
accepted, the British police have traditionally been able to
secure compliance without resort to the use or threat of force
that is associated with other policing systems. Thus, whereas
the typical American 'cop' will patrol the streets of even the
quietest country town wearing a Sam Browne belt on which
conspicuously hangs a gun in a quick-draw holster, ammunition pouches, a canister of Mace gas, handcuffs, and a long
nightstick, all of which overtly display the coercive power
that underwrites his authority (Rubenstein, 1973), the British
police officer normally displays no weaponry at all. The
British 'bobby' does not need to display a formidable
appearance as a barely veiled threat, because his legitimate
authority ensures that compliance will be readily forthcoming.

The ability to secure compliance without the veiled threat
of the formidable appearance further strengthens the police
officer's authority, for he becomes a non-threatening figure.
The notion of policing by consent points to the fact that the
ordinary citizen need feel no fear of the police, since, devoid
of the means of imposing compliance by force, the police
officer cannot be a threat. Compliance must be willing and
based on an acceptance of police legitimacy, because it cannot
be anything else. Thus, the very vulnerability of the British
police has been turned to advantage, because it reinforces the
citizen's obligation to obey. The less of an intimidatory
presence the police are, the more they are respected, and the
more willing are citizens to comply with their directions.

Being vulnerable, the police have — both individually and
collectively — had to negotiate acceptability. Storch (1975)
has described how, in its infancy, the police needed to
negotiate a *modus vivendi* with working-class communities

virtually street by street. When it came to policing crowds, the assumption of full responsibility from the military meant that the lethal longstop was no longer available, and only a style of policing which was acceptable would prevent the police being overwhelmed. Geary (1985) has described how picketing was transformed throughout the first half of the twentieth century from 'stoning and shooting' to ritualized 'pushing and shoving' as both sides arrived at a mutually acceptable compromise. This is typified by the practice of police using their authority to stop vehicles entering strike-bound premises so that pickets could address the occupants.

Lacking coercive might, the police could not 'throw their weight about'. This bred respect rather than fear, and respect engendered compliance.

## Policing with Coercion

So long as police authority is accepted, the virtuous circle remains intact, but once legitimacy is denied, the police must rely upon naked power. The fact that few encounters between the British police and members of the public are confrontational does not mean that police authority goes totally unchallenged. When it does, the police are authorized by law to coerce compliance. Beneath the benign appearance of the British bobby lies the irreducible and world-wide reality that the police are ultimately a coercive force. It is this that creates the dilemma.

Section 3 of the Criminal Law Act 1967 allows anyone to use force for a lawful purpose.

A person may use such force as is reasonable in the circumstances for the prevention of crime, in effecting or assisting in the arrest of offenders or persons unlawfully at large.

Nevertheless, it is the police who have become specialists in the use of legitimate violence. Thus, the law expects the ordinary citizen to retreat from a threat before using force in self-defence (Ashworth, 1975; Harlow, 1974), whereas it is the duty of the police to enter threatening situations in anticipation of using force. Officials other than the police may be legally entitled to use force in specific conditions, but tend, nevertheless, to leave the exercise of coercion to the police. For example, police may accompany social workers to apprehend psychiatric patients in need of compulsory treatment and also bailiffs in the process of evicting trespassers. It is the police who have the authority to use force, and it is they who may ultimately be responsible for the use of lethal force. For example, it is virtually inconceivable that any other citizen could lawfully decide to shoot someone using a high-powered rifle with a telescopic sight as might a police officer acting as a sniper against an armed criminal or terrorist.

## Policing with Restraint

The second pillar of legitimate police authority in Britain is that force has been used with restraint. This is often described as the 'doctrine' or the 'principle' of 'minimum force'. But it is not a legal doctrine or principle, for the law imposes the apparently less rigorous criterion of what is 'reasonable in the circumstances' — a vague and, according to many legal commentators, an unsatisfactory criterion.[2] Yet, it is by the more rigorous standard of 'minimum force' that the police are commonly judged.

'Minimum force' simply means using no more force than is necessary to achieve a lawful purpose. Like the law itself, this principle relates the amount of force that can be used to the circumstances, and does not place any absolute restriction on how much force may be employed. If a person can be arrested by simply being asked to accompany the officer, there is no need for him to be grabbed and forcibly frog-marched to the police station. On the other hand, a rampaging gunman may justifiably be shot and killed by a police sniper if there is no less forceful alternative.

The police themselves recognize that public confidence in the police is achieved, not by conformity to the legal standard, but by their acting ostentatiously in accordance with the more demanding *moral* prescription of 'minimum force'. Hence the mistaken shooting of Stephen Waldorf (see pp. 19–21) was successfully defended in count as the use of 'reasonable force', but was widely condemned as a breach of the doctrine of 'minimum force'.

## Policing Criminals or Citizens

Whilst the principle of minimum force may permit quite extreme force to be used in particular circumstances, *any* use of force detracts from the benign, non-aggressive image that the British police have tried to cultivate. The underlying reality is laid bare — the police are, ultimately at least, a coercive force. This detracts from their authority, because, as Bittner (1970; 1975) has persuasively argued, public tolerance of violence has diminished over the recent past, and the association of the police with violence is itself contaminating. The sight of police officers fighting with others is likely to occasion the reaction that the police are little better than the hooligans they arrest. Since the role of the police as specialists in legitimate violence uniquely exposes them to involvement in violent encounters, they are also uniquely exposed to contamination.

This contamination is minimized, and legitimacy maintained, when the law is coercively enforced against those identified as criminals, for criminals are, by definition, outside the moral community. As Klockars (1985) has pointed out, the great advantage of defining the police mission as the prevention and detection of crime is that such a definition does not threaten those within the moral community of respectable society. The police can safely occupy the persona of the moral hero battling with the forces of evil.

Whereas the criminal can be presented as the 'bad guy' who deserves no better, this is often not the case in public-order policing, which frequently entails the police acting coercively against those who are, at least arguably, *within* the moral community. Denied the moral high ground, the police are obliged to use force (albeit usually only holding and pushing) against 'ordinary decent people'. At best, this can become a battle between moral equals; at worst, it raises the spectre of oppressive policing and the suppression, not of

crime, but of dissent. However, if the policing of public
disorder is undertaken by officers who are recognizably
'ordinary coppers', then these fears can by minimized
because of the positive association of these officers with the
'fight against crime'. The threat posed by the possession and
use of the paraphernalia of riot control is that the police are
no longer *recognizably* 'ordinary coppers', but become
likened to a different, and alien, breed of police—the riot
squad who are associated less with fighting crime and more
with brutal suppression of protest. As Reiner (1985a: 72) has
remarked: 'Dixon is out and Darth Vader is in, as far as riot
control goes.'

## Developments in Police Use of Force

The remaining chapters will be devoted to an examination of
these developments in armed policing and riot control. It will
not be solely a technical or tactical discussion, because, for
the reasons given above, policing is not simply an exercise in
instrumental rationality, it is symbolic as well. We will
return frequently to the dilemmas posed by the competing
demands of strategy, tactics, and technology on the one
hand and public acceptability on the other.

However, technical considerations—concerning weaponry and tactical deployments—cannot be avoided, nor
should they. This book has benefited from the unprecedented
access afforded by the Metropolitan Police to hitherto
confidential documents and other information; and a detailed
exposition is contained in the appendices. Appendix A
describes policy on armed operations, and Appendix B deals
with public order. Readers who wish to avoid reading the
technical detail may simply use these appendices as a
reference section.

Both appendices refer exclusively to the policy, weaponry,
and tactics of the Metropolitan Police. This is much less
limiting that might at first appear. First, most armed
operations and major public-order incidents take place within
the Metropolitan Police District. Second, because of the
demands that have been made upon them, the Metropolitan

Police have been at the forefront of development in policy, weaponry, and tactics. Amongst other innovations, they were the first to establish a dedicated firearms team (D11), and it was they who developed the long riot shield. Third, because the Home Office insists on common minimum standards in both armed and public order policing, what the Metropolitan Police do is very much the same as what is done in any other police force in England or Wales.

The main body of the text concentrates upon the issues that have arisen in connection with these two areas of policing. The text begins with a brief review of the recent history of developments in armed policing and riot control. Taking the mid-1960s as a convenient starting point, Chapter 2 will outline the path trodden by British policing. In Part II, attention will focus on the issues that have arisen from the organization of armed policing. Chapter 3 considers whether too many officers are authorized to carry firearms; whether selection and training is rigorous enough; and whether specialization is the answer. In Chapter 4, attention will shift to the weaponry and tactics employed in armed operations. Do the police shoot to kill, and is there any alternative? Are the police now armed to the teeth, or do they require yet more lethal weapons in their armoury?

Discussion then shifts, in Part III, from armed policing to riot control. Chapter 5 explores fears about the growing, and undoubted, paramilitarization of the police, and suggests that, although it does contain dangers, it also offers advantages. Chapter 6 discusses the problems — legal, tactical, and political — that arise from the police use of force in public-order policing. Chapter 7 discusses the overtly political aspects of public-order policing and the part played by the 'politics of explanation'. Part IV concludes by returning to the broad issues of the position of the police in society. The principal issues will be the contradiction between the *principle* and the *tradition* of using 'minimum force'.

# 2

# The Eclipse of 'Dixon of Dock Green'

## Introduction

In the 1950s and early 1960s there was considerable public pride in the British police. Geoffrey Gorer (1955) was able to report that the public viewed the constable as the epitome of the ideal citizen, and Michael Banton (1964) felt it necessary to justify research on the police as an institution despite the fact that it was working well. A particular cause for pride was that the British bobby could police the streets unarmed and without presenting an aggressive image. The popular stereotype of the British police was the avuncular figure of George Dixon in *Dixon of Dock Green*. This weekly television series presented a low-key image of policing: if criminals had to be arrested at all, this was achieved with no more force than a restraining hand and the command, 'You'd better come with me, m'lad'.

The intervening period has seen a significant transformation. The media's fictionalized police officer is the gun-toting member of some mythical specialist unit, like 'CI5' in the TV series *The Professionals*, whose members spend most of their time screeching around in cars and shooting it out with criminals and terrorists. Whilst no more fanciful figures in their own way than George Dixon, they do indicate a fundamental change in the image, if not the reality, of policing. The credibility of that image is reinforced by the increasingly common portrayal of actual police officers in the news media. When journalists wish to illustrate an article on policing, they now reach not for the library picture of a bobby in traditional uniform talking to a child, but the picture either of an officer at Heathrow Airport carrying what appears to be a machine-gun or of an officer wearing protective clothing baton-charging rioters. The modern British police officer has thus come to be equated on the one hand with his American armed cousin and on the other with his European paramilitary counterpart.

By what route have we travelled from *Dixon* to *The Professionals*? Essentially, there have been two paths which eventually and tragically converged in 1985. The one path has led the British police towards the increasing, and increasingly public, use of firearms. The second has led to a progressive paramilitarization of policing civil disorder. The first part of this chapter will describe how the British police have changed from a rarely to an occasionally armed force. The second part will describe the evolution of the riot control function.

## From Unarmed Bobby to Armed Cop

*The watershed*

It is always difficult to establish the existence of a historical watershed, but it seems clear that 1966 marked a fundamental change in the approach of the police to armed operations. Hitherto, official policy on armed policing was notable for its absence despite the fact that the Metropolitan Police has never been an entirely unarmed force. Firearms have always been available to police officers, and in 1883 permission was granted for officers on the outer divisions to carry revolvers during night duty (Gould and Waldren, 1986). Force policy was, however, consciously to minimize the force's preparedness for, and competence in, using firearms. Guns were resorted to only occasionally and the police gave low priority to training, relying instead upon the experience some officers had gained from their military service (Gould and Waldren, 1986; Hoare, 1980).

In the very rare cases where arms had to be used the British police showed an almost endearing incompetence and seemed quite proud of a total unfamiliarity with their weapons and sensible methods of dealing with such cases. (Greenwood, 1979: 1)

The assumption seemed to be that if the problem was ignored it would go away. Two events conspired to change all that.

In 1965 capital punishment was abolished for all categories of murder. Since 1957 capital punishment had been restricted to the murders of on-duty police and prison officers, murders committed in the furtherance of other crimes, and murders committed through the use of firearms or explosives. Now Parliament had decided to remove the special protection afforded to the police, and it was feared by opponents of that measure, which included most police officers, that criminals would have little reason not to kill police who sought to arrest them. Those fears apparently received almost immediate confirmation in August of the following year, when three unarmed detectives were callously gunned down as they tried to stop and question a gang of known criminals, led by Harry Roberts, who turned out to be armed (*The Times*, 13 August 1966). An unprecedented wave of revulsion at the callousness of the crime and sympathy for the police swept the nation. From the perspective of the police, it seemed that they were now entering a new era in which they would find themselves confronting armed and dangerous criminals far more frequently than they had in the past. Just lurking over the horizon, and about to make itself felt, was a threat of an altogether greater danger — terrorism. The rules of the game' looked as though they were about to change, and the police in the mid–1960s decided that they had better be prepared.

The amateur phase was about to end, and the safety of officers and the public would now depend on highly trained and disciplined men being able to act as a professional body. . . . The police would no longer be able to pay lip service to gun training, police firearms would be public knowledge, and their effective use would involve tactics which were alien to the British Bobby image. (Hoare, 1980: 72)

### Responding to the Armed Threat

The most concrete expression of that changed emphasis was the establishment of the Metropolitan Police Force Firearms

Unit, which subsequently became famous under its organizational designation 'D11'. D11 was to have a dual role: on the
one hand to train officers who needed to carry firearms, and
on the other to provide specialist armed support if it was
needed. By the 1970s certain special units and squads
contained many authorized firearms officers (AFOs) and, in
addition, approximately one in ten patrol officers was
similarly authorized. By 1972 the Home Office had issued
official 'guidance' (a euphemism for an instruction) on the
types of weapon and ammunition approved for police use.
There was now an official policy on police use of firearms.

This transformation remained largely invisible to the
public until 1972, when PC Peter Slimon (who was on armed
protection duty at a nearby embassy) walked into a bank in
Kensington, central London. What Slimon confronted in the
bank, however, were not terrorists but commonplace armed
bank robbers, who had already shot a foreign tourist in the
legs because of his failure to comply quickly enough with
their demands. The ensuing exchange of shots left Slimon
seriously wounded from a shotgun blast and two robbers
shot and wounded, one of whom was subsequently found
after having bled to death from his wounds (*The Times*, 28
December 1972).

PC Slimon was regarded, not as an armed aggressor, but
as the victim of armed crime, and received much public
sympathy as a result. As the decade progressed, he was to be
joined by another armed protection officer who would also
show considerable courage before falling victim to an armed
criminal. In 1974 Princess Anne and her husband, Captain
Mark Phillips, were returning from an official engagement.
As they drove down the Mall towards Buckingham Palace in
her official limousine, the Princess was attacked by a
deranged man, Ian Ball, attempting to abduct her (*The
Times*, 21 March 1974). Her limousine was rammed by the
man's car and then her assailant leapt out, firing wildly from
two hand-guns. Her bodyguard, Inspector Beaton, was only
able to fire one shot before his weapon jammed and he was
shot three times, receiving severe injuries. Having shot
several passers-by who tried to intervene, the assailant was
eventually overpowered and arrested by unarmed police

officers attracted to the scene by the sound of gunfire. The assailant was eventually found to be unfit to plead by reason of insanity, and was committed to a secure psychiatric hospital (Gould and Waldren, 1986: 150–2).

In both of these incidents the police could properly be regarded as clearly fulfilling their duty. The public might lament the need for any police officer to have to be armed, but there was little basis for criticism of police action. However, criticism was notable for its absence in other incidents which, at least in retrospect, offered the opportunity for public controversy. Just a few months after Slimon's shoot-out with bank robbers in Kensington, members of the Special Patrol Group[1] responded to a reported hostage-taking at India House — the Indian embassy in London. India and Pakistan were then at war, and three Pakistani youths had invaded the embassy, two of them armed with what appeared to be pistols and the third with a sword. When the SPG officers arrived, and with the situation still fluid, two officers received authorization to draw weapons from the armoury box carried on board their vehicle and to enter the embassy. In the lobby they confronted the three youths and, seeing the pistols being used to subdue the hostages, the officers opened fire, killing two youths and capturing the third. Only then was it discovered that the pistols being used by the youths were replica weapons incapable of firing bullets (*The Times*, 21–5 February 1973). Whilst regrettable, the shooting at India House was regarded by public opinion as understandable. After all, the police officers were not to know that the pistols held by the two young would-be hostage-takers were replicas. The young men themselves had presumably intended that they should appear sufficiently authentic so as to convince their hostages. What public criticism there was directed itself towards the manufacture and importation of such replicas.

Nor was there much criticism when, later in that same decade, police shot and killed Michael Calvey during an attempted armed robbery of a supermarket which the police had staked out on the basis of a tip-off (*The Times*, 11 and 12 December 1978; Gould and Waldren, 1986: 172–3). Upon their arrival the robbers were challenged by an armed detective. As Calvey began to swing his loaded, double-barrelled, sawn-off shotgun towards the officer the detective fired, and Calvey was shot and killed. There was the potential for criticism, since Calvey had been hit in the back. However, public opinion accepted without demur the evidence of the pathologist which showed that Calvey had been in the act of turning towards the officer when he was fatally shot. The allegation made by Calvey's widow that her husband had been gratuitously slain received little serious attention.

Events in London could not be isolated from similar incidents occurring elsewhere involving armed police. Here, too, the police use of firearms occasioned regret rather than alarm. The killing of Paul Howe in 1979 by officers from the Essex Constabulary was one such instance. Police had sought to arrest Howe, a young man with a history of mental illness, but he took a hostage and hijacked a car at gunpoint and was chased for twelve hours as he sought to escape. During this time Howe fired several times at other road-users as well as at the pursuing police, but fortunately without hitting anyone. He vainly attempted to hijack a cargo ship, and eventually took several more hostages in the Castle public house in the quiet country village of Ramsey. Having released most of his hostages, and the remainder having escaped, Howe fired a fusillade towards surrounding police, injuring one officer. He then emerged and walked towards the police cordon, and as he walked around a vehicle behind which an armed officer was taking cover he was shot and killed. Public reaction was that this was a regrettable, but unavoidable, loss of a young life (*The Times*, 22 May 1979).

Much less regret was expressed at the killing of William Hughes, an escaped prisoner who, whilst on the run, murdered four members of the Moran family in Derbyshire, took Mrs Gill Moran hostage, and hijacked her car in an attempt to escape. Intercepted by police, Hughes threatened to kill Mrs Moran with an axe, but was shot dead by officers who were able to approach the car from the rear without being seen. The officer who shot Hughes and another who grappled with him as he died, preventing him striking his hostage with the axe, were treated as heroes (*The Times*, 28 April 1977).

From the vantage-point of the 1990s, what is striking about these and various other incidents occurring in the 1970s was the absence of any publicly expressed anxiety about the use of firearms by the police. The public trusted the British police to act with restraint in such circumstances. That reputation for restraint received dramatic vindication by the way in which two highly publicized sieges were handled by the Metropolitan Police during the mid–1970s. One siege was at the Spaghetti House restaurant, where a gang of robbers took hostages when their robbery attempt was interrupted by the arrival of the police (*The Times*, 29–30 September 1975). An even more spectacular siege was the containment of four IRA terrorists in a flat in Balcombe Street, in central London. The terrorist gang had been pursued into the apartment after falling into a police trap, and there they had taken a middle-aged couple hostage. For more than a week the terrorists and the hostages were surrounded, until they eventually surrendered to police in the glare of television lights. The police were widely commended for their patience (*The Times*, 7–13 December 1975).

Indeed, if there was criticism it was that the police showed an excessive disinclination to resort to force in such circumstances. The Iranian embassy siege in 1980 was ended by an assault by the SAS, but not until the terrorists had begun killing hostages. Some commentators wondered at the time whether that assault should have commenced earlier. However, this criticism was overshadowed by the heroism of an ordinary constable, PC Trevor Lock, who had been on guard at the embassy and was overpowered during the terrorist attack. The terrorists, obviously believing that no British police officer would be armed, did not bother to search him. So he retained his revolver, concealed beneath his uniform jacket, throughout his captivity. During the SAS assault he overpowered one of the terrorists and held him at gunpoint (*The Times*, 1–6 May 1980; Gould and Waldren, 1986: 179–81). When asked later, during the inquest into the deaths of the terrorists, why he had not killed the man, he replied that the police were trained to use minimum force to arrest, not to kill.

### The shooting of innocent people and the loss of trust

Although there had been mounting public concern regarding the use of firearms on the streets of London and other major cities, the police had succeeded in avoiding censure. However, the assumption, held by most articulate public opinion, that the British police were restrained in their use of force and would only use firearms as a last resort was to be seriously dented by two shooting incidents in which innocent people were the victims of police bullets. The first occurred in 1980 when, following a shooting and a chase, in which police were fired upon, a man took a pregnant girl, Gail Kinshen, hostage in a Birmingham council flat. As police began to deploy around the apartment, the man suddenly burst out of the flat into a darkened passage, firing at surrounding officers from a shotgun. The police returned fire, but instead of hitting the man, they struck Gail, whom the man was holding as a human shield but whom the police were unable to see in the darkness (*The Times*, 13 June 1980). She died shortly after from her injuries, and the man was eventually tried for her murder (*The Times*, 28 March 1981). However, the fact that it had been police bullets which had killed this unfortunate girl led to considerable public controversy, and to doubts being expressed about the professionalism of the officers involved.

The damage inflicted upon the reputation of the police by this incident was as nothing compared to the shooting of Stephen Waldorf, which was to mark a second watershed in the recent history of armed policing in Britain (*The Times*, 15–17 January 1983). The London Metropolitan Police had formed a special squad of detectives to search for the highly dangerous escaped criminal, David Martin. Martin had escaped from custody as he awaited trial for a series of armed robberies and for the callous shooting of a police officer. On the first occasion on which he had been arrested, he had pulled a gun and tried unsuccessfully to shoot one of the officers, DC Finch. In the struggle that followed Finch had been able to overpower Martin, but only after the latter had been shot by another officer. Even then Martin had not desisted: despite his injury, he attempted to draw a second concealed weapon and shoot Finch, who was now lying on top of him. Only after Finch struck him across the face with his service revolver was Martin finally subdued.

The highly resourceful Martin had escaped from custody during one of his periodic appearances in court for a remand hearing. A team of detectives, which included the same DC Finch who had struggled with Martin, was given the responsibility of recapturing him. Wire-tapping the telephone of Martin's girlfriend, the police overheard the couple arrange to meet and travel together to a location outside London. Martin's girlfriend and brother were followed and at the prearranged venue met a third man who bore a striking resemblance to the wanted man, and whom police assumed to be their quarry. The three then travelled together in a hired car towards the agreed destination. Slowed to a near-stop by the London rush-hour traffic, the officer in charge of the police squad ordered Finch, who was in a car following shortly behind the suspect vehicle, to walk along the footpath and check whether the passenger in the car was indeed Martin. As Finch approached the car, his apprehension at again confronting Martin grew, so in anticipation he drew his service revolver. Looking into the car, he perceived Martin's distinctive features. The passenger made a sudden move. Finch, fearing that Martin had recognized him from their previous encounter and was reaching for a gun, panicked and opened fire. Other pursuing officers, hearing what sounded like a gun-fight, rushed to their colleague's assistance. They too opened fire at the passenger. A total of fifteen shots were fired, eight of which hit the man who now lay sprawled half in and half out of the car; but he was not dead. Knowing Martin's capacity to continue fighting, Finch ran forward and hit the man on the head with the butt of his gun, fracturing the man's skull. It was, alas, only then that the awful truth dawned — the man was not Martin, but

Stephen Waldorf, a freelance television producer who had a marked physical resemblance to Martin (Gould and Waldren, 1986: 187–8).

As surgeons miraculously repaired the damage done to Waldorf's body, the Metropolitan Police were surveying the damage that had been done to their reputation for restraint. Officers had shot and severely wounded the wrong man, a man who could not have actually posed any danger to the police because he was unarmed at the time. Eventually, Finch and another officer who had joined in the shooting, DC Jardine, were charged with the attempted murder of Stephen Waldorf, as well as a series of lesser charges. The jury acquitted the two men on all counts after a trial lasting over a week. The jury concluded that officers had made a tragic mistake, but held that they had not acted 'unreasonably' given the circumstances (*The Times*, 13–20 October 1983).

If the individual officers concerned were found 'not guilty', the same could not be said the of Metropolitan Police, whose procedures and practices had been revealed in a very poor light. These events merely served to confirm Greenwood's prophetic remarks:

In no field is the price of incompetence so high as in armed operations. . . . No subsequent action, no recriminations and no compensation can bring to life the innocent citizen or the police officer needlessly killed. Nothing will destroy confidence in the police more thoroughly than the apparently ill trained and ill disciplined policeman who kills or maims the innocent or who, through his incompetence, fails to protect the public from a dangerous offender. (Greenwood, 1979: 3)

The official response to the tragedy was to set up a working party, under Assistant Commissioner Geoffrey Dear, fundamentally to review firearms policy and practices. The numbers of officers authorized to carry firearms was reduced, the length of training was increased, and the rank of those able to authorize the use of firearms raised. The police were forcefully reminded by the public outcry that it was regarded as preferable that a gunman should escape than that innocent people should be placed at risk of being shot by the police (Gould and Waldren, 1986: 189–91).

*A new scepticism*

What changed most profoundly, perhaps, was the public's trust in the police to use firearms responsibly. A new scepticism amongst articulate opinion was now less prepared to accept the police version of events. The police had lost the presumption of innocence that the public had hitherto granted them, and now all their actions were to be subjected to much greater critical appraisal. Incidents which would previously have gone unremarked now initiated critical scrutiny from the media and public commentators. Had Gail Kinshen and Stephen Waldorf remained the only innocent victims of police bullets, it is possible that scepticism would have declined with the passage of time. Unfortunately, they were not to be the last victims. In Birmingham in 1985, armed officers searching a house following the arrest of an armed robber shot and killed the man's five-year-old son, John Shorthouse, when he suddenly jumped from his bed and startled the officer (*The Times*, 25–7 August 1985). In London, only a few weeks later, armed officers, again searching for a suspected armed robber, shot and severely wounded his mother, Mrs Cherry Groce, leaving her permanently disabled (*The Times*, 29–31 September 1985).

Again, the officers responsible for these shootings, PC Chester and Inspector Lovelock, were tried for manslaughter and malicious wounding respectively, but acquitted of all charges. The official response, contained in the ACPO working party report of 1986, was once again to limit further the number of officers permitted to carry firearms, to place even greater reliance on dedicated, specialized firearms teams, and to show yet greater caution in authorizing armed operations. These measures, however, could not restore the reputation for restraint which the police had earlier enjoyed.

The mistaken shootings of Stephen Waldorf and Cherry Groce and the accidental killings of Gail Kinshen and John Shorthouse fundamentally transformed the public response to armed operations, especially where shots were fired. Circumstances which in the past would have been regarded as regrettable but understandable now began to realize their full potential for controversy. Thus, following a two-day siege of a van in Philbeach Gardens in which the escaped murderer, James Baigrie, had sought refuge, the fugitive shot and killed himself after police fired CS gas into the van in an effort to force his surrender (*The Times*, 22 October 1983). The outcry that followed was led by the then Opposition Home Affairs spokesman, Clive Soley, who demanded to know why the police had not waited longer (Gould and Waldren, 1986: 196–9). Criticism was equally strident after two robbers were confronted in a North London post office in 1984 and shot as they reached into the bags they were carrying (*The Times*, 15 June 1984): the police belief that the bags contained guns (when, in fact, they did not) was regarded much more sceptically than had earlier incidents in which officers had made erroneous, split-second decisions.

Whereas the public had previously been prepared to accept that a police officer could not know whether the gun his adversary was holding was real or a replica (as at India House), or was loaded or unloaded, such tolerance was no longer offered. When the robber, Denis Bergin, was shot and killed as he burst into Sir John Soane's Museum in central London, wielding a unloaded shotgun presumably with the purpose of intimidating his victims (*Sunday Times*, 8 February 1987), there was chorus of criticism. Earlier that same year, at a road-block in a quiet Somerset lane, Glyn Davies approached armed police officers who were preventing him from continuing in his attempt to obtain custody of his daughter by holding her at gunpoint; he not only ignored warnings to stop and lay down his weapon, but pumped the loading mechanism of his shotgun as if making ready to fire. Ten yards from the road-block he was shot dead; but he was found to have expended his ammunition when firing earlier at pursuing police (*The Times*, 23 November 1987). In both cases, the fact that the firearms used by the deceased were unloaded at the time they were shot aroused public anxiety. Strangely, criticism was most acute in the case of the museum robbery: for example, Frank Dobson MP, an Opposition front-bench spokesman, was reported as saying, 'I am shocked. We need an immediate independent inquiry. Police are loafing around with guns far too much'; and a policy adviser to the Association of London Authorities remarked, 'Arming gun-crazy cops and telling them to shoot on sight is no solution in a democratic society' (*Sunday Mirror*, 8 February 1987). The inquest jury returned an open verdict.

Even when robbers are caught with loaded firearms which they are clearly prepared to use, controversy is not extinguished. Two armed robbers were shot dead and a third wounded when police intercepted an attempted robbery on an armoured security van outside an abattoir in Plumstead, East London, in July 1987. Challenged by a PT17 tactical firearms team to lay down their weapons, one robber threatened the driver of the security van and the other two levelled their guns at the policeman, who shot all three (*The Times*, 10 July 1987). Comparing the museum and abattoir shootings, a national newspaper commented at the time: 'In both cases, police had staked out a robbery target. In both cases, the robbers were armed. In both cases, so far as is known, police procedures were followed. But, in both cases too, it was only the police who fired, not the robbers'. The editorial concluded: 'It does look as though . . . the police are more prepared to carry the fight to the criminals than they used to be. It may not actually be a shoot-to-kill policy — such a thing would be illegal — but it may look like one to the professional armed robbers' (*Guardian*, 10 July 1987).

Given these comments, it might seem that, if adherence to proper procedures does not ensure that public anxiety is quelled, then allowing the suspects to open fire first might do so. In fact, the tide of public concern is no longer stemmed even in these apparently straightforward circumstances. Thus, John Cartwright MP demanded a public inquiry into the shooting of armed robbers in his Woolwich constituency (*Daily Telegraph*, 24 November 1987) when, surrounded by a tactical firearms unit and challenged to lay down their weapons, one of the robbers opened fire, hitting the Inspector in charge of the firearms team in the leg. The return fire from the police killed one of the three robbers, Anthony Ash, and wounded a second. Considerable attention was given by the news media to a witnesses description of the police being lined up 'like a firing squad' (see *Daily Mirror*, 24 November 1987).

*Protecting the public and the Hungerford massacre*

A different, but no less damaging, kind of scepticism was aroused by two incidents that occurred in the mid–1980s. The first took place throughout the 1985 Christmas holiday period, at Northolt, London. Errol Walker was besieged in a block of flats, having killed the friend of his estranged wife, and then taking the victim's child, Carlene, hostage at knife-point. A protracted siege came to an unplanned end when a PT17 officer, seeing Walker alone on the balcony, tried to prevent him from returning to the flat in which his hostage was being held captive. Unfortunately he failed, but this precipitated an immediate assault on the flat, using distraction devices. As police entered they found Walker in the act of stabbing his four-year-old hostage and he was shot — the first person to be shot by PT17 officers in the nearly twenty years that the unit had been in existence (*The Times*, 2–4 January 1986). What caused concern was that these highly trained, specialized officers were seen to be acting with less than consummate expertise.

Concern about the ability of the police to protect innocent citizens from homicidal criminals was to reach a crescendo in the horror and outrage prompted by the Hungerford massacre, when Michael Ryan randomly killed sixteen people in a quiet country town. For reasons that will remain the object of speculation, Michael Ryan shot dead a young mother as she picnicked with her two young children in nearby Savernake Forest. As he then drove towards Hungerford he robbed a petrol station and fired more shots, fortunately hitting no one. When he returned to Hungerford he proceeded to shoot randomly at anyone who came into view. By the end of the day, after he had been cornered by armed police in a local school and eventually committed suicide, sixteen innocent people lay dead. It was the worst incident of its kind in British criminal history (*The Times*, 20 August 1987).

How had it been allowed to happen? Why had armed police not responded more quickly? Why had they not cornered and, if necessary, killed Ryan earlier? Why had they allowed Ryan to kill so many innocent people? Was this, as one television programme was to allege, 'a basic failure of the police' (Edwards, 1988)? The coroner dismissed these criticisms by explaining that this was the cost of having a largely unarmed police force. Nevertheless, the criticism served to confirm the second part of Greenwood's prophecy. For he had warned of the consequences, not only of the police shooting the innocent, but also of their failure 'to protect the public from a dangerous offender' (Greenwood, 1979: 3).

*Police firearms policy*

It has not only been shooting incidents that have aroused public anxiety; so too has general police firearms policy. The decision to equip bodyguards with the Heckler and Koch MP5K sub-machine-gun, in anticipation of the summit of Western leaders in 1984, had caused a furore, with the Labour Opposition demanding that these weapons be withdrawn (Gould and Waldren, 1986: 192–3).

However, anxieties were aroused even more conspicuously by the decision overtly to arm uniform police at London's Heathrow airport in 1986. This decision followed attacks by Palestinian terrorists on airports in Rome and Vienna, where they had killed a large number of passengers waiting at the El Al check-in points. However, it represented a fundamental break with tradition, for hitherto even armed uniformed officers had been required to carry their weapons covertly. The sight of British police officers carrying a sub-machine-gun type of weapon seemed to many to be the final abandonment of their unarmed image. Nor was this controversy limited to critics outside the police. When the Police Federation's magazine, *Police*, contained a cover photograph of divisional riflemen posing with their rifles, it prompted a police officer to write:

I cannot help saying in the first instance, after 30 years public service, how disappointed and dejected I feel. This is not what the public wants to see and indeed, not what the public should see, although I accept the necessity, from time to time, to be prepared for such armed conflicts. All you have done is display our organization in such an abhorrent 'macho' image, that such weaponry would only be matched by counter-weaponry.

What seems to have concerned people is that, having abandoned the cautious 'amateurism' of the previous era, the British police had apparently adopted the aggressive approach more commonly associated with American and Continental styles of policing.

An incident in January 1987 highlighted another form of armed deployment arousing public anxiety (*The Times*, 30 January 1987). Two men were pursued south along the M1 by officers from the Nottinghamshire Constabulary. When they were eventually halted between junctions 12 and 13 in Northamptonshire, they fired at the police who had stopped them. However, the police were quickly able to return fire because theirs was an 'armed-response vehicle', in which firearms were routinely carried and available for use on the authority of an assistant chief constable. The public discussion that this incident prompted revealed that Nottinghamshire were not alone in deploying such vehicles. The Home Office Working Group received evidence that two other forces — West Yorkshire and Hampshire — had such a policy (Home Office, 1986*a*). The Metropolitan Police acknowledged that they too had an armed-response vehicle, manned by members of the Royalty and Diplomatic Protection Department, whose officers protect sensitive locations such as embassies, and people at risk of assassination or attack, such as Ministers of the Crown.

In fact, there is nothing new in this kind of deployment, especially in London (Roberts, 1973). It was officers from such a vehicle, then the responsibility of the Special Patrol Group, who responded to the hostage-taking at India House in 1972, where they entered and shot dead two youths. In 1977 this responsibility was transferred from the SPG to the Diplomatic Protection Group (as it was then known) and assigned to a vehicle with the call sign 'Ranger 500'. Although dedicated to diplomatic protection — it was one of the first vehicles to respond to the shooting outside the Libyan Peoples' Bureau in which WPC Yvonne Fletcher was killed (*The Times*, 18 April 1984) — the officers who man this vehicle are still police officers and can be deployed to armed incidents occurring within the central London area (see reply to Mr Blom-Cooper, Home Office, 1986*a*). It should be remembered that PC Peter Slimon was an armed protection officer *en route* to an embassy in January 1972 when he encountered armed robbers, one of whom he shot dead.


## From 'Bobbies on the Beat' to 'Riot Police'

*Convergent trends: the shooting of Cherry Groce and the Brixton riot*

The shooting of Mrs Groce in 1985 was to represent the final convergence of two trends which had progressively undermined the image of the unarmed, benign 'bobby' in the eyes of articulate public opinion. Following that shooting, widespread rioting erupted in the Brixton area of London in which she lived. During that riot two people were killed and, not for the first time, the public saw on their television screens the image that has come to parallel that of the 'armed cop' — riot police equipped with crash helmets and visors, wearing flameproof overalls, carrying shields, clashing with rioters.

Compared to the development of armed policing, the origins of this parallel development are more difficult to specify, for the Metropolitan Police have long found it part of their duty to subdue the riotous behaviour of their fellow citizens. Indeed, one of the main reasons for the introduction of the 'New Police' by Sir Robert Peel in 1829 was in order to control the mob without recourse to the army (Critchley, 1970). By the mid–1960s it seemed that public protest was a genteel affair, typified by members of CND staging sit-down demonstrations in Trafalgar Square, prompting the police simply to lift protesters bodily into waiting vehicles for transportation to the police station. There seemed no need even to retain the Riot Act on the statute-book, and in 1967 it was repealed.

Whether it was a mere coincidence that the repeal of the Riot Act was followed by an upturn in violent mass disorder (Smith, 1987), or whether the participants in such disorder were following a pattern established elsewhere in the world, by the end of that decade styles of protest became decidedly less genteel (Clutterbuck, 1980). The fashion for 'direct action' by students pressing their demands upon university administrators led to a series of more or less violent confrontations with the police on both sides of the Atlantic. In America, the campus riots in protest at American involvement in the Vietnam War reached a climax during the 1968 Democratic Party Convention in Chicago, where protesters clashed with baton-wielding police (Walker, 1968). On the Continent, too, student protesters clashed violently with police in West Berlin and, most notably, in Paris during the summer of 1968 (Hanley and Kerr, 1989). In Britain, 1968 was also to witness a significant departure from the genteel style of public protest. Outside the American embassy in May and October that year, over 10,000 protesters gathered to denounce American involvement in the Vietnam War, amid scenes of what were regarded as unprecedented violence (*The Times*, 31 May and 23 October 1968). This was followed in 1970 by the campaign to sever sporting links with South Africa and the violent disruption of the Springbok rugby tour (*The Times*, 22 May 1970; Clutterbuck, 1980). Even pop festivals came to be associated with disorder which reached its climax at Windsor in 1974, when police attempted to prevent an illegal concert being held in the Great Park amid scenes of considerable violence (*The Times*, 30 August 1974).

Another manifestion of Britain's 'agony' (Clutterbuck 1980. was the area of industrial relations, which was also becoming increasingly associated with violent disorder. Confrontation with the Heath Government grew in the wake of the Industrial Relations Act, coupled with the attempt to impose a statutory wages policy. Together, these policies led to prolonged and bitter strikes, with violent confrontations on the picket-line. This reached its now legendary climax with the confrontation between striking coal-miners and their supporters, on the one hand, and Birmingham Police, on the other, at the Saltley coke works in 1972 (*The Times*, 11 February 1972). After the first appearance of a new tactic — mass flying picketing — the police admitted defeat and closed the gates of the coke depot. This led to the formation of the

police National Reporting Centre to improve the effectiveness of mutual aid arrangements, whereby a police force can
lend personnel to a neighbouring force facing extraordinary
problems. It also prompted the change, in function and title,
of civil-defence mobile columns into what became Police
Support Units (see pp. 307–9).

Despite increasingly violent incidents of public disorder,
the police continued to feel that they were able to control
these events without recourse to special equipment and
tactics. Indeed, it was thought that the traditional appearance
of the British bobby acted as a restraint against excessive
violence on the part of the crowd. The police who held back
a demonstrating crowd or picketing workers were not some
alien force, but the ordinary coppers who told people the
time, returned lost children to their parents, and prevented
crime. The tactic of physically holding a crowd, so that
police and protesters came into close proximity, was seen
also to reduce violence, since it discouraged the throwing of
missiles because the police did not present a distant and
anonymous target. The supposedly good-natured pushing
and shoving was regarded as all part of the game, and
demonstrated the innate superiority and civilization of the
British, in contrast to their European counterparts and
American cousins.

It was the violent termination of the 1976 Notting Hill
carnival that was to witness the first overt departure from the
traditional methods of policing public disorder (*The Times*,
31 August 1976). The scale of the assault upon the police at
that carnival convinced the Metropolitan Police of the need
for protective equipment. In 1976 the police were forced to
defend themselves using whatever came to hand, including
dustbin lids and empty milk-bottle crates. Not only did the
disorderly crowd inflict numerous injuries, but it showed the
police to be impotent in their primary responsibility of
maintaining 'the peace'.

The protective equipment comprised a modification to the
traditional helmet and the development of a large perspex
shield. The insertion of a reinforced lining and the addition of
chin-straps which would hold the helmet on the head
transformed this hitherto ornamental item of uniform into an

effective form of protection. This development aroused little public concern, since it produced no discernible change in the appearance of the police officer. What did create concern was the appearance of plastic shields behind which officers could obtain protection from missile attack. Although the shield in question bore little resemblance to the shields used by Continental police forces, its introduction was widely seen as marking a shift towards an alien and unwanted system of public order policing.

The shield quickly saw 'active service' during a march by the neo-fascist National Front through the London Borough of Lewisham in 1977, which provoked a predictably violent response from militant left-wing organizations under the banner of the Anti-Nazi League. Police officers escorting the National Front marchers, as well as the marchers themselves, came under missile attack and the shields were deployed (*The Times*, 14 August 1977). The fact that the police were perceived by many commentators to have been in the position of defending fascists did little to enhance sympathy or respect for their role. This, together with the deployment of shields, was interpreted by many as a threat to the principle of 'policing by consent'.

The provocative actions of the National Front continued to punctuate the 1970s with violent confrontations at Ladywood in Birmingham (*The Times*, 17 August 1977), Manchester (*The Times*, 9 September 1977), the East End of London (*The Times*, 17 August 1977), and many other cities (Clutterbuck, 1980). Nor were violent confrontations between the National Front and anti-fascist groups novel. There was already a martyr to the cause of anti-fascism, Kevin Gately, who was killed at Red Lion Square (*Sunday Times*, 4 October 1974). The National Front had arranged to hold a meeting at Conway Hall, and anti-fascists staged a counter-demonstration. The police allowed the counter-demonstration to process along one corner of the square, and most demonstrators were content to do so. However, a small faction tried to charge through the police cordon and gain access to the hall. There was fighting as police on foot and on horseback forced the crowd out of the square. During the course of this action, Kevin Gately was killed by a blow to the head; but Lord Scarman (1975) accepted that it was unlikely that he had been struck by a police officer as some critics had alleged.

No such exoneration followed the killing of Blair Peach in Southall, 1979; indeed, his death was to have an impact on the policing of civil disorder comparable to the effect that the Waldorf shooting had on the use of firearms. During the general election campaign of 1979, the National Front exploited the provisions of legislation designed to ensure fair play between competing political parties to hold a provocative meeting in an area of high Asian settlement, Southall. Predictably, anti-fascist organizations mobilized a counter-demonstration which erupted into violence, including the throwing of missiles and firing of flares at police lines, and the police suffered several serious casualties. During the dispersal of a crowd occupying a side street from which missiles had been thrown, a demonstrator, Blair Peach, was struck on the head[2] — in all likelihood by a police officer — and subsequently died of his injuries (*Daily Telegraph*, 24 April 1979).

As quickly as Peach achieved the status of a martyr for the cause of anti-fascism, so the Special Patrol Group (who had been in the forefront of police action and were responsible for the baton charge during which Peach died) came to represent the fall from grace of the British police. A much-publicized inquest, together with an internal police inquiry and a self-appointed committee of inquiry, were unable to determine which officer struck the fatal blow, but became the vehicles by which considerable damage was inflicted on the reputation for restraint of the British police (Dummett, 1980*a*; 1980*b*). Civil libertarian and other groups mounted a campaign to demand the disbandment of the SPG and, following some of the disclosures about the activities of some members of this group, their role as a specialist public order unit was progressively played down until they were assimilated into the Territorial Support Groups (TSGs) set up under the force reorganization of 1986.

Worse, much worse, was still to come. The disorders that had occurred so far had been directed at others, for example, anti-fascists trying to prevent the National Front marching and holding meetings. In these situations the police were accepted by public opinion as impartial keepers of the peace, in their own phrase, 'the jam in the sandwich'. What was to happen next was that the police themselves would become the object of violence. In April 1980, police in Bristol were attacked by a large crowd as they attempted to mount a raid on a cafe in a predominantly ethnic-minority district from which they believed alcohol was being unlawfully sold (*The Times*, 3 April 1980). Eventually, the police were forced to withdraw entirely from the area for several hours as they awaited reinforcements from neighbouring police forces, and earned a public rebuke from the Home Secretary (*The Times*, 3 April 1980). Almost exactly a year later, violence again erupted, this time in the Brixton area of south London (*Sunday Times/The Times*, 11–13 April 1981). Again, the target of the rioters was the police themselves. According to Lord Scarman (1981), the rioting was a spontaneous explosion of antagonism against the police, who were perceived by the black community to be both racist and oppressive.

Disorder was to reach an even greater peak of ferocity during July of that year, when rioting erupted in the northern cities of Liverpool (*The Times*, 6–9 July 1981) and Manchester (*The Times*, 9–12 July 1981), followed by dozens of lesser disturbances in cities throughout Britain, including renewed rioting in Brixton. However, it was in Liverpool that the most severe rioting was to occur; after three days of continuous disorder with a police force exhausted and suffering increasing casualties, the decision was taken to use CS gas for the first time on the mainland of Britain. The non-availability of projectiles suitable for use in civil disorder meant that CS gas was delivered by methods designed for use against barricaded criminals, and some people suffered serious injuries as a consequence. Nevertheless, it had the desired short-term effect and the riots subsided. However, further serious damage had been done to the reputation of the police, who were tainted by allegations of racism and of sliding into increasingly aggressive means of countering civil disorder.

Although most attention focused upon the causes of the disorder, it was also apparent that, despite the possession of shields, the police were still ill-prepared and ill-equipped for dealing with disorder of such ferocity, particularly the petrol bombs which had been used against the British police for the first time in their history. For the police, there were two urgent responses needed: first, to restore their relations with the ethnic minorities; second, to improve their capability of dealing with serious civil disorder. The type of equipment made available represented a clear break with tradition. Henceforth, officers in such situations would be equipped not only with shields but also with crash helmets and visors, and they would be clad in flameproof overalls. Authorization was granted for police on the mainland of Britain to acquire stocks of CS gas and plastic baton rounds, and the Home Office commenced trials of water cannon. Training was to be improved and many forces followed the lead of the Metro-politan Police in establishing dedicated units specializing in public-order policing. Inevitably, invidious comparisons began to be drawn between the inner cities of mainland Britain and the situation in Northern Ireland.

However, it was not in the inner cities that this new approach to policing civil disorder would conspicuously be revealed, but in the even more sensitive arena of industrial conflict. A foretaste of what was to come occurred, in 1983, outside the *Warrington Messenger* newspaper plant, when striking print workers and their supporters attempted for-cibly to close the premises and met equally forcible resistance from police, some of whom were equipped with riot gear (*The Times*, 30 November 1983). However, it was the year-long miners' strike, which began the following March, that was to see the most violent picket-line clashes. After the closure of Cortonwood colliery, the Yorkshire area was called out on strike and asked for support from other areas of the National Union of Mineworkers. They were joined by Scotland, and both areas received the endorsement of the national executive of the union. For a number of complex reasons, the national executive found it expedient not to call a national strike, but to rely upon federated areas deciding to join the growing movement. However, not all areas decided to strike, and those areas that did not were subjected to picketing by strikers from other coalfields. The centre of the

strike was in Yorkshire and the main bastion of resistance
was in the adjacent Nottinghamshire coalfield. Thus, large
numbers of Yorkshire pickets travelled south into Nottinghamshire, and at the Ollerton colliery on 17 and 18 March
some 10,000 pickets assembled. There was considerable
disorder and one man, a picket, died after apparently being
struck by a missile (*The Times*, 18 March 1984).

There then began the largest peacetime policing operation
in Britain. At any one time, up to 14,000 police officers from
forces outside the coalfields were drafted into those areas to
maintain the peace, or, in the view of the pickets, to protect
'scab labour' and thus break the strike. Disorder reached a
new peak for an industrial dispute, and was epitomized by a
confrontation between pickets and police at the Orgreave
coking plant near Sheffield. On 18 June an estimated 12,000
pickets confronted some 3,000 police, many of the latter
equipped in protective clothing and carrying shields. Horses
were used to charge into the crowd, and 'snatch-squads' of
police rushed forward to make arrests (*The Times*, 19 June
1984). The events resembled nothing so much as a medieval
battleground, and although the police eventually triumphed
and the coking plant was not forcibly closed by pickets, it
was at further cost to their traditional image. Many in the
Labour movement expressed strong antagonism towards
the use of such paramilitary tactics in an industrial dispute.
The Labour Party's annual conference witnessed an angry
debate on policing methods in which delegates denounced the
policing operation (*The Times*, 2 October 1984). As the
eventual return to work by isolated individuals began to
grow and was met by the inevitable violence of the pickets,
these paramilitary tactics were increasingly in evidence.[3]

Hardly was the strike over than further violent confrontations were to be seen in vivid detail on television. When Leon
Brittan, then Home Secretary, visited Manchester University
Students' Union, police charged into students occupying the
union steps (*The Times*, 15 March 1985). In the fighting that
followed, a number of students sustained injuries, and a
subsequent Police Complaints Authority inquiry was highly
critical of police action. The PCA was similarly critical of the
policing of another violent confrontation that occurred as the

'peace convoy' sought to breach an injunction preventing them from gaining access to Stonehenge on the occasion of the summer solstice (*The Times*, 2 June 1985). During a violent confrontation in a beanfield near Stonehenge, television viewers saw police with batons drawn battling with hippies. Although comparable scenes of violence only recurred infrequently, the confrontation between hippies and police in Wiltshire was to become an annual event for the remainder of the decade.

It was rioting in the inner cities that was to bring 1985 to its violent apogee. In the Birmingham district of Handsworth, rioting claimed the lives of two Asian sub-postmasters who died as a result of arson. The ferocity of the violence had prevented the police from gaining access to the area for some hours, and during that time severe damage was done to business premises, including the post office in which the Asian men died (*The Times*, 10–14 September 1985). Perhaps the most notable feature of that riot was the reaction of local Labour MPs, who, in stark contrast to earlier riots, showed little sympathy for the supposed grievances of the rioters.

A matter of only a few weeks later saw further rioting in Brixton following the shooting of Mrs Groce (*The Times*, 29–31 September, 1985). In contrast to Handsworth, the police enjoyed little moral advantage, given the event which had provoked the riot. However, it was notable that, in contrast to earlier riots, the police were able to gain the upper hand more quickly and bring the situation under control within twenty-four hours, although two people were killed during the rioting. However, that tactical effectiveness was not to be seen at the third riot of that summer, in Tottenham, north London, when police would face unprecedented violence and suffer their first fatality in such circumstances since 1833 (*The Times*, 7–12 October 1985).

Following a controversial incident in which police searched the house of a suspect and, during an altercation between the police and the family, the suspect's mother, Cynthia Jarrett, suffered a heart attack and died, protest demonstrations were held outside the local police station. During the evening rioting erupted on the nearby Broadwater Farm council estate, the construction of which resembles a fortress, with many elevated walkways from which rioters could hold police at bay. Rioters attacked police not only with missiles and the now all too familiar petrol bombs, but also with knives and machetes, some attached to long poles. Most ominous of all, a variety of firearms, including at least one shotgun and a .38-in revolver, were used against police officers. Severe casualties were inflicted upon the police by the rioters, and PC Keith Blakelock was hacked to death as he and a group of officers protecting a fire engine and its crew were attacked by a machete-wielding mob.

The Broadwater Farm riot would earn a place in police history not only because of the murder of PC Blakelock. It was also the first occasion that plastic baton rounds were deployed operationally by the police on the mainland of Britain. In the event, they were not actually fired because the scale of the rioting had subsided by the time they arrived, but if that particular Rubicon was not crossed that night, the police certainly found themselves beginning to wade across it.

If disorder subsided from the peak of ferocity experienced at Broadwater Farm, it did not disappear. Prolonged industrial conflict was to be the scene of yet further violent picket-line clashes. In January 1986 News International, publishers of the *The Times* and other newspapers, dismissed all members of the major printing unions and moved production to a new plant at Wapping in east London. The following year was punctuated by a series of violent confrontations, which reached a peak on the night of 24 January 1987. Demonstrators supporting the strikers turned over a lorry and then hurled a total of three and half tonnes of rubble at police guarding the plant; the police replied with foot and mounted charges into the crowd (*Sunday Times*, 25 January 1987). Following many complaints of police misconduct, the Police Complaints Authority held an inquiry. Twenty-seven officers were charged with various offences, but after six cases had been dismissed at the committal stage (*The Times*, 4 May 1989) the prosecutions of all but three officers collapsed (*The Times*, 27 March 1990). This did not prevent publication of a highly critical summary of the PCA inquiry report which accused some officers of indiscriminate violence (*Police Review*, 23 February 1990).

As the 1980s came to a close, there reappeared scenes of violent political protest. These protests centred mainly around two issues: the publication of Salman Rushdie's *The Satanic Verses* and the introduction of a new system of local taxation, the community charge (more commonly known as the 'poll tax'). In the autumn of 1988, Muslims in Bradford began a campaign to have Rushdie's novel banned on the grounds that it was blasphemous. There were a series of demonstrations and ritualistic book burnings. The situation became much more serious with the passing of a 'death sentence' on Rushdie by Ayatollah Khomeini (*The Times*, 15 February 1989). This sparked a number of violent demonstrations in various cities throughout the summer and autumn of 1989. For example, a demonstration in Dewsbury, West Yorkshire (*The Times*, 26 June 1989) led to police in riot gear battling with Muslim demonstrators and a public house being wrecked by rioters.

The poll tax aroused a similarly protracted series of disorders throughout March and April 1990, as a succession of local authorities met to set the charge and protesters gathered outside town halls. In one week there were at least twelve serious outbreaks of disorder connected with the tax (*Independent on Sunday*, 11 March 1990) and police at Hackney in east London charged crowds with batons and horses (*The Times*, 9 March 1990).

This violence reached its peak at a massive demonstration in Trafalgar Square, organized in protest at the tax, which degenerated into one of the worst political riots of recent times (*Sunday Times*, 1 April 1990).

Throughout this entire period, football hooliganism represented a continuous source of violence and disorder. However, disorder was only indirectly involved in the two incidents that created the greatest shock waves: the deaths of fifty-six people in a fire at Bradford City football ground (*Sunday Times*, 12 May 1985), and ninety-five Liverpool fans who were crushed to death at Hillsborough football ground in Sheffield (*The Times*, 17 April 1989). Both disasters arose mainly because of the antiquated stadia in which they occurred, but the need to maintain public order was to the fore as first Lord Justice Popplewell (*The Times*, 25 July 1985) and then Lord Justice Taylor (*The Times*, 5 August 1989) held their inquiries. The Hillsborough report drew particular attention to the dangers of confining fans behind fencing designed to prevent them invading the pitch and attacking rivals.

## Conclusions

The developments in public order and armed policing have led many to conclude that the British tradition of 'policing by consent' is seriously endangered, if it has not already been abandoned. The controversy surrounding these developments has been fuelled by the general politicization of policing throughout the 1980s. Following the election of the Conservative Government in 1979 with a strident 'law and order' mandate, and the immediate implementation of the significant pay increases recommended by the Edmund Davies report whilst the remainder of the public sector was being subjected to reductions in expenditure, the liberal and left in British politics became increasingly critical of the police. A number of chief constables eagerly joined the political debate over such issues as the growing number of deaths in police custody, police accountability and control, and police race relations (Reiner, 1985a).

Not only were significant sections of the political left generally antipathetic to the police, but many of the central issues related to incidents in which a significant measure of force had been used by the police. The killing of Blair Peach raised issues of race relations and, the effectiveness of internal police investigations, as well as public-order policy and tactics. Inner-city riots prompted much discussion of police racism and the harassment of black youth. The miners' strike brought into vivid focus issues of police accountability. Almost overnight, it seemed, the police had become a legitimate target of left-wing criticism.

Notions like that of 'community policing' attempted to revive the myth of Dixon of Dock Green, but it became increasingly clear that Dixon had faded into history. The prevailing image of the police was no longer his avuncular features, but the much less agreeable outline of the visored helmet.

# PART II

# 'Armed Police'

# 3

# The People for the Job?

## Introduction

In the quarter of a century since Harry Roberts and his associates gunned down the three unarmed detectives in Shepherds Bush, police use of firearms has been transformed. Many officers now receive special training and are authorized to carry guns; there are special squads and departments, some of whose members are permanently armed. The armoury available to the police has expanded to include hand-guns (both revolvers and self-loading pistols), pump-action shot-guns, carbines, and sub-machine-guns, as well as sniper rifles (see Appendix A for details).

So obviously alien to the British police tradition are these developments that it is not surprising that they have provoked a number of controversies. Foremost amongst these are questions regarding the number of officers authorized to carry firearms and their fitness for doing so. These questions have been raised following the shootings of Stephen Waldorf, John Shorthouse, and Cherry Groce. Wider issues have also been raised about the kinds of weapon used, especially the carbines at Heathrow Airport. Other issues, though no less important, have received less public attention. This and the following chapter will consider these problems.

## The Numbers Game

A matter of recurring concern is the actual number of officers who are authorized to carry firearms and the frequency with which those firearms are actually carried.[1] Much of this concern seems to have been fuelled by an uncritical acceptance of the figures (reproduced as Fig. 1 and Table 1)

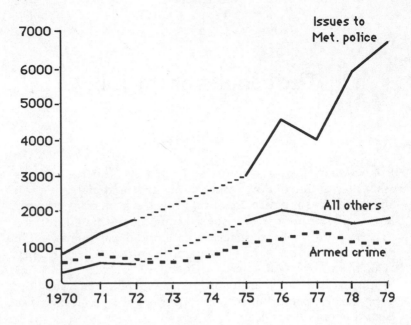

Fig. 1. Firearms issued to police 1970–1979. Reproduced (computer enhanced image) from Hoare, 1980.

*Note*: The same axis is used for the amount of armed crimes *and* the number of firearms used.

contained in an M.Sc. dissertation written by a serving police officer (Hoare, 1980: 74). He concludes:

It is no surprise that the Metropolitan Police averages 76% of the national total of issues, but they are now seen to be breaking steeply away from what appears as an established equilibrium in the rest of the country. This rise does not coincide in any way with known armed crime, but it is likely that a good deal of this upsurge is due to terrorist activity in London.

Others have concluded that these figures simply show a lack of firm control and supervision on the part of the Metro-

TABLE 1. Police use of firearms compared to armed crime, 1970–1978

| Year | Issue of guns | | | Firearms crime | | Armed robbery Total |
|------|------|------|------|------|------|------|
| | Met | Provinces | Met as % | Total | Serious | |
| 1970 | 803 | 269 | 75 | 1,358 | 524 | 47,888 |
| 1971 | 1,344 | 591 | 69 | 1,734 | 633 | 63,333 |
| 1972 | 1,712 | 525 | 77 | 2,070 | 599 | 53,999 |
| 1973 | – | – | – | 2,466 | 549 | 48,777 |
| 1974 | – | – | – | 2,828 | 716 | 65,000 |
| 1975 | 2,863 | 1,689 | 63 | 3,850 | 1,069 | 95,888 |
| 1976 | 4,414 | 1,953 | 69 | 4,632 | 1,189 | 107,666 |
| 1977 | 3,933 | 1,814 | 68 | 5,302 | 1,371 | 123,444 |
| 1978 | 5,835 | 1,627 | 78 | 5,672 | 1,138 | 99,666 |

*Source*: Hoare, 1980.

politan Police (Benn and Worpole, 1986; Blom-Cooper in Home Office, 1986a).

An immediate problem in deciding whether police are or are not over-reacting is in establishing what they are reacting to, for the Home Office statistics on firearms offences have long been inadequate. Hoare points out that relatively trivial offences of criminal damage and assault caused by youngsters using air weapons were until recently included in the statistics along with much more serious offences such as armed robbery. Through a careful reanalysis of the data, Hoare (1980: ch. 7) was able to distinguish between the trivial and the serious, and we remain indebted to him for this. It is a distinction that the official statistics now also incorporate (Home Office, 1986b). Unfortunately, in other respects Hoare gave a misleading interpretation of the data.

Let us begin by considering the claim that the number of firearms issued to Metropolitan Police officers is 'breaking steeply away from what appears as an established equilibrium in the rest of the country'. In addition to Hoare's original data, Table 1 also provides the number of 'issues' in the Metropolitan Police expressed as a percentage of the national total. This contradicts the suggestion that the Metropolitan Police figures are 'breaking steeply away' from the rest of the country. In fact, throughout the 1970s they formed a U-curve, from roughly three-quarters at the beginning of the decade, dropping to two-thirds during its middle years, and rising again to just over three-quarters by the end of the period. The confusion seems to have arisen from the failure to appreciate the difference between the *absolute numbers* of guns issued by the Metropolitan compared to other police forces and the question of their proportionality. As in any escalating trend, a constant proportional difference produces an increasing absolute difference.

Next, let us consider the view that the increase in firearms issued to police did 'not coincide in any way with known armed crime' (Hoare, 1980: 74). If this was in fact true, there would be no statistical correlation between the number of armed robberies (the single offence accounting for the vast majority of 'serious armed crimes' and for which there are reliable figures) and the number of firearms issued to police. The absence of such a correlation is computed as 0, whereas, if there were a perfect correlation (such that every increase in armed crime was matched by a corresponding increase in police firearms issued), the correlation coefficient would have a value of $+1.0$. In fact, the correlation between the trend in serious armed crime, as defined by Hoare, and the trend in the issue of firearms to Metropolitan Police officers was $+.85$, and that between armed robberies and the issue of police firearms was $+.79$. The comparable figures for the police outside London was $+.97$ in relation to both serious offences and armed robberies. There was, in short, an extremely close relationship between the occurrence of serious armed crime and the issue of firearms to police.

In addition to the general failure to distinguish between absolute numbers and a *proportional* relationship in an escalating trend, there is the further problem of not comparing like with like. Hoare compares the number of *armed offences* to the number of *occasions* when firearms were *issued* to individual officers. Both were increasing during the 1970s, but because the number of police firearms issued in the Metropolitan District increased from 803 in 1970 to 5,835 in 1978, and serious firearms offences rose from 524 to 1,138 during the same period, the size of gap obscures the similar trend. However, the 'gap' is more apparent than real, because armed offences are not directly comparable in scale to the number of weapons issued to police officers. First, even if police are dealing with a single armed suspect, there would always be many more than a single firearm issued, not least because armed officers should always be deployed in pairs, and prudence dictates the use of more than a single pair of armed officers. Second, a serious armed offence may involve *several* offenders using firearms, whereas each 'issue' of police firearms refers to *a* gun being issued to *one* officer. Thus, if police were searching for several armed persons who together had committed one offence, then obviously the number of guns issued to individual officers may increase accordingly. Third, if an armed operation persisted over a number of days, then the number of guns issued would also increase accordingly. For example, the attempted armed robbery at Sir John Soane's Museum in 1987 had involved four armed officers waiting for three days to intercept these armed men (*Police Review*, 12 February 1987). Under the procedures in force during the 1970s, this would have amounted to twelve 'issues'. It is thus virtually inevitable that firearms issued to police will outnumber armed robberies to a considerable degree. It was to prevent erroneous conclusions such as these being drawn from the published figures that the basis for calculating the use of police firearms was changed in 1983 from the number of guns issued to individual officers to the number of 'armed operations'. Under this system the 'stakeout' at Sir John Soane's Museum would have constituted a single 'operation'. However, it is unfortunate that official figures on the total number of guns issued are no longer available, since this would give the most complete picture.

Even had Hoare's interpretation of the data been correct, it is far from clear whether it indicated an over-reaction. As Hoare's figures on serious armed crime show (Hoare, 1980: 46–54), there was a qualitative change in the mid–1970s towards a greatly increased use of firearms, especially shotguns—a particularly fearsome weapon (pp. 283–4). As the use of such weapons became much more prevalent during the 1970s (see Hoare, 1980), so officers would quite reasonably

take the obvious precaution of carrying weapons with which
to defend themselves and others whenever there was reason
to believe that they might encounter armed criminals. To use
an analogy, it is not surprising that the blood transfusion
service responded to the AIDS epidemic by screening *all*
blood products, despite the small number of people who
have been found to be carrying the HIV virus. Whilst this
response could be portrayed as statistically disproportionate
to the scale of the prevalence of the problem, it is not so,
because the risk is so serious (that is, life-threatening) that *any*
increase in frequency amounts to a *qualitative* change in the
level of risk. So it is with the growth in armed crime during
the 1970s. What is surprising is not that the police now issue
firearms much more frequently than they did in the past, but
that their use of firearms has remained so closely related to
the actual incidence of serious armed crime. Had they truly
over-reacted, then *every* reported armed incident, or suspected armed criminal to be arrested, would have prompted
an automatic armed police operation, with a consequently
massive increase in the carrying of guns by police.

Not only has such a massive increase in armed policing *not*
occurred, but the tendency is in the opposite direction. For
the police have responded to public concern about the
number of AFOs and the procedures for issuing firearms by
gradually reducing the former and strengthening the latter.
On the other hand, in the wake of the Hungerford massacre
there has been criticism of the reduction in the numbers of
armed police on the grounds that they are insufficient to
provide a swift response to such an incident (Edwards, 1988).
Perhaps the lesson to be drawn from this controversy is that
in this regard the police simply cannot win (Waddington,
1988).

## Selection and Training

Another issue that has frequently been raised in connection
with the police use of firearms is the adequacy of selection
and the quality of training. Concern has been expressed
about the ability of armed officers to perform satisfactorily

under the acute stress that is bound to accompany an armed operation. There seems to be a fear that volunteers for the position of AFO will be people unhealthily attracted to guns. Some faith seems to have been placed in the use of psychometric tests to discover which officers have a healthy attitude towards firearms and to predict how they will respond to stress. Unfortunately, after experimenting with several possible psychometric tests, the Home Office Working Party concluded (Home Office, 1986*a*) that none had proved satisfactory. The reason is probably two fold: first, there is no satisfactory data base upon which to rest correlations between test scores and operational competence; second, it is likely that it is the nature of the situation, rather than the character or temperament of an individual officer, that is the principal determinant of behaviour in armed operations, as in so many areas of human activity.

Nevertheless, selection of officers for training as AFOs is not taken lightly. Currently, selection occurs at two levels: the commander of the division or squad must first satisfy himself that officers sent for training have proven themselves suitable, and, secondly, instructors must also be satisfied as to the suitability of the trainee. If at any time an officer's suitability comes into question, his authorization is withdrawn. Despite the fact that these are subjective judgements, they seem more likely to be valid compared to psychometric tests which, at best, can only consider a few variables.

From the opposite point of view, it has been suggested that the concern to avoid selecting people with an 'unhealthy' interest in firearms actually militates against the selection of suitable individuals. Yardley and Eliot (1986*b*) claim that officers 'will be actively discouraged from private firearms ownership', with the result that they will only gain familiarity in handling weapons during their periodic refresher training (see also Yardley and Eliot, 1986*c*). Whether or not forces outside the Metropolitan Police adopt such a policy cannot be affirmed or denied here, but certainly it is the case that many instructors and AFOs in the Metropolitan Police belong to gun clubs, and there is a long tradition of recreational shooting organized by the Metropolitan Police sports and social clubs (Gould and Waldren, 1986).

The unsupported allegation that the police avoid selecting officers with a sporting interest in firearms detracts from the more serious point made by Yardley and Eliot (1986a), namely that, compared to the training given to drivers of police vehicles, the length of time devoted to training AFOs is grossly inadequate. A basic driving course lasts four weeks, and most drivers will have the opportunity to practice some of their driving skills, at least, on a daily basis. AFOs, on the other hand, receive a basic course of ten days (and prior to 1983 it lasted only five days) and have the opportunity to practice officially four days per year. Indeed, it seems that only successive tragedies have wrenched the necessary resources from the authorities to extend training even to this meagre ration. It took the murder of three unarmed detectives in 1966 for the police to abandon 'amateurism' and begin systematic training at all. It was the Waldorf shooting which prompted a major internal inquiry — the 'Dear report' — resulting in extended training being given to officers. The shootings of John Shorthouse and Mrs Groce likewise provoked a major review and innovations such as 'Level II' teams. Only in the wake of the Hungerford massacre have armed-response vehicles been deployed. The explanation why progress seems only to occur in the wake of disaster will be more fully examined in Chapter 10.

For the moment, it should be appreciated that the resource implications of firearms training are considerable. There are fifty-six officers engaged full-time in firearms training in the Metropolitan Police. In 1986 the training commitment amounted to 19,630 man-days for officers who would otherwise be available for other duties. In line with the Dear report, the force intends to double the amount of refresher training from four to eight days annually, thus adding a further 7,500 man-days to that total. Added to this is the cost of practice ammunition, targets, building and maintaining ranges, testing instructors for the level of lead in their blood, and much more besides. The annual budget for firearms training in 1985–6 amounted to approximately £2 million. Thus, it is not difficult to appreciate the resistance of policy-makers to committing further resources in view of the Government's financial management initiative which insists that tangible benefits should result from expenditure. Thus, the Dear report's proposal to extend refresher training to eight days a year has only begun to be introduced and will be gradually phased in, because of its financial implications. Furthermore, there is the laudable desire not to take officers away from street duties unnecessarily. It is partly in order to maintain control over the size of the training commitment that the number of authorized officers has been reduced, so that henceforth they will be fewer but better trained.

There is no doubt that training has improved substantially since 1966; nor is there much doubt that training in the Metropolitan Police compares favourably with that provided by other forces in Britain or overseas. However, there is equally no doubt that much room exists for improvement, particularly in standards of marksmanship and tactics, at both initial and refresher training levels. During initial training, officers are taught to fire their weapon at a static paper target on a practice range in good light. They repeat the same 'shoot' usually ten times, and will know for how long the target will be exposed. For only one brief session are they presented with still photographs and videos portraying a variety of actual scenes which require them to consider whether or not to shoot. However, even this technology is limited, for whilst the scenarios can be changed so as to avoid familiarity, they are played out no matter what action the officer takes short of opening fire. He is a passive observer of circumstances until he decides to shoot. There is no opportunity for officers to be presented with simulated incidents in which moving targets have to be distinguished from innocent bystanders under varying conditions of light and heat.

Attempts are made by instructors within their limited resources to improve marksmanship skills during refresher training. Officers are increasingly exposed to tests which require them to be seated, or to walk around, or fend off an imaginary bystander, or to shout a warning. The ingenuity shown by instructors in devising these tests within the constraints they face is commendable. However, for an officer training to use the Heckler and Koch MP5 to be faced with six targets, one of which is nominated by the instructor for him to engage, is a far cry from confronting one or more terrorists in a crowded terminal building.

Yardley and Eliot (1986*b*) have argued for more realistic training, involving officers engaging other people with wax bullets which inflict minor injuries but are not lethal. They have gone further, and suggested that some training exercises should involve the use of live rounds to simulate the experience of genuine combat. These suggestions were rejected by the Home Office Working Party on the grounds that they laid too much emphasis on 'engagement' rather than 'containment' (Home Office, 1986*a*). This is a reasonable argument, for police officers are not soldiers, and a successful strategy is designed to ensure that there is a peaceful conclusion to the incident, not a shoot-out. However, whilst this is generally true there *are* some officers who might need to engage armed persons. These include officers at Heathrow airport who might find themselves in an exchange of fire with terrorists; their being equipped with the Heckler and Koch MP5 carbine is justified precisely on the grounds of their possibly needing to engage terrorists. Much the same seems to apply to officers in the Royalty and Diplomatic Protection Department and also 'Level I' officers who might have to execute a hostage rescue (see Appendix A). For these officers, at least, there might be some merit in training along the lines suggested by Yardley and Eliot (1986*b*). Since this suggestion was made and rejected, technological developments have made realistic simulated combat more readily attainable without the risks inherent in the proposals made by Yardley and Eliot, by using balls of paint that can be fired from normal operational firearms.

On the other hand, the Working Group was surely correct in insisting that for the vast majority of officers the emphasis should be upon 'containment' rather than 'engagement'. If officers avoid confrontations, so that they do not need to decide when and when not to shoot under conditions of extreme stress, then this is much more likely to ensure that innocent people are not mistakenly shot. However well-trained and mentally stable a person might be, there is always the possibility that in making a split-second decision they will do so in error. Adequate tactical training avoids the futile quest for a cadre of superhuman individuals to whom firearms can be entrusted.

Given the emphasis upon 'containment' rather than 'engagement', however, the amount of time devoted to tactical training seems inadequate. The basic course includes a number of tactical exercises in containment, the interception of vehicles, and 'ambushing' armed robbers (see Appendix A for details). These are of immense value, especially when videotaped for later replay to the officers concerned, to whom mistakes can be pointed out. However, the opportunity for such tactical exercises, even during a two-week course, are limited. Trainees are not brought up to a standard of proficiency, they are simply shown how *deficient* they are, in the hope that given this knowledge they will exhibit caution in actual operations. This would be less regrettable if subsequent refresher training included tactical exercises designed to build upon the basic training. Unfortunately, this only occurs during the *annual* refresher course, because neither time nor facilities allow for such exercises to be carried out on a quarterly basis.

Not only is refresher training insufficient to provide adequate rehearsal of tactics, it is also insufficient for the maintenance of simple marksmanship skills. A three-month lapse, during which an officer might not even have handled a gun, is a lengthy period. The sheer familiarity with the weapon shows a noticeable deterioration during this time.

Although training has improved considerably in recent years, therefore, there seems to be much more that can be done. Senior officers concerned with firearms training are acutely aware that this is so, but are constrained by budgetary restrictions. Certainly, the cost implications of substantial improvements in training will be considerable. What the Metropolitan Police and the Home Office must balance is the cost of less than complete competence against the likely gain from greatly improved training, especially tactical training. Given that one bungled operation can, apart from causing death or injury to innocent persons, spark a riot and do immeasurable harm to the reputation of the police, it would seem that a substantial improvement in training is needed to restore that balance.

## Generalists or Specialists?

One way of trying to achieve some balance between costs and rewards is to concentrate resources upon a relatively small group of people who can be highly trained. This seems to be the direction in which policy on firearms has been moving during recent years and seems likely to develop in future. The Home Office Working Party report of 1986 certainly endorsed such a move, and in the Metropolitan Police this took the form of establishing the 'Level II' teams (see Appendix A). The success of these teams is likely to lead to their establishment on each of the eight territorial areas, with officers trained to this level operating armed-response vehicles. If this occurs, the role of the divisional AFO will become residual.

The advantages of specialization are clear enough: a small group of officers can be removed from general policing commitments and dedicated to firearms training and operations, ensuring the highest standards of competence. Also, the same officers work together as a team, thereby coming to know each other's capabilities and acquiring trust in one another, so that they can act as a cohesive unit rather than as a collection of individuals. Their frequent exposure to operational conditions familiarizes them with the vagaries of actual operations, so that they are less likely to be caught off-guard. Élite status raises morale, and can become an incentive for maintaining strict discipline. All these advantages have been demonstrated by the Force Firearms Unit throughout its existence.

Equally, there are evident disadvantages in specialization: an inevitable corollary is that a limited number of officers will be placed repeatedly in the position of having to confront armed criminals and terrorists. Apart from the risk to which this exposes such officers, it also means that these few officers will be repeatedly called upon to decide whether to open fire or not. Whilst such highly trained men may be best able to make this decision, it does place an enormous burden upon few shoulders and exposes them also to accusations that they are 'gun-happy' if, and when, they decide to open fire, particularly if they do so on more than one occasion.

Another problem arising from specialization is how much expertise is needed and how readily available it should be. There is now sufficient demand in London for one Level II team per territorial area, but these officers are trained only to use the standard Model 10 revolver — not the more exotic weapons that might be needed for certain operations. At present there seems little likelihood that there would be sufficient demand to justify establishing a dedicated Level I team for the London area, because its more sophisticated skills are not required so often. Indeed, the expansion of Level II teams might siphon away demand for Level I officers, who would be needed only for the most specialized tasks. Even in London, where the threat of armed crime is greatest, there would seem to be little reason to establish SWAT squads on the American pattern, as favoured by Yardley and Eliot (1986c). Indeed, not even the police in the crime-ridden cities of the USA find it necessary to retain wholly dedicated SWAT (Special Weapons and Tactics) teams. It seems inevitable that the operational and training roles will continue alongside each other for the forseeable future.

There is also a distinct advantage to the dual 'burden' (Yardley and Eliot, 1986c) of an operational and instructional role for Level I officers: the combination of an instructional and élite operational role enhances the status of training. When a member of an élite operational squad instructs trainees to give priority to caution and safety, this cannot be dismissed as theoretical advice divorced from operational reality, to be safely disregarded. If this is the advice of one of the famed 'blue berets', then it carries considerable authority.

### Command

Increasing specialization has increased the 'professionalism' of the officers who are called upon to carry guns. Unfortunately, the same cannot be said of the senior officers who might be placed in command of a firearms incident. Command, it seems, remains the bastion of the tradition of 'amateurism'.

Officers to whom guns are issued will rarely be above the
rank of Inspector and will, therefore, be subordinated to the
decisions of unarmed senior officers who plan the operation
or assume command once it has begun. Whereas the AFO at
the scene will have received possibly two week's initial
training and regular refresher training, the senior officer who
commands him may be, and in the past frequently has been, ·
wholly untrained.

Amongst AFOs there circulates a host of horror stories
concerning instructions that have been given to armed
officers by their superiors. For example, it is alleged that in
one incident an armed intruder was thought to be in a house
and so two AFOs attended, along with two dog-handlers.
After a brief wait during which no activity could be seen
within the house, the senior officer formed two pairs, each
comprising an AFO and a dog-handler. He then instructed
one pair to enter through the front door and the other
through the rear to search the premises. Thereby, he violated
firearms policy on several counts: he needlessly placed
officers in a situation which might have resulted in a
confrontation with an armed criminal in which they or he or
some innocent person might have been shot; he sent a search
group in without either a support group or cover group; he
instructed them to enter through separate entrances, instead
of the same entrance, with the result that they might have
suddenly encountered each other in circumstances which
could have precipitated an exchange of fire; had the gunman
been encountered, say, in the ground floor hallway, and had
there been an exchange of fire with him, officers entering
from the front might have been firing towards officers
entering from the rear and vice versa; and the dogs and their
handlers were untrained in working with firearms. Fortunately, the gunman had escaped and nothing untoward
occurred.[2]

This and other similar stories may, of course, be apo-
cryphal, but gain credibility from what has been publicly
revealed about the management of armed operations in cases
that have resulted in court action. DC Finch, for example,
was sent alone and without protective cover to look into the
yellow Mini car which was thought to contain David Martin.

It is hardly any wonder that when he saw a person whom he believed to be Martin make a sudden movement, he panicked and opened fire. In fact, Finch should never have been placed in that situation, and certainly should not have been allowed to go unsupported and without cover possibly to confront a person known to be armed and highly dangerous. Other incidents, too, have raised equally serious issues about the management of armed operations. The former Chief Fire-arms Instructor said in evidence during the trial of Inspector Lovelock for the malicious wounding of Mrs Groce that the operation violated the 'golden rule' of avoiding confrontation (*The Times*, 13 January 1987).

Mistakes of this kind might occur for several reasons, not the least of which is ignorance. Untrained tactical com-manders may simply be unaware of the lethality of certain types of firearm. It is alleged that the phrase 'He's only [*sic*] armed with a shotgun' all too frequently falls from the lips of senior officers! Thus, armed operations have, in the past, been too often conceived and implemented like their un-armed equivalents — the use of firearms by police being treated as an 'added extra'. Considerations other than those given priority by firearms instructors can take precedence. For example, CID officers will wish to secure and preserve evidence that might otherwise be destroyed during the course of a lengthy siege.

The time-hallowed means of arresting wanted persons and securing evidence is to surprise them early in the morning, with a sudden and overwhelming force. Thus, the door is opened with a sledgehammer and officers rush in, often with little notion of who, apart from the wanted person, is in the premises and where they are located. In an unarmed operation this approach may have considerable advantages, but when guns are being carried by the first officers to enter the premises there is the potential for disaster. What is surprising is not that very occasionally a startled officer fires a shot which kills or injures an innocent person, as happened in the cases of John Shorthouse and Mrs Cherry Groce, but that this happens so rarely.

The Metropolitan Police are aware of this problem, and have instituted an urgent programme of senior officer training, designed to inform those who command such operations of the proper tactics to adopt. During the two-day course they are informed of the need to contain a situation and ensure that officers are protected behind suitable cover at an appropriate distance from the threat. The destructive power of the shotgun is demonstrated, so that they do not minimize the risks of such weapons. Trained senior officers, it is hoped, will resist the temptation to opt for an 'early morning turnover' when they suspect the wanted person is armed. Instead, they are advised to contain the premises with a cover group and keep innocent bystanders away with a perimeter group. Only when the situation is secured should they telephone or communicate in some other way with those inside the premises and invite them to surrender. By pursuing the strategy of defensive caution that their AFOs are taught, it is hoped that mistakes can be avoided.

However, it is difficult to disagree with the conclusion of Yardley and Eliot (1986c: 26):

> any senior officer who is to command marksmen cannot do that job effectively unless he has some degree of proficiency in, and understanding of, the tactical use of firearms himself. This cannot be accomplished in a course lasting a couple of days.

The problem arises from the fact that armed operations are still, thankfully, beyond the daily experience of most senior officers and, therefore, inevitably enjoy only a marginal position amongst the many issues to be considered. It is only when an armed incident arises or operation is planned that this factor comes to the fore, and then two days' training at some time previously is an uncertain bulwark against habit and competing demands. Senior officers may feel daunted by the demands on manpower, the disruption to the life of the community, and the high public profile required by a containment operation, particularly if it is not certain (only strongly suspected) that the person is armed. The problems were illustrated by an incident in 1988, when police in Preston surrounded a bank thought to contain armed robbers and their hostages. After a wait of more than two hours police entered the bank to find the supposed hostages locked in the vault, the robbers having escaped (*The Times*, 16 September 1988). The only thing left to show for the operation was a large commitment of resources, the bringing of the town centre to a virtual halt during the morning rush-hour, and ridicule in the popular Press, who paid no attention to safety of the hostages.

To counter these influences, the Metropolitan Police have since 1987 introduced a system of requiring Commanders to contact PT17 for advice and guidance on any armed operation that might be contemplated. This is, apparently, working well, and senior staff at PT17 report that they have been able to exercise greater influence over the conduct of armed operations than in the past. Nevertheless, difficulties remain, not least with the advisory role of the firearms officer acting as a 'tactical adviser'. This officer, who may be a local AFO or a member of PT17, will almost certainly be junior both in rank and experience to the man he is 'advising'. No doubt, the influence of the PT17 specialist will carry far greater weight than that of a local AFO, but PT17 officers cannot be readily available in all instances, and it is in the early stages of an unanticipated incident that errors are likely to occur. Thus, whilst one must concur with the view that 'a good commander should never be unwilling to ask subordinates for their opinions' (Yardley and Eliot, 1986c), this remains a classic example of a contradiction between rank and expertise in an hierarchical organization. The 'incident commander' is expected to do what his title implies — 'command'—and this may seem inconsistent with accepting the advice and guidance of subordinates.

In the light of all this, there is a striking complacency in the Home Office Working Party's endorsement of the advice in the Manual of Guidance issued by the Association of Chief Police Officers to all British police forces:

a tactical adviser should always be consulted. He should be, or should have been, an authorized firearms officer himself and should have extensive background knowledge of tactical solutions, deployment, communications, and option and contingency planning. The tactical adviser should not himself be part of the operation and may be of *any rank*.   (Home Office, 1986a: 12; emphasis added.)

The Working Party's recommendation 'that chief officers be reminded of the importance of ensuring that the commanders of armed operations always consult a tactical adviser' also appears insufficiently forceful.

As specialist teams come to play an increasingly important role in all firearms operations and incidents, there seem correspondingly compelling reasons to give them full responsibility for the management of the entire operation. A parallel could be drawn with the way in which responsibility is handed over to the military when the latter act 'in aid of the civil power', as happened when the SAS assaulted the Iranian embassy in 1980. Likewise, if an armed team are to be deployed, for example, to effect the arrest of a wanted person, responsibility could be formally be assigned to them for the implementation of this goal which, when completed, would be returned to the incident commander. To compromise the safety of innocent members of the public, police officers and even suspects, in the name of hierarchial and territorial authority seems wholly unjustifiable.

## Legal Liability

The suggestion that at least some senior officers are less than wholly competent in managing armed operations raises the thorny issue of who should be held liable in law when operations go wrong.[3] At present, as officers are continually reminded during their initial and refresher training, the individual officer is deemed to be responsible for his actions. Thus, it was DCs Finch and Jardine who were tried for the attempted murder of Stephen Waldorf, PC Chester who was tried for the manslaughter of John Shorthouse, and Inspector Lovelock who stood trial for the malicious wounding of Mrs Groce. In each of these cases it was the officer holding the gun who was held accountable. Yet in each of these cases, serious questions were raised about the management of the operation for which the officer in the dock was not, and should not have been held, responsible.

Of course, officers who use their weapon recklessly must be held responsible for their actions. However, when a senior officer orders a subordinate to enter a situation where he might confront an armed suspect and be required to make a split-second decision whether to shoot or not, it seems unjust for the officer to be required to shoulder the responsibility alone if an innocent person is injured or killed in these circumstances. Unfortunately, the response of the authorities to the various incidents which have given rise to public concern has not been to deal effectively with the problem. After the Waldorf shooting, the Home Office issued new guidelines which the Police Federation magazine, *Police* (May 1983), rightly paraphrased as 'Whitelaw tells police: "You're on your own"'. One does not need to endorse the view of the Police Federation that 'armed officers should have some form of legal protection indemnity from prosecution' (*Police Review*, 23 October 1983) to recognize the injustice of heaping such responsibility exclusively upon the shoulders of officers who are unlikely to hold a rank above that of sergeant.

*Team work*

The problem is particularly acute when, for tactical reasons, it is impossible for officers to act solely on their own initiative. Force riflemen who might be required to implement a 'sniper option' might need to have their fire co-ordinated so as to shoot a number of suspects simultaneously. It is simply impractical to expect an officer glazing through a telescopic sight to be aware of the wider circumstances that might justify him opening fire. Indeed, if he were to exercise such a measure of discretion he could jeopardize the entire action and place hostages at risk. For all practical purposes, such a rifleman must trust the judgement of the 'fire marshal' and act on his command, but the law refuses to acknowledge the legitimacy of 'superior orders'.

A similar situation arises in hostage rescue operations. Officers who are required to burst into a room, identify and engage any hostile person, and rescue hostages cannot be expected to deliberate as to the 'reasonableness' of the particular circumstances they will find once they enter the room. It must be accepted, as a practical necessity of the speed with which such an operation is implemented, that any armed person encountered will be shot. Again, the officer bursting through a door or window will have to trust the judgement of his superiors that such a measure of force is justified in law. He has no practical alternative, but the law seems not to recognize this fact.

As will be seen later, when discussing the policing of public disorder, there are occasions when the perfectly proper emphases given in law to the discretion and responsibility of the individual constable is simply inappropriate. As Stobart (1989) has convincingly argued, the law should recognize that there are occasions when police officers must act in concert under the orders of their superiors and, therefore, when those superiors must also accept their share of legal liability for the action taken.[4]

*Passive non-compliance*

Additional problems regarding the legal liability of armed officers arise from the conservative policy adopted towards armed operations described above. Officers are instructed to use a firearm only as a last resort in conditions where killing a person could be justified as 'reasonable force' under section 3 of the Criminal Law Act, 1967 (see Appendix A, p. 290). Whilst every use of force must be justified as 'reasonable *in the circumstances*' and these circumstances cannot be precisely stipulated in advance, certain problems do recur with sufficient frequency to demand greater attention. In particular, it sometimes happens that an armed person will refuse to comply with instructions from surrounding officers, perhaps threatening to breach the containment, but not act in such a way as to immediately threaten life.

The difficulties that arise were dramatically illustrated by an incident which occurred in 1982. David Martin, the escaped, armed criminal for whom Stephen Waldorf was mistaken, was eventually captured in an underground train tunnel after being pursued by armed police. Cornered in the tunnel and surrounded by armed police, Martin was commanded to surrender, but persistently refused to do so, whilst at the same time making no overtly hostile movement. He simply stood defiantly refusing to comply with police instructions. The surrounding officers knew how dangerous Martin was, and that he was perfectly capable of a last suicidal gesture in order to take a police officer with him to the grave (he later committed suicide in prison). After some minutes of this 'Mexican stand-off', officers rushed and overpowered him, whereupon it was revealed that he was unarmed. When Glyn Davies tried to breach the police cordon (see p. 23), he placed the police trying to prevent his escape with a shotgun in a dilemma: either to shoot and probably kill him, or to allow him to breach the containment and thus expose other innocent people to danger. Had Davies's gun been loaded and had he escaped and been able to take hostages, the refusal of the police to shoot may have been viewed as reckless.

Nor is this a unique situation by any means. Indeed, it is so common in the USA that it is colloquially known as 'suicide by cop'. Foolhardy behaviour on the part of people suspected to be armed places the police in a delicate and undefined legal position, for would it be 'reasonable' in such circumstances to open fire?

## The 'fleeing felon'

The issue of whether it is 'reasonable force' to shoot an armed person who is not, *at that instant*, presenting a direct threat to life, does not end with those who seek to breach a containment. What of the gunman who is in the act of escaping? Many countries, including the USA (Condon, 1985) Canada (Chappell and Graham, 1985), and Australia (Harding, 1970) explicitly allow their police to open fire upon 'fleeing felons' who satisfy various other criteria regarding the gravity of the offence and likelihood of being armed. Cases in Northern Ireland in which members of the security forces have shot and killed escaping suspected terrorists (Asmal, 1985) have suggested that such action is lawful under statutory authority identical to section 3 of the Criminal Law Act, 1967. Yet the situation remains desperately unclear because the question of 'reasonableness' is a matter of fact to be decided by a jury according to the particular circumstances. Whilst juries in trials of police officers accused of criminal conduct following the tragically mistaken or accidental shootings of Stephen Waldorf, Cherry Groce, and John Shorthouse have been sympathetic to the dilemmas facing the armed police officer, inquest juries have been less so. An 'open verdict' was returned by the inquest jury inquiring into the death of Denis Bergin, who was shot as he burst into Sir John Soane's Museum in Holborn waving a sawn-off shotgun which turned out to be unloaded. If these circumstances did not amount to a clear case of 'lawful killing', then shooting a gunman in order to prevent his escape seems even more questionable.

The confusion over what is permissible has not been helped by the remarks made by Mr Justice Mars-Jones during the trial of Hussein Said for the attempted assassination of the Israeli ambassador, Sholom Argov. The would-be assassin had fired only one shot from his automatic weapon, hitting the ambassador in the head, when his weapon jammed and he ran off, still clutching his sub-machine-gun. He was pursued by the Ambassador's protection officer who, having shouted a warning fired one shot at the escaping gunman, wounding him. During the trial the defence submitted that unnecessary force was used to make the arrest. Summing up, however, the judge commented that not only did the officer act lawfully and properly in shooting to prevent an armed and dangerous man from escaping, *he would have been neglecting his duty had he not done so* (Gould and Waldren, 1986: 188–9). Whilst unexceptionable in the circumstances of this case, this statement places the armed officer in an unenviable position in that, if faced with an armed person who seeks to breach a containment, he may be guilty of using unreasonable force if he opens fire and neglecting his duty if he does not.

### An unclear and unsatisfactory law?

There has been criticism of section 3 of the Criminal Law Act from civil libertarians (Asmal, 1985; Kitchin, 1988), lawyers (Harlow, 1974; Ashworth, 1975), and police officers, all of whom protest about the vagueness of the 'reasonableness' criteria. At first sight there is much to complain about. 'Reasonableness' might cover a multitude of sins and allow the police (or security forces in Northern Ireland) to exploit the latitude it offers them. On the other hand, as noted above, from the perspective of the police officer, what is or is not reasonable may represent a legal fog in which he must operate.

It is unlikely that any more explicit legal stipulation will actually circumscribe police action any more than it already does. The police already impose restrictions upon themselves which are far more constraining than any interpretation of the word 'reasonable' is likely to have. Not only that, those non-legal restrictions can have *de facto* legal significance when they are introduced into evidence about the facts of the case. Thus, during the trial of Inspector Lovelock, attention was drawn to the safety rules, particularly to that which said, at the time, 'Do not point a gun at anyone unless you intend to use it'. Prosecution counsel argued that, by pointing the gun at Mrs Groce, Inspector Lovelock must have formed the intent to shoot her, or else been in breach of the safety rules.

Public anxieties could perhaps be assuaged if the more restrictive philosophy actually governing police use of firearms was to be stated in the form of 'codes of practice'. Whilst not being statutory requirements, these codes could indicate to all concerned what is expected of the police in armed operations. Officers could still argue that a departure from these rules was 'reasonable in the circumstances' as they uniquely encountered them — the advantage of this being that the law would not need to try and foresee every situation in which lethal force might need to be employed. Statutory attempts to do precisely this have tended to produce a much *less* restrictive framework than that which has actually applied in Britain (as in relation to the 'fleeing felon' rule mentioned above, pp. 63–4). Thus, the codes of practice would almost certainly forbid firing at or from a moving vehicle (which is a restriction not imposed in any of the countries referred to above), but under extreme conditions the courts might still judge it perfectly 'reasonable' for an officer to breach this rule. Such a code would provide the basis for proper conduct without creating a legal strait-jacket. In any event, a shooting incident is automatically referred to the Police Complaints Authority for an independent inquiry.

*'To err is human, to forgive is not force policy'*

Criticism of police behaviour in relation to the use of firearms often concentrates less on what actually or allegedly happened and more on the satisfactory or unsatisfactory subsequent investigation of the incident (Asmal, 1985; Kitchin, 1988). The suspicion persists that the police will close ranks and cover up any misdeeds committed by their colleagues — seemingly a propensity to be found worldwide.[5]

In other jurisdictions, where the possession and use of firearms by the police are commonplace, there may be genuine problems of accountability. In Britain, the use of firearms by police is so exceptional that it seems incapable of avoiding the closest scrutiny. In each of the most controversial shootings, where innocent people were the victims, the officers concerned were tried for serious criminal offences. The fact that no convictions were achieved meant that, in each case, after close public scrutiny before an independent jury, the officers were acquitted of criminal conduct.

Nor is there evidence that police close ranks and protect officers involved in controversial shooting incidents; indeed, the available evidence points in the opposite direction. The behaviour of some senior officers towards subordinates who have shot people in the line of duty suggests a tendency to abandon those who might cause embarrassment or controversy. The Home Office report on post-shooting trauma (Manolias and Hyatt-Williams, 1988) remarked: 'Quite frequently little consideration seems to have been shown about the welfare of firearms officers' (p. 11), adding that this behaviour amounted to 'callous or even cruel treatment' in some cases (p. 14). Fortunately, the identification of 'post-traumatic stress disorder' as a medical condition has led to the implementation of rules and procedures which should prevent similar excesses in future. Officers involved in shooting incidents now and in future will be immediately placed on sick leave and offered professional counselling and support.

Nevertheless, problems remain: officers involved in shootings are removed from any operational role for the duration of any investigation and this can cause irritation and resentment, since it might appear both to him and his colleagues as a punishment for doing his duty. The onerous responsibility of carrying a gun does not cease with the decision to open fire or not, for having decided, in a split second, to fire, the officer will find a host of others eager to second-guess his decision — such is the price of the rule of law.

## Should Police Be Armed at All?

This chapter has concerned itself so far with problems concerning the numbers of armed police, the training they receive, the frequency with which arms are carried, the adequacy of command, and the legal liability of the armed officer. All of this is predicated on the assumption that it is right for at least *some* officers to be armed some of the time. However, this assumption has been radically challenged by Jacobs and Sanders (1986), who conclude that police should not be armed at all. They argue, first, that arming the police for their own self-defence transfers the risk of injury, however remote, from the police to innocent third parties. Since there is nothing to choose between an injury to a police officer and injuries to other innocent people, there is no reason to advantage police to the disadvantage of the public. Secondly, they point out that the risk to police officers from armed criminals may be no greater, and possibly less, than the danger to other groups, such as postmasters and security guards. If police have a claim to be armed for their self-defence, so too do these other groups; and this would transform Britain into an armed society like the USA, a development which would be contrary to the wider public interest. Fourth, in reply to the argument that the State owes a duty to those upon whom it imposes hazardous responsibilities, they claim that the State owes an equal duty to many other groups of citizens which it discharges with less care than it does its duty to the police. For example, the State does not properly safeguard threatened minorities, whereas it lavishes resources upon law and order. They conclude that access to guns is a privilege. A just and democratic society cannot give privileges to one group and withhold them from another unless the first group has a greater right to, or need for, that privilege. At present the police have no greater right to, or need for, firearm protection than countless other groups of people. (Jacobs and Sanders, 1986: 13)

Although this argument will appear to many to be ridiculous, and has been ridiculed, it serves the useful purpose of challenging us to justify why police, and police alone, should be allowed to carry firearms. Such a justification actually obliges us to recognize the reality that police are not merely 'citizens in uniform', but are 'monopolists of force in civil society' (Bittner, 1970) with duties that the rest of us do not share. In fact, Jacobs and Sanders (1986: 12–13) acknowledge this when they note: 'Police officers are unusual in that the state places them in jeopardy and does not allow them to retreat from danger.' Hence 'egalitarian grounds' do not apply; if they did, then police would not be obliged to tackle armed people. The authors' dismissal of this argument on the grounds that the State does not discharge its obligations to 'threatened minorities' and others is specious, even supposing it to be factually correct. The State *explicitly* imposes upon police officers certain duties which expose them to danger, whereas even if it disregards entirely—even as a matter of policy—racial violence, it places no duty on those who suffer such violence to expose themselves to this danger. In any case, even if it is true that the State discharges its responsibilities to the police more adequately than it does for other citizens, such a failure does not excuse it from discharging its duty as completely as possible.

Nevertheless, it remains true that arming the police may displace the risk from them to innocent persons killed and injured accidentally. However, even this argument is not nearly as simple as Jacobs and Sanders make it sound, for refusing to arm the police might also expose innocent third parties to danger. For example, unarmed police would be impotent to prevent armed terrorists from slaughtering passengers in an airport terminal. Thus, the danger is not simply transferred from the police to other citizens, but from the police *and* one group of innocent citizens to other innocent citizens. Of course, much the same applies to the ambulance and fire services, for in speeding to convey someone to hospital or extinguish a fire they too expose other citizens to the risk of accidental death or injury. Perhaps this is what the authors have in mind when they make an exception 'where the safety of the general public would otherwise be jeopardised' (Jacobs and Sanders, 1986: 13). Once this point is conceded, however, the absolute refusal to allow police to carry firearms is renounced, to be replaced by the question of how many firearms should be issued under what circumstances. As has been shown above, the police have pursued and are continuing to pursue a cautious policy in this regard.

*Weighing the dangers of armed confrontation*

An alternative to not arming the police is to avoid armed confrontation if at all possible. As is explained more fully in Appendix A the preferred option is always to contain and to negotiate a peaceful surrender. Nevertheless, there are some occasions where confrontation is initiated by armed police, particularly when intercepting armed robbers. This inevitably occurs in a public place where innocent people may be present and shots are likely to be exchanged in potentially chaotic circumstances as criminals seek to avoid capture. It is also a situation in which armed police are most likely to make a split-second decision about whether or not to shoot. If the police are in possession of sufficient information to mount an interception, why not arrest the criminals at a time and place of their own choosing, when the hazards of armed confrontation are minimized?

The police response to this type of question is that this is the course of action they *do* pursue whenever possible, but that it is not always possible. Robbery Squad and other officers who repeatedly deal with serious crimes point out that information which justifies an interception may not be sufficient to establish a prosecution. For example, an interception may be mounted on the basis of gossip and hearsay, or an informant may simply not be prepared to give evidence in court. Juries have shown themselves unwilling to convict suspected armed robbers on 'conspiracy' charges even when they have been found in possession of what seems straightforwardly incriminating evidence. Armed robbers, it seems, make it a habit not to come into possession of their most incriminating accessories (masks, guns, and so forth) until the very last moment before the robbery commences. An overt police presence at the scene might prevent the commission of a robbery of which the police had prior warning, but only the arrest and conviction of the robbers will prevent them from committing another robbery at another place without police knowledge.

The alternative might be for the police to allow the robbers to commit the robbery, secure good evidence of their involvement by the use of evidence-gathering videos and photographs, and then arrest the criminals later. This may not be possible when robbers are masked; and even if identification could be guaranteed, there is always the danger that a robbery of which the police had prior intelligence goes wrong and some innocent third party gets hurt. In the latter circumstances it is likely that there would be a public outcry, and at least possible that the police could be held to be in neglect of their duty. Equally, if robbers who are surrounded by armed police behave as inexplicably as did Anthony Ash and his companions at Woolwich in 1987 and initiate a gun-fight, the police are open to the criticism that they exposed innocent bystanders to danger. This is simply another of the inescapable dilemmas that surround police use of firearms.

### Should the Police be Routinely Armed?

If the view that the police should be completely disarmed is rejected, are there not compelling grounds for routinely arming *all* police officers? In the wake of the Hungerford massacre, police were criticized for the slowness of their response. It was suggested that, had armed police been more readily available, then Michael Ryan could have been cornered and captured or shot before he had killed as many people as he eventually did kill (Edwards, 1988). Whilst this argument only challenged the wisdom of the official policy of reducing the number of AFOs, it is consistent with the wider argument that if all police were routinely armed they would be better able to protect the public from armed criminals and terrorists.

It is also argued by Greenwood (1987) that routinely arming the police would reduce the likelihood of mistakes and accidents such as the Waldorf, Groce, and Shorthouse shootings. He claims that current policy marginalizes the use of firearms, so that, when police find it necessary to deploy armed officers, they and those accompanying and commanding them find the whole situation unfamiliar. Routinely handling firearms would encourage officers to regard their gun as just another item of equipment to be used when necessary.

Together, these arguments stand Jacobs and Sanders (1986) on their proverbial head. They amount to saying that the public would be better safeguarded by a routinely armed police than by having police use of firearms restricted. However, it is no more convincing than its antithesis, for it seems to be based on no firm empirical foundation.

The notion that routinely armed police would be able to intervene more quickly and decisively to prevent recurrences of incidents like the Hungerford massacre seems plainly to be false. It is worth noting that the Hungerford massacre occurred on the first anniversary of an incident in Oklahoma, where a postal worker shot dead eight of his colleagues. The presence of a routinely armed police did not prevent that massacre, any more than it prevented the murder of thirteen people in and around a McDonald's hamburger restaurant in San Ysidero, California, a year previously, or the shooting of several primary-school children in Chicago in 1988. There have been similar episodes of rampaging killers massacring large numbers of innocent people in Belgium, France, and Australia, all of which have routinely armed police. The reason for such a loss of life before police can effectively intervene seems to have been the same as the reasons for the hesitant police reaction at Hungerford — speed and chaos. Although the Hungerford shootings spanned an hour, most incidents of this kind are over in a matter of minutes. By the time the police arrive, most of the carnage has taken place. In addition, police rarely have a clear idea of what has happened and who the perpetrator is or where he is to be found. By the time these uncertainties have been resolved, the person has usually been cornered and/or run out of ammunition. In any case, unless officers were to be routinely armed with high-velocity rifles (an escalation in police weaponry which is rare even in the USA), they would be no match for someone like Michael Ryan, who was armed with a semi-automatic assault rifle. In this event, a specialist firearms team would need to be mobilized and deployed, all of which takes time.

Nor is there any firm empirical foundation for the argument that greater familiarity with firearms would prevent tragic accidents. The fact is that we simply do not know and cannot easily discover whether those police forces throughout the world that are routinely armed are or are not more competent in their use of firearms than are the British police. The USA does not collect statistics regarding the numbers of people shot by police and the circumstances in which they are shot. However, occasional Press reports and research studies featuring police use of firearms reveal that mistakes certainly do occur. Again, systematic evidence about mistaken shootings by Continental police forces is notable for its absence, but incidents have come to attention which indicate that here too mistakes and accidents occur. For example, Dutch police attempting to capture an escaped German convict shot and killed his hostage (*The Times*, 23 June 1989). Perhaps the most tragic example of incompetence was the attempt to free Israeli hostages from their Palestinian captors during the Olympic Games held in Munich in 1972. This brief catalogue of failings by other police forces is not designed to excoriate them, but merely to correct the claim that familiarity with firearms breeds competence.

There are also strong grounds for arguing that routinely arming the police constitutes a hazard for public and police alike. Even in countries whose police are exposed to far more violence than in Britain, most police work does not involve firearms. In these numerous hostile, but unarmed, confrontations the officer's gun can be more of a hindrance than a help. It is worth noting that around a third of American police officers who are killed on duty are shot with their own gun. Thus, in anticipatory self-defence officers must adopt tactics when dealing with everyday incidents which offer additional protection from the threat of having their gun snatched from them (Rubenstein, 1973). What this tends to encourage is the use of firearms, not as a weapon of last resort, but as the primary weapon. FBI instructors confirm that an officer would 'draw down' upon people in any hostile encounter as a matter of course. If this practice became commonplace in Britain, it would lead inevitably to a massive escalation in the use of force and doubtless to a deterioration in police–public relations.

Police–public relations would also suffer from the need for officers to adopt a defensively antagonistic approach to *all* police–public encounters so as to protect their weapon in non-confrontational encounters with ordinary citizens. Armed police tend to adopt the habit of turning the 'weak hand' side of the body towards anyone who approaches them, so that their gun is furthest from the person (Rubenstein, 1973). Unfortunately, this posture tends to be widely perceived as aggressive, since it bears a close resemblance to a boxing stance, and discourages non-confrontational contact between police and public (see Waddington, 1989 for further discussion).

## Conclusions

Policy in Britain has been conservative: the arming of police was precipitated by the growth in armed crime and terrorism; systematic training was only begun once it became clear that it could no longer be avoided; and the intention is to maintain only small teams of highly trained, specialized officers for armed operations. On the other hand, it must be said that, whilst caution in this area of policy-making is generally to be commended, it seems that it has been adopted by default. Developments have been forced upon policy-makers by events. The Home Office Working Party report (Home Office, 1986*a*), though in many ways a sensible document, gives little indication that the problems of dealing with armed operations have been fully appreciated. One hopes that it will not require another disaster to promote still further developments in training and operational arrangements.

# 4
# 'Deadly Force'

## Introduction

Although the police have always used firearms they have been reluctant to acknowledge it too openly. Their fear, that to do so would promote public concern, has proven well-founded. Controversial incidents, especially tragic mistaken and accidental shootings, have raised not only issues of selection, training, and supervision, but also anxieties about an aggressive style of policing. It was seen in Chapter 2 that condemnation of 'trigger-happy' police has followed even the most apparently justified shootings of armed robbers by police. It was also noted how public anxieties were aroused by the sight of officers openly carrying what appear to be sub-machine-guns at Heathrow airport.

What seems to be at risk, so far as many onlookers are concerned, is whether the traditional commitment to the principle of 'minimum force' is in jeopardy. Therefore this chapter will consider whether tactics are unwarrantably aggressive and whether the weapons used are more lethal than they need be.

## 'Shoot to Kill'?

Perhaps one of the most serious worries is that armed officers are taught to 'shoot to kill'. This concern seems to underlie such casual remarks as that made by Tony Banks MP, following the Sir John Soane's Museum shooting: 'Too often police are shooting first and questioning later' (*People*, 8 February 1987). These anxieties have been most fully and forcefully articulated by Sarah Manwaring-White (1983) who, after an apparently thorough review of police weaponry and tactics, concludes:

it is obvious that an increasing number of officers are being trained to shoot to kill and more are trained every year. They are told to aim at the chest area and to do whatever is necessary to protect their colleagues and the public. . . . Training has become a matter of course and 'shoot to kill' has replaced the old instruction of using a gun as the last resort in self defence. (pp. 130–2)

This allegation is given apparent credence by her quoting the injudicious remarks of two Chief Constables: John Alderson, then Chief Constable of Devon and Cornwall, who is reported as saying, 'We are prepared to shoot to kill in the interests of society if necessary', and John Duke, the late Chief Constable of Hampshire, who is quoted as saying, 'The gun is not made for protection, nor made to injure or to frighten. It is made to kill, and police officers being trained to use it when necessary in Hampshire are being trained with this in mind' (Manwaring-White, 1983: 117). More recently, the then parliamentary adviser to the Police Federation, Sir Eldon Griffiths, MP, was quoted as saying that the police 'always shoot to kill' and do so as a matter of duty (*Sun*, 10 July 1987). Of course, the term 'shoot to kill' has acquired added significance in the context of allegations that security forces in Northern Ireland adopted a 'shoot to kill' policy, by which is meant 'summary execution'.

In fact, Manwaring-White's case is flimsy and ill-informed. Let us consider the points made in reverse order. Perhaps the statements made by the two Chief Constables were ill-advised and made without consideration of how they might later be used by critics such as Manwaring-White. Yet, even as they stand, they do not offer support for Manwaring-White's extravagant conclusions. Alderson is saying no more than is and always has been the truth, for as 'monopolists of force in civil society' (Bittner, 1975) the police must be prepared ultimately to use lethal force to fulfil their mandate to protect the public. Thus, if it is necessary to shoot and kill a terrorist machine-gunning passengers in an airport lounge, this will be the duty of the police. This is not a revolutionary change: the police used firearms to engage anarchistic terrorists at the 'Siege of Sidney Street' (Gould and Waldren, 1986: ch. 7). What has changed is the scale of preparedness made necessary by the growth in armed crime and terrorism.

Mr Duke, too, is uttering no more than a truism. A gun is not designed to fend off bullets: it is only effective when fired, and when it is fired at someone it is likely to prove fatal. When he says that Hampshire police officers are trained with this in mind, he is doing no more than repeating the generally accepted guidance on police use of firearms. Metropolitan Police policy, as taught to all AFOs, is quite explicit on this:

An authorized firearms officer is trained to shoot at a given area — usually the torso. Any shot aimed at that target area is likely to result in grievous bodily harm being caused. Therefore, if an officer shoots with the intention not to kill the suspect, but to stop him, he must realize that a possible consequence is the death of the suspect. He must therefore believe before he shoots that causing grievous bodily harm or possibly killing the suspect is reasonable under those particular circumstances and that the conditions of Section 3 Criminal Law Act 1967 apply.

It follows that, if the circumstances would not justify the killing, there must be no attempt to stop a suspect by shooting merely to wound him.

There are, then, two related but separable points to be considered. The first is that the purpose of shooting someone is not to kill them, but to stop them committing some extreme act. The goal is not death, but total and immediate incapacitation. The second point is that the consequence of shooting someone is probably, although not inevitably, that they will be killed. The policy is cautious, rather than cavalier in the manner suggested by Manwaring-White, because it insists that police can open fire only when they would be justified in killing the person, even if death does not result. In contrast to the impression conveyed by Manwaring-White, the policy is conservative, for it insists that firearms be used only as a last resort in the most extreme circumstances.

The reference made by Duke to using guns to 'frighten' people also leads, in fact, to the opposite conclusion to that arrived at by Manwaring-White. Two of the six safety rules which AFOs must learn by rote and be prepared to recite whenever challenged, state, 'Never draw your weapon from the holster unless you have occasion to use it' and 'Never

point a firearm at anyone unless you are prepared to shoot'.
In other words, officers are specifically warned *not* to draw
their weapons and point them simply in order to intimidate
someone. Drawing a gun from the holster is a serious matter,
which must be reported to senior officers, and is not to be
undertaken lightly.

If the purpose of shooting at suspects is to stop rather than
kill them, why is it necessary to fire twice in 'sense of
direction' shooting (see p. 293)? Police are trained to fire two
shots in rapid succession when firing 'sense of direction'
because these shots are fired at close range when immediate
incapacitation is absolutely essential given the imminence of
the threat. In view of the urgency of the situation and the lack
of time in which to take aim, one shot might miss the armed
person; and in the time it would take to appreciate this the
suspect could have fired and killed the officer or some other
innocent person. Moreover, if only one bullet struck the
person there is no guarantee that it would totally incapacitate
and prevent the suspect returning fire. The shooting at the Sir
John Soane's Museum provides a good illustration of the
difficulties that can arise in such circumstances. One of the
bullets fired at Denis Bergin actually struck the butt of the
shotgun he was carrying. Only one bullet struck his body.
The other man who was shot was hit by a single bullet in the
arm. In the confined space of the hallway of the museum, a
failure totally to incapacitate an armed person could easily
prove fatal to the police or other innocent people.

## Returning fire?

If the police must only open fire when justified in using lethal
force, should they not wait until their adversaries open fire
upon them? In other words, are the police 'shooting first and
questioning later', as Tony Banks, MP, suggested? This
question has arisen, of course, most acutely in those cases
where unarmed people have been mistakenly shot, but also
when individuals carrying *unloaded* weapons or replicas have
also been shot by police.

If officers were to be constrained only to draw their own
weapon when confronted by a person who also had a weapon

drawn, or only to point it when another was intending to shoot, or to fire only when fired upon, then this would be tantamount to inviting them to commit suicide. To draw a weapon from the holster, especially when that weapon is concealed under a tunic or jacket, would take much too long. A person armed with, say, a shotgun, would have ample time to aim and fire before the police officer's weapon had cleared the holster. Only to point a gun when an officer intends to fire it would, again, expose that officer to undue risk from a sudden attack. To fire only when fired upon is a prescription for serious injury or death. Thus, officers must be allowed to draw their gun from the holster when they reasonably apprehend that there is an armed threat. Similarly, it is essential that officers should fire their weapon when they reasonably anticipate that an armed person is *about* to open fire.

### Warnings

The extent of the danger to which armed officers are exposed when confronting armed suspects is illustrated by the fate of three policemen engaged upon armed operations. The first, PC Peter Slimon, was shot as he shouted a warning to bank robbers in 1972. The second was Inspector Dwight Atkinson, who was shot in the leg as he called out a warning to armed bank robbers in Woolwich in 1987. The third, and most tragic, was PC Brian Bishop of the Essex Police, who was shot and killed by an armed robber whom he and his colleagues intercepted at Frimley in 1984. Bishop died as he challenged the robber to surrender with his gun drawn and pointing at the robber. Nevertheless, the latter was able to fire both barrels of his sawn-off shotgun from within a bag that he was carrying. The shots killed Bishop and seriously wounded his colleague standing near to him. A shot fired by a third officer armed with a shotgun gravely wounded the gunman, but was not quick enough to save Bishop and his colleague. Although having his gun drawn did not save Bishop, to require officers in similar circumstances to keep their weapon holstered would significantly increase the risk to them.

The fate of these officers puts other, more controversial, incidents into proper perspective. For example, the killing of Michael Calvey in 1978 has been criticized because he was hit in the back during a raid on a supermarket in Eltham by a shot fired by officers lying in wait. The pathologist explained at the inquest that the wound indicated that Calvey had been in the act of turning towards the officer when hit. A fully loaded double-barrelled shotgun was in his possession at the time, and was recovered from the scene. Had the officer not fired when he did, allowing Calvey to aim the shotgun towards him, he might well have suffered the same fate as Bishop. An even more striking parallel with the murder of Bishop was the shooting by police of two robbers at a North London sub-post office in 1984. When challenged, one of the robbers reached into a holdall he was carrying. Fearing that it concealed a shotgun, the officers opened fire, wounding the man and his accomplice. Upon inspection the bag was found not to contain a weapon (*The Times*, 15 June 1984). Of course, the officers could not have known that at the time, and had the bag indeed contained a gun they too might have been killed as Bishop was later to be killed. Inevitably, armed officers may be called upon to make a split-second decision which might, with hindsight, prove to have been made in error. An erroneous decision to open fire might lead to the injury or death of an innocent person; the opposite error may result in the death or injury of the officer himself.

Of course, the police cannot be licensed to fire upon suspects no matter what the circumstances, nor does the law allow them to do so. They can only use such force as is 'reasonable in the circumstances'. However, when it comes to judging what is 'reasonable in the circumstances', the actual hazards of armed operations must be kept in mind. The possession of a gun does not make a police officer invulnerable, and he must make split-second decisions upon which his life and the lives of others might depend. This undoubtedly creates a recurring dilemma, not least for the officer holding the gun, but it is not a dilemma that can be eliminated by imposing such restrictions on police officers as would repeatedly place their lives in jeopardy.

*'Shooting to wound'*

A third point raised by the quote from John Duke regards so-called 'shooting to kill' as opposed to 'shooting to wound'. As Duke remarks, guns are designed to kill, not merely to injure, and the official guidelines explicitly forbid officers to attempt to stop a suspect by shooting to wound him or firing a warning shot. Why not shoot simply to wound or to knock a weapon from a person's hand? It would seem a humanitarian alternative to shooting with the knowledge that one is likely to kill. It would also seems to accord faithfully with the doctrine of 'minimum force'. Having passed the threshold at which recourse to firearms becomes necessary, this surely avoids inflicting more injury than is required to subdue an adversary. A person shot in the lower limb might well drop any weapon he was carrying and thus be rendered harmless. It seems difficult to disagree with Blom-Cooper (1988):

Even if prevention [of a crime] dictates some incapacitation of the terrorist before effecting his capture, it may be unnecessary or unreasonable to use deadly force. Warning shots overhead, or in an emergency to avoid an escape, a shooting to injure or maim but not to kill may suffice.

If such a policy were to be implemented, however, far from reducing death and serious injury, it would be likely to increase them.

There are four reasons why this is so: first, shots intended to wound are likely to miss. Limbs are very much more difficult to hit than the torso, especially in the highly charged conditions of an armed confrontation. It is, therefore, more likely that shots aimed at the limbs will miss their target completely (this, of course, being the intention of shots fired as warnings). In this event two dangers arise: the first is that, having missed its intended target the bullet will hit someone else and cause injury or death; the second is that, having missed the person at whom the shot was aimed, the intended target will carry out his threat.

Second, a wounded person is unlikely to be incapacitated either totally or immediately. Even if shots fired at the limbs strike their intended target, it is far from certain that they would have the intended effect. Compared to the trauma that normally follows being shot in the torso, gunshot wounds in the limbs inflict only relatively slight injury. Even if a person fell to the floor having been shot in the leg, he might still retain hold of a weapon and be capable of using it. There is a further danger: shots fired at the limbs are highly likely to pass through their target, retaining enough velocity to inflict serious injury or death upon anyone unfortunate enough to get in the way.

The third objection follows from the first two, for if shots aimed at the limbs failed to incapacitate totally and immediately, either because they missed or did insufficient injury, police officers would become inclined to open fire at a lower level of threat. To do otherwise would be to gamble with the life that was being threatened: a shot which failed to incapacitate, might allow the adversary to kill innocent people. There would need to be sufficient time to allow some assessment to be made of the effects of each shot. If the shot had missed or failed to incapacitate, a further shot may be necessary. Delaying to the last possible moment before opening fire would not leave enough time to make such an assessment and take *any* corrective action before the threat was executed.

This leads to the fourth objection; if police were to open fire at a lower level of threat, albeit with the intention of wounding, the result is likely to be an increase in serious injury and death. Mention has already been made of the danger posed to innocent bystanders by shots that miss or pass through a limb. There is also the likelihood that shots fired with the intention of wounding will actually kill. Errors of aim are likely to result in shots intended to hit the limb actually hitting a vital organ. Even when the bullet strikes its desired target, there is no guarantee that it will not ricochet off bone or a hard object carried by the person and cause unintended serious injury or death. For example, Errol Walker, shot as he stabbed his hostage at Northolt in 1985, was shot in the shoulder, but the bullet ricocheted, striking him in the side of the head, causing him serious injury although it did not kill him. If police officers were to follow the guidance offered by Blom-Cooper and fire at the lower torso, this likelihood becomes much greater, since, if the bullet misses the abdominal arteries, there is a strong probability that it will hit the pelvis and ricochet with unknowable consequences. These are more than hypothetical possibilities: evidence from Australia (Harding, 1970) and Canada (Chappell and Graham, 1985) suggests that a significant proportion of dubious killings by police arose from shots fired with the intention of warning or wounding.

It might be objected that even if *some* adversaries were inadvertently killed by shots intended to wound, this is preferable to *all* of them being shot with the intention of killing. This would be so if those shot at a lower level of threat would, in any case, have been shot at a later stage of the incident at an extreme level of threat. It is probable that at least some incidents would never reach the most extreme threat level, and so people would be shot with the intention of being wounded who would not be shot at all if the expectation was that they would be killed. Therefore, the likelihood is that a 'shoot to wound' policy would result in more people being shot, a proportion of whom would be killed.

The balance of advantage seems to lie — where policy currently places it — in favour of having recourse to firearms only *in extremis* and doing so with the intention of inflicting grievous, if not fatal, injury. To do otherwise would be to invite a lowering of the threshold at which recourse to firearms was made and thereby possibly to cause the unintended greater loss of life. The cost of this approach is that when shots *are* fired they must inflict sufficient injury to incapacitate immediately and utterly.

## Man-Stopping Bullets

This brings us to the question of the weaponry issued to police, particularly the type of ammunition used and whether it is gratuitously injurious. Benn and Worpole (1986: 64) make the extraordinarily ridiculous claim that the .38-in

Smith and Wesson is 'a large calibre revolver originally developed for hunting in the US and known there as the "grizzly-bear killer". No other European countries issue their police with such large hand guns, guns which it seems lack the double-safety devices of other pistols.' In fact, the Model 10 Smith and Wesson was originally designated as the 'military and police' revolver, for this was always its intended market. The use of hand-guns for hunting is a relatively recent development, arising from the production of particularly powerful weapons, all of which chamber ammunition of much heavier calibre than the .38-in cartridge. Yet even these particularly powerful weapons would not be used against an animal as large as a grizzly bear.

Apart from these errors of fact, this and other similar comments reveal two areas of confusion: that between the revolver and the propellant power of the ammunition fired, and between revolvers and self-loading pistols. This section will examine the first source of confusion and the following section will consider the second.

There is no simple correspondence between the calibre of a gun and the power of the ammunition it can fire. A .38-in revolver may be capable of firing any one of several types of ammunition which vary in their power and, hence, muzzle velocity. The .380-in, or '.38-in short' as it is sometimes known, is the least powerful; the .38-in standard is next most powerful; that is followed by the .38-in special and the .38-in special + P; and finally the .357-in Magnum is the most powerful.

Contrary to the impression conveyed by television and cinema portrayals of armed police, there is no such weapon as the 'Magnum'. Thus, when Clint Eastwood says, in the 'soliloquy' from *Dirty Harry*, 'This is a Magnum .44-in, the most powerful hand-gun in the world . . . so all you've got to ask yourself is "Do I feel lucky today?"' he is talking nonsense: it is a Smith and Wesson Model 29 that he is pointing at the 'bad guy'. The term 'Magnum' refers, not to the gun, but to the propellant power of the round fired by the gun. In fact, just to confuse matters, the .357-in Magnum round is the same diameter as the .38-in round (the difference in nomenclature arising from where on the cartridge the measurement is taken). The difference between these rounds is the power of the propellant and the length of the cartridge case which accommodates it.

Confusion arises because not all .38-in rounds can be fired from the same gun. As the power of the round increases, so too does the length of the cartridge case. This is partly due to the need to accommodate the propellant itself, but also ensures that weapons which are not designed to withstand greater pressures cannot fire the more powerful cartridges. Thus, a .357-in Magnum round would fit into the chamber of a Smith and Wesson Model 10, but it would protrude beyond the length of the chamber, thus preventing the cylinder from being closed and the bullet fired. However, any of the various .38-in rounds could be fired from a revolver capable of firing Magnum ammunition, because the length of the cartridge would be less than that of the chamber. The round that is currently approved by the Home Office for issue to the police is the .38-in special + P 125 grain bullet, about which more will be written later.

Confusion is, perhaps, compounded by the fact that some police officers are issued with weapons which *are* capable of firing Magnum ammunition, even if they do not do so. For example, until recently Model 19s and 28s were issued to members of Level I teams, who also act as instructors. Why issue revolvers capable of firing the Magnum round, if this round is not actually used? Any gun designed to fire a Magnum round tends to be more robust than its counterparts designed to fire less powerful ammunition, because this round when fired imposes greater stress upon the weapon. Thus, an additional advantage of supplying Model 19s and 28s to instructors, who use them quite frequently in training and instruction, is that they are more durable. Moreover, heavier weapons tend to be more accurate. In short, the fact that some officers may be equipped with revolvers capable of firing more powerful ammunition does not mean that they will actually fire the most powerful ammunition the gun is capable of chambering. In sum, to say that the Smith and Wesson is a 'large-calibre revolver' (Benn and Worpole, 1986: 64) is simply to confuse the weapon and the power of the ammunition.

It is equally misleading to compare the Smith and Wesson .38-in revolver with the 9-mm self-loading pistols traditionally used by Continental, and increasingly carried by American, police forces. In fact, the 9-mm parabellum round is almost exactly the same diameter as the .38-in round. Moreover, just as .38-in ammunition has its more or less powerful variants, so too does 9-mm ammunition. However, it should be added that, because of the enclosed construction of self-loading weapons, as compared to the open construction of the revolver cylinder from which gases can escape other than through the barrel, 9-mm ammunition actually has a *higher* muzzle velocity than comparable revolver ammunition. This invalidates the second element of Benn and Worpole's assertion.

Nevertheless, it must be acknowledged that there *has* been a drift towards the use of more powerful ammunition by police during the recent past. The 158-grain .38-in Special replaced the .380-in, and more recently it in turn has been replaced by the 125-grain .38-in special + P round. The decision to change from the .380-in to the .38-in special was dictated by problems in the supply of ammunition, which is governed to a significant extent by the large American market. The switch from the 158-grain .38-in special to the 125-grain .38-in special + P was made in order to provide the police with ammunition which had greater stopping power. However, it is a type of round which in 1973 was refused to the Metropolitan Police (Gould and Waldren, 1986: 202) and was described by the *Daily Telegraph* as being 'softer and flat-nosed so as to spread on impact' (quoted in Gould and Waldren, 1986: 201).

There may appear to be some substance, therefore, to claims that the police are using more powerful ammunition than they need and which, from the *Daily Telegraph's* description, appears to be a form of 'dum-dum' bullet apparently outlawed by international treaty. Indeed, the decision to adopt semi–jacketed, semi–wadcutter ammunition (see p. 278) was taken in the knowledge that it departed from the strict letter of the Hague Conventions of 1889, 1899, and 1907, the provisions of which British and European governments have extended unilaterally to the police. These conventions stipulate that *military ammunition* must be fully jacketed round-nosed, and not designed to disintegrate or explode upon impact. It explicitly forbids 'hollow-point' bullets, commonly referred to as 'dum–dum' bullets. However, these conventions have never applied to policing; they have simply been extended by analogy.

The choice of a semi-wadcutter, semi-jacketed round departs from the Hague Convention in so far as the bullet is not fully jacketed and might, therefore, be seen as gratuitously lethal. In fact, the 125-grain revolver bullet and its 95-grain parabellum equivalent were chosen because, in practice, their fully jacketed predecessors were found to be *more* likely to disintegrate upon hitting a person. Specifically, it was discovered that the metal jacket became detached from the lead bullet after striking bone. Thus, it is contended that the semi-jacketed bullet, whilst departing from the strict letter of the Hague Conventions, complies with its spirit and is not *designed* to expand or fragment. At the same time, a lighter, faster bullet was thought to offer greater 'stopping power'.

*Stopping power*

This calls for some clarification of the notion of 'stopping power'—a discussion which for the moment will be restricted to low-velocity bullets like those fired from revolvers. Bullets do not simply puncture the flesh, causing loss of blood, nor does the impact energy of the bullet knock a person off his feet. Low-velocity bullets fired from pistols, sub-machine-guns, and shotguns (and typically used by police) inflict catastrophic injury in the course of rapidly decelerating as they pass through bodily tissue. According to the size, shape, weight, and velocity of the bullet, the transfer of kinetic energy from it to the tissue creates a cavity of varying size and shape. The larger the cavity the more massive is the loss of blood and other bodily fluids, the greater the shock, and the more likely is damage to vital organs, causing rapid incapacitation and possibly proving lethal (Dawkins, 1989).

A bullet should be designed so that it is likely to come to

rest *within* the body of the person shot (in other words, it should not over-penetrate). This is for two reasons: first, it ensures that no other person is hit by a bullet that has passed through the 'primary target', unlike the holiday-maker hit by a bullet fired by the SAS soldiers in Gibraltar (*Independent*, 21 September 1988). Second, but more important, it results in *all* the kinetic energy of the bullet being deposited within the person shot, thus maximizing the amount of injury inflicted.

A failure to inflict maximum injury, and thereby fully to incapacitate, exposes innocent people to danger because the threat can be executed. There is always the real risk that, even as the adversary dies, he may fire a shot or detonate explosives that will injure or kill innocent people. Therefore, once the point is reached when opening fire is justified, the overriding consideration must be to incapacitate the opponent totally and immediately. Using ammunition which inflicts only limited injury, even though it too is often fatal, is to compromise the achievement of incapacitation. Since killing the adversary is justified in these conditions, and death is the likely consequence of being shot, compromising on the amount of injury inflicted is not only potentially dangerous to others but also an exercise in futility.


*Is British police ammunition powerful enough?*

Conformity with the stipulations of the Hague Conventions hitherto, and the continued reluctance to depart from them, testify to the conservative minimalist approach of the British authorities over the years. But the question must be asked: is policy on ammunition too conservative and minimalist? As noted above, police officers are instructed to fire two shots in rapid succession when firing by 'sense of direction' in order totally to incapacitate an armed antagonist. Experience gained at the Plumstead abattoir shooting in July 1987 indicated that when paired shots strike a person they may indeed incapacitate effectively. That same incident also demonstrated that where only a single shot hits a person, he is not necessarily incapacitated and might continue to pose a threat. At Plumstead the robber who survived, though knocked to the ground by the shot, still retained hold of his weapon and might have returned fire had he not been overwhelmed by other armed officers. This replicated the experience of the shooting at Sir John Soane's Museum, where one of the raiders was shot in the arm but was able to escape from the scene before being arrested by pursuing officers. Even more alarming was the fact that one armed robber was shot five times in an exchange of fire with detectives who intercepted a post office robbery in East Acton in 1988 whilst he, in turn, shot and wounded two of the detectives (*Independent*, 16 December 1988). Therefore, there is no guarantee that an armed person struck by a single shot will not be able to return fire, shoot innocent third parties, or detonate explosives. This raises the issue of whether there are good grounds for *increasing* the power of the ammunition supplied to armed officers.

If the police were to adopt more powerful ammunition, the most likely choice would be to use either .38-in special + P or .357-in Magnum hollow-point bullets. The .357-in Magnum hollow-point is virtually universal amongst American police forces, including the FBI, who set the standard of 'best practice' in these matters. The hollow-point configuration causes the bullet to expand rapidly upon hitting flesh and thereby to decelerate, creating a large cavity in the torso. The grounds for using the Magnum cartridge is that its enhanced velocity is needed to produce the expansion of the bullet upon impact. Indeed, there seems to be a trend amongst American police forces to use still heavier calibre ammunition such as .41-in, .44-in, and .45-in, because of the additional stopping power afforded.

Obviously, bullets of a hollow-point configuration, fired at greater velocity and possibly of heavier calibre, are likely to prove more lethal, but lethality should not be confused with stopping power. It is possible that ammunition that lacks stopping power can still prove lethal. The robber shot by PC Slimon in 1972 subsequently died, but did so some time later from loss of blood and was *not* immediately incapacitated by the .380-in bullet that struck him. Some people shot by police using the semi-jacketed, semi-wadcutter bullets have died, but others have survived. Nor does it seem that the use of hollow-point bullets will inevitably kill those who are shot by the police, since American experience indicates that only a third of police shootings prove fatal (Milton *et al.*, 1977).

Use of hollow-point ammunition is a clear breach of the Hague Conventions, but are the standards imposed by those conventions appropriate or prudent when applied to police work? The fully jacketed ammunition stipulated by the conventions tends to over-penetrate, thus proving less effective and more dangerous to innocent bystanders than alternative rounds which the conventions forbid. These are important considerations relating to any police ammunition, but are of particular significance in regard to close-protection officers, who are armed with .38-in Special + P ammunition, and riflemen, who are currently issued with .308-in or .223-in fully jacketed ball ammunition of military design.

Protection officers, for whom the most serious threat is an assassination attempt made at close quarters by someone in a crowd, need ammunition which is most likely to incapacitate a possibly drugged or crazed assassin with minimal risk of over-penetration. Greenwood argues that for this role it is 'irresponsible' to use anything other than hollow-point ammunition (1979: 296), whilst Yardley and Eliot (1986c) prefer the recently developed 'Glaser safety slug', a fully jacketed round containing a number of small pellets which are released within the body of a person shot once the outer casing strikes him, causing enormous injuries, and rejected by the Home Office for this reason. Either of these rounds is more likely to incapacitate even a determined attacker with little risk of over-penetration or ricochets than is currently issued ammunition. However, despite these purely technical advantages, the Home Office has rejected the use of this kind of ammunition because it would inflict injuries which are considered to be ethically unjustifiable and inconsistent with the Hague Conventions.

Achieving a balance between technical suitability and ethical acceptability is even more difficult in the case of high-velocity rifle ammunition. The police are currently permitted to use only ball ammunition of military design which strictly complies with the provisions of the Hague Conventions. However, high-velocity ammunition of this kind is almost invariably lethal, because once the muzzle velocity of a bullet exceeds 2,000 feet per second (and the .308-in Steyr bullet has a muzzle velocity of 3,000 feet per second) it causes a particular kind of injury to the person. As it passes through the body the bullet creates a tremendous shock wave ahead of, and all around, its path. This causes the large exit wounds and enormous injuries for which these weapons have become notorious. Not only is the injury from such a weapon likely to prove fatal, but the bullet is almost certain to over-penetrate and, moving with such velocity, could hit others with devastating consequences.

The danger of over-penetration is illustrated by the injuries suffered by Governor Connally of Texas who was wounded during the assassination of President Kennedy in Dallas in 1963. One of the bullets, which is thought to have struck the president in the back of the neck, is then believed to have exited through the front of the throat and hit Connally, who was seated in front of Kennedy in the same car. The bullet hit Connally in the back and then exited from his chest and struck him in the wrist, eventually coming to rest in his thigh upon which his hand was resting. Fortunately, Connally survived; others might not be so lucky.

If the danger from ricochets is added to that of over-penetration, the unsuitability of this kind of ammunition becomes even more evident. A bullet that missed its target might have a range of up to two miles, and if it struck a substantial object and ricocheted its subsequent path could not be predicted. This could pose a considerable hazard to innocent people quite remote from the scene of the confrontation.

High-velocity weapons are necessary for riflemen because, used at long distance, they must retain their accuracy. The problems of over-penetration and ricochets could be mitigated, however, if not solved, by the adoption of some kind of soft-nosed bullet, such as the ROTA ammunition manufactured by Royal Ordnance which disintegrates upon impact and will not, therefore, ricochet. These rounds would cause horrendous injuries to anyone they struck, and would almost certainly prove fatal. However, the high-velocity ball ammunition now issued to riflemen is hardly less lethal. It seems that the desire not to be seen to adopt a type of ammunition most injurious to the suspect has overruled concern for the safety of innocent people who might suffer the fate of Governor Connally, or worse.

Treating the Hague Conventions as an analogy for the doctrine of 'minimum force' leads to the police being equipped with ammunition which is unsuitable to their role. The principle of 'minimum force' does not apply to military engagements in time of war, and the conventions do not apply to police confronting terrorists and armed criminals who, themselves, are not signatories to the conventions and cannot be expected to be bound by them. If the conventions are not treated as an analogy, and the doctrine of 'minimum force' is approached directly, then the ethical justification for more powerful, and thereby injurious, ammunition becomes evident. Yet such a conclusion invariably provokes a howl of outrage and the accusation that the doctrine of minimum force is being abandoned.

## Minimum Force and Lethality

The objection that using more injurious ammunition would violate the principle of 'minimum force' is to appeal to an unduly simplistic conception of that principle. Put simply, the doctrine of minimum force means that no more force should be used than is *necessary* for the accomplishment of a lawful purpose. What goes unrecognized is that *necessity* has two quite distinct aspects which are of crucial operational importance to the use of firearms by police. The first is that force should not be employed until it becomes essential. Thus, although there may be occasions where a pre-emptive use of force may be expedient in order to extinguish any likelihood of threat, it is normally expected that force will only be used *in response* to some threatening action of the adversary. Force, in other words, should not be used 'just in case' the adversary poses a threat, but only after that threat has materialized.

The second aspect is that the force used should only be sufficient to overcome resistance. No matter how much harm is threatened by an adversary, the amount of force used should be limited to that which is necessary to subdue him, otherwise the use of more force would be gratuitously punitive.

When police use non-lethal force, both corollaries of the doctrine are readily applicable. For example, a police officer should only strike someone with his truncheon if that person poses a threat sufficiently serious and imminent to make hitting him a necessity. Having struck him with sufficient force to disable, the police officer would be unjustified in administering any further blows. By contrast, the use of firearms entails crossing a threshold which precludes the application of this second restriction.

Because firearms are inherently lethal weapons, they can only be justifiably used in the most extreme conditions of an immediate threat to life. Primacy is thus accorded to the first element of the minimum-force doctrine — that firearms should only be used as a last resort. Paradoxically, this effectively renders other considerations redundant, for in life-threatening circumstances it is imperative that incapacitation be both total and immediate. To do otherwise might allow the adversary to carry out his threat after he has been hit. Instant and complete incapacitation entails inflicting nothing less than devastating injury, since the circumstances are so extreme that there is no room for error. This can *only* be achieved with any reliability by bullets that inflict the kind of injury that has hitherto been regarded as ethically unaccept-able. Inflicting such injury *is* to use no more force than is necessary, for to inflict lesser injury in such extreme circumstance might prove ineffective. If, instead, an effort is made to minimize the injury inflicted on an armed adversary, this merely transfers the risk of death and injury from him to the innocent. Using insufficiently injurious ammunition does precisely this — place innocent lives at risk.

*Eliminating the threat and 'shooting to kill'*

A similar problem arises in regard to the number of shots fired at an armed adversary. For although this issue has arisen with shootings in connection with terrorism in Northern

Ireland, it has implications for police on the mainland of Britain.

When terrorists and armed criminals mistaken for terrorists have been shot by the security forces, the great number of shots fired has been equated with a breach of the doctrine of minimum force. The pathologist at the Gibraltar inquest into the shooting of three Provisional IRA terrorists thought to be in possession of remote detonating devices capable of exploding a nearby bomb described the SAS soldiers' action as a 'frenzied attack' on precisely the grounds that each had suffered multiple gunshot wounds (*Independent*, 9 September 1988). It is taken to be axiomatic that shooting someone repeatedly, even after they have collapsed, cannot be consistent with using minimum force, simply because so much force is actually used. On the basis of the previous argument in relation to ammunition, there would seem to be every reason to use such devastating force when circumstances have reached such a perilous extremity. If they have not reached such an extremity there is no justification for shooting at all.

It might appear that to shoot someone twice in rapid succession is sufficient to achieve the purpose of total and immediate incapacitation, and so it might be in many instances. The trouble with relying on this measure of force alone is that it cannot reasonably assure total and immediate incapacitation in all circumstances, for some people show a tremendous capacity for sustaining injuries of this magnitude and still continuing to fight. This is illustrated by the armed confrontations between FBI agents and two armed bank robbers in the Miami suburb of Suniland in 1986, and between police and Palestinian terrorists at a Rome airport in 1985 (Edwards and Menzies, 1986). In both cases, adversaries continued to inflict death and injury upon others despite having sustained multiple and ultimately fatal gunshot wounds.

How can a person fail to be incapacitated after suffering such wounds? First, differences in physique affect the likelihood of incapacitation: more muscular, heavier, and larger people are able to sustain more injury than their smaller, lighter counterparts. Second, scientists have been aware for over a decade that people secrete 'natural opiates' when in a state of physical arousal which act as an analgesic and thereby immunize them against the pain and trauma of gunshot wounds (Snyder, 1986). Third, some criminals and terrorists may take synthetic drugs, such as heroin and its derivatives, which also have an analgesic effect. Fourth, and finally, there is the increasing likelihood that terrorists, in particular, will wear body armour, thus reducing their vulnerability to low-velocity bullets fired at the torso.

In these circumstances, to rely on firing (at most) paired shots only at the torso is to risk ineffective incapacitation of armed opponents and the consequent danger of injury and death being inflicted upon innocent people. The alternative is to use a significantly greater measure of force to ensure, so far as is possible, total and immediate incapacitation. It is reported that the FBI has changed its tactical procedures. The emphasis is now upon 'threat elimination', that is, agents are instructed to keep firing their weapon at their opponents until the threat posed by the suspect is eliminated (*Hand-gunner*, November 1988). Using the increasingly common 9-mm self-loading pistols, this could mean firing up to eighteen shots, and double this number with a change of magazines. This, of course, was the tactic employed by the SAS soldiers during their 'frenzied attack' on the terrorists in Gibraltar. Similar concerns were expressed after soldiers shot three betting-shop robbers on the Falls Road, Belfast, some thirty times (*The Times*, 15 January 1990).

In both incidents attention was also drawn to evidence that the deceased had been shot whilst lying on the ground, which led to the accusation that the soldiers had administered a gratuitous *coup de grâce* (Kitchin, 1988). As Blom-Cooper (1988) has noted: 'It is one thing to fire a fatal shot at an escaping prisoner, himself armed and intent upon shooting to kill. It is altogether different to use overkill — to do something more than is strictly appropriate.' Is firing a fusillade of shots at a person, even after he has collapsed, 'more than is strictly appropriate'? If a person poses an immediate armed threat such action is appropriate, for such a person will only be incapacitated if he is physically prevented from aiming the weapon and pulling the trigger. Firing repeated shots is most likely to achieve this purpose, for the impact of each bullet will cause at least momentary trauma until the person releases his grip on the weapon.

Not even the firing of repeated shots to the torso will necessarily prevent a terrorist from triggering an explosion even though he is lying gravely, even fatally, wounded. Such a threat would be eliminated only when *all* movement is arrested by shooting the person in the head, with the intention of severing the brain stem and thus preventing all motor functioning. Similarly, a gunman threatening a hostage could be prevented from reacting to having been shot himself only if shot in the head.

In short, in some circumstances it may be wholly justifiable under the doctrine of minimum force to inflict the most devastating injury upon an adversary by firing a fusillade of shots possibly at the head and even after the person had collapsed.[1]

## Self-Loading Pistols: Firepower and Safety

It is the capacity to fire multiple shots in rapid succession that is the distinct advantage of the self-loading pistol when compared to the revolver. The Glock carries seventeen rounds in the magazine, and this fire-power is further enhanced by the speed with which magazines can be exchanged, so that in a sustained gun-fight an officer could have as many as thirty-four rounds readily available. It is this capability which has encouraged increasing numbers of American police forces to exchange revolvers for self-loading pistols. Its value was shown during an exchange of fire between police and armed robbers in Harrow, north London, when a PT17 officer expended fifteen rounds.

This kind of weapon also has attractions for critics of the police, for, unlike revolvers, the self-loading pistol is usually equipped with a safety catch. It is to this type of weapon that Benn and Worpole are invidiously comparing the .38-in revolver when they say that the latter 'seems to lack the double-safety devices of other pistols' (1986: 64). They are not alone in voicing such concern. The issue arose most pointedly during the trials of PC Chester and Inspector Lovelock. The defence in each of these trials was in essence the same: that the gun was accidentally discharged by a startled officer. This, not unnaturally, led to questions about the safety of the revolvers issued to these officers and anxiety that they seemed to lack 'safety catches'.

In fact, revolvers are not as a rule fitted with 'safety catches': the safety of a revolver relies upon its firing mechanism, for a revolver fired in 'double action' is an inherently safe weapon. This calls for some explanation of 'double-action' versus 'single-action' shooting. Double action means that, when the revolver's hammer is in the closed position and then the trigger is depressed, the cylinder rotates and the hammer is forced back until it drops forward under the pressure of a spring on to the firing pin, causing the round in the chamber to be fired. This requires between 10 lb. and 13 lb. of pressure on the trigger of the Smith and Wesson Model 10, and the trigger must travel some considerable distance in order to operate the mechanism. This makes double-action shooting an inherently safe procedure. Single action, on the other hand, means that in the case of a revolver the hammer is manually retracted until it locks (sometimes called 'cocking' the hammer), which in consequence rotates the cylinder, positioning the next round in line with the barrel. Then the merest touch on the trigger (3 lb. in the case of the Model 10) releases the hammer which fires the round. The advantage of this mode of shooting is that the reduced pressure upon, and shorter distance travelled by, the trigger allows greater accuracy. For that reason, single action is favoured by competition marksmen. However, it is obviously much less safe, since inadvertent pressure on the trigger would be sufficient to fire a round accidentally.

Until the report of the Home Office Working Party (1986a), Metropolitan Police officers were instructed in how to fire the revolver in both single and double action. This was justified as necessary because it was a feature of the weapon, and it was important for officers to know how it operated. It was also thought to have some operational value for carefully aimed shooting at long distances; accuracy at 25 metres is undoubtedly improved when firing single-action. However, the evident dangers inherent in this procedure convinced the

Home Office Working Party that this mode of firing the
weapon was too dangerous to be continued. There have been
suggestions that under stress officers might place the gun in
single action without realizing they have done so, and
certainly news film of an armed incident in Oldham 1972
shows a supposedly trained AFO doing precisely this and
then pushing the gun, still in single action, into his pocket!

The situation now is that AFOs are familiarized with
single-action shooting, but are instructed never to use it
operationally. What is not clear is why police revolvers
continue to retain the facility for firing in single action. Some
American police forces have adapted the internal mechanism
of their revolvers to prevent this mode of firing, and the
simple expedient of removing the hammer–spur would make
it extremely difficult to cock the hammer. The fact that the
Metropolitan Police have not taken such action, relying
instead upon a simple proscription, seems to reveal a
touching faith in the efficacy of rules and the influence they
might have over officers in a tense and possibly frightening
situation. Surely, if single-action shooting is inherently
dangerous, then the means of doing it should be removed.

Critics seem not to be convinced of the inherent safety of
revolvers, preferring instead the self-loading pistols that
Continental police tend to use (Benn and Worpole, 1986).
Indeed their preference is shared by many police officers in
Britain and North America who find reassurance in the fire
power of such weapons. Whether self-loading pistols are as
suitable for police work as either side of the argument
imagine is, at least, debatable.

*Self-loading pistols: unsuitable complexity*

It is important to recognize the important differences
between the self-loading pistol and the revolver. In a
revolver, each round is placed into its individual chamber
and, as the gun is fired, the cylinder revolves, bringing each
chamber in succession into line with the barrel and firing–pin.
The round itself, once positioned in the chamber, does not
move. By contrast, the rounds in a self-loading pistol are
taken out of the magazine and pushed into the breech very

rapidly. This is a complex and forceful mechanical process which is more likely to result in the weapon jamming because the round is not properly seated in the breech. Jamming may also occur if a bullet misfires and does not create sufficient pressure to operate the mechanism. When this occurs the slide has to be retracted manually, to eject the jammed round. Sometimes the round can be so badly jammed that the gun has to be disassembled to clear it. When a jam does occur, the weapon is incapable of firing any more shots until the jam is cleared. The Walther PP (a standard Continental police pistol) carried by Inspector Beaton when acting as Princess Anne's bodyguard was of this design, and jammed after he had fired one shot at the man attempting to abduct her. Once this occurred, and having been wounded, he was virtually powerless to protect the Princess (Rae, 1987). Revolvers, on the other hand, are mechanically much simpler, and therefore there is less likelihood that things can go wrong. If they do go wrong and the round does not fire for some reason, then all that is needed, save for the most improbable circumstances, is for the handler to squeeze the trigger once again, thus revolving the cylinder and bringing another round into position and firing it.

The sheer mechanical complexity of the self-loading pistol, which demands a very high standard of handling skill, makes this a weapon of limited use for police officers who may have to use the weapon in an emergency. Even in the safety of the practice range the complexities of handling the gun cause difficulties.

A further problem arises from the complexity of the firing mechanism: the need for the user to adopt a sound firing position. Unless the arms are locked so that the recoil from the gun can be fully absorbed by the user, the energy from the recoil can dissipate. This can result in the slide mechanism failing to work adequately and the gun jamming. Such a firing position is taught to users of both self-loading pistols and revolvers, but in an actual gun-fight an officer acting under stress or possibly injured might not be able to adopt an ideal firing position. For example, PC Slimon shot an armed robber after he himself had been shot and was lying on the pavement. It is highly improbable to suppose that he achieved this feat by adopting the prescribed firing position. Had he not been using a revolver, with its simple mechanism, it is less likely that he would have been able effectively to return fire.

Yet another problem arising from the complexity of the mechanism is the restrictions it places on the type of ammunition used. Because the round has to be transferred from the magazine to the breech before being fired, the gun is designed to fire fully jacketed, round-nosed bullets. A fully jacketed bullet has the lead bullet encased in a steel, copper, nickel, or brass sleeve or coat. This enables it to resist any distortion as it is wrenched from the magazine and slammed into the breech. Travel from magazine to breech is aided by a round-nosed bullet shape, which most readily slides up the ramp and into position. Unfortunately, as noted previously, fully jacketed round nosed bullets tend to over-penetrate. In 1986, therefore, it was decided to make available to officers authorized to carry the Browning or Glock an alternative semi-wadcutter, semi-jacketed round, that is, one with a flattened nose which is unsleeved and is therefore less likely to over-penetrate. Unfortunately, its shape means that it is rather less likely to travel easily up the ramp and into the breech. In particular, the condition of the magazine is critical, as any distortion of the lip might cause a jam to occur.

The complexity of this type of weapon demands not only the very highest handling skills, but also a degree of care and maintenance that could only reasonably be expected if it was the sole property of a particular individual, rather than being shared amongst a collection of AFOs.

Why, then, is this weapon so popular amongst firearms-trained police officers? What attracts users to such a weapon is its fire-power, rate of fire, speed of reloading (for all the user need do is remove the empty magazine, replace it with a full one, and release the catch), and its slim shape and lightness, which make it easier to carry and conceal. Perhaps another, but undeclared, reason for the popularity of self-loading pistols is that they are a 'prestige' weapon, restricted to the Force Firearms Unit and officers of the Heathrow airport Security Section.

The undoubted advantage of this type of pistol is its fire-power, and there are good grounds for issuing it to officers who might become engaged in a sustained gun-fight with terrorists and determined criminals. Fortunately, very few armed officers can anticipate such confrontation, and for most police work the revolver seems adequate. The fire-power of revolvers can be enhanced by devices which speed reloading, and which are used by Level II teams. 'Jet loaders' carry six rounds in a cylinder which complements the revolver cylinder and a mechanism which allows all six rounds to be injected into their respective chambers simul-taneously and rapidly. The only disadvantage with this is that it prevents topping up a revolver once a few shots have been fired; on the other hand, it offers a rapid and reliable method of reloading which enhances fire-power.

Whilst the self-loading pistol may be appropriate for officers who are highly skilled in their use, such as Level I teams, it would seem that the disadvantages of this kind of weapon outweigh the advantages for more general use. Only if the use of drugs by armed criminals becomes much more prevalent would the advantages of self-loading pistols outweigh their disadvantages. Even when this kind of weapon is issued to highly specialized officers, it would seem prudent (in view of the fact that armed police should always be deployed in pairs) for the partner to be equipped with the more reliable revolver. Alternatively, the British police may follow their American colleagues in allowing armed officers to carry an additional, back-up gun in case the primary weapon fails to operate or its ammunition becomes exhausted.

### The catch in the safety argument

Another important difference between the two types of weapon is that, whereas revolvers can be fired in single or double action, a self-loading pistol is fired predominantly in the single-action mode. The mechanism of the self-loading pistol is operated by the recoil from the previously fired round, not by the depression of the trigger. Thus, each time a round is fired the mechanism pushes the hammer into the single-action position where the lightest touch on the trigger (5 lb. in the case of the Browning and 7 lb. for the Glock) causes the hammer to fall and the round in the breech to be fired, which in turn activates the mechanism and pushes the hammer into the single-action mode. Since a live round sits in the breech ready to fire and the hammer is cocked, there is always the danger that an inadvertent touch or even a jolt may cause a shot to be fired. It is because self-loading pistols are so delicately poised in single action that they are almost universally equipped with safety catches. Unlike the revolver, the self-loading pistol is not inherently safe and, therefore, safety has to be added by means of an external locking mechanism which prevents the trigger being depressed and a round being fired unintentionally. Once the safety catch is released in anticipation of opening fire, however, there is a greater risk of an accidental discharge than there would be with a revolver. Yet it seems strange that, when single-action shooting with revolvers has been discontinued on grounds of safety, there should be pressure from within the force and outside it to adopt a type of weapon that fires in single action.

Traditionally, self-loading pistols, like the Browning, operated *only* in single action and were carried 'locked and cocked'. When the gun is drawn from the holster, the safety catch is released by the thumb so that as soon as the gun is aimed it is ready to fire. Technical development has, paradoxically, both increased *and* decreased the safety of such weapons. On the one hand, many modern self-loading pistols incorporate a double-action mechanism for the first round fired, thereby enhancing safety. When the weapon is loaded, like all self-loading pistols, the first round is placed into the breech by 'racking' the slide manually. A catch is then depressed which causes the hammer to fall, but the gun does not fire because the hammer is not allowed to make contact with the firing-pin. When the first round comes to be fired, the trigger is depressed and this causes the hammer to open and fall onto the firing-pin as in double action (although, of course, there is no cylinder to rotate). This gives an extra margin of safety with respect to the first shot fired and obviates the necessity of applying a safety catch, but thereafter the recoil slide mechanism ensures that all subsequent rounds are fired single-action. On the other hand, manufacturers have made safety catches easier to release, thus arguably reducing the safety of the gun. The Glock 17, for example, incorporates the safety catch into the trigger so that as the user squeezes the trigger the first few pounds of pressure release the safety catch and the next few pounds cause it to fire, all in one action. The Heckler and Koch P7 incorporates the safety catch into the butt of the gun which, when gripped, releases the catch.

*Safe handling*

The safety of weapons is not guaranteed by safety catches or other mechanical features which can be disengaged. The way in which a weapon is handled is much more important for ensuring that it is safe. As the trials of PC Chester and Inspector Lovelock illustrate, there is the danger that innocent people might be accidentally shot as a result of an armed officer being startled. For example, Inspector Lovelock explained how, as a shape loomed out of the darkness, he tensed, causing the gun to fire.

The likelihood that such an accident will occur is increased by the stance adopted by armed officers. The 'isosceles' stance involves holding the butt of the gun with both hands, arms pushed forward and locked at the elbow, with the knees flexed. The reason for locking the elbows is that under extreme stress muscular control can be diminished, especially in the limbs, causing the condition known colloquially by some American police as the 'liquorice arm'. Massad Ayoob, whose system of gun-fighting is founded on the need to overcome stress, insists that the isosceles position is the most robust stance yet devised (Ayoob, 1984). Unfortunately, since the upper body is locked when adopting this stance, the muscles of the trigger finger are amongst the few parts of anatomy that are left free to contract if the officer is startled.

This danger is reduced by the practice of never fingering the trigger until the last possible moment—even a drawn weapon is held with the finger resting outside the trigger guard. In the event of the officer being startled, the trigger could not be inadvertently squeezed. However, there are difficulties concerning this practice, for normally the finger rests along the frame of the gun in the outstretched position and, if it becomes necessary to finger the trigger, it is simultaneously repositioned and bent around the trigger. Unfortunately, the weakness in this practice is that under stress there is a tendency to exaggerate the contraction of the finger muscles as the finger wraps around the trigger, thus making an accidental discharge likely. Ayoob recommends that, even when resting outside the trigger guard, the finger should always be kept bent, so that no further muscular contraction is required when fingering the trigger; all that is necessary is that the finger is repositioned, and the likelihood of accidental discharge is minimized. This seems to be a sensible recommendation which should be incorporated into training.

## Non-Lethal Weapons

The prospect of non-lethal weapons being developed to replace the disagreeable necessity to use lethal firearms has long held a fascination for lay commentators. The impetus for the development of non-lethal alternatives to firearms in the USA came from the 1985 decision of the US Supreme Court in the case of *Tennessee* v. *Garner*, which restricted the right of American law enforcement personnel to shoot at a 'fleeing felon'. This has prompted the development and use of electrified batons ('sting sticks'), barbs that fasten to the skin and carry an incapacitating electric current ('Tasar'), bags containing shotgun pellets which expand upon being fired from a shotgun so as to stun and disable those who are hit ('bean bags'), and tranquillizing darts.

Unfortunately, no complete replacement for lethal firearms has yet been found. The reasons for this go to the heart of the problem of using minimum but effective force. To use a non-lethal weapon as a direct substitute for lethal firearms would require that it should incapacitate the adversary as totally and immediately as a lethal firearm. However, this would involve inflicting such trauma that it is likely to prove as deadly as a firearm, at least to some people. That is, an electric shock, or stunning impact from a 'bean bag', or anaesthetic drug capable of reliably causing total and immediate incapacitation would inflict so much injury that it is likely to prove fatal itself. If less injury is inflicted, then total and immediate incapacitation cannot be reasonably guaranteed.

What these kinds of weapon *can* offer, and have been used for in America, is a means of dealing with situations before they reach the stage at which the use of potentially lethal force is justified and where total and immediate incapacitation is *not* essential. A man holding police at bay with a knife or a person holding a gun, but not threatening anyone directly, might be overpowered with such a weapon. For example, had the police at the Northolt siege been able to disable Errol Walker when he appeared alone on the balcony adjoining the flat, they might not have had to shoot him as he attempted to stab his hostage.

The problem is one of calibrating a measure of injury needed to disable a dangerous person without its becoming life-threatening. This is immensely difficult given the vagaries of physical differences amongst human beings: the force needed to disable a body-builder could easily kill a 'seven-stone weakling'. Thus, although referred to as 'non-lethal', these weapons have actually caused the deaths of some of those against whom they have been used, whilst others seem to be have been almost totally unaffected by these weapons. As has been noted earlier, not even bullets will have the same effect on all those shot.

The introduction of this kind of weapon, far from resolving the problems of police use of deadly force, actually compounds them. If weapons of this type were to be employed, then potentially lethal force would be employed *not* as a last resort, but at a lower level of threat. True, the likelihood that these weapons would prove fatal is much less than that of firearms, but there remains a likelihood, however small, that they will kill. Thus, the police would need to make an even finer calculation than they now are obliged to make, between the amount of force to be applied as opposed to the level of threat presented by their adversary.

One weapon that seems particularly promising is the 'low energy' version of the ARWEN baton round, which contains a sack of CS powder that ruptures on impact. This, however, like any comparable weapon, is likely to inflict serious injury on at least some people and may even prove fatal in particular circumstances. This weapon was developed by Royal Ordnance in the early 1980s as a replacement for the baton gun used for riot control, in which capacity it has been the victim of the wider campaign waged against the use of plastic baton rounds (see pp. 195–208) and of financial restrictions on procurement by the Ministry of Defence (Waddington, 1989).

## Sub-machine-guns

Of all the weapons issued to the police, those which have attracted most criticism are the Heckler and Koch MP5 and MP5K. It is the MP5 that is carried by some officers at Heathrow airport.

The issue is not whether terrorists pose a serious threat to diplomats, politicians, and airports. The fact that they do is evidenced by attacks such as the attempted assassination of Sholom Argov, the Israeli ambassador, in 1983 and the grenade and machine-gun attack at Rome and Vienna airports in December 1985, which resulted in two passengers being killed and forty-seven injured at Vienna and thirteen killed and seventy-six injured at Rome. The fact that Heathrow is not immune to terrorist activity was vividly illustrated in 1986, when Hussein Hindawi attempted to plant a bomb on board an El Al airliner departing from Heathrow, and, in 1988 by the destruction of Pam Am Flight 103 which blew up over Lockerbie *en route* from Heathrow to New York. Unfortunately, these are only the most recent of a series of similar attacks staged in different parts of the world over the past twenty years. The issue *is* whether the overt deployment of officers carrying the Heckler and Koch MP5 is operationally effective.

The grounds upon which the deployment of the MP5 was justified were twofold: as mentioned in Appendix A, its magazine of thirty rounds affords sufficient fire-power to engage terrorists in a prolonged gun-fight. At Rome and Vienna, terrorists attacked the El Al check-in queues with Kalashnikov AK47 assault rifles which had two magazines of thirty rounds each taped together, so that once the first magazine was exhausted the second could be inserted by the simple expedient of inverting the magazine and pushing it home. This meant that, within the space of a few seconds, the three terrorists at Vienna and the four at Rome each had the opportunity to fire sixty rounds at a rate of 600 rounds per minute. The total attack at Vienna, including a car chase and second gun-fight with police, lasted just seven minutes and that at Rome lasted only fifty-five seconds (Edwards and Menzies, 1986). Given that the police may need to confront that kind of fire-power, it is argued that *they* need the fire-power of a weapon like the Heckler and Koch MP5.

The second reason for requiring a carbine is that police may need to engage terrorists at relatively long distances. Terminal buildings provide large open areas affording little cover, and the piers connecting the various gates for boarding aircraft are enormously long corridors, again offering restricted cover. In addition, airports include large open areas where terrorists might attack airliners waiting to take off. The maximum effective range of the hand-gun is optimistically estimated at 50 metres. Rifles can fire accurately over much greater distances, but suffer from problems of over-penetration. A carbine firing a normal 9-mm pistol round can provide the additional range without much risk of over-penetration should a gun-fight occur under these circumstances. Fired single-shot from the shoulder and having little recoil, the MP5 is justified as much more accurate than any hand-gun but no more injurious.

The deployment of the MP5 at Heathrow created a furore, principally on the grounds that it was a sub-machine-gun unsuitable for use in a crowded airport. Yardley (1986) explicitly doubts whether it was meant to be fired from the shoulder, or whether it was intended to fire only single shots, and added that in any case the ammunition used was unsuitable. Like others, he sees it as a symbolic victory for terrorists, not only unlikely to deter further attacks but likely actually to increase the danger to armed officers, who would become the first targets for any attacker. What validity is there in these criticisms?

As already explained, the gun can only fire single shots and officers are instructed only to fire aimed shots from the shoulder. Why not, then, use a dedicated carbine which would not be confused with a sub-machine-gun, and avoid all the negative connotations of the latter? Yardley argues that such a weapon could fire a round more suitable to police needs. He points out that the Heckler and Koch MP5 normally fires a 9-mm, round-nosed, fully jacketed round, which, as mentioned previously, tends to over-penetrate, lacks 'stopping power' thereby, and tends also to ricochet. However, dedicated carbines are magazine-fed weapons which also normally fire round-nosed, fully jacketed rounds. Moreover, in fact the Metropolitan Police now issue a semi-wadcutter, semi-jacketed round of less power than the military 2Z round to which Yardley seems to be referring. This bullet does not over-penetrate as easily as its military counterpart, nor is it so likely to ricochet, although it is more prone to jam the firing mechanism. Of course, these same rounds could be used in a dedicated carbine with the same advantages and disadvantages. An advantage in doing so might be that they could not be confused with sub-machine-guns, and thus not convey such an aggressive militaristic image. However, dedicated carbines such as the Martini have the appearance of a rifle and must, like the MP5, be carried openly. It is doubtful whether they would be any more acceptable to public opinion.

A second, and altogether more substantial, challenge is contained in a report on the Rome and Vienna terrorist attacks written by Chief Superintendent Edwards and Detective Sergeant Menzies of the Sussex Police, who were at the time responsible for security at Gatwick airport (Edwards and Menzies, 1986). After visiting Rome and Vienna airports in the wake of the terrorist attacks of 1985, they too dispute the operational effectiveness of carbines or sub-machine-guns for use *within* airport buildings. Their report points out that, despite the fact that at least some of the officers who engaged the terrorists at both Continental airports were armed with sub-machine-guns only one officer used this weapon, and he did so in single-shot mode. The authors of this report remark that at Vienna: 'It is significant that although armed with the Steyr sub-machine-gun the offiers chose the 9-mm pistols as the more appropriate weapon for use inside the terminal.' At Rome: 'The majority of the rounds were fired from Beretta pistols . . . The sniper overlooking the concourse could not fire because of the confusion below.' They conclude: 'The use of machine-guns by police in the terminal building is not recommended because of the numbers of passengers that could be reasonably expected', and 'Hand guns used by trained officers can compete effectively against sub-machine-guns in close combat.'

Advocates of the Heckler and Koch MP5 amongst Metropolitan Police firearms instructors reply to this argument by pointing out that it is often the practice on the Continent, where officers are permanently armed with handguns, to use the sub-machine-gun as the back-up weapon rather than the primary weapon. Officers at Heathrow armed with the Heckler and Koch MP5 are trained to regard this as their primary weapon and their hand-gun as their back-up. Hence the Heckler and Koch MP5 is carried in the 'high port' position which facilitates ease of use, being very rapidly aimed and fired from the shoulder.

If, for whatever reason, officers at Rome and Vienna airports used pistols successfully against terrorists armed with AK47s, what purpose is served by equipping officers with carbines? What remains unclear from the Edwards and Menzies report (1986) is how much success the Rome and Vienna officers actually enjoyed. It appears that the terrorists were shot repeatedly but were not incapacitated until all their ammunition had been expended. Had the police used the firepower of a sub-machine-gun, it is, perhaps, possible that they could have fired a sustained hail of bullets at the terrorists (aiming preferably for the head) and caused sufficient injury to disable them before they completed their murderous attack.

Where the report does undermine the justification for deploying the Heckler and Koch MP5 at Heathrow is in its finding that the only officers able to engage the terrorists were those immediately on hand, who did so at close range. At Vienna, the report notes: 'Of the number of police officers inside the terminal building only 2 were in a position to respond to the attack by using firearms, the remainder were

thwarted by the number of passengers who were running
away from the attack.' A similar situation occurred at Rome,
where only three of the ten or more officers on duty in the
terminal were able to engage the attackers. Thus, the report
concludes: 'Because of the number of passengers likely to be
in the check-in area it is probable that a small number of
officers will be able to respond to a terrorist attack.' Apart
from pointing to the need to place available officers at
strategic locations, this also suggests that the extra range
afforded by the Heckler and Koch MP5 will not be needed.
On the other hand, an attack on a pier or gate area may
require officers to engage terrorists at some distance.
Nevertheless, Edwards and Menzies do recommend that
automatic weapons be available for the area outside the
terminal, where confrontations might occur at greater
distances.

Whether or not it is operationally effective, is the
deployment of the MP5 a symbolic victory for terrorism?
Whilst the sight of a police officer carrying what appears to
be a sub-machine-gun will be commonplace to the international traveller, it obviously damages the unarmed image
of the police in the eyes of the domestic population.
Certainly, photographs of officers carrying this weapon seem
frequently to adorn newspaper and magazine articles on the
police, especially anything remotely to do with firearms.
This might be an acceptable price to pay if it deterred
terrorist attacks. On the one hand, it might be argued that the
possession of such weapons did not deter the attacks on
Rome and Vienna, where police are routinely and much
more heavily armed than in Britain. On the other hand, it
could be contended that the heightened security at airports
since 1985 has caused terrorists to avoid any repetition of this
kind of direct assault, even if they have simply changed their
tactics in favour of hiding bombs on board aircraft. What
cannot be validly argued is that carrying such a weapon
endangers the police. Yardley claims: 'The irony is that high
profile security is ineffective. At the most obvious level
because walking around in uniform and carrying a sub-
machine-gun is akin to walking around with a target pinned
to you.' (1986: 20). The terrorists at Rome and Vienna had
ample opportunity to shoot the police before opening fire on

the passengers, but chose not to do so. Indeed, at Rome they paid no attention at all to two officers standing either side of the stairs from which they launched their attack.

## Sub-machine-guns and 'minimum force'

Important though Heathrow airport has become as the most visible example of armed policing, the use of sub-machine-guns is not limited to this location. It was noted above that some protection officers may carry a sub-machine-gun under particular and closely monitored circumstances. Officers of PT17 train in its use both as a single-shot and as an automatic weapon. The advantage of using the MP5 in automatic mode is *not* that it can spray whole areas indiscriminately; on the contrary, automatic fire would be used in *close-quarters* encounters. A single burst lasting less than a second would discharge a number of shots faster than they could be fired as single shots. In a confrontation with terrorists or desparate criminals threatening to kill hostages, automatic fire at close range would allow the almost instant delivery of severely incapacitating force. An adversary hit by a hail of automatic gunfire would have much less opportunity to open fire or detonate explosives than had he been shot once or twice with single shots.

Although this can, as argued above (pp. 93–6), be justified within the doctrine of minimum force by the need to eliminate a threat by total and immediate incapacitation, the devastating injuries that the use of automatic fire is intended to inflict has caused controversy. What is ironic is that the controversy concentrates so exclusively upon the use of sub-machine-guns. It is this weapon that has come to symbolize the supposed threat to the principle of minimum force, whereas the shotgun is relatively publicly acceptable. This is so despite the fact that shotguns loaded with 'SG' (see pp. 283–4) have the potential.to hit a person with the equivalent of nine .32-in unsleeved bullets — the equivalent of a firing squad. Fired at more than 15–20 metres, there is a strong probability that some of the pellets will miss their target entirely and pose a danger to innocent bystanders. If any weapon is designed to spray bullets it is the shotgun. Loaded with a single rifled slug, the shotgun can achieve accuracy, but at a cost of inflicting massive injuries.

The sub-machine-gun, for all its negative public image, is a weapon whose use is much more consistent with the doctrine of minimum force. A single 9-mm round can be fired from a sub-machine-gun, or a succession of shots can be fired *depending upon the circumstances*. Thus, the amount of force used can depend upon the level of threat presented, whereas a shotgun will deliver a devastating hail of fire whatever the level of threat.

In view of this, there are strong grounds for arguing that shotguns should be weapons of last resort, and that the sub-machine-gun should replace them as the standard inter-mediate-range long-arm.

## Overt versus Covert Carrying of Guns

It is not only the *fact* that police carry what appears to be a sub-machine-gun that seems to arouse so much public anxiety, but that they are *seen* to do so. In Britain, not only do armed officers in plain clothes covertly carry firearms, so too do armed officers in uniform. This is quite unusual, if not unique, amongst police forces throughout the world. On the one hand, this prevents the public being alarmed by the sight of visibly armed police, and avoids a distinction being drawn between armed and unarmed officers. On the other hand, it significantly hampers an armed officer who might need to draw his gun from the holster hidden under his tunic, as it did when PC Trevor Lock was overpowered by terrorists attacking the Iranian embassy before he could draw his gun. Officers in shirt-sleeves have an even greater problem, for the only opportunity for carrying the gun covertly is in a holster inside the trouser pocket, which makes the gun extremely difficult to draw in an emergency. Officers in some forces are equipped with a special pouch covered by a flap secured by velcron, which can quickly be ripped open and the gun drawn. Even so, this is obviously a more difficult manœuvre than simply drawing the gun from a holster worn openly on the hip.

There are also anomalies, especially at Heathrow airport,

where members of the Security Section are permanently armed. Amongst the officers in this section, a distinction is drawn between those who overtly carry the Heckler and Koch MP5, and who are, therefore, allowed also to carry their hand-gun overtly, and those who are simply armed with hand-guns which they must carry covertly. It is argued by some officers, first, that since the Heckler and Koch MP5 is carried overtly any damage to the unarmed image of the British police has already been inflicted, and second, that the justification for carrying the Heckler and Koch MP5 is that a terrorist attack may occur suddenly, without warning and be of such brief duration that an officer may need immediately to return fire. The same surely applies to other officers of the Security Section, each of whom might be impeded in drawing his covertly carried hand-gun from the holster under the same circumstances. A second anomaly is that officers who carry guns covertly cannot be easily distinguished from unarmed officers engaged on 'general duties'. In the event of a terrorist attack, insofar as police might be the targets of the attackers, unarmed officers will be at as much risk as their armed colleagues. However, there is a compensating advantage that not knowing which police officers are or are not armed may cause terrorists to overestimate the odds they might face in mounting an attack.

There seems little reason to doubt that the effectiveness of armed officers in combating a terrorist attack would be enhanced if they wore their firearms overtly. The difficulty lies in weighing these quite tangible benefits against the damage that this would do to the image of the unarmed, non-aggressive British bobby. The response of the Home Office Working Party (1986a) to the suggestion that weapons should normally be carried overtly was hostile. They insisted that overtly carrying weapons, such as the Heckler and Koch MP5, is an exceptional measure in response to exceptional conditions.

*Guns for concealment*

An issue related to the overt versus covert carrying of weapons is the type of weapon that should be issued to officers in plain clothes who must, of necessity, carry a firearm covertly. It was for officers engaged on these duties that the Walther PP was originally provided, because it is a compact weapon. However, when that weapon was withdrawn in 1974 it was replaced by the short-barrelled, five-chamber version of the standard Model 10 Smith and Wesson, the Model 36 (Home Office, 1972). In 1983 the Model 36 was, in turn, replaced with the six-chamber version of the same weapon, the Model 64, which is of stainless-steel construction.

The justification for choosing the Models 36 and 64 is that their two-inch barrels make them easier to conceal and less cumbersome to carry routinely. However, the disadvantage of this weapon is that it is less accurate over long distances (Greenwood, 1979; Harold, 1974). This is now officially acknowledged, since officers authorized to use the Model 64 need only qualify in aimed shooting at a maximum of 15 metres, compared to the 25-metre range of the Model 10. The short distance between the foresight and backsight on the Model 64 means that it is difficult to achieve accurate alignment, and any small error at the point of aim is magnified with increased distance. Moreover, the stainless-steel construction reflects light and often obscures the sight-picture, making this weapon particularly difficult to aim. On the other hand, it is thought that this weapon is unlikely to be used at long distances, for it is mainly issued to officers engaged on close-protection duty where they may have to combat an attack at close quarters. However, the only occasion to date where a protection officer has been called upon to use a short-barrelled revolver — the attempted assassination of Ambassador Argov — involved him shooting a carefully aimed shot at the escaping would-be assassin who was 15 metres away (see p. 64).

A further disadvantage is that the short barrel reduces the muzzle velocity of any round fired from the 800 feet per second of the Model 10 to approximately 600 feet per second. It was probably for this reason that detectives armed with Model 64s found that five shots were needed to incapacitate one of a gang who opened fire on them during the East Acton post office robbery (*The Times*, 16 December 1988). The reduced stopping power of a much slower bullet is particularly serious in regard to armed bodyguards, and further strengthens their need for more potent ammunition if the short-barrelled revolver is to remain the weapon with which they are issued.

The advantage of concealment over accuracy and stopping power would be more convincing if the length of barrel were critical to concealing a revolver. Unfortunately, the most difficult features of any revolver to conceal are the cylinder and the butt, which, in the case of the Model 64, are virtually identical to the Model 10. It seems difficult to disagree with Greenwood (1979) or Harold (1974), who argue that the balance of advantage lies with the longer-barrelled revolver, particularly since the 'pancake holster' makes even this bulky weapon easy to conceal. However, if concealment is of such overriding importance, then it would seem that a self-loading pistol, similar to the Walther PP, is what is required.

## Armed-Response Vehicles

Just as the police are concerned about damaging their unarmed image by overtly carrying firearms, so they have sought to avoid the charge of having armed police 'roaming the streets of London'. Thus, instead of having a small number of armed officers on stand-by, ready to respond to incidents, divisional AFOs have been obliged to retire to the nearest station and draw a weapon specially from the armoury. It now seems likely that this will change, and that there will be a small number of vehicles on patrol which permanently carry firearms and whose crews are quite highly trained in their use. It will be they that will provide the initial response to armed incidents in future.

Hitherto, the police and the Home Office have been reluctant to endorse the deployment of armed-response vehicles for reasons which appear less than convincing. The Home Office Working Party (1986a) saw no reason 'to commend the practice to chief officers', apparently on the grounds that such vehicles require that crews be trained both as drivers and as AFOs. However, this is hardly a compelling objection, since dog-handlers have long been trained to drive emergency vehicles as an additional skill, and there seems no reason why AFOs should not similarly be trained. Moreover, there seems to be a correlation between driving skill and marksmanship. The principal concern amongst policy-makers seems to have been the controversy that such a move might occasion. However, in the wake of the Hungerford massacre and the McLaughlin (1988) report, official attitudes seem ready to change. Indeed, they have already changed in many forces nationwide who now deploy armed-response vehicles. The irony is that, as the McLaughlin report made plain, armed-response vehicles would probably have made no difference to the outcome of the Hungerford massacre, save possibly to have increased police casualties.

Far from being viewed with trepidation, such a development has a number of advantages. In the past, when an armed incident was reported, the first police officers likely to arrive at the scene would have been unarmed. They would have done whatever they could to protect members of the public and contain the gunman, but their effectiveness in doing so was likely to have been hindered by their being unarmed. Moreover, these unarmed officers were highly vulnerable and may have fallen victim to a gunman, as did PC Brereton during the Hungerford massacre in August 1987 and PC Carlton who attempted to intercept armed robbers in Coventry in December 1988. When armed officers eventually arrived, they might have done so singly and have had to form themselves into pairs at the scene. This might have involved being paired with another officer whom they did not know, or had not worked with closely, or with whom they had not trained — an obviously unsatisfactory situation given the seriousness of the circumstances. An armed-response vehicle, by contrast, is not only likely to arrive first, but would contain a pair of officers of Level II standard who work and train together regularly. The weapons carried in the vehicle would be the same as those with which the crew regularly train, and not some unfamiliar and possibly unsuitable gun drawn from an armoury. Thus, the crew would be in a position to establish an effective containment from the outset.

What is less clear is why these vehicles need to *patrol*.

Clearly, the purpose that they will serve is one of an emergency response to armed incidents. Surely, it is imperative that they should be able to reach any point within the area for which they are responsible in the minimum amount of time. Patrolling means that, when armed officers are needed, they may be far from the scene of the incident and possibly engaged in some other task. Armed response is genuinely 'fire brigade policing', and it seems appropriate to adopt the same strategy as the fire brigade. Thus, the armed-response vehicle should be based at a static strategic location from where it can reach all points in the area in the minimum time. Officers on stand-by could then have weapons and body armour readily to hand, instead of being expected to stop their vehicle and don equipment. There could be no accusation that police were patrolling the streets with firearms, and the weapons themselves would remain securely inside a building rather than in a relatively insecure car. The officers could be occupied on duties which could quickly be abandoned. The only loss would seem to be to that shibboleth 'preventative patrol', which seems to achieve little besides the wasteful consumption of fuel.

## Drifting Towards an Armed Police?

The prospect of certain police vehicles routinely patrolling with firearms on board raises the genuine issue of whether, in responding to armed crime and terrorism, the British police are drifting gradually but inexorably towards becoming routinely armed, as are virtually all their counterparts throughout the world. The danger is not only that, as the growth in crime and terrorism pose an increased threat, the police will be drawn towards ever more frequent deployment of armed officers, but also that it is more difficult to reverse direction once an escalatory step has been taken.

An example of this kind of 'ratchet effect' can be seen at Heathrow airport, where the Heckler and Koch MP5 was deployed in response to the attack on Rome and Vienna airports. Whilst until recently authority for carrying these weapons was granted each month by the Home Office and the firm wish amongst senior officers of the Metropolitan Police to remove these weapons once it is safe to do so, it is unlikely that they will be withdrawn in the foreseeable future. If these weapons were to be withdrawn, and this decision were to be followed by a terrorist attack at the airport, it seems reasonable to suppose that the public outcry would be enormous. The police and the Home Office would be condemned for failing adequately to protect the public, as they were following the Hungerford massacre, when a spurious connection was made between that incident and reductions in the number of AFOs (Edwards, 1988).

Only the clearest indication that the risk to airports has been significantly reduced, if not eliminated, will encourage those in authority to take such a decision. However, it is in the nature of terrorist activity that it does not easily permit such a conclusion to be drawn. It is difficult to identify a point at which tension has lessened sufficiently to warrant a degree of disarmament. Whereas a particularly horrendous incident can precipitate an escalation towards armed policing, few comparable events can prompt a compensating de-escalation.

## A Task for the Police?

If it is necessary for armed protection to be routinely provided at airports and elsewhere, is it appropriate that this should be a responsibility of the civil police, given the damage that it inflicts upon their unarmed reputation? There seems to be a strong case for assigning *some* armed tasks to a separate agency.

The police, particularly the Metropolitan Police, have always performed various guarding duties: there have always been police bodyguards, and they have usually been armed. The growth of international terrorism has caused this function to be extended massively. Airports throughout the UK are protected by armed police; the Royalty and Diplomatic Protection Department (RDPD) guard persons and places at risk from terrorist attack; beyond the civil police, the Atomic Energy Authority police (see *Time Out*, 22 October 1986) and Ministry of Defence police both provide armed protection for sensitive installations. Whether performed by members of the civil police or not, the tasks they perform are essentially the same, and distinguish them from the remainder of the police service. This is partially recognized in the case of the RDPD, whose vehicles have a distinctive maroon livery. All these departments of the Metropolitan Police or separate police forces perform a quasi-military, rather than police, role of providing protection from external attack. As already mentioned, it makes little sense to imagine police 'containing' a terrorist attack upon an airport terminal: the task of armed officers must be to engage and defeat.

Perhaps it is time that serious consideration is given to establishing a national paramilitary security force to perform these guarding duties. If they wore a uniform which distinguished them from the police, they would be free to carry weapons overtly without undermining the traditional image of the unarmed British police. Directly responsible to government, the cost of such a corps would not be obscured by its inclusion with other police functions and inevitable competition for resources within the police budget. In areas like airport terminals, the separation of function would avoid anomalies and confusion, leaving the police to deal with routine policing tasks whilst the security force simply guarded against terrorist attack.

Even if this strategy were adopted, it would not eliminate the need for some police to use firearms some of the time in connection with 'normal' crime. This is likely to amount to two or three armed operations per day in the Metropolitan Police District, as now, or even more. So long as this is a regrettable necessity, the police must commit themselves to maintaining and enhancing the professional approach that has been increasingly evident since the mid–1960s. There is no likelihood that PT17 will disappear — nor should they.

## Conclusions

'Minimum force' is not what it seems: using less 'aggressive' tactics, weaponry, and ammunition may simply shift the danger of death and injury from armed aggressors to innocent victims; guns with safety catches may be more dangerous than those without; a sub-machine-gun/carbine is less lethal than a shotgun; the use of armed-response vehicles would not amount to an escalation, but would allow fewer specialized officers to provide an effective response to armed incidents. However rationally defensible these propositions and proposals, they confront the reality of 'public acceptability', which is often uninformed and emotional. Thus, practices continue which not only are less effective, but in some cases are more likely to result in error and needless injury.

# PART III

# Riot Police

# 5

# Paramilitary Policing

## Introduction

Just as the sight of a police officer carrying a gun is regarded as foreign to our policing traditions, the appearance (especially throughout the 1980s) of officers wearing special helmets and clothing, carrying shields, and deployed in squad formations has reinforced the fear that Britain has imported the methods of alien policing systems. (For details see Appendix B.) By their appearance, function, and deployment these officers are seen to be set apart from ordinary constables. Symbolically, they represent a coercive, even oppressive, style of policing, designed to secure compliance by force rather than consent. Like the armed officer, the riot police shed the image of vulnerability in favour of a 'formidable appearance'. Are we abandoning the British policing tradition and replacing it with a paramilitary style of policing, even a 'third force'?[1]

## 'Paramilitarism'?

The anxieties aroused by the apparent paramilitarization of the police are clear enough, but unfortunately the reasons for such alarm are left largely unexplained. It seems to be taken as axiomatic that the creation of a 'third force' or paramilitary organization of the entire police force must be a threat to civil liberties and an abrogation of 'policing by consent'. Given that many other liberal democracies have paramilitary police forces of one kind or another,[2] it seems rather xenophobic to view these arrangements with such horror. But if paramilitarism is inherently a 'bad thing' we should be reasonably clear about what is being condemned. What, precisely, is meant by 'paramilitarism'? And what is seen as threatening to the British police tradition in 'paramilitarism'?

The extent of the confusion that surrounds the term 'paramilitary' is indicated by a brief examination of the French police system, which is taken by many to epitomize the Continental style of policing. The archetypal paramilitary 'third force' is often assumed to be the French CRS (*Compagnies Républicaines de Sécurité*). However, the CRS is, in fact, neither paramilitary nor a 'third force'. It is the *gendarmerie* that is truly paramilitary, in that, whilst performing police duties, it is accountable to the Ministry of Defence and could be used in a purely military capacity in time of war. It thus forms a 'third force' in the sense that it occupies a position between the military, and the police. The CRS, by contrast, is unambiguously part of the civil police (the Police Nationale) responsible to the Minister of the Interior. Yet it is the CRS who have gained the fearsome reputation for suppressing disorder by forceful means and having the function of a 'third force', whilst the *gendarmerie* are apparently regarded with some affection by the French public, the equivalent of the British country bobby who polices small rural communities (Stead, 1983; Roach, 1985).

So, when anxieties are voiced about the creation of a British 'paramilitary' police system or a 'third force', what is meant? It is possible to identify three overlapping elements to what is normally regarded as 'paramilitarism': whether police officers have civilian or non-civilian status; their organization and structure; and the restraint shown in the use of force.

## A civil force

It is perfectly true that when the Metropolitan Police was introduced in 1829, and provincial police forces were created in its wake throughout the following fifty years to form a nationwide system, every effort was made to distinguish the 'New Police' not only from the discredited arrangements it replaced, but also from the existing policing systems on the continent of Europe (Emsley, 1983). By contrast with the centralized paramilitary police used by Continental regimes to subdue and repress a hostile and non-compliant population, the British police were to be seen as a distinctly civil force which would support, not undermine, the traditional liberties of the British people. It was not necessarily so high-minded either in conception or practice, but this was how the 'police idea' was presented and is often still remembered. Peel actually wished to re-create the Irish Constabulary (a national, politically controlled, paramilitary force) on the mainland of Britain, but opposition from a landed aristocracy that feared both the cost and the threat to liberty, in alliance with the lower classes, who feared tyranny, prevented the realization of that ambition. Perhaps for reasons of expediency more than principle, Peel created a distinctly civilian 'New Police' (Critchley, 1967; Emsley, 1983; Stead, 1977; 1985).

The civilian status of the New Police was immediately obvious from their appearance, for they were attired in civilian rather than military-style clothing. The original uniform was that of a top hat and dark frock coat. The constable carried a rattle to summon assistance and a baton with which to defend himself, but these were hidden from view. The aim was to convey the impression that the constable was simply 'a civilian in uniform'. His legal powers were little more than those granted to members of the public. In the words of the 1929 Royal Commission,

The police of this country have never been recognized, either in law or by tradition, as a force distinct from the general body of citizens. . . . a policeman, in the view of the common law, is only 'a person paid to perform, as a matter of duty, acts which if he were so minded he might have done voluntarily'. (*Royal Commission on Police Powers*, 1929)

This was always something of a myth, and one which has progressively departed from reality over the past 150 years. In reality, the police officer has both the legal and social authority to do much more than the ordinary citizen. However, myths are important in social life, and the myth that surrounded (and to some extent continues to surround) the British police is that they are a civil police, not remote from the public. Indeed, the clamour for 'community policing' seems to reflect a desire to restore the police officer more clearly to such a position (Alderson, 1979).

## Paramilitary organization

Another respect in which the 'New Police' were a distinct-
ively civilian force lay in the status of the individual officer.
He held the medieval office of 'constable', to whom the
common law granted original powers and discretion in their
exercise. In law, therefore, each police officer, no matter
what his rank, was a constable with equal powers and
responsibilities. Unlike the soldier, the constable could not
plead that he acted under orders from higher authority, since
no superior rank could intervene between the constable and
the law.[3] This clearly distinguishes the British police from
paramilitary police forces throughout the world. In a
paramilitary force, command is hierarchical, because the
capacity for coercive might is promoted by concerted and
disciplined action. If a force is to coerce a resistant population, its commanders must be confident that, if and when
they give the order to open fire, their subordinates will do so
immediately and competently. Discipline ensures compliance
with instructions, no matter how unpleasant or dangerous
they might be to the individuals charged with carrying them
out. There is no room in such an organization for individual
discretion; the force must operate as a single unit under the
direction of its commander, who is responsible for its
actions.

Instead of being 'a civilian in uniform', the paramilitary
police officer should be divorced from the civilian population
and owe first loyalty to his force. To be removed from the
civil population and stationed in separate barracks encourages
group solidarity amongst members of the force, and also
discourages the establishment of loyalties to those whom
they might be called upon to suppress. Thus alienated from
the civil population, a paramilitary police would have less
compunction in using force than would a civil police
enmeshed in a web of affiliation with local people.

A colonial force also has the advantage that it lacks ethnic
affinity with the civil population. A domestic paramilitary
police cannot easily do the same; but the maintenance of a
mobile force, to be used anywhere within the boundaries of
the country, can ensure that few affinities are shared between

the force, temporarily stationed in an area, and the resident population. Mobility means that political control cannot be exercised locally, for a force might well be used in an area other than that in which it is barracked. Thus, paramilitary forces tend almost invariably to be instruments of the central government, sent wherever they are needed to suppress disorder or revolt. The fact that they serve the central, rather than the local, administration is another reason why paramilitary forces tend to be seen as remote from the civil population.

Thus, it is not simply the paramilitary organizational structure *per se* that is objected to, but what that structure facilitates — the oppressive use of force. Paramilitary police forces blur the line between the police function of using force to arrest suspected offenders and bring them before the courts and the military function of defeating and destroying an enemy. A paramilitary police uses its superior might to suppress. Protective equipment, offensive weaponry, and the deployment of officers in squad formations are associated with the capacity to impose order by naked coercion. Once such a measure of force is possessed by the State, so too is the potential to use it for tyrannical purposes.

Discussion of the use of force itself will be deferred to the next chapter. What needs to be considered first is whether British policing has become organized along paramilitary lines, and whether this is as deplorable as the critics maintain.

## 'The British Police Advantage'

The lack of such a capacity to suppress disorder by force, far from being a weakness of the British police tradition, has actually been its strength. It was argued in Chapter 1 that the unarmed British bobby, whose appearance was the very opposite of the formidable invincibility of his Continental and colonial counterparts, achieved levels of public compliance which were exceptional when judged by international standards, however grudgingly such compliance may have been given by the lower classes. Unable to coerce the public by naked force, the police had little alternative but to arrive at mutually acceptable arrangements.

Police engaged in public-order duties were not deployed in squads, but as an assembly of individuals. Once they had been allocated to a particular location, the action taken by officers at the scene remained a matter of individual discretion. There were no prescribed public-order tactics and little, if any, training in public-order policing. This rather chaotic and muddled approach to public order distinguished the British police from their counterparts throughout the world, yet by the 1960s it had come to be regarded as conferring the 'British police advantage' (Bowden, 1978). It was 'winning by appearing to lose', and 'win' the police often did. Throughout the 1950s and 1960s, there were not the scenes of police–public confrontation that were witnessed abroad.

Police could 'win by appearing to lose' because picketing and political protest were conducted with restraint. Orderly picketing, conducted by a handful of pickets and supervised by a nominal police presence, could achieve its goal. Trade union solidarity meant that there was no need forcibly to close premises as had been the tactic during the early years of the trade union movement. Moreover, the respectability enjoyed by the trade unions, especially their close connection with the Labour Party, inhibited them from supporting forcible closure. The violence and disorder that would inevitably accompany such tactics would only rebound to the electoral disadvantage of the political arm of the Labour movement (Geary, 1985).

Also, during this period political protest was muted, again possibly because of the existence of the Labour Party. The Campaign for Nuclear Disarmament staged marches and acts of civil disobedience such as sit-down demonstrations in Trafalgar Square. CND believed that the election of a Labour government would lead to the achievement of their aims, and when the Wilson Government was elected in 1964 the Committee of One Hundred officially disbanded (Clutter-buck, 1980). Thus, both labour unrest and political protest were pursued through constitutional channels because this held out the prospect of success.

As Chapter 2 documented, during the 1960s this situation changed dramatically: the police stopped 'winning by appearing to lose' and started actually to 'lose', and the response was to introduce changes designed to 'win'.

## The rise of a national riot police

What was to become one of the most controversial developments — the capacity of the police to act on a national scale — was not an invention of the 1970s, but a resurrection and enhancement of arrangements that had long existed. Throughout the nineteenth century it was common practice for the military to be summoned to assist the police in controlling civil unrest (Critchley, 1970). In the 1890s police forces were officially encouraged by the Home Office to enter into arrangements whereby they could offer each other assistance if faced with circumstances that threatened to overwhelm them. Police forces had previously made such arrangements on an *ad hoc* basis, but this was unsuitable and, as Morgan (1987) notes, allowed parsimonious police authorities to rely upon military assistance for which they did not pay instead of neighbouring police for whom they would be required to foot the bill. For some years the Metropolitan Police performed the function of a national public-order reserve, being dispatched to trouble spots as an alternative to military intervention. Indeed, it was the ability of central government to dispatch the Metropolitan Police that was instrumental in the evolution of a solely civil response to major incidents of public disorder (Geary, 1985; Morgan, 1987). The Desborough Committee of 1919 (see report published in 1920) placed the provision of what has come to be called 'mutual aid' on a firm footing, and the 1964 Police Act now provides the statutory framework whereby forces can obtain aid from their neighbours.

The concern felt about industrial unrest in the wake of the First World War was translated into a system of central-government civil-contingency planning (Jeffery and Hennessy, 1983) which had direct implications for the police. From its very beginning, the police force was an integral part of a nationally co-ordinated response to civil emergencies. As

Morgan (1987) documents, the inter-war years saw the evolution of greater central direction of the police by the Home Office, because of concern at the growth of industrial and civil unrest. As strikes caused increasingly national rather than merely local dislocation, government concern grew. Moreover, as the government itself intervened directly in industrial relations, especially when it greatly expanded its own role as an employer with nationalization after the Second World War, so it became increasingly difficult to distinguish between employer–employee conflict and unconstitutional attempts to bring down the elected government.

Renewed anxiety about the ability of the police to maintain public order prompted a review of civil contingency planning (Jeffery and Hennessy, 1983), and particularly the police role within it. In particular, the ability of the police to expedite mutual aid in case of a nationwide emergency was enhanced by the establishment of the National Reporting Centre (NRC; now known as the Mutual Aid Co-ordinating Centre). The centre is housed at Scotland Yard, and is staffed by officers seconded from provincial police forces to the Public Order Forward Planning Unit, and supplemented by Metropolitan Police officers. It receives requests for aid, which are then matched to resources available from 'aiding' forces. In so far as it performs a central co-ordinating role, it is in a strategic position to pass on information and intelligence from one force to another.

It was the dissemination of information and intelligence that produced much of the controversy during the miners' dispute (Coulter *et al.*, 1984; *Sunday Times* Insight Team, 1985). The factual basis for such concern was scanty, to say the least. A journalist overheard one conversation in which officers at the NRC relayed information regarding the movement of pickets from one force to another. He gained the impression that the NRC were instructing the force to whom the information was being passed to intercept the pickets (Kettle, 1985). Against that should be set such clear evidence of local police autonomy as the refusal of some chief constables either to accept officers from particular forces, because, for example, they believed them to be too aggressive in their appearance, or, alternatively, to provide the numbers of officers that the NRC were requesting.

Whilst fears about the role of the NRC seem less than securely grounded, what cannot be denied is the extent to which central government played a dominant role in the dispute, and the fact that local police authorities were effectively by-passed (Spencer, 1985; Loveday, 1986). Public pronouncements by the Attorney-General and Home Secretary seemed designed to encourage the police to take an uncompromising approach. Changes in the law on picketing, although not part of the criminal law, clearly indicated what Parliament regarded as the limits of tolerable conduct. For example, the codes of practice issued under the Employment Act 1980 state that 'The main cause of violence and disorder on the picket line is excessive numbers', and continues, 'Large numbers on a picket line are also likely to give rise to fear and resentment', before concluding that there should be no more than six pickets at any entrance (McCabe *et al.*, 1988: 29). Hence, it is authoritatively indicated to the police that large numbers of pickets are likely to create conditions that amount to a breach of the peace. However, in this respect, as in others, this was far from being unprecedented; it merely continued the process begun in the aftermath of the First World War: central government exercising influence by 'advice' and 'guidance'. What the miners' strike finally revealed was the capacity of the British police to act collectively in response to a national emergency.

## A national riot police created by stealth?

The development of an integrated national structure for responding to public disorder was effectively conducted in secret, not least the most recent introduction of the NRC/MACC. This aspect has been repeatedly criticized for undermining democratic accountability and control. McCabe *et al.* (1988) rightly complain that under conditions of national emergency, such as the miners' strike, the power of chief constables has been greatly expanded, the role of the local police authorities diminished and the influence of central government has come to predominate without any compensating accountability to Parliament. McCabe *et al.* make recommendations designed to reverse many of these developments, re-emphasizing local political control and placing the direction of policing during national emergencies on a firm constitutional foundation, proposals which raise issues of *realpolitik* and desirability.

The demand for increased local political control is not limited to public-order policing, but it is in this connection that it becomes most acute. For in policing public disorder, senior officers are able to exercise their discretion to implement policies most directly. It was the Chief Constable of Birmingham who, in 1972, ordered that the gates of the Saltley coking plant should be closed (Clutterbuck, 1980); the Chief Constable of Avon and Somerset withdrew his officers from the St Paul's district of Bristol during the riot in 1980 (Joshua and Wallace, 1983); and the Assistant Chief Constable of South Yorkshire commanded the police at Orgreave in 1984 (Jackson, 1986). Since this exercise of police discretion also occurs in connection with politically sensitive issues, critics maintain that here, at the very least, the police should be subject to democratic control (McCabe *et al.*, 1988).

As a matter of *realpolitik*, however, it is in connection with policing public disorder that local political control is *least* likely. It would require central government unilaterally to cede influence that it has steadily acquired over the past sixty years or more. That influence was acquired for politically compelling reasons by governments as ideologically different as Stanley Baldwin's inter-war Conservative Administration and Clement Atlee's post-war Labour Government (Jeffery and Hennessy, 1983). The political compulsion is simply that central government is held electorally responsible for civil disorder, especially when it causes national disruption as it threatens to do when strikers seek forcibly to close premises. As 'law and order' has become a controversial political issue, it seems even less likely that government will allow others, possibly of an opposed political party, to determine policing policy.

Of course, central government has never totally abdicated from the maintenance of public order. Before extending its influence over the police, the government could call upon the army. Indeed, it was partly to limit the role of the army in internal affairs that governments came to exercise increasing influence over the police. In the unlikely event that responsibility for public-order policing were to be devolved to local level, central government would retain direct control over the military, and might revert to using it as in the past. Indeed, there have been suggestions that, frustrated by the inability of the police to control flying pickets during the first few days of the 1984–5 miners' strike, central government privately warned chief constables that, if they were unable to maintain order, the army would be called in. It is highly improbable that, in a unitary State like Britain, central government would deny itself a national capability to restore public order. Instead of having recourse to the army, it is always possible that the central government would overtly create a national 'third force' directly under its control. More probable, perhaps, is that any legislation which restored local political control would also contain reserve powers allowing ministers to direct the police in times of emergency.

One of the more perplexing aspects of this debate is that many of the advocates of local political control are also neo-Marxists (Coulter *et al.*, 1984; Lloyd, 1985), whose analysis seems wholly at odds with their prescriptions. If the police are, as is so often maintained, oppressive agents of the capitalist State, then it is simply unrealistic to demand their effective emasculation through local political control. The capitalist ruling class is hardly going to accede tamely to their oppressive apparatus becoming subject to local democratic control. If this is a prescription to be implemented after the socialist revolution, then it would appear redundant, since public disorder is unlikely to arise in conditions of universal harmony.

*Realpolitik* aside, there remain serious misgivings about the desirability of placing the policing of public order either under local political control or even on a firm constitutional footing. Both prescriptions are frequently offered on the basis of first principles — namely, that the existing situation is undemocratic. However, it seems often to be also the case that critics envisage that such a change will have positive consequences for civil liberties which they perceive to have

been progressively eroded. For example, those who objected
to central influence during the miners' strike seemed reasonably to believe that Labour Party-dominated local police
authorities in the coalfields would be more favourably
disposed to the strikers. Whilst this may indeed have been
true of this strike, it is by no means inevitable that local
political control will always ensure protection for the
underdog. In contrast to the support shown by local
authorities for the miners, the police received the full support
of the Cheshire County Council during the dispute at the
*Warrington Messenger* newspaper (Scraton, 1985), as they did
from all political parties on the Wiltshire Police Authority
when it came to the decision to prevent the 'Peace Convoy'
from reaching Stonehenge (National Council for Civil
Liberties, 1986). Local control would not guarantee that the
police would be employed in ways that liberal and radical
critics would like.

Nor is it apparent that placing the policing of public
disorder on a firm constitutional foundation would have the
desired effect. Having documented the gradual expansion of
surreptitious central government control over the policing of
industrial disputes, which she views with evident disfavour,
Morgan (1987: 280) concludes:

By comparison with the industrial history of many other countries,
Britain has coped reasonably well with bridging the gap between
an efficient police and democratic accountability. Apart from their
use in labour disputes, the police seem to have remained broadly
popular with the local community. Despite the deaths at Feather-
stone in 1893 and at Liverpool and Llanelli in 1911, British labour
relations did not experience the habitual violence and loss of life
that punctuated the history of the United States from the 1892
Homestead strike to the stay-in strikes at Flint, Michigan, in 1937.
The fearful carnage between a para-military state police and
industrial workers evident in France, Germany, Italy and many
other European countries down to 1939 again found no echo in
Britain.

In other words, police in countries like the USA, who were
under local political control and where citizens were protected by a Bill of Rights, saw *more, not less,* violence.

Why was there this difference? We can only speculate, but

perhaps the authorities in Britain, acting on constitutionally shaky ground, were careful not to go too far. Where the constitutional ground was firmer, the authorities felt confident in exploiting it to the full. If so, the desire for constitutional tidiness could result in the very opposite of what its advocates envisage.

When polemical condemnation is stripped away, what is clear is that the organization of public-order policing, brought to public attention by the miners' strike of 1984–5, is not a breach with the past. The scale of that operation was conditioned by the nature of the strike and the tactics employed by the National Union of Mineworkers. During the 1974 strike, when support for it was solid, there was no comparable mutual-aid operation in the police force, despite the activation of the NRC, because there was no public disorder.

### Does a 'third force' now exist in Britain?

Whether a departure from tradition is in question or not, the issue remains: does Britain now effectively possess a 'third force'? Discussion of this issue has been bedevilled by a failure to distinguish clearly between function and structure. In the early 1970s the creation of such a 'third force' was seriously deliberated, but ultimately rejected (Bowden, 1978), as it has been periodically since it was first mooted in the 1920s (Jeffery and Hennessy, 1983; Morgan, 1987). However, whilst the creation of a separate, centrally organized force found little favour, the need effectively to maintain and restore public order was never seriously challenged. It was the introduction of a 'third force' into the policing *structure* that was rejected, not the *function* of the police to control civil disorder (see Gregory, 1985).

Structural changes which were introduced in the early 1970s and those that have occurred subsequently were designed to provide an *alternative* structure to that of a 'third force'. Critics will no doubt complain that the end is still served, albeit by slightly different means. However, this is a dispute about the end rather than the means. Critics seem to fear that protest and dissent, rather than disorder, is being suppressed. If *this* is their criticism, then objecting to the structural means employed to achieve that end is as irrelevant as it is invalid. A 'third force' is precisely what it says it is: a force, like the French *gendarmerie*, or, more accurately, the West German *Bundesgrenzschutz* (Gregory, 1985), separate from either the police or the army. No such force exists in Britain.


## Squads not Individuals

The reason why some people may genuinely fear that a 'third force' has been created is that when police are now deployed in public order situations they are no longer an assembly of individuals, but are formed into squads under a hierarchy of command akin to military formations. This makes the police a more formidable force, since they act in concert and can be expected to follow the orders of superior officers, rather than exercising individual discretion.

It is perfectly true that developments in public-order tactics rely increasingly upon police acting as a co-ordinated unit, rather than as disparate groups of individuals. As such they are more formidable, giving the authorities a potentially much more powerful instrument for repression, if they choose to use it. At the same time, there is a compensating advantage for protesters in deploying the police in this manner: they act as a *disciplined body*. It is the ability to deploy personnel in co-ordinated, disciplined units that is one of the defining features of military organization. Not only does this allow the police to act more effectively to maintain order or quell disorder, it also means that greater control, supervision, and, therefore, discipline can be maintained. Since policing civil disorder is conducive to indiscipline, effective control and supervision is an essential precondition for policing with 'minimum force'. As Reiner (1984: 54–5) remarks:

There is an important issue here which critics of the police have not reflected on enough. In violent confrontations, a 'non-militaristic' response by police (i.e. without adequate training, manpower, coordination, and defensive or even offensive equipment) could mean that injuries will be multiplied. This doesn't just mean injuries to the police, but also to others who will suffer from undisciplined and excessive violence from constables who lose their cool or their courage. If the use of violence by the police is necessary, it must be handled efficiently rather than aggravated by incompetence or default. Scarman is right to argue that 'policing is . . . too complex a job to be viewed in terms of a simplistic dichotomy between "hard" and "soft" policing styles'.

Here Reiner is echoing the earlier remarks of Marx (1970), who noted that the non-militaristic organization of the American police had probably contributed to excessive force being used by them during the 'long hot summers' of ghetto rioting.

Policing civil disorder engenders fear, anger, and frustration amongst officers who are often too close to the action to understand what is occurring. The feeling that one has lost control and is at the mercy of unpredictable events only heightens anxiety. The opportunity to take forceful action allows not only for the expression of these emotions, but is exhilarating in its own right.[4] For all these reasons, it is essential that officers engaged in public-order situations are carefully supervised and controlled, for internal controls on behaviour are unlikely to prove reliable. Traditional methods of public-order policing did not provide for this, for police were deployed in loosely organized groups and left to take what action they felt was desirable in the circumstances they faced. The disorganized shambles that represented the initial response to the disorders in St. Paul's, Bristol (Joshua and Wallace, 1983) is a good illustration of how ill-co-ordinated and ineffective traditional methods actually were. This was not a singular failure, by any means: police action at Red Lion Square was hardly more co-ordinated (Scarman, 1975; Gilbert, 1975), nor was the policing of the National Front meeting at Southall in 1979 (Dummett, 1980*a*; 1980*b*). In conditions of such chaos and confusion, frightened and frustrated police officers are unlikely to act with calm detachment. Indeed, as both Dunning *et al.* (1987) and Morgan (1987) both extensively document, the policing of public disorder in the first half of the twentieth century was often accompanied by significant use of force and an apparent absence of discipline.

Moreover, in conditions of such disorganization random arrests are likely to be made, such as that of the Policy Studies Institute's researcher, Stephen Small, arrested during the 'New Cross Massacre: Black People's Day of Action' protest march in March 1981. He records his experience in the report, *Police and People in London,* and it is an instructive and credible insight into how public-order policing can appear from the receiving end:

When a number of skirmishes broke out several hundred yards in front of me and quite near to Blackfriars Bridge I was in the centre of a thick crowd of demonstrators who were marching towards the bridge itself. . . . Shortly after the commotion and running about began, the police, who were walking alongside the marchers on either side of the road, suddenly formed a cordon across the road some twenty or thirty yards in front of me. There was a lot of confusion as a result of this cordon and people were peering over the heads of those in front in order to see what was going on. The crowd was becoming very dense as the marchers at the back, apparently unaware that a cordon had been formed, were still walking towards the bridge. At this stage I was physically separated from my companions and I was being pushed by the pressure from behind towards the cordon. As I moved nearer to the cordon I, too, tried to see what was going on ahead. As the pressure of the crowd was becoming too strong I reached the actual cordon itself and I tried to move along the cordon to the right hand side of the road (that is, facing the bridge). I was right next to the line of policemen, and was occasionally pushed into them by the crowd. At one point a police officer pushed me back with his chest and there was a sharp retort in Patois from the black person whom I was shoved into. At this part of the road there was a deep ditch and a long dug-out where pipes were being laid.

Amid all the confusion and noise (and there was still a lot of skirmishing ahead of the cordon) the open-backed transit van with the loud-speaker on it drove towards the cordon. The cordon was originally very straight but now had a considerable bend in it. Several officers unlinked arms to allow the van to pass the cordon and the rest of the cordon gave way with many officers unlinking arms. A lot of people were carried through the cordon as this happened and I jumped over the ditch ahead of me as I too was carried through. As I jumped over the ditch I fell on the floor but immediately arose and began to rub my hands which were sore from the fall. The van had passed the cordon, people were pushing past the police and running past me on both sides as police officers were apparently trying to stop them and reconstruct the cordon. The next thing I saw was a very irate policeman running directly at me and my spontaneous response was to turn and move out of his direction. As I moved the officer began to shout 'You're nicked, you're nicked' and chased after me. As I moved through a crowd of people about ten yards ahead of me there was a group of 15–20 policemen and I slowed down and bumped softly and accidentally into one of them. He had apparently seen the first policeman chasing me, and he grabbed hold of my arm. The officer in pursuit of me grabbed hold of my other arm and said 'You're nicked you bastard!' (Policy Studies Institute, 1983*b*: 148–9)

It would be illuminating to read how the police officers involved in this incident perceived what happened. One can only speculate, but it seems probable that with disorder occurring behind them and crowd pressure building to the front, the officers in the cordon were apprehensive. The collapse of the cordon was probably attributed to crowd violence by those officers who were unaware that some of their colleagues had unlinked arms to allow the van through. The surge of the crowd through the disintegrating cordon and the scuffles that probably accompanied it would only increase fear that the police were losing control of the situation. The sight of a young man, who had apparently been one of those to break the cordon, brushing dirt from his hands could well have been interpreted by the 'irate policeman' as evidence of involvement in missile-throwing. The fact that when challenged and pursued the young man ran off would serve to confirm that suspicion, which would be further reinforced when Small collided with the other officer. When subsequently, Small's friend appeared and began remonstrating with the officers, this was doubtless regarded as yet more 'aggravation' which confirmed yet again the guilt of those in custody (for a police officer's view of an actual confrontation, see *Police Review*, 24 May 1985).

This account does not allow us easily to brand one side or the other as guilty and the other as guiltless. It is possible to explain such confrontations as the product, not of wilfulness or malign motives on either side, but of the confused circumstances in which both parties found themselves. Confusion is, perhaps, the inevitable accompaniment of

public protest and disorder, but it should be minimized as far
as possible for the benefit of all concerned. This demands
concerted, co-ordinated, and disciplined conduct on the part
of the police. Allowing individual officers or small contin-
gents to act as they see fit is not a recipe for concerted, co-
ordinated, and disciplined conduct. The consequence, in the
above example, was that arms became unlinked to allow a
van to pass through, with the result that the cordon
disintegrated, the police lost control, and Small was arbitrarily arrested in the ensuing mêlée.

## A disciplined body

Given the circumstances of public protest and disorder,
disorganization of this kind cannot entirely be eradicated;
however, recent developments in the supervision and control
of officers make uncoordinated and undisciplined action less
likely.

The basic level of organization for public-order policing is
the Police Support Unit (PSU), into which is built unprecedented levels of supervision. Each PSU comprises two
'serials' of constables, each under the direct supervision of a
sergeant, with the whole unit under the command of an
inspector. In instances of serious disorder, the PSU remains
together as a single body and is deployed as such. Supervis-
ing officers can, therefore, retain a measure of direct control
in a manner that is utterly denied them in the less coherently
structured    arrangements    associated    with    'traditional
methods'. It is the inspector who commands his officers in
how, for example, to advance. He can order them to advance
with their shields at 'the carry', or in 'Indian file', or he can
establish a shield cordon. It is he who decides in which
direction to advance, and whether and how to turn a corner.
If it is necessary to enter premises, it is he who decides how it
is to be done and in what order his officers should do it, and
he can quickly enter himself if there is resistance within the
building that needs to be subdued.

None of this will totally ensure that undisciplined conduct
will never occur. As My Lai[5] demonstrated, even disciplined
soldiers acting as a unit can commit acts of the most extreme

savagery. However, a clear chain of command through the inspector and sergeants does establish clear lines of control and accountability. It means that senior officers can easily deploy and keep track of large numbers of officers. Contingency plans and tactics rely, not on every individual officer knowing what to do, but on the thorough briefing of a limited number of supervisory officers in the responsibilities of their PSU. Because these advantages are so obviously beneficial, Metropolitan Police tacticians have suggested that PSUs ought to be organized into yet larger units to be called something like Police Support Groups, there are, however, no plans to implement this at present.

The deployment of officers engaged in public order policing in squads is not a development to be deplored, but one to be welcomed. It promises to introduce a measure of discipline that is a necessary condition for the exercise of 'minimum force'. However, that promise has yet to be fully realized. As debriefings following major disorders and as, occasionally, public expressions of dissatisfaction (*Police,* October 1985) make clear, the policing of disorder still remains quite chaotic. If the promise of disciplined effectiveness is to be realized, it is essential that senior officers are able to command and control the operation effectively.

*Command and control*

Adequate command and control is, then, essential, to ensure not only that police can effectively maintain or restore public order but also that they can retain discipline under conditions most likely to undermine it. Now that officers on the street are deployed in formations which allow for that discipline to be imposed, attention has concentrated upon command and control exercised at the highest levels (see pp. 326–8).

As mentioned previously, considerable problems have arisen behind the scenes of disorder with the command and control operation. Internal post-riot reviews have repeatedly exposed deficiencies in effective deployment, relief, and refreshment of officers on the scene, as well as liaison between different branches of the force and external organizations, such as London Transport. The remedy has been to distinguish 'slow-time' and 'quick-time' decision-making, assigning the former to the Gold commander and control room and the latter to the Silver commander and control room.[6] Gold determines the overall strategy, and his control room ensures that officers are regularly refreshed and relieved, whilst Silver 'fights the battle' by deploying officers and setting immediate objectives. It is the task of Bronze commanders, who are directly in charge of officers at the scene, to decide how objectives are to be achieved and by whom. When appropriate, the Silver commander can use a mobile control room so as to remain close to the scene of disorder, where he can liaise directly with his Bronze commanders (Power, 1988).

There is no doubt that the distinction between slow-time and quick-time decision-making is a valid and valuable one. Relieving the Silver commander of the need to worry about when any particular PSU was fed, or to keep track of how long officers have been on duty, will allow him to keep track of the operation and decide on tactics. At the same time, Gold control should ensure that there is no unnecessary repetition of what has happened previously, where some officers have been on duty uninterruptedly for sixteen hours, whilst other 'fresh' officers that could have relieved them were not deployed.

Despite its obvious advance over previous structures of command and control, this system still suffers from two drawbacks: the first organizational and the second conceptual.

### The limits of the military analogy

The principal problem that afflicts the 'Gold, Silver, Bronze' system of command is that of 'arcing'. The intention is that command should follow the military model, with the Gold commander setting the strategy, which is translated into tactical deployment and objectives by the Silver commander to be implemented by the Bronze commander. Information should flow upwards through the chain of command, from Bronze through Silver to Gold. However, tacticians complain that Gold commanders display a tendency to abandon the chain of command and instruct their Bronze commanders directly when the situation becomes critical — communication is short-circuited, hence the term 'arcing'.

The solution to the problem is seen to lie in the education of prospective Gold commanders, instilling in them an appreciation of the need to allow their Silver commanders to get on with the tactical implementation of their strategy. However, the problem is more fundamental than this solution allows. 'Arcing' suggests that the Gold, Silver, and Bronze division of responsibility and levels of command is a misguided and inappropriate attempt to equate police and military organizations. This system confuses the valid and necessary distinction between 'slow-time' and 'quick-time' decision-making with a false, quasi-military analogy regarding the chain of command.

The fundamental flaw in the chain of command is that the most sensitive decisions will be taken by the Silver and Bronze commanders, *not* Gold. It is they who will be 'fighting the battle' whilst the Gold commander sits back and hopes that the strategy he has laid down is correct. Gold control is concerned with important logistical matters, but not with matters for which anyone is likely to be held ultimately accountable before a disciplinary or judicial tribunal. By contrast, a decision by the Silver commander, say, to deploy mounted officers may very well become highly controversial and reflect upon the Gold commander and the officers under his command. Thus, monitoring such a decision over the radio, the Gold commander is almost compelled to intervene if he believes the decision to be imprudent, for he will be held responsible not only for the strategy but also for its execution. Indeed, the need for the Gold commander to monitor the decisions of the Silver commander distracts him from his supposed purpose, which is to make strategic and 'slow-time' decisions.

To some extent, simple amendment to the Gold, Silver, Bronze hierarchy would remedy these deficiencies: that is, to make the subordinate Silver commander responsible for 'slow-time' logistical decisions and his superior, the Gold commander, responsible for strategy and its tactical implementation. This would no doubt entail some amendment to the metallic designation of respective commanders. It would also provoke other difficulties, most acutely that of liason with community leaders. At present, the Gold commander has the opportunity of liaising with local community leaders in a place remote from the fray. If the Gold commander were actually responsible for tactics, as well as strategy, he would be unable to discharge this function. However, the extent to which community leaders would wish to be remote from the fray, as opposed to being seen publicly representing their community to police officers on the spot, is open to doubt. Those who might wish to liaise in more tranquil surroundings may find a second-in-command an acceptable deputy, especially if they are assured that the senior officer is taking responsibility for the conduct of the operation.

In another respect, the division of responsibility between Gold and Silver commanders exposes a more fundamental limitation to the applicability of the military analogy to the policing of public disorder. The fighting of a military battle is something for which preparations can be made and strategy determined. Even if the military are in a defensive position, they can assess the strengths and weaknesses of their presumed adversary and attempt to predict his likely strategic options. By contrast, policing civil disorder, like policing in general, is almost entirely reactive. Civil disorder can erupt almost anywhere at any-time. There may be prior indications, although the experience of using 'tension indicators' has yet to prove its worth. But if violence can erupt in a 'community policing' showcase like Handsworth for no apparent reason, it can occur anywhere.

Occasions when such a strategy can be worked out well in advance will be limited to pre-planned events, not spontaneous disorder. Thus, raids like that on Broadwater Farm estate in 1989 (*The Times*, 30 September 1989) can be planned with quasi-military precision, because, quite unusually, this was an operation *initiated* by the police. Much more frequently, the police will be responding to disorder, and even if that disorder is confidently predicted, the initiative will rest, not with them, but with those who create the disorder, and this will negate any attempt to formulate a strategy. For example, at the Notting Hill Carnival in 1987 disorder was confidently anticipated because Operation

'Trident', which had rid the area of drug-dealing in the weeks preceding the carnival, had created antagonism and a desire for revenge in some quarters. Shield units were deployed in reserve, and had received intensive training in the weeks prior to the event. Strategic options had been devised: for example, the direction of dispersal was determined in advance and a pattern of cordons to facilitate this had been prearranged. When disorder broke out, the plan swung impressively into operation and met with considerable success, despite the inevitable unforeseen difficulties.

However, not even this carefully planned operation could anticipate every contingency. For instance, when the violence erupted police established a cordon sealing off All Saints Road at its junction with Westbourne Park Road in accordance with the plan for dispersing people from the area. After the violence had subsided, but with the dispersal of carnival-goers still continuing in line with the strategic plan, it was clear that this cordon was coming under considerable pressure from a large crowd of people attempting to regain access to All Saints Road. The Bronze commander at the scene decided to allow people to pass through the cordon at a controlled rate so as to avoid what was developing into an ugly scene. He judged that the majority of people trying to gain access to All Saints Road wished to do so in order to make their way home northwards, and that the dispersal plan did not allow for this. On this occasion, it was essential to reverse the broad tactical plan to *prevent* the recurrence of disorder. The 'strategy' had to be overridden because of the compelling need to maintain order.

In less predictable circumstances, as when policing marches, demonstrations, and football matches, the strategy cannot be determined clearly in advance, because it will depend upon the exact nature of the disorder that erupts: whom it involves, and where and when it occurs. The matter is more fundamental than merely observing, as is instilled into every military tactician, that tactics should be flexible so as to achieve the strategic goal. The fact is that in policing the strategy is always fixed: it is to maintain or restore order. What passes for 'strategy' is nothing other than general tactics, but tactics must be flexible, since the police should take whatever action is reasonable at the time to maintain or restore the peace. But if tactics are to be employed flexibly then general tactics must be capable of being revised or reversed so that order can be preserved or restored.

In stark contrast to the military, police tactics in public order situations will, or should, emerge *in response* to the situation as it develops. Since policing is so reactive, all that senior officers can do in anticipation of disorder is to offer general guidelines and principles that they wish to be followed in the event of disorder erupting. How, then, can the police act with the co-ordination and discipline previously commended as necessary for ensuring the use of no more than minimum force? The role of senior officers is to maintain an overview of the whole operation, and to influence its course by making decisions as the situation unfolds to ensure as much co-ordination as possible. Officers at street level cannot be expected to appreciate that by pushing a disorderly crowd in one direction they are aggravating the situation elsewhere. This can only be appreciated by senior commanders who, remote from the immediate disorder, can comprehend the whole scene. Yet, the senior commander is not determining strategy in the sense of some grand plan, he too is merely acting tactically albeit within wider horizons. His strategic goal must be to do whatever is prudent to restore and maintain 'the peace' — a goal imposed by his office and shared with every other police officer of whatever rank.

To propose, then, that the most senior officer, occupying the position of Gold commander, should sit back and allow subordinates to make crucial tactical decisions is little short of prescribing the abdication of command. 'Arcing' is not an aberration, but a recognition on the part of Gold commanders that they need to maintain direct control of the operation so that it conforms as closely to their wishes as possible.

Fortunately, the problem only rarely arises, since most pre-planned public-order operations involve only 'slow-time' decision-making, because no disorder occurs — at least for the vast majority of the time. The work of Gold control is principally that of booking officers on and off duty, and keeping them refreshed meanwhile. However, even this low-key aspect of public-order policing is not free from controversy.

### 'A waste of time'

A corollary to the essentially reactive nature of even the policing of large scale, pre-planned public-order events is that sufficient officers need to be available to deal with any likely contingency. The need to be able to respond effectively in the event of the 'worst-case scenario' dictates that more than enough officers will be deployed on all but the rarest occasions. For example, following the disorder that had occurred at the Notting Hill carnival during 1987, a considerable number of officers, around 10,000 in total, were deployed a year later. Shield serials needed to be kept on stand-by lest disorder reoccurred. It is taken as given, in the context of the British tradition of policing public order, that such officers should be kept out of sight. The presence of large numbers of police, some equipped in protective clothing, would be seen as intimidatory — more in keeping with the strategy of the 'formidable appearance' of Continental police forces than the minimum-force strategy traditionally adopted in Britain. However, keeping large numbers of officers hidden from public view can amount, literally, to a waste of time. Certainly, many officers spend many hours at such events whiling away their time, watching films, reading books, playing cards, or improvising games of cricket. Tedium is far more typical of public-order policing than is the exhilaration of action.

### Central or local control?

A problem which also arises from the need to deploy so many officers on public-order duties is simply keeping track of them all — the 'slow-time' decision-making undertaken by Gold control. Given the resources available to the Metropolitan Police this should be easy, but these resources are in danger of being squandered.

At the cost of some £5 million, the public-order control

room, known as 'GT', was computerized and came on-line in mid–1987: an impressive complex, in which information can be received, updated, combined and analysed so as to aid decision-making and transmitted almost instantaneously. For example, various PSUs will come on duty at different times at widely dispersed home stations, so that some will reach their 'ground assigned' whilst others are still in transit. A commander might wish to know simply how many PSUs he has available for deployment and how many are *en route*; or he may find it useful to know what types of officer are at his disposal—how many shield or mounted serials? Alternatively, he may need to be aware of which PSUs came on duty first so that they can be dismissed earliest. Any of these inquiries and many more can be answered immediately. Moreover, the computer stores all the information that passes through it for later inquiry, so that should, for example, a complaint be received regarding officers at any particular location, it will be a relatively easy matter to discover who was assigned to that position at the relevant time.

Unfortunately, the provision of this installation was overtaken by events, for during the period of its construction the force had been reorganized into eight semi-autonomous areas, each of which had at least one public-order control room, all of which lacked the sophistication of the newly computerized control room at Scotland Yard. Area control rooms operate with the primitive technology of magnetic wipe-clean boards around the walls and messages conveyed by a 'runner'. The result is that the lag between a deployment and its being recorded on the magnetic board can be of the order of three-quarters of an hour. This contrasts unfavourably with the almost instantaneous sharing of information in computerized control rooms and the capacity to analyse deployments immediately. In the computerized control room the commander knows, moment by moment, how many officers and of what type he has available and where they are located.

Not only has the decision to equip each area with its own autonomous control room wasted the valuable central resource, it has also been unnecessary—a needless retreat into technological primitivism. First, since all directions are communicated by radio or telephone, there is no need for 'slow-time' control to be undertaken by each area. Operators many miles from the scene can keep track of which officers have booked on, and when they were last refreshed, just as easily as those only a few miles from the scene. With advanced technology, operators in a distant control room can probably do so much better than those in a relatively close, but antiquated, control room. Second, this decision entails the sevenfold replication of control room facilities through-out the force—one for each of the areas outside central London (the central area being able to use the facilities at Scotland Yard). Third, it also requires a similar replication of staff trained to operate each control room. Fourth, given the relative infrequency of such events, the staff in any given area control room are likely to be less familiar with procedures than are centrally located staff who would frequently operate such a control room.

The only significant disadvantage of using such a central control room would seem to be that, under current arrange-ments, the Gold commander may be remote from the situation and unable to liaise either with his junior com-manders or community leaders. However, if the roles of gold and silver were to be reversed, as suggested above, then this objection loses much of its force. If it is still thought essential for the 'slow-time' commander to be physically nearer the scene than central London, there need be no technological obstacle. That part of the central control room now known as 'the bridge', where the commander sits with his immediate support staff, could just as easily be replicated on board a mobile 'bridge' and transported to a police station near the scene. Since the information received at the 'bridge' is conveyed electronically, it is unnecessary for the 'bridge' and its occupants to be in the same place as operators receiving and processing information. A mobile 'bridge' could be plugged in to a secure land-line installed at any one of several police stations throughout the area. This is no more difficult than providing terminals for the existing computer-aided dispatch and message-switching system. The savings made in not replicating control rooms throughout the Metro-politan Police District might well offset some of the cost of such a mobile 'bridge'. Moreover, such an arrangement

would introduce a welcome measure of flexibility in locating
this component of the control room, for a fixed installation
can come under attack itself, as did the control room at
Brixton during the 1985 disturbances.


## Intelligence


Another reason for radical and liberal criticism of public-
order policing is the growth in the intelligence function.
During the miners' dispute there were repeated accusations
of Special Branch infiltration and telephone-tapping. Why
serious and large-scale threats to public order should be
excluded from intelligence-gathering is not made clear by the
critics. Few complaints are made about the gathering of
intelligence against organized criminals or terrorist groups.
Public disorder can result, and has resulted, in severe physical
damage, injury or death, not to mention considerable
disruption. Gathering accurate information from which the
proper conclusions are validly drawn (the intelligence function) not only enables an effective police response but also
avoids excessive policing.

These gains of adequate intelligence were nicely illustrated
at the Henley regatta in 1985, which was policed by the
Thames Valley force, and observed closely by the author.
This annual event, attracting many thousands of people,
occurred in the wake of the inglorious end to the miners'
dispute and the immediate aftermath of the disorder connected with the 'Peace Convoy' near Stonehenge. The
militant left-wing newspaper *Class War* had announced that it
was to be the opportunity to 'bash the rich' — a follow-up to
its earlier attempts to 'stop the City' by disrupting financial
centres in Leeds and the City of London. The problem for the
police was to maintain order without presenting the kind of
high-profile presence which would achieve by default the
militants' aim of disrupting the event. Because the police
were in possession of good information which enabled them
to identify and keep track of the movements of *Class War*
activists, a minimal police presence could be maintained
overtly whilst other officers remained in reserve. This

information also meant that 'punks' and others who might erroneously be thought to be *Class War* militants were not confused with the real activists, thus avoiding confusion amongst the police and the needless harassment of innocent people.

Immediately before 3.00 p.m., officers on routine public-order duty were warned that the militants intended to disrupt traffic on the only bridge across the Thames. Officers on stand-by were brought forward. Just as the militants assembled outside a hotel at one end of the bridge, police were able to encircle and contain them. After shouting slogans for some minutes, the militants dispersed, defeated.

If the police had not gathered accurate intelligence, the militants might well have achieved their purpose and public order would have been disrupted. Not only that: in the police action which would undoubtedly have followed, it is probable that both police officers and protesters would have been hurt. The absence of accurate intelligence might also have caused the police to overestimate the extent of the threat, because of the confusion of militants with ordinary young people who dress in punk fashion. Stark (1972) argues that it was the *lack* of accurate intelligence that led some American police forces to over-react to anti-Vietnam War demonstrations. In the absence of accurate intelligence, rumour and hearsay gain credibility, with sometimes un-pleasant consequences.

The value of the intelligence function extends beyond the acquisition of 'secret' information about what a group intends to do in the future. There is also a need for 'real-time' intelligence about what is happening at any given moment. One source of such information is from officers at the scene. During the miners' strike, for example, officers at various intersections would monitor the flow of vehicles and report heavy concentrations, thus allowing control rooms to estimate where flying pickets might be heading and take anticipatory police action. However, in many crowd situations the view of officers in direct contact with the crowd is always limited by their position on the ground. It is in providing an overview that technology can be of valuable assistance. Fixed television cameras on high buildings can provide immediate information about the numbers and density of crowds at particular locations, the activities of offenders within crowds (such as 'steamers' running through the crowd robbing people), and patterns of movement of the crowd as a whole. To know which way a crowd is moving and how big such a crowd is is invaluable to an operational commander at the scene. In addition to fixed cameras, the 'heli-tele' carried on board one of the force's four helicopters can provide real-time television pictures of spontaneous disorder or moving events such as marches.

## Should There Be a Third Force?

If the advantages of a paramilitary response to public disorder are so great, why not follow the lead of other policing systems who have much greater experience of policing civil unrest, and introduce a national riot police? This has been advocated not only by conservatives who fear a threat to constitutional government from radical dissident groups but also by some liberal commentators, who see such a force as a means of protecting the traditional image of the British civil police (Morris, 1985). A separate paramilitary force dedicated to public-order duties would allow the civil police to continue to 'police by consent' in the traditional manner.

This superficially attractive proposal suffers from a number of practical flaws. First, such a force would be expensive to maintain, since there are insufficient riots (even during the soccer season) to keep it occupied. This would have two likely consequences:

(i) The paramilitary police would acquire various ordinary policing duties which would blur the distinction between them and their civil police counterparts, thus undermining the traditions that such a division of labour is designed to uphold.

(ii) Even with these additional tasks to keep them employed, it would remain very expensive to maintain such a force and so it would be kept small in number to minimize costs. Therefore, when deployed in their public order role they would need to compensate for their lack of manpower by greater fire-power. It is for this reason that this type of force tends to be associated with the doctrine of the 'formidable appearance'. This does not mean what it means in the ACPO tactical options manual — that once disorder has begun the police should present a 'no-nonsense' image. It means that *before* any disorder has occurred, the paramilitary police present a formidable appearance as a veiled threat. It seems that often the consequence of so doing is to provoke the very disorder this strategy is designed to prevent.

Second, however mobile such a force might be, it is unlikely to be on hand to deal with every, or even many, spontaneous outbreaks of disorder. If, in order to provide a speedy response, such a force were distributed throughout the country it would either be enormously expensive or, more probably, spread too thinly to make much of a contribution. It is, therefore, highly likely that the local civil police would have to contain a riot, at least during its initial stages, before being relieved by their paramilitary colleagues. In addition, if disorder were widely dispersed, as it was during the miners' strike, it is highly unlikely that any paramilitary force would be large enough to cope unaided by the local civil police. Consequently, the civil police would still find themselves having responsibility for riot control. The benefits that would supposedly accrue from such a separation of function would be lost — the civil police would continue to find themselves expected to 'pat kids on the head one day and then shoot with plastic bullets the next' (*Police*, November 1986: 9).

Third, if the local civil police were to be relieved by a paramilitary force, there would be problems in arranging such a handover. The local civil police might well be reluctant to cede responsibility, just as they now contemplate calling for military assistance with utter horror — as confession of abject failure. Moreover, since the *raison d'être* of a paramilitary force is its separate command structure, it would operate within the territorial area of the civil police but outside their control. The civil police might fear that under these conditions they would be left to pick up the pieces after the paramilitary force handed responsibility back to them.

An alternative to a permanent, specialized, paramilitary police is a part-time reserve force, along the lines of the US National Guard in its riot control role. This is an alternative that British governments have toyed with in the past. During periods of major industrial conflict, especially during the 1920s, various forces were temporarily raised to maintain public order (Morgan, 1987). The Special Constabulary originally fulfilled this role, being empowered on an *ad hoc* basis to assist the regular police in containing anticipated episodes of civil disorder. However, this experience has not always been a happy one, for special constables and similar units lack the discipline of their regular counterparts. Indeed, it was the savagery of the part-time yeomanry in suppressing disorder in the early nineteenth century that provided one incentive for establishing a professional police.

Experience of the National Guard in America has been mixed. During the Detroit riot of 1967, both the National Guard and the local police appeared significantly less disciplined than units of the regular army. Of course, it was a National Guard unit that opened fire on college students at Kent State University who were protesting at the invasion of Cambodia in 1972. On the other hand, the Walker report (1968) into the disorders that accompanied the Democratic Party Convention at Chicago in 1968 concluded that the military discipline of the National Guard made them both more effective than the civil police and less prone to over-react to the taunts of the protesters.

Whether such an alternative would be considered preferable to the option that still remains, of asking for military assistance, seems doubtful. The use of either seems conceivable only in the most extreme circumstances; and serious though recent disorders have been, they have not yet reached these levels.

## Paramilitarism: Curse, Blessing, or Just Unavoidable?

So long as the threat of serious disorder exists and it remains the duty of the police (as opposed to some other body) to suppress it, paramilitarism will have some value. Of course, full-blown militarism has never truly been absent, for the option has always existed of calling on the army to aid the civil power. Those who hanker for some mythical 'Golden Age' ought, perhaps, to recall that it was in those halcyon days that troops sometimes confronted and even opened fire on pickets and protesters. If the military are not to be relied upon, then the police must be able to deploy as an effective and disciplined body. No doubt the motivation for developing such a capability has been to enhance effectiveness, but it has the added advantage of allowing senior officers to exercise greater discipline and control over subordinate ranks. Probably nothing will eliminate undisciplined conduct on the part of individuals or small groups of officers, but paramilitary deployment allows a degree of control that traditional methods could not hope to match.

The association of paramilitarism with restraint may seem odd, for it is the coercive potential of militarized policing that is cause for concern. The paramilitary police of authoritarian systems from communist Eastern Europe to apartheid South Africa do not leap to mind as models of restraint. The anxiety aroused by the paramilitarization of the British police is not restricted to their organization and deployment, but extends to the weaponry now available and the tactics used. Are the police 'tooling up' to suppress a dissident civil population?

# 6

# The Use of Force in Public-Order Policing

## Introduction

The central concern lying at the heart of complaints about the paramilitarization of the British police is the use of force. Observers have concluded from seeing officers dressed in protective attire that they have adopted not only the appearance of 'alien' riot police but also their exemplars' more aggressive tactics.[1] In fact, contrary to this popular belief, public-order tactics in Britain have not been imported from overseas. They have grown organically, with their roots firmly planted in tradition. Indeed, this has been the cause of some of the problems that have afflicted this aspect of policing, for although the police have moved some considerable distance up the hierarchy of force, they have done so in the manner of a person climbing a mountain backwards: keeping the terrain that has been covered clearly in view, but having little idea of where they are or where they are going. Perhaps it is time to stop and take some bearings.

## 'Pushing and Shoving': The Continuation of a Tradition

The method of controlling the vast majority of public-order situations is as it always has been: the police form cordons to demarcate areas the crowd can occupy from those that they cannot. Most cordons are passive, since most crowds comply readily. Compliance is secured, not by force, but through prior discussion and agreement. The research conducted by

David Waddington and his associations (1988) illustrates, *inter alia*, that police seek to negotiate whenever they can and that negotiation is an important, indeed crucial, element in the preservation of order. Even when crowds try to breach the cordon, the most common response is still that of officers holding and, if necessary, pushing back the crowd.

It is clear that most observers and critics are not concerned about the vast majority of public-order events which occasion no disorder. What causes concern is the few that do and particularly those that involve the use of protective equipment. It is to these that we will now turn. Before doing so, it should be appreciated that we will be discussing the small minority of public-order events, and that a forceful response to disorder is still a rarity.

## The Use of Protective Equipment

The introduction of the long shield in 1976 and the subsequent acquisition of riot helmets and flame-resistant overalls did not represent the breach with traditional methods of policing public disorder that has often been claimed. It sought merely to offer defensive protection to otherwise unprotected officers dressed in ordinary uniform. The ordinary police helmet was reinforced, but every effort was made to retain the traditional appearance of the British bobby.[2]

Tactically, too, the aim was to retain the traditional methods of policing disorder. Shield tactics are an extension of the traditional notion that police cordons hold and push back a crowd, even if safety dictates that this is done from a distance. Progress is slow, partly because the shield is heavy and cumbersome and because the shield unit of five men are huddled together in the 'rugby scrum' formation, which also inhibits rapid movement.[3] Moreover, whilst the long shield does provide satisfactory head–to-toe protection from attacks made by people to the front of the officers, it offers no protection at all against attacks made from the side or rear. Thus, a cordon proceeding, say, along a street is always vulnerable to attacks from side streets, or from buildings lining the route. Cordons are instructed to stop and check that any side street or other opening is clear before crossing and, ideally, other officers to the rear will cordon off such streets and openings once the forward units have advanced along the street. Shield units must take care not to push a crowd in such a direction that they are channelled to the sides and able to encircle the police or attack them in a pincer-type movement.

Turning into side streets can be extremely hazardous for shield units, particularly at T-junctions and crossroads where the crowd might split. To turn any corner involves pivoting, like guardsmen on parade, trying to maintain a straight line, for otherwise one shield unit can advance too far in front of its companions and become vulnerable to attack from the side. If rioters have split, with some turning one way and others turning in an alternative direction, it is essential that sufficient shield units are available simultaneously to cordon off as many streets as are occupied by the crowd. Even so, shield units are inevitably exposed to missiles thrown over the heads of their colleagues from rioters behind them. The vulnerability of shield units to attack from the sides and rear, and the consequent necessity to muster sufficient officers to cordon off avenues of attack, further slows the rate of police advance. All a crowd need do is to turn a corner and they will find they are allowed ample time in which to reform and rearm.

At the time of the 1976 Notting Hill carnival, the provision of such an essentially defensive piece of equipment as the long shield and the subsequent development of tactics in its use was perfectly understandable. After all, the level of violence to which officers were exposed on that occasion, though regarded at the time as exceptional, was modest by comparison with what was to happen later. When more extreme violence did erupt, the police response was to provide additional protective equipment: a visored helmet to protect the head, flame-resistant overalls, and portable fire extinguishers to protect against fire. Yet this development continued to build upon the traditional notion of holding and gradually pushing back the crowd.

This remains fundamentally different to Continental and

colonial methods, despite superficial similarities. In Britain, it remains the case that large numbers of officers maintain close physical proximity to the crowd, holding and gradually pushing it back. By contrast, Continental and colonial police rely on relatively smaller groups of highly mobile officers aggressively dispersing the crowd. The cowering posture of British police behind their long shield is the very antithesis of the 'formidable appearance' associated with Continental and colonial riot police. To the extent that the British police have been reluctantly obliged to adopt more aggressive tactics, they have continued to maintain fidelity with their traditions. The baton charge and use of mounted officers continue to be the principal offensive tactics.

What might be read by some as an apologia for the adoption of a more aggressive style of public-order policing is not offered here with any commendation. On the contrary, if the British police are guilty of anything, it is a failure to appreciate the nature of the task of quelling serious disorder. They, and many others, remain blinded by their traditional image of policing public order without recourse to overtly aggressive tactics. From the vantage-point of 1990, the development of police public-order tactics is confused and out of touch with reality.

## Arresting Offenders

The commitment to maintaining tradition can clearly be seen in the efforts the police continue to make to *arrest* those amongst a violent crowd who commit offences. Arresting wrongdoers is, of course, the task which typifies the police function and reinforces their image of enforcing the law against criminals, rather than stifling dissent. However, there are considerable obstacles to achieving the successful arrest and prosecution of offenders in these circumstances. The collapse of various trials associated with disorder at St Paul's, Bristol, at Orgreave and other sites during the miners' strike, and at the 'Battle of the Beanfield' near Stonehenge all demonstrate how difficult it is to bring successful prosecutions. The practical problems are, first, that it is almost always difficult, and sometimes impossible, to effect an arrest at the scene of the disorder. Either the crowd is too dense or the level of hostility is such as to make it too dangerous for officers to get close enough to offenders to make an arrest. Second, even when an arrest is made, either at the scene or later, it is difficult to obtain evidence which establishes beyond reasonable doubt that a given individual committed a particular offence. The chaos and confusion that inevitably surrounds such events confounds attempts to establish a clear link between, say, the damage caused by a missile and the person who threw it. Even when the offence is extremely grave, such as the murder of PC Keith Blakelock, clear and solid evidence of guilt is often absent. Winston Silcott and others were convicted of PC Blakelock's murder on the basis of incriminating statements made after the event, which were challenged in court by the defence and are still disputed by organizations like Amnesty International.

The Metropolitan Police have attempted to overcome these problems through two strategies. The first has been the introduction of 'evidence-gathering teams' (see pp. 333–4). Their purpose is to gather good-quality evidence of individual commission of serious offences. The results of this use of photographic evidence are extremely impressive, making it difficult for offenders to deny that they were present and requiring them to provide some explanation of their actions. Photography allows for facial identification, but even where people wear masks it is sometimes possible to identify them from the clothes they were wearing. After disorder has occurred, local officers can scan through photographs and try to recognize individuals; and when, later, people are arrested for run-of-the-mill offences, they too can have their identities checked to see if they are wanted.

The use of such evidence-gathering techniques has undoubtedly increased the likelihood that individual wrong-doers amongst a disorderly or riotous crowd can eventually be brought before the courts. However, as offenders become more aware of these possibilities, they will doubtless take every available opportunity to obscure their identity. If offenders are to be captured, it is best for them to be detained at the scene, rather than later. It is to the achievement of this goal that the second strategy is directed. This has been to enhance the role of 'arrest squads'.

Small squads of officers, known more commonly as 'snatch squads', have always been envisaged as having a role in public-order policing. Their task is to run through the police cordon from the rear and arrest members of the crowd. They do this in various manœuvres, most commonly as a four-man team. Half of the unit is usually equipped with a small shield, and has the function of protecting the arresting officer or officers. The arresting officers seize the alleged offender and bring him back behind the police cordon. Enhancement has taken the form of introducing greater organization and control of arrest squads, for the danger previously was that arrest squads would arrest whomsoever they were able to arrest and against whom there would often be limited evidence. Now the aim is carefully to target particular individuals, perhaps acting in co-ordination with evidence gatherers such as those operating remote video cameras. However, in instances of severe rioting, when the need to arrest those committing very serious offences is obviously most imperative, it might be simply too danger-ous for arrest squads to operate.

However successful the police are in arresting specific wrongdoers, either at the scene of disorder or later, this does not address the fundamental problem of policing civil disorder, which is to restore peace and tranquillity *there and then*, not only to arrest individuals whom the courts can punish at some time in the future. As Sir Ralph Dahrendorf expresses it: 'There is clearly something pathetic about the arrest of 39 soccer hooligans if hundreds were involved in breaking up terraces, attacking rival fans and finally the police, looting shops and injuring innocent bystanders' (1985: 34). As Dahrendorf goes on to point out, the real threat of riotous disorder, apart from the specific crimes that might be committed during its course, is the challenge to the 'rule of law' by groups too large to be effectively punished. Put simply, riots demonstrate that when significant numbers of people act in concert, they can get away with it. Quelling disorder requires that the crowd, which is the vehicle for disorder, be dispersed, if necessary by force. Unfortunately, the implications of dispersal are avoided by the emphasis given to arrest. The fiction is maintained, even in the Metropolitan Police's tactical manual, that force will be targeted against specific wrongdoers.

## Dispersal

Because a crowd is an entity in itself, the most sensible strategy to combat a violently disorderly mob is to *disperse* it. A dispersed crowd is no longer a crowd, and, lacking coherence, loses its awesome potential for violence and destruction. Its members cannot commit criminal offences with such impunity, since there is much greater opportunity for officers to gain physical access to the offender when there is no solid mass to obstruct the former. If a dispersed crowd can be kept moving, there will be limited opportunities for its members to acquire debris and other sources of missile ammunition, as well as fewer opportunities to throw them.

Current public-order tactics, maintaining the traditional approach, are not directed towards the dispersal of the crowd. Indeed, quite the opposite strategy is taken, albeit by default. Currently, the aim in controlling a non-violent crowd seems to be to *attract* it rather than to encourage it to disperse. Once the crowd becomes violent, the slowly moving police cordon becomes the focus for activity, so that, instead of dispersing a crowd, it draws the crowd together. Since the speed of advance is inevitably slow, a violent crowd has ample opportunity to throw missiles and rearm, as well as build barricades to slow the advance even further. The result, as the police have come to recognize themselves, is that the long-shield cordon has become an 'Aunt Sally'.

### Speed and flexibility

Recognizing that the long-shield units lack sufficient speed to effect the dispersal of rioting mobs, police tacticians have sought means of introducing greater speed. This has involved the replacement of the long shield by smaller, lighter alternatives which allow officers to move more freely and yet offer them some measure of protection. Initially, officers were deployed as separate 'short-shield' Police Support Units (PSUs) positioned to the rear of the long-shield cordon. The long shields provided the basic defensive cordon, whilst the task of the short-shield units was to run through the gaps in the long-shield cordon, dispersing the crowd and making arrests. As the short-shield units did this, their long-shield companions would advance as quickly as possible to overtake the short shields and restore a defensive cordon. By this leap-frogging manœuvre it was hoped to achieve a more rapid advance.

This remains the basic manœuvre, but an additional variant is the deployment of officers, not as separate short- and long-shield PSUs, but as a single PSU/TSG in what is called the 'mix-and-match' formation: a PSU/TSG consisting of twenty constables, two sergeants, and an inspector will consist of two long-shield units and twelve short-shield officers. Thus, it is hoped that, in the earliest stages of disorder, a few PSUs/TSGs will possess sufficient speed and flexibility quickly to disperse a disorderly crowd before it poses too great a threat.

Unfortunately, there remains a basic flaw in this man-œuvre: the continued reliance upon the long shield to provide the defensive cordon. For however quickly the short-shield officers proceed to disperse the crowd, their rate of advance will always be governed by the speed of the long shields. If they move too far ahead of the long-shield units, they will lack adequate defence and be vulnerable to attack. Thus, the crowd will have repeated opportunities to reform and rearm whilst the long shields move up to secure the defensive cordon.

## Dispersal, mobility, and the use of vehicles

Effective dispersal of a crowd requires that the police should be able flexibly and rapidly to attend where there is any concentration. It is the recognition of this fact that lies at the heart of the strategy of 'aggressive mobility' which informs public-order policing in most other countries, and is particularly associated with Continental and colonial policing systems. It has also been recognized *ad hoc* by police facing serious public disorder in Britain in the past.

One of the riots that occurred in the summer of 1981 took place in the Moss Side district of Manchester. Initial disorder occurred on 8 July, during which time Moss Side police station was attacked. The following day the Greater Manchester Police adopted the *ad hoc* tactic of deploying groups of officers in vans who were able to arrive speedily at scenes of disorder and chase away those responsible. Having done so, they reboarded their vehicles and raced to the next scene of disorder. In fact, the tactic was remarkably successful when compared to those employed elsewhere during that summer. Within twenty-four hours the rioting had largely been quelled.

It is worth quoting from the Chief Constable's report:

The fast deployment of men in vans, rather than on foot or in cumbersome police coaches, was also determined by recent experiences in other police areas. Lines of police officers with riot shields, remaining static or moving slowly forward towards a riotous assembly, can only, at best, contain the situation. Policemen are presented as targets for fire bombs and all types of missiles. In such large groups officers are immobile and not unnaturally this has an adverse effect on police morale, particularly when there is aerial bombardment . . .

The use of vans enabled many small groups of officers to be deployed in an extremely fast and flexible way which had the effect of disorienting the rioting crowds and facilitating the arrest of many offenders.   (Anderton, 1981: 3–4)

It is noteworthy that, although available, long shields were not used by officers engaged in this operation.

The strategy employed in Manchester was not entirely a novel one. In 1958 the Notting Hill race riots met the same *ad hoc* response, with similar success. Here, too, quite small numbers of officers were deployed in vehicles to break up hostile or provocative assemblies. Despite scenes considered outrageous at the time, the situation was policed by many fewer officers than has occurred since in comparable situations (Moore, 1988).

It seems that the lessons of Moss Side and Notting Hill have still not been fully assimilated. Effective dispersal requires the police to move at a speed equal to, if not greater than, that of the dispersing crowd. This can only be achieved effectively using vehicles from which lightly equipped officers can alight to chase the crowd and harry dispersed groups of disorderly people. The vehicle itself, properly protected, takes over the defensive role currently performed by long-shield units. Obviously this will involve potentially costly damage being inflicted on such vehicles; but officers have suffered serious injuries whilst forming cordons, and it is surely preferable that vehicles rather than people should be exposed to such risks. Moreover, a vehicle can use its speed and, if necessary, its strength in a defensive capacity should it be subjected to severe attack. It can retreat more effectively than can officers on foot.

Vehicles offer other advantages too. First, they can be used to carry equipment which is either too heavy or cumbersome for officers to carry on foot. For example, some tactics involve the police using high-intensity lighting, the glare from which prevents members of the crowd seeing what the police are doing and serves also to disorientate them slightly. These 'dragon lights' could easily be installed on vehicles instead of, or in addition to, being carried by individual officers, and would provide an additional height advantage.

Second, vehicles could carry equipment used to warn disorderly crowds to disperse. At present, there is considerable difficulty in providing adequate warnings before baton charges are made or special weapons are deployed. The sheer volume of noise made by disorderly or riotous crowds defeats most hand-held public-address systems. Vehicles could be equipped with very loud PA systems or could be used to display visual warnings, for example, on illuminated display boards.

Third, vehicles could be used as a temporary place in which securely to hold people who have been arrested. Arresting offenders tends to be incompatible with effective dispersal, since arresting officers will be required to remove the prisoner to some secure accommodation usually well to the rear. The time taken to convey the 'prisoner' to such accommodation and complete initial documentation upon arrival results in the officers being unavailable at the scene of disorder. A vehicle which was in the immediate vicinity, literally only a few yards away, could be equipped with a secure cage into which arrested people could be temporarily placed, allowing the arresting officers to return rapidly to the dispersal operation.

Finally, vehicles could also provide immediate protected accommodation for injured officers, in which first aid could be rendered.

The obstacle to the development of such tactics lies, not in any objection to the compelling operational reasons for them, but from their 'aggressive' appearance. The slow-moving long-shield cordon is a mere extension of the traditional 'pushing and shoving', but 'aggressive mobility' is regarded as 'alien'. True, these *are* tactics more commonly associated with Continental and colonial styles of policing public disorder. It seems that the British police will be obliged eventually to adopt more aggressive dispersal tactics based on the use of vehicles as the only logical response.

What *can* be said in favour of current public-order tactics is that close supervision by senior officers can readily be maintained. The difficulty with 'aggressive mobility' is that officers end up as dispersed as the erstwhile crowd and, therefore, much more difficult to supervise. At least the use of the cordon, by concentrating officers together, means that their actions can be supervised by a few senior officers on the spot. However, once the police resort to their sole offensive dispersal tactic — charging into the crowd — supervision and control become the first casualties.

### Baton Charges

When the slow-moving cordon proves incapable of achieving enforced dispersal of the crowd, the police in Britain have traditionally resorted to the baton charge. This owes its origins to Francis Place a supporter of the Reform Movement in the 1830s, who at the same time feared revolution if protests were not effectively policed. He advised Superintendent Thomas of the infant Metropolitan Police to cease the practice of trying to make selective arrests amongst the crowd. Instead, he advised that

> when he saw a mob prepared to make an attack, to lead his men on and thrash those who composed the mob with their staves as long as any of them remained together, but to take none into custody; and that if this were done once or twice, there would be no more such mobs.   (Quoted in Palmer, 1988)

As Palmer records, this tactic was implemented on 9 November 1830 and became an instant success, since, although injuries were inflicted, these were rarely fatal, in stark contrast to the lethal sabres and rifles of the military.

This same tactic has until very recently been incorporated into various manœuvres, involving both mounted and foot police, currently employed by the Metropolitan Police. Yet tradition is not an infallible guide, for this is a tactic which is both legally debatable and tactically flawed.

### Incapacitating offenders

The debate about the legality of the baton charge was initiated at the Orgreave riot trial, when counsel for the defence succeeded in obtaining the disclosure of certain public-order manœuvres, contained in the hitherto secret ACPO *Tactical Options Manual*, and referred to by the Assistant Chief Constable whilst giving evidence at the trial. The manœuvre that caused most controversy was that of charging into a violent crowd to arrest offenders and disperse the remainder.

> Long shield officers deployed into crowd and deployed across the road. Behind long shield units are deployed all the short and round shield officers with batons. On the command the short shield officers run forward either through and/or round the flanks of long shields into the crowd for not more than 30 yards. They disperse the crowd and *incapacitate* missile throwers and ring leaders by striking in a controlled manner with batons about the arms and legs or torso so as not to cause serious injury. Following the short shield units the long shield units advance quickly beyond short shields to provide additional protection. Link men from the long shield units move in and take prisoners.   (Quoted in McCabe *et al.*, 1988)

McCabe *et al.* remark: 'It is not surprising that defence counsel at the Orgreave trial described this as an incitement to commit criminal assaults' (p. 50) and Brewer *et al.*, (1988: 24) consider the manœuvre 'legally dubious'.

Only one conclusion can be reached with any certainty, and that is that *no one knows what the law is in this regard*. The question of the legality of various public-order manœuvres has yet to be decided by the courts, for neither criminal nor civil proceedings have been brought to test it. This uncertainty itself *must* be considered deplorable, for it leaves both police and members of any crowd without guidance as to what forceful action may lawfully be taken by the police.

Given that we are in the realms of speculation, what are the grounds for believing that this and, by implication, other similar manœuvres are of dubious legality? The legal basis for using force is section 3 of the Criminal Law Act 1967 (see p. 7). In addition, it seems that the common law allows the police a less circumscribed authority to use force to prevent a breach of the peace, or to restore it once it has been breached. Clearly, deliberate acts of brutality by police officers in any circumstances are and should be illegal. But this is only incidentally the problem. The central issue is: how much force can the police *lawfully* use to suppress, not the actions of particular individuals, but a state of general disorder?

The problem is not the *amount* of force the police are entitled to use in quelling disorder, since the police can lawfully use quite extreme force, if it is warranted by the circumstances. For example, if firearms are used during the course of a riot, as they were at Broadwater Farm, there would seem every justification for the police to reply with lethal force against those responsible. Certainly, police officers are entitled to use their truncheons to incapacitate offenders, if that is necessary and justified by the circumstances. Moreover, an officer may lawfully use force in order to *prevent* an offence which has not yet been committed, if force is necessary and justified by the circumstances.

What is at issue is whether a senior officer commanding others can issue a blanket instruction to officers to use incapacitating force against anyone — even 'missile throwers and ring leaders' — without regard to whether such force is necessary to arrest or subdue any particular person. If an officer engaging in this manœuvre moves into the crowd and encounters a previously identified missile-thrower, or someone throwing missiles at that moment, is he permitted in law to strike that person an incapacitating blow with his truncheon, even if alternative, less forceful, action (such as arrest) would suffice? It seems highly unlikely that he is. Section 3 would seem, from its wording, to envisage force being used only when it is required to overcome *individual* resistance. The extract from the manual, cited above, on the contrary, seems to invite officers to strike missile-throwers with incapacitating blows whether or not that measure of force is needed to overcome a resisting person. Other officers, the 'link men', then follow behind and arrest those who have been incapacitated. But what if the person could be arrested without receiving an incapacitating blow? Of course, it is possible that when the officers charge into the crowd they might encounter individuals who cannot be arrested or prevented from committing further offences by any other means, and in those circumstances the officers would be justified in using a greater measure of force. However, the amount of force employed would depend upon the *particular circumstances* surrounding the individual concerned. It is the *global* nature of the instruction to 'incapacitate missile throwers and ring leaders' that is of doubtful legality. A senior officer who issued the instructions contained in the ACPO Manual might find himself liable to prosecution for inciting his officers to commit criminal assault, and officers who carried out those instructions would also risk prosecution for assaulting those whom they struck.

The police would doubtless respond to these arguments by pointing out that this is just one of several alternative manœuvres that a senior officer could employ in the circumstances. If it were tactically feasible to arrest missile-throwers, then the officer would employ a manœuvre designed to achieve that purpose, for example, deploying 'snatch squads'. However, the general conditions may be such that arrests cannot be made. For example, there may be insufficient police officers available, and the disorders may be so serious (possibly life-threatening) that no other action would achieve the aim.

The issue turns on the scope of 'the circumstances',

referred to in section 3. Do they include the general conditions or merely the behaviour of the individuals against whom force is used? One can easily envisage a situation where the general circumstances might seem to justify the use of significant force, but resistance by any given individual does not. Suppose that serious disorder is occurring, property is being destroyed, and innocent lives jeopardized by arsonists. Relatively few police officers have assembled, but given the scale of disorder their senior officer feels compelled to take some action in defence of life and property, as well as towards restoration of the peace. He deploys his officers in the manner described in the extract from the ACPO manual. In the course of the manœuvre a 'missile-thrower' is struck and injured as he, say, tries to escape. Was the force employed against the 'missile-thrower' 'reasonable in the circumstances'? If 'the circumstances' are taken to be the whole situation — the severity of the disorder and the limited means available to combat it — then the use of such force may be justified. If 'the circumstances' extend only to the moment when the officer struck the 'missile-thrower' as he attempted to escape over the wall, then it is unlikely that the use of that measure of force would be justified. Until the courts have occasion to interpret the meaning of section 3, no one knows what, precisely, 'the circumstances' actually means.

### Baton charging to disperse

Much of the debate surrounding the disclosure of the extract from the ACPO manual cited above has concentrated upon the incapacitation of missile-throwers and ringleaders. However, this at least retains the notion that only those who are guilty of wrongdoing will be injured, and that force is used as ancillary to arrest. Yet the most acute problems arise from the delphic phrase, 'They disperse the crowd'. Elsewhere, the manual refers to baton charging a crowd solely for the purposes of dispersal, omitting any reference to making arrests. Although the manual provides no explanation of how dispersal is to be achieved, the implication seems to be—and training confirms—that it is envisaged that members of the crowd will be struck with truncheons. If the use of force against suspected offenders is a grey area, the use of force for the purpose of dispersal is positively fog-bound.

The crux of the issue here is whether police can use force against individuals *who may not be guilty of any serious offence.* The principle of individual culpability, enshrined in English criminal law (that a person is liable to legal penalty only for the actions they have committed), and the whole tenor of section 3, seems to suggest that, however disorderly the actions of some other participants in a crowd, merely to be present at the scene of disorder is not to commit any offence and, therefore, that to be subjected to attack by baton-wielding police officers would be to suffer an 'unreasonable' use of force. If so, this would present formidable obstacles to effective public-order policing, for in many situations it will present the police with two alternatives: either doing nothing (because arrest is not feasible given limited resources) or taking action which is unlawful.

In particular, if this is (as seems likely) the legal position, it renders the baton charge virtually redundant as a manœuvre, for its purpose is to create fear amongst the crowd as a whole so as to *intimidate* its into members fleeing from the scene. The threat of injury caused by the batons or the fear instilled by horses being ridden towards them in 'a way indicating they do not intend to stop' is intended to induce members of the crowd to flee and thereby disperse. Such a tactic, therefore, entails threatening to inflict potentially serious injuries[4] upon those present, and is actually likely to result in the innocent and guilty members of the crowd alike being attacked. There are several reasons why this is likely to occur.

1. The use of force in a baton charge is inevitably and unavoidably indiscriminate. Even if officers have identified wrongdoers prior to the commencement of the baton charge, it is highly likely that, as they run the thirty metres towards the crowd, their targets will disappear in the ensuing mêlée as people seek to escape the onrushing police. On making contact with the crowd, there would be no one to hit, and the aggressive appearance of the charge would be revealed as an empty gesture. It is highly improbable that in these circumstances officers would restrain themselves from striking out at whomever they happened to encounter. The result,

as Gregory (1987: 18) notes, is that the 'more commonly seen' baton charge is 'a full force charge petering out into apparently random attacks on demonstrators and even passers-by'.

2. The baton charge is not only indiscriminate because of this unavoidable practicality: it is indiscriminate by design. Its purpose is to instil fear and thus induce the crowd to flee. This is achieved through exemplary deterrence: sufficiently serious injuries are actually or potentially inflicted upon arbitrarily selected individuals so as to induce others to comply (by dispersing) for fear that they too may suffer the same fate. Unless the police are seen to be willing to inflict injury upon those amongst the crowd who do not flee, the threat is not credible and there is no incentive to evacuate the scene. Force must be used indiscriminately, because otherwise those who had not themselves done anything to warrant falling victim to a baton-wielding officer would have nothing to fear and, hence, no incentive to flee. Whilst the police are reticent about admitting it (even to themselves in their confidential manuals), baton charging *is*, in fact and by design, indiscriminate, and people are likely to be struck arbitrarily. Those who are struck are likely to include those who do not, or cannot, escape from baton-wielding or mounted officers. For example, during the poll tax riot in Trafalgar Square, television viewers saw a hapless woman knocked to the ground by mounted officers charging missile throwers.

3. A baton charge, by its nature, is also arbitrary, in so far as it exposes those at the front of any crowd to the greatest risk of injury. Others in the crowd only a few ranks towards the rear have no incentive to flee, since they are unlikely to suffer injury. The vast majority of a large crowd may even be unaware that a baton charge is in progress. Thus, those at the front, with the greatest reason to escape, may be inhibited from doing so by those behind them with much less reason to leave. So even if the crowd, *as a whole*, has a means of escape, a baton charge is unlikely, in practice, to afford a means of escape to those most directly affected, because it offers no incentive to others at the rear of the crowd to evacuate the scene. Not only is this unfair to individuals

exposed to injury, it also limits the tactical effectiveness of baton charges.

4. The exemplary application of force means that whilst the total amount of force *employed* by the police may be *proportionate* to the scale of the disorder, the amount of injury *suffered* by an arbitrarily selected person is likely to be *disproportionate* to any particular offence he has committed. Thus, whilst there may be ample justification in using a given amount of force to disperse a violently disorderly crowd, there may be less justification in inflicting a serious (possibly lethal) injury upon any particular member of it. Those who fall victim to the baton charge are often justified in asking, 'Why me?'.

The problem is clearly illustrated by the events surrounding the death of Blair Peach at Southall in 1979 (Dummett, 1980*a*; 1980*b*). There seems to be little doubt that the disorder in the streets surrounding Southall town hall had reached a level which justified dispersal. Even the NCCL inquiry accepted that the crowd was violently disorderly. Immediately before the fateful baton charge along Beechcroft Avenue, an officer had suffered a multiple fracture of the jaw from a missile thrown from that direction. The dispersal of the missile-throwing crowd in Beechcroft Avenue was clearly necessary, and the force used was, *in general*, proportionate to the scale of the disorder. The problem was that, in striking Blair Peach, with whatever instrument was used, a fatal injury was caused, and this was clearly an excessive penalty for any individual to suffer for simply having been amongst a disorderly and violent crowd (for no evidence was adduced of his involvement in any specific offences).

5. The baton charge is directed towards the crowd as an entity, with the purpose of breaking its coherence and preventing concerted action, and not against disorderly or violent subgroups within the crowd. Crowds are rarely homogeneous: they often contain those who are eager to engage in violent confrontation with the police and others who are prepared to take a more passive and less violent approach. For example, it was a small contingent of the International Marxist Group, amongst an otherwise peaceful group of anti-fascist protesters, who initiated violence at Red

Lion Square in 1974 (Scarman, 1975). In responding to the violence emanating from this section of the crowd, however, police action to drive back and disperse the protesters inevitably involved using force against previously passive participants. Baton charges, in particular, are likely to occasion complaints from passive participants of unnecessary and excessive use of force by police officers, and of the police being 'out of control'. Many police officers believe that 'Sod's Law' dictates that whoever is seriously injured will emerge as a paragon of virtue.

6. It is anticipated that the crowd will obligingly scatter as the police rush towards them but, if it does not, the legal (as well as tactical) flaws of the baton charge become even more apparent. Suppose officers are instructed to 'clear' a street by making a baton charge and, as they do so, a significant number amongst the crowd respond by passively standing with their hands on their head, or indicating by some other gesture that they present no threat and will meekly submit to arrest. The baton-charging officers are now presented with a dilemma: should they continue with the baton charge or stop to arrest those who have surrendered? To do the former would allow some members of the crowd to get behind police lines, where, if they decided once again to become active rioters, they could pose a considerable threat. If the officers cease the baton charge, in order to stop and arrest those who have 'surrendered', then the tactic of 'clearing' the street will have failed. This may seem a small objection, but if, say, the purpose in 'clearing' the street were to disperse a crowd some of whom were committing arson, then the failure to complete the action might result in death or injury to innocent victims. Finally, if only some officers stopped to arrest those surrendering whilst their colleagues continued with the baton charge, then the depleted ranks of the charging officers might risk becoming engulfed by a larger, hostile crowd.

7. Once a crowd is actually beginning to leave the scene of disorder, the tactic of dispersal would appear to have succeeded, and there would seem to be no need for further recourse to force. However, it may be imperative to ensure a

rapid and complete dispersal to prevent the crowd re-forming and possibly causing further disorder. It may also be necessary to channel a dispersing crowd so as to prevent its congregating in vulnerable locations, such as shopping areas. But what powers and responsibilities would the police have if some members of the crowd appeared deliberately to be dallying? Such a person might be arrested under the constable's common-law powers to prevent a breach of the peace, and may be guilty of obstructing a police officer in the performance of his duty (Smith, 1987). However, like any other arrest in a public-order situation, this would deplete available manpower at a possibly crucial moment. In view of that, could the police legitimately use even such a modest amount of force simply to push laggards in front of them?

It is probably because of this legal uncertainty that the police seem unwilling to admit, even to themselves, that there are occasions in which they must use force other than for the purpose of arresting offenders. Hence the coy references to 'missile throwers and ring leaders' to suggest that only those deserving injury will be struck with batons. However, the truth that force is used to instil fear and intimidate everyone in a crowd into fleeing is revealed in the description of manoeuvres involving mounted officers. It is simply unrealistic to expect mounted officers to make an arrest. In so far as they use force, they do so to cause fear and thereby dispersal. To disperse a violent crowd, therefore, horses are ridden towards it in manner designed to *give the appearance* that they are at full gallop—which they are not—and are unable to stop—which, in fact, they *are* able to do. When members of such crowds and onlookers later complain that police horses charged them and wonder that no one was killed and protest at the panic caused, they are unknowingly testifying to the success of the manoeuvre. The intention is precisely to create such fear amongst all those present.

## A public-relations disaster

Whilst the aim is to instil fear, rather than to cause injuries, baton charging is a tactic which tends to elicit negative impressions of the police who appear to be 'out of control'. Public opinion and members of the crowd alike tend to respond to the intimidatory impression given by the baton charging police, rather than to the absence of serious injury. Thus, quite apart from the legal difficulties that arise from its use, baton charging often results in adverse publicity. Published accounts of baton charges, almost always given by highly respectable members of the crowd who were engaged in no unlawful activity, tend to emphasize the arbitrariness and aggression of the police.

For example, the London Strategic Policy Unit briefing paper, *Policing Wapping* (1987) quotes the following news report:

A *senior nurse* from Ilford had never witnessed such police violence: I was separated from my husband and friends and they came at us with truncheons. If I hadn't been pulled away I would have been under the hooves. Then the riot police came and put the boot in. They kicked anybody on the floor and the verbal abuse was unrepeatable. I am shattered.' (*Guardian* 17 February 1986; emphasis added)

Similarly, the *Observer* of 21 June 1987 carried the following account of a violent picket outside South Africa House, written by Lynne Reid Banks, described in the heading as 'middle-aged, middle-class' and as one who 'reluctantly went along':

it was a shock when the raid happened. A large new group of police struck without warning from the rear of the crowd (i.e. from the road). They plunged in, grabbing about a dozen demonstrators, mainly black and bundled them away . . . . And abruptly—as I was trying to move away—a policeman reached across the barrier and, seizing me by the arm and shoulder, shoved me forcibly to one side . . . . Then I saw Norma in the crowd, looking frenzied. 'They've hurt Steven!' she was shouting.

Thus, it can be the police who emerge as the 'villains' and the demonstrators who appear to be the 'victims'. The fact that police action is not unambiguously lawful and undertaken in conformity with set procedures only adds to the negative public image.

*Baton charging and excessive force*

The most damaging publicity that can arise from baton charging is the sight of officers engaging in what seems clearly to be excessive force. Television pictures of a police officer apparently hitting a prostrate picket repeatedly with his truncheon at the Orgreave coke works during the miners' strike did immense damage to the police reputation for restraint. Unfortunately, such incidents, and worse, are likely to recur, for baton charging is inherently conducive to the use of excessive force.

As a tactic the baton charge is almost impossible to control. As a result, not only are individual officers not restrained by the presence of senior officers from resorting to excessive force, but there is also the danger that officers will become stranded and vulnerable to attack. Under training, officers are instructed to charge for only a limited distance to some predetermined objective. They are expressly forbidden to pass any kind of junction, and even more emphatically told not to follow the crowd around a corner. To contravene either of these proscriptions is to court disaster, for officers passing a junction could be cut off from their colleagues by rioters coming around and behind them; and to chase rioters around a blind corner could be to run straight into a trap. However, senior officers privately concede that, once a baton charge is initiated, it is largely beyond their control to direct. The police *are* 'out of control'.

The reason why baton charges are difficult to control is known colloquially in the Metropolitan Police as 'the red mist'. This refers to a potent cocktail of psychological conditions which diminishes *any* person's self-control, and from which police officers are not exempt. Baton charges require officers to act aggressively in conditions of relative anonymity: they will certainly be in uniform; they may be wearing protective clothing with visors to obscure their facial features; and they will almost certainly be acting, not as individuals, but as a group. The target of their actions will not be other individuals, but an equally anonymous collectivity—'the crowd', 'Them'—who will have insulted and physically attacked 'Us'—the police. Officers' anger and frustration will thus have been aroused, and a baton charge will allow retaliation in conditions which minimize individual responsibility. The violence that the police employ in response is seen, certainly by the police themselves, as justified—upholding the law—a feeling that inhibits restraint. Baton charging is also physically arousing because of the exertion involved. In striking members of the crowd officers are likely to experience pleasure, not because they are sadists, but because they will undergo a reduction in physical stress which is experienced as pleasurable and which will encourage them to repeat the aggressive action. Psychologically, these are conditions virtually designed to encourage aggression and violence.[5]

Added to this volatile mixture, the human physique makes it extremely difficult to strike people in a manner other than that which will inflict serious injury. Whilst officers are instructed to strike people with their batons only on the arms, legs, and torso, and are forbidden to hit people on the head, this is an unnatural action which is likely to be forgotten in the heat of the moment. The natural inclination is to strike downwards, as one would with a hammer, and the most likely target of such a motion is the opponent's head. Not only is striking at the arms and legs unnatural, it is also incompatible with running: to strike with a downward motion whilst running simply involves an extension of the normal movement of the arms, whereas to strike with a lateral swing at a person to the front of oneself involves slowing down or coming to a halt.

### Long truncheons

Officers carrying a shield encounter a further problem: if the shield is held across the body as protection from attack, it also becomes an obstacle to striking with the baton. It was for this reason that long batons were acquired, since they afford the additional reach needed. This may appear to be a break with tradition, but in fact represents a return to the more substantial truncheon with which earlier generations of police were routinely equipped and to the 'night-stick'—a common item of equipment until the late 1960s. This fidelity to tradition does not make the long truncheon any more welcome, however, since it merely exacerbates the problems already identified.

Officers are instructed to use the long baton, in a baton charge, to strike at the legs of crowd members so as to incapacitate them. The tactic envisages the squad of officers comprising two ranks: the leading rank makes contact with the crowd striking at the legs, whereupon the following rank runs between the officers in the front rank and also administers blows to the legs so as to force the crowd to retreat. This manœuvre is repeated, with each rank 'leap-frogging' the other and compelling the continued retreat of the crowd.

However, this tactic is both confused and potentially dangerous. If the purpose is to incapacitate someone, then the long baton used in the prescribed manner might be a suitable weapon. It is conceivable that, in the course of disorder, it may become necessary to knock some people to the ground rather than using less forceful means to arrest them. But if this is the purpose for which the long baton was envisaged, then its use in this 'leap-frogging' manœuvre is inappropriate, for this tactic cannot be used against selected targets: in practice, the batons can only be used against those members of the crowd who happen to be to the fore and with whom the leading rank comes into contact. The aim of continuous 'leap-frogging' would seem to be to enforce the retreat of *the crowd as a whole* by striking people at least arbitrarily, if not indiscriminately.

If dispersal is the aim, then the use of a heavy, long baton is inappropriate for two reasons. First, it is subject to all the legal objections raised earlier. Second, it is tactically counter productive, because if people are struck incapacitating blows to the lower limbs they will be unable to flee. Indeed, the tactic envisages that incapacitated individuals will be arrested. This will be undertaken by 'arrest squads' following behind the ranks of long-baton officers. But with what offences would these incapacitated individuals be charged, and on what evidence? Arresting incapacitated people requires that the officer striking the person will give evidence at a later date, but in the confusion of such a manœuvre it is unlikely that they will even be able to remember whom they have struck, still less why they struck any particular individual. In a vain attempt to overcome this evidentiary problem, tacticians have suggested 'tagging' each incapacitated person with a label containing the number of the officer who struck him, or using polaroid photographs of the officer and the incapacitated person together. Such suggestions have rightly been exposed to some ridicule from operational officers. It would not only involve officers in repeatedly pausing to 'tag' or be photographed, and thus defeat the object of a dispersal operation, but, in the chaos of such a manœuvre, it would expose officers to risk of attack as they diverted their concentration away from the crowd, who might still be close at hand. In practice, it is more likely that those people incapacitated by blows from long truncheons would be left to litter the ground.

The particular danger of using long batons is that their additional length increases both the weight of the implement and the speed achieved by the tip when delivering a blow, because the tip travels through a much wider arc. The result is that the energy imparted at the point of impact is much greater and the injury inflicted is likely to be more severe than that inflicted by an ordinary baton. Equipping officers with such a weapon, in conditions so conducive to stimulating aggression, where the natural inclination is to strike downwards at the head, seems highly questionable. It should, perhaps, be noted that the Hong Kong Police no longer issue long batons to their riot police because even this highly militarized force fears that it cannot impose sufficiently disciplined use of this weapon.

Why, then, have we not witnessed many more serious injuries arising from police baton charges? The most immediate answer is that Britain has been quite fortunate in experiencing little serious disorder in the recent past. Historical accounts (Geary, 1985; Morgan, 1987; Dunning *et al.,* 1987) suggest that in less placid times the injuries inflicted by such means *were* considerable. In addition, it should be noted that one of the few advantages of the baton charge is that it is rather difficult for a police officer wearing protective clothing to catch rioters who will have twenty to thirty metres' head start. Unfortunately, this advantage is offset by the fact that it is the halt and lame that are most vulnerable to being caught (witness the arrest of David Bell at Orgreave, as described in Jackson, 1986).

### Can the use of force against innocent bystanders ever be justified?

It would be tempting to conclude that the indiscriminate use of force is never defensible. However, any such restriction on the use of force by the police would have possibly unwelcome consequences. Suppose that police attempt to arrest wrongdoers committing serious offences, or seek to prevent a serious offence, or try to rescue a victim, in conditions where large numbers of passive bystanders and onlookers obstruct them. Making their way through the crowd to achieve their purpose might involve the officers in pushing people aside, with the result that some of these innocent bystanders are injured. If force could not be used against innocent parties, then the law becomes the proverbial ass. This would render unlawful not only dispersal tactics but almost any attempt at making an arrest in a crowd or forcefully pushing through a crowd to assist someone in distress. Indeed, it would make even the traditional holding and pushing of a crowd (which involves using force against the front ranks of it) of questionable legality. If, on the other hand, such forceful action were to be considered proper *in these circumstances*, what difference is there between using force to barge a way through the crowd and using the same amount of force to put the whole crowd to flight to achieve the same purpose (which is what dispersal amounts to)?

It seems clear that there are circumstances where it is quite proper for force to be used to disperse a crowd, and that this will inevitably entail the indiscriminate use of force against members of that crowd. The question then arises of the legal and tactical conditions under which that force should be used.

### Removing batons

To some extent, the above discussion is of historical interest because, in the face of these criticisms, their own internal

review, and the experience of policing Wapping, the Metropolitan Police had decided to abandon the *baton* charge and to
discontinue the use of the long truncheon entirely. It seems
likely that other forces will follow suit, although for the
present baton charging remains in the ACPO *Tactical Options
Manual*. It is now envisaged that officers will simply charge
into crowds without using their batons for the purpose of
dispersal. They may, of course, continue to use their batons
for self-defence.

Will this change make any material difference? It is
unlikely that it will. The logic of the charge remains the
same — to instil fear sufficient to cause a crowd to flee. The
psychological conditions will also continue to apply: angry
and frustrated officers will be let loose on the crowd. The
difficulties of command and control will persist, indeed, will
be exacerbated: officers will be tempted to draw and use their
truncheons in 'self-defence'. Indeed, in so far as the absence
of drawn truncheons is likely to diminish the fear that a
charge instils in members of a crowd, they will have less
incentive to flee, and there is a correspondingly greater
likelihood that crowd and police will come into physical
contact. Hand-to-hand fighting with injuries to both sides is
thus likely to occur. This is not a recipe for disciplined action
by the police, nor does it overcome the problems of legality,
for force is still being used indiscriminately for the purpose of
dispersal. It is likely that those arrested in such circumstances
will be arbitrarily selected, and that there will be insufficient
evidence against them.

In conditions of disorder it is not the *baton* charge that
needs questioning, but the baton *charge*.


*Effectiveness against large crowds*

The preceding discussion has proceeded on the assumption
that charging at crowds in order to disperse them is in fact,
effective. Indeed, it often *is* effective when disorder is
sporadic and committed by relatively small groups. The
limits of its effectiveness are shown when it is used against
large gatherings such as those at Wapping and the anti-poll
tax riot in Trafalgar Square. On both occasions, baton and

mounted charges often consisted of brief forays into the crowd which temporarily retreated before mounting a counter-attack and forcing officers to retreat. This to-and-fro seems only to embolden the violent members of the crowd, who see themselves as having defeated an apparently superior adversary.

The tactical problem of using charges as a means of dispersing a large crowd is that only very limited force can be applied from the perimeter. Most of those in the crowd will have no incentive to flee because they are at no risk. On the contrary, baton charges present a spectacle which tends to attract even the more passive members of the crowd to 'where the action is'. Instead of being scattered, as in a genuine dispersal, the crowd remains coherent, and in so far as it is forced to retreat, it enters new areas in which further damage to property may be inflicted, and where missile ammunition can be acquired.

## The Alteratives

Two problems arise from the use of 'traditional methods' of policing public disorder — legal and tactical. The legal basis for crowd dispersal is, at best, precarious. Since any enforced dispersal is likely to involve indiscriminate force, the law should clearly acknowledge and regulate its use. Given that such indiscriminate use of force will be applied to the innocent and guilty alike, it is equally essential that the tactics employed should ensure that only minimum force is applied to any particular person.

## The Need for a Riot Act?

Historically, the solution to the problem of using any measure of force for the purpose of dispersing a crowd was to transform all those present into offenders (Smith, 1987). Under the Riot Act, all those remaining in an area one hour after the Act had been read by a Justice of the Peace were guilty of the offence of riot. This was a felony punishable by death, mainly, it seems, to buttress the military, who could — and not infrequently did — use gunfire to disperse riotous mobs. The repeal of the Riot Act in 1967 deprived the police of an explicit power of dispersal, and denied crowds, the safeguards of legally established procedures to be followed prior to dispersal. The Public Order Act, 1986, although widely attacked as an instrument of oppression (see e.g. Greater London Council, 1986), failed to restore a clear power of dispersal which would authorize the use of force for this purpose, despite the Public Order White Paper's (Home Office, 1980) recommendation.

There are genuine problems with, and objections to, the reintroduction of such a power. Lord Scarman remained unconvinced of the need for it after the matter had been raised during the course of his inquiry into the Brixton disorders of 1981 (Scarman, 1981). It is sometimes difficult for members of a crowd to hear or see the instruction to disperse; they could thus be subjected to forceful police action because they remained in ignorance of the dispersal order. Even those who heard the instruction and wished to comply with it might find it difficult actually to leave the scene because of the density of the crowd. Others may unwittingly enter a disorderly situation after the dispersal order has been issued and remain unaware of that order until dispersal is enforced by the police. Since a dispersal operation is likely to extend over quite a considerable area, some innocent people might find themselves overtaken by events and vulnerable to police action. For example, a dispersing but still violent crowd might invade a shopping area, and innocent shoppers could find themselves being pursued by baton-wielding police. Finally, there is the difficulty posed by residents of an area subject to a dispersal order. They might be participants in the disorder, but retreat only to their doorsteps, perhaps inviting others to join them, thus frustrating the dispersal instruction. This could be overcome by the imposition of a curfew, but since in most instances the residents of an area are those most directly victimized by the disorder, this might seem an unjust penalty to inflict upon the innocent.

Some of these difficulties could be overcome. For ex-

ample, warnings could repeatedly be broadcast over powerful PA systems, carried either on vehicles or on helicopters
and supplemented by visual signs. In any event, if disorder
reached levels that justified recourse to forceful dispersal
tactics, it is highly improbable that even passive participants
would be unaware of the mayhem going on around them.
Nevertheless, the likelihood that passive, if not wholly
innocent, participants are likely to suffer forceful police
action designed to disperse the crowd of which they happen
to be members does present a difficulty.

The public interest would be served by the provision of an
explicit dispersal power, for procedures could be stipulated
before such action was taken. Moreover, since the enforced
dispersal of a crowd arises from the decision of a senior
officer, legal accountability could be enhanced. At present it
is the individual officer who strikes someone with his baton
who is held responsible in criminal and civil law for his
individual actions. The senior officer who commands him
and who decided to mount a charge is not similarly held
accountable to law. Counsel was asked by the Police
Federation to give an opinion on the legal position of the
police officer who uses his truncheon in a public-order
situation. In the opinion, counsel remarks:

the fact that the individual police officer has been ordered to strike
the demonstrators with his baton would not provide that individual
officer with any defence under existing criminal law. It would, in
my opinion, mitigate against any sentence imposed on the officer
but would not be a defence to any charge of assault. (*Police*, May
1986: 12)

If such a dispersal power were to be enacted, then responsibility for the total manœuvre could be placed on the shoulders
of those whose decision it is to employ it.


### 'Alien Methods'

The reintroduction of a dispersal power still leaves open the
question of how enforced dispersal should be tactically

achieved. Despite the many serious objections to the traditional baton charge as a tactic of crowd dispersal, it continues
to be regarded by articulate public opinion as preferable to
the importation of alternative weapons and tactics which are
denounced as an escalation in the use of force. The
assumption seems to be that breaking with the British
tradition of public-order policing entails breaking with the
principle of 'minimum force'. In fact, the opposite is true:
many of the weapons and tactics devised by police and
internal security forces who have much greater experience of
controlling serious disorder are less injurious to the individual than are traditional British methods. The irony is that
the principle of 'minimum force' is achieved best by weapons
and tactics that have nothing to do with traditional British
policing methods.

If the aim is to disperse a disorderly and violent crowd then
it is essential that only sufficient force necessary to compel
members of the crowd to escape should be used. Knocking a
few of them to the ground with police batons is bound to be
regarded as an excessive use of indiscriminate force. A more
appropriate measure of force can be achieved by two means:
equipping officers with weapons which inflict unpleasant but
limited injury when used against individuals and/or the
global application of a mildly noxious stimulus.

### Close-quarters Weapons

*If* officers are to continue to disperse violent crowds by
charging at them with a view to intimidating crowd
members into dispersal, it is essential that the weapons used
should strike a balance between causing sufficient injury to
provide an incentive to disperse and not inflicting more
injury than is strictly necessary. This the regular police
truncheon does not do, for it is designed as a means of self-
defence which can be used with incapacitating force. What is
required is a weapon which, although it might look fearsome
(for the main purpose of its use is to intimidate), has a low
impact energy.

A number of alternatives present themselves. The first
group are variants of the traditional baton that have been

successfully used elsewhere. Unfortunately, although the weapons themselves are quite suited to the task for which they are used, they are associated with oppressive regimes, thus conferring upon them unpleasant connotations. The sjambok, despite its unfortunate association with the repressive apparatus of the apartheid system, is a weapon which is designed to inflict unpleasant and painful injuries which are unlikely to prove severe. It is ironic that the weapons used by such oppressive regimes tend actually to inflict *less* serious injury than those traditionally used in a liberal democracy.[6]

Another alternative is to use advanced technology, such as various instruments for transmitting electric shocks, so-called 'sting sticks'. When used as a means of totally incapacitating violent people they have been found to be unreliable. American police forces which have experience of these devices complain that, when used against fleeing suspects, they merely cause the escaper to run even faster. However, in a dispersal context this is precisely what is desired. The aim is not to incapacitate totally, but to inflict sufficient pain and discomfort to act as an incentive for the person to leave the scene.

Much the same applies to the use of Mace gas, which may be more suitable in public-disorder situations than in other violent encounters, for whilst it too has proven unreliable as a means of total incapacitation, it does inflict such discomfort as to act as a powerful incentive to disperse. Mace is an irritant agent which is delivered by means of an aerosol spray held by the police officer. It gained an unpleasant reputation following its liberal and often punitive use by members of the Chicago Police against anti-Vietnam War demonstrators causing disorder at the 1968 Democratic Convention (Walker, 1968). Unpleasant and excessive though the actions of some police officers undoubtedly were on that occasion, it is worth noting that even this very liberal use of mace seems to have had no lasting ill-effects upon those exposed to it. The same cannot be said about others who have been the victims of similarly excessive use of police batons.

A recently developed means of delivering an irritant agent is made by the ISPRA company. It consists of an irritant, based on CS agent, delivered as an aerosol cloud to distances of around twenty metres using $CO_2$ as the propellant. Officers carry a quite large canister of agent and propellant in a harness, and activate the aerosol by the depression of a trigger which releases a cloud of irritant agent towards the crowd. If a person is engulfed by the aerosol, not only is the normal debilitating reaction caused, but the agent also causes intense skin irritation, producing a burning sensation and thereby giving rioters an even more compelling incentive to flee. The amount of irritant contained in the canister and its range and spread, together with its debilitating effects, mean that only a few officers equipped with such a device would be needed to disperse a relatively large crowd.

The alternative weapons discussed so far are all designed to be used at close quarters. As such they have two drawbacks in common with the baton charge they might be used to replace. First, whilst less injurious than the traditional baton, any weapon of this kind is likely to be used against an arbitrarily selected few amongst the crowd. The person left with a weal or with their eyes smarting is unlikely to appreciate that the measure of force to which he has been subjected represented a careful balance between providing an incentive to disperse and avoiding excessive injury. Second, since these weapons would be used instead of batons in a police charge, there remain the difficulties of maintaining command and control. Moreover, since some of the weapons would be of little use to incapacitate determined attackers, officers might find themselves at greater risk of retaliatory assault by members of the crowd, especially if they became isolated. Inevitably, officers would need to retain their ordinary truncheons for self-defence, with the possibility that some of them might use it in preference to alternative weapons.

In sum, whilst these weapons may have their place in the arsenal of riot control technology, hand-to-hand combat is not something to be encouraged. It is better if police maintain a distance from a riotous crowd and deliver any noxious stimulus from afar.

### Globally applied mildly noxious stimuli

The baton or mounted charge amounts to the application of a noxious stimulus — fear. Unfortunately, fear is not distributed equally throughout the crowd, nor is the consequence of being struck by a baton 'mild'. Moreover, the attempt to instil fear may prove counter-productive, for the display of aggression is as likely to encourage a violent response as it is to put a crowd to flight. The alternative is directly to apply some mildly noxious stimulus to the entire crowd. There are currently available three means of doing this, used in various jurisdictions elsewhere, but only one of which is authorized for use by the British police.

*CS agent*   The first use of CS agent on the mainland of Britain occurred in Liverpool during the riots of 1981. This was severely criticized by many commentators,[7] not least for the fact that the projectiles used to deliver the agent were not designed for use in public order and were responsible, it seems, for some serious injuries. The projectiles were, in fact, mainly 'ferret' cartridges, designed to be fired from shotguns and designed for use against barricaded gunmen. The Chief Constable of Merseyside, Kenneth Oxford (1981), has acknowledged that ferret cartridges were unsuitable for the purpose for which they were used.

What is often overlooked by critics, both of this particular action and the use of CS agent in general, is the fact that this was an act of admitted desperation. With an exhausted force, suffering heavy casualties, the police were close to defeat. Traditional policing had failed, even when it had been supplemented by PSUs provided under mutual aid arrangements and equipped with the latest instruments of coercive policing — the long shield. The violent and disorderly crowds that threatened to overwhelm the police had to be dispersed, but the police possessed no effective means of doing so. They resorted to the only alternative at their disposal and, although not intended for that use, it succeeded in its purpose. The crowd dispersed and order was restored.

Critics of the subsequent decision to allow British police forces to stock CS smoke in projectiles designed for use in situations of civil disorder should ask themselves what alternative they would offer. If a police force finds itself in the position of the Merseyside Police, would they allow it to be overwhelmed? If so, what would be the consequences for the rioters and non-rioters alike? It is unlikely that the authorities would stand meekly aside and allow a major city, or a substantial part of it, to be consumed by a rioting mob. If the military were then to be deployed, it is highly improbable that they would refrain from using more force than the civil police whom they replaced. If the police are not to be overwhelmed, and if traditional methods have failed as comprehensively as they failed in Toxteth, then recourse to CS smoke, or some comparable alternative, will become necessary. This is the dilemma that critics seem reluctant to confront. To protest that it is not for them to propose alternatives to the use of such weapons is simply irresponsible, for to deny the police an option without an alternative will itself have consequences. Without access to adequate protective equipment, the police at Handsworth in 1985 were impotent to quell the riot in its early stages, with the result that innocent people lost their lives (Dear, 1986).

Although there are various ways in which CS agent can be delivered, the most common is by some form of projectile. The canister discharges a smoke which carries the CS agent and which, when inhaled, causes the aversive reaction of coughing, nausea, and streaming eyes.[8] It is a most unpleasant experience and one from which all but a very few people seek to retreat. It is, therefore, a very effective dispersal device. The use of 'air-burst' projectiles enhances the effectiveness of CS smoke: instead of a single canister delivering the smoke, a series of smaller canisters are ejected from a parent canister above the crowd, so that there are several sources of smoke.

For the purpose of dispersal, CS smoke has a distinct advantage over the baton or mounted charge. Not only does it apply a sufficiently unpleasant stimulus generally for everyone to want to leave the scene, it can do so in ways that allow effective means of escape. The contradiction in baton charge tactics, already mentioned, is that the crowd must have a means of escape to the sides and rear, but when the crowd is large (when dispersal is most likely to be necessary) those most likely to suffer injury, and to have the greatest incentive to leave, will be those at the front who have the least opportunity to escape because of the weight of numbers behind them. CS smoke can be applied selectively to portions of the crowd immediately adjacent to avenues of escape.

Gradually, the smoke is applied to those towards the front, who can now leave, because those behind them have already dispersed. Under these relatively controlled conditions, members of the crowd are less likely to be injured by police batons which they cannot escape or by the panic reaction of those who are trying to escape.

A principal objection to the use of CS smoke is that it is inevitably indiscriminate; indeed, it is so by design, for it seeks to administer a noxious stimulus to *all* who are present at the scene, whatever the level of their individual involvement in the disorder. The problem arises in connection with innocent bystanders or local residents, who may be as severely afflicted by the CS agent as members of the crowd. This is a genuine problem, but not as significant as is often claimed. After all, whilst undoubtedly extremely unpleasant, CS smoke is not dangerous (despite spurious claims to the contrary — see Wright, 1977; 1978). Careful scientific evaluation has concluded that even if inhaled in a closed room for an extended period of time, CS smoke is unlikely to have any permanent ill effect, even for someone suffering from respiratory disease.[9] Moreover, the chemical composition of CS is such that, when dispersed, it quickly combines to form a molecule which cannot be inhaled, and which tends to descend towards the ground in the form of small droplets. Bystanders and nearby residents may be alarmed at the sight of whirling smoke, but it seems that the CS irritant remains active for only a short time. In any event, what has to be weighed when assessing the utility of CS smoke or any other dispersal device is whether the need to quell disorder justifies any damage that is likely to be inflicted on innocent parties.

Tactically, the problem with using CS irritant is that police officers would need protection from its effects in the form of respirators or face masks, either of which will reduce mobility because they hinder breathing. Follow-up man-œuvres designed to keep the crowd moving would need to rely on vehicles, although mounted officers could be used, because horses are impervious to the effects of CS.

*Water cannon*  Another way of enforcing dispersal which is commonly employed elsewhere, but currently unavailable to the British police, is the water cannon. This vehicle has been evaluated by the Metropolitan Police, but eventually rejected by the Home Office. A great deal of confusion and misunderstanding surrounds its use.

The advantage of the water cannon over other weapons designed to enforce dispersal is that it is less indiscriminate than, for example, CS smoke and yet can deliver a noxious stimulus to virtually all members of a disorderly crowd. Water is most effective when used at low pressure to drench large numbers of people and thus induce them to disperse. In addition, dye can be added to the water to provide lasting identification of participation in the disorder, and CS agent can also be added to cause an even more noxious experience. Delivering CS agent by a water jet has the added advantage that it cannot swirl in the wind nor inadvertently drift into surrounding premises. Also, since the agent is mixed with the water as it enters the nozzle, the use of CS can be switched on and off at will. Likewise, the jet of water can be electrified to enhance the unpleasantness of the experience and encourage flight. The use of high pressure is much less effective and not often used. However, the high-pressure jet can be used to extinguish fires, such as flaming barricades.

Tactically, water cannon could fill a gaping void in contemporary public-order strategy — static defensive formation. Despite the fact that public disorder has historically been associated with strikes, where police have protected plant and workers from pickets, current public-order strategy is premised upon fluid street rioting — as witnessed by the comparatively infrequent inner-city disorders of the 1980s. Continuous forward advance against riotous pickets makes little sense, given that the factory gate is the focus for disorder. A dispersed crowd is likely to reassemble outside the premises it wishes to close. All that now occurs is continuous skirmishing between pickets and static lines of police, with the ·latter becoming precisely the 'Aunt Sally' that is now considered anathema in other circumstances of disorder. Water cannon are appropriate for this situation, for they can maintain sufficient distance between pickets and police to prevent further missiles being thrown. Being static, the water supply can often be continuously replenished, and there is no problem of manœuvrability.

On the other hand, water cannon are alleged to have a series of well-known disadvantages. It is sometimes claimed that these vehicles expend their supply of water quickly and, therefore, need frequently to be recharged. This is a misunderstanding of the notion of the 'rate of flow'. If the water were to be discharged in an uninterrupted stream, the supply would be exhausted in a matter of minutes, depending upon the size of the tank. However, this is not how the water is normally used. It is usually fired in short bursts, and in this mode can be made to last some considerable time, some estimates suggesting up to two hours. However, it *is* true that the water cannon will need to be supplemented by a bowser which can resupply it, when necessary. Also false is the claim that the vehicle is inevitably unwieldy because of its size and weight. In fact, it is no more unwieldy than a large fire engine, which usually carries the same quantity of water and is approximately the same size.

A genuine difficulty is conspicuousness, for the sight of a water cannon may itself provoke the disorder it is designed to combat. Provocation is difficult to assess, for those who are intent on violence will find almost anything provocative. Unlike CS irritant, however, which can be delivered from instruments carried by an single officer and which can remain stored away until needed, water cannon are difficult to hide or disguise.

A further disadvantage is that the vehicle itself may be subject to attack and, therefore, needs physical protection by officers with shields. Also, it seems that such vehicles should not be deployed singly, when they can become vulnerable to attack, but should be deployed in groups, each supporting the other. This would mean the expenditure of considerable amounts of money to provide sufficient vehicles, which would also need to be deployed strategically throughout the country if they were to be available in the event of spontaneous disorder. In addition, there would be considerable costs involved in maintaining sufficient trained crews to operate the machine and specially trained officers on foot to protect it and engage in co-ordinated manœuvres with it. It seems likely that, given the infrequency with which this kind of vehicle would be needed, the Government has concluded that it would not be cost-effective.

*Smoke*  The third commonly used device is non-irritant smoke. This is used to divide a crowd into sections, since it seems that people are generally disinclined to enter smoke. However, it has the drawback that, because police officers are also people, they too tend to be disinclined to enter smoke. In any event, the Government has so far been reluctant to authorize its use.

## Minimum force

All these weapons involve the application of less force to any given individual than that which is likely to befall the victim of a traditional police baton charge. The experience of being struck with a baton lighter than the traditional truncheon, or receiving an electric shock from a 'sting stick', or inhaling gas, or being drenched with water, will be very unpleasant. It is so by design: the purpose is to compel people to disperse by imposing a significant disincentive to remaining at the scene. Yet the amount of force applied to any specific person is much more consistent with the principle of 'minimum force' than being arbitrarily struck with a length of wood.

All the methods of applying noxious stimuli from a distance have the added advantage that the officers who apply the noxious stimuli do so without making direct contact with the crowd, and remain under the control and supervision of their superiors.

Before leaving the question of dispersal, it should be noted that this tactic does not exclude making arrests; indeed, it can facilitate this. As the crowd disperses, arrest squads can (provided the crowd is not too violent) more easily gain physical access to suspected wrongdoers and make arrests. Moreover, filter cordons can be situated along the direction of dispersal, with the task of trying to detain those identified as having committed offences. Of course, many offenders would escape, but this, unfortunately, seems to be the inevitable corollary of civil disorder.

## Incapacitation

So far, we have discussed the use of force either to arrest or to disperse: the first objective involves using as much force as is required for a clearly lawful purpose, whilst the second should involve the use of minimum force to cause superficial pain and discomfort sufficient to induce dispersal. The use of force to incapacitate involves a more controversial step, since here violence is used to render a person incapable of acting in a criminal manner, but without the aim of immediately arresting him. It is one more irony of the law that the use of quite extreme force against selected people committing serious offences seems to fall more straightforwardly within section 3 of the Criminal Law Act than does the use of much less force against third parties as a dispersal tactic, provided the force used was proportionate to the seriousness of the act and circumstances precluded alternative action.

Not only may incapacitating use of force against selected individuals be lawful, but it seems clearly to be morally preferable to the inevitably indiscriminate use of force to disperse. The principle that a person should only be responsible for the actions they, and they alone, have committed, remains intact (Smith, 1987). If a person who is about to throw a fire bomb is knocked to the ground, that would appear a quite just and proportionate use of force. In some situations it might be impractical for the police to intervene in any other way to prevent serious offences being committed. For example, they may simply lack sufficient resources to do otherwise, or it may be too dangerous to approach closely enough to effect an arrest.

There can be little doubt that, in serious disorder, individuals are likely to commit acts which might justify their incapacitation. However, if incapacitating use of force is called for, it is essential that it be inflicted only upon those individuals committing actions which clearly justify its use. It was seen earlier that it is not incapacitation *per se* that is objected to by critics (McCabe *et al.*, 1988; Brewer *et al.*, 1988) but the global instruction to incapacitate 'missile throwers and ring leaders'. If particular missile–throwers were incapacitated selectively and in order to prevent them from throwing their missile, this would appear to pose little legal difficulty for the police. The issue is not whether such force can lawfully be employed, but how such a selective use of force can be tactically administered. The baton charge is an inappropriate manœuvre for achieving selective incapacitation because, as the officers run towards the crowd, conditions will probably change. Missile-throwers might cease to throw missiles and seek to escape, whereupon the justification for incapacitating them diminishes.

Both tactical and legal considerations are most directly satisfied by the employment of means which incapacitates a selected person at the time that he is committing the serious offences the prevention of which justifies this level of forceful action. The most appropriate means of achieving this goal is by some form of projectile which inflicts an incapacitating, but sub-lethal, injury upon a selected wrongdoer at the instant he commits the offence. The projectile which is currently available for this purpose is the plastic baton round (PBR), more colloquially known as the 'plastic bullet', and certainly the most controversial weapon in the police public-order armoury.[10] Its use is regarded, almost universally, but not entirely rationally, as the worst imaginable scenario[11] — 'the Ulsterisation of our cities' (Ouseley, 1987;). Brewer *et al.* (1988: 35) warn ominously: 'The next notch is the ratchet of public order policing is likely to be made by the use of plastic bullets, CS gas having been used for the first time during the urban riots in Liverpool in 1981.' In fact it is, with certain important qualifications, the most appropriate means of incapacitating wrongdoers in riotous situations.

*Plastic baton rounds*

The history of the plastic baton round itself demonstrates something of the confusion that has existed regarding the use of force to disperse a crowd as opposed to its use for incapacitation. It seems that the first baton rounds were used in Hong Kong, and were made of wood. This weapon had a dispersal function, for it was intended to be fired from a shotgun at the ground ahead of the rioting mob, so as to ricochet and strike the lower limbs. In such a role it was highly unlikely to prove incapacitating, but would obviously offer a strong inducement to flee. As public disorder grew in Northern Ireland and the British army sought an effective weapon, a rubber equivalent to the Hong Kong baton round was developed. This too was a dispersal weapon, designed to be used in exactly the same way as its Hong Kong predecessor. It was used in action in Northern Ireland by the British army until 1975. Unfortunately, it was the cause of three deaths during that period, and was eventually withdrawn in favour of the plastic baton round.

What is rarely acknowledged or appreciated is that the plastic baton round, though very similar in design, is fundamentally different in conception to either of its predecessors. This is *not* a dispersal weapon; it is designed for incapacitation. Instead of being fired at the ground ahead of the rioters, so that its unpredictable subsequent flight would strike random members of the crowd, it was designed to be fired directly at identified individuals.

The L5A4 PBR is a cylindrical slab of solid PVC plastic, 4.5 in. long and 1.5 in. in diameter, weighing 4.75 oz. and fired from the L67 launcher. The baton round used by the police on the mainland is exactly the same as that now used in Northern Ireland, but in the past the propellant power of the Northern Ireland variant was higher (the charge being 45 compared to 25 grains), and it was designed to be fired from a greater distance. This explains the difference between the speed and effective range quoted for the two weapons. The currently available baton round has a velocity officially estimated as 120 m.p.h. and an effective range of between 25 and 50 metres, compared to the 160 m.p.h. and 30–60 metre range attributed by observers to the previous Northern Ireland version. In the Metropolitan Police this weapon can only be issued on the authority of the Commissioner, and deployed under the direct supervision of a 'designated officer' of senior rank. Its immediate use would normally be preceded by a warning to rioters. The weapon is designed to be fired at the lower part of the body of individuals, not indiscriminately, and will be discharged only on the command of the specialist weapons commander, who is directly in command of the baton gunners. However, it is the individual gunner who is ultimately responsible for opening fire, as is the case with the use of lethal firearms. Each 'baton gunner' is assisted by a 'spotter' who both protects him and advises him regarding the fate of his shots.

Tactics envisage three basic manœuvres: first, baton gunners operating with the assistance of shield units; second, gunners operating on their own; and third, gunners firing from vehicles. The originally conceived manœuvre was for the baton gunners to be deployed with a long-shield PSU/TSG, who provide protection. The gunners then take aim from the appropriate side of the shield wall (right-handed gunners firing from the right-hand side), and in a crouching stance. The specialist weapons commander gives the command to engage and the gunners fire at selected individuals, chosen either by the commander or by themselves. They may fire individually, in a volley, or in an ordered sequence, as dictated by the commander. The guns continue to fire until ordered to cease fire by the commander. It is envisaged that, once firing ceases, either the shield cordon will advance or arrest squads will move forward, but either way those incapacitated by the baton rounds will be apprehended. If injured they will be taken to medical teams for immediate treatment and thence to hospital. Following treatment, they would be arrested and charged with the offences that they were committing and which justified discharging the baton round at them. Meanwhile, should further contact be made with rioters, the gunners could be commanded to open fire again. This is the manœuvre that has received wide publicity through the news media.

This tactic has recently lost favour because the presence of the shield cordon is thought likely to attract missiles, thus making the task of the gunner all the more difficult. The alternative is to leave the gunners relatively free to find appropriate cover (for example, behind vehicles or street furniture) and to fire from those positions.

Since it is assumed that rioting would have reached an extreme pitch before the use of baton rounds would be authorized (as, in fact, was the case at Broadwater Farm), it is considered unlikely that either manœuvre described above would be feasible. For shield units and baton gunners to advance to within twenty-five metres of such a ferocious mob would be highly dangerous. Thus, it is anticipated that vehicles would be used to offer protection. The vehicles may either be PSU personnel carriers, or, more probably, the armour-plated Land Rovers specially acquired for the purpose. The latter possess a small porthole with a detachable cover through which the baton gun is aimed and fired, observed by the spotter from an adjacent porthole. Firing from a vehicle in this manner would have the additional advantage that the officer would not need to have his visor down and would, therefore, be better able to aim his weapon.

*PBRs: lethal weapons?*

What makes this weapon particularly controversial is the deaths, particularly of children, that its use has caused in Northern Ireland. The fact that fourteen people have been killed by plastic baton rounds, added to the three killed previously by the rubber predecessor, have led some campaigners to claim that the weapon is so dangerous that it should be withdrawn (see particularly Information on Ireland, 1987). The European parliament has been sufficiently convinced to pass motions calling for the use of baton rounds to be discontinued. The potential lethality of this weapon has become accepted as a commonplace, so much so that even the police are wary of using it. Senior officers, likely to find themselves in command of public-order operations, are officially warned that PBRs can inflict serious or fatal injuries. Is the plastic baton round as dangerous as its critics maintain?

There is no doubt that PBRs are designed to inflict serious injury, for that is how people are incapacitated. However, the fact that such injury is caused by design and that some people have been killed by accident or misuse are not grounds for prohibiting the use of PBRs on the mainland. The fact remains that baton rounds are a *sub-lethal* weapon, a step in a graduated hierarchy of force to be applied in riotous circumstances. As the European Commission on Human

Rights observed in its rejection of a claim brought by the
parent of a thirteen-year-old boy killed by soldiers in 1976,
the PBR used in Northern Ireland was 'less dangerous than
alleged'. Since the commission's conclusions fly so squarely
in the face of the many accusations made by the critics of this
weapon and its use, the issue deserves detailed consideration.

The following account of Brian Stewart's tragic death is
contained in the publication *They Shoot Children* (Information
on Ireland, 1987: 13):

Brian Stewart was hit in the face by a plastic bullet fired by soldiers
of the King's Own Scottish Borderers soon after 6 p.m. on 4
October 1976. He had just left his home in Turf Lodge, West
Belfast, and was standing on a corner. Several eye witnesses said
there was no rioting in the area at the time. The British army made
a number of contradictory statements attempting to justify the
shooting.

Elsewhere (p. 21), the publication adds: 'The inquest jury
returned an open verdict. In a civil action, the judge accepted
the army's claim that Brian was rioting, but his family
disputes this.'

Mrs Stewart made application to the European Commission on Human Rights in 1982, claiming that the use of PBRs
on the occasion of her son's death was in breach of the
European Convention on Human Rights and, additionally,
that their use in Northern Ireland was discriminatory since
they had been used predominantly against Catholics. The
Commission found that 'the death of Brian Stewart resulted
from the use of force which was no more than absolutely
necessary in action lawfully taken for the purpose of quelling
a riot.' It went on to add:

The Commission notes that the use of the plastic baton round in
Northern Ireland has given rise to much controversy and that it is a
dangerous weapon which can occasion serious injuries and death,
particularly if it strikes the head. However, information provided
by the parties concerning casualties, compared with the number of
baton rounds discharged, show that the weapon is less dangerous
than alleged.

The nub of the issue is the casualty and fatality rates, for, as
an official briefing paper notes, 'Baton rounds are not free

from risk' (Brittan, 1985). However, as it rightly continues, 'No method of controlling such rioting is entirely safe'; indeed, people have been killed on the British mainland after having been struck by police engaged in baton charges or after colliding with police vehicles driven at crowds during the course of civil disorder. The Home Office estimated that between 1970 and 1984 (when fourteen people had been killed by rubber and plastic baton rounds) 'Over 7,000 baton rounds have been fired for each fatality that has occurred' (Brittan, 1985).

The publication *They Shoot Children* places a different interpretation on the data, complaining that a global estimate, like that used by the Home Office, fails to distinguish plastic baton rounds from the rubber version. It computes that the plastic baton round has a fatality rate of one in 4,000 firings, compared to one in 18,000 firings of the rubber baton round. It concludes that the plastic version is even more dangerous than its rubber predecessor. However, it is notable that between 1970 and 1975 (when they were withdrawn) there were nearly 56,000 rubber baton rounds fired compared to only just over 45,500 plastic baton rounds over the period 1974–84. The reason for this disparity in the frequency of use lies in the different purpose for which these weapons are employed.

As previously noted, the rubber baton round was designed and used as a dispersal weapon, to be fired so as to strike indiscriminately the lower limbs of crowd members, whereas the plastic version is an incapacitating weapon designed to be fired at selected targets. Consistent with their purpose, the rubber baton rounds would have been fired more liberally so as to induce dispersal and in a manner least likely to strike the vulnerable parts of the upper torso and head. The expectation would, therefore, have been that only minimal injuries would result. When, in fact, the use of the rubber baton round resulted in three deaths it was found to be 'unacceptable', since killing people is incompatible with the deliberately indiscriminate use of weapons with the aim merely to disperse. By contrast, the plastic baton round is likely to be fired with more economy at those presenting a clear threat and in conditions which justify inflicting an incapacitating injury, and often in conditions that justify the use of lethal force itself. The more discriminating purpose for which the plastic baton round was designed could be expected to cause more serious injuries — at least sufficiently serious to incapacitate.

The issue is not, then, whether serious injuries are caused, but whether the injuriousness of the weapon is proportional to the scale of the problem. Whether the use of baton rounds on any given occasion is proportionate is a matter of fact for a jury to decide, and will depend on the circumstances. What can generally be said is that the severity of disorder occurring in Northern Ireland is such that a fatality rate of this magnitude does not seem disproportionate. However one interprets the data, it remains the fact that literally thousands of baton rounds (of either version) have been fired without causing fatal injury. This compares favourably with comparable situations elsewhere in the world, even liberal democracies. For example, twenty-one people were killed by police and National Guardsmen during five days of rioting in Detroit in July 1967 (Kerner, 1968). The *relative* casualty rates indicate not only the greater restraint shown by the security forces in Northern Ireland compared to their counterparts elsewhere, but also demonstrate the value of the plastic baton round in providing a sub-lethal option for dealing with serious rioting.

Once the focus shifts from the fatality and casualty rates to the circumstances of individual cases, it also becomes clear that in many instances the fatal baton rounds were fired in circumstances for which they were not intended. According to the accounts of individual deaths contained in *They Shoot Children*, a high proportion of fatalities resulted from baton rounds fired at close quarters and not at the prescribed distances. Tobias Molloy was killed 'by a rubber bullet fired at point blank range'; Michael Donnelly was shot at '15–20 yards range'; Paul Whitters was 'shot . . . in the head from about seven yards range'; Nora McCabe was shot at 'a range of about six feet'; Peter McGuiness 'was shot at point blank range'; and John Downes 'was shot from about five feet'. Thus, six of the fifteen fatalities allegedly died from shots fired within the minimum prescribed range of 25–30 metres.

The fact that the baton rounds were fired at shorter distances than are prescribed, even if accurate, does not prove any misuse on the part of the security forces. An RUC police officer or soldier can use 'such force as is reasonable' in performing his duty and if he, or someone else, is under sufficient immediate threat as to justify using potentially lethal force he is entitled to employ whatever means are at his disposal, be it a firearm or a baton gun. This is neatly illustrated by what must have been the most widely publicized death to occur as a result of a baton round, the killing of John Downes. Downes was killed by an RUC reserve constable, Nigel Hegarty, in August 1984, during a police operation to arrest the Noraid spokesman Martin Galvin, who had gained illegal entry to Northern Ireland. Galvin had been addressing a crowd when the RUC moved in. The crowd responded by obstructing the police. During the ensuing mêlée Downes rushed towards a police officer wielding a stick. The officer's colleague, Hegarty, caught sight of Downes rushing passed him, turned, and fired his baton gun at almost point-blank range, killing Downes. Hegarty was charged with manslaughter but acquitted, the court accepting his defence that he reasonably believed his colleague was in serious danger and employed no more force than was necessary to prevent the threat being carried out. Legally, it would have made no difference whether Hegarty had shot Downes with a baton gun or any other type of firearm.

It is argued in *They Shoot Children* that a weapon of this kind will almost inevitably be abused and fired at less than its prescribed minimum range. Flagrant abuse is a possibility, of course, but perhaps a more serious danger is that, in the confused circumstances of a riot, officers may well find themselves in circumstances that are, or are *perceived* to be, life-threatening and be tempted to use their baton gun in preference to alternatives that may be just as effective but less injurious. Given this risk, it is essential that such weapons be deployed only in conditions of the strictest supervision. However, the risk that officers might make too ready a recourse to such a weapon must be balanced against the likelihood that officers will find themselves in conditions of disorder that they are unable to control, with the result that innocent people (including the officers themselves) may be killed.

It might appear, however, from the high proportion of children and young people amongst those killed by PBRs that these weapons are used too liberally against vulnerable youngsters who, as Rosenhead has observed, 'are too young to be a threat to the security forces' (Information on Ireland, 1987: 27). In fact, Rosenhead's sentimentality is misplaced, for children do pose, and have posed, a considerable threat to members of the security forces. A petrol, acid, or blast bomb is dangerous in the hands of anyone, be they a child or an adult. Certainly, the Commission on Human Rights was satisfied that the firing of a baton round at thirteen-year-old Brian Stewart was justified in the circumstances.

Nevertheless, it may be objected that baton rounds present a risk of serious injury or death not only to active participants in riots, adults or children, but also to innocent bystanders. Of course, distinguishing the innocent bystander and the active participant is not at all easy, especially in retrospect. It is remarkable how frequently, according to *They Shoot Children*, those killed by baton rounds were simply innocent bystanders who were not even at the scene of any disorder. Even if credulity is strained by these accounts, it cannot be denied (and the security forces in Northern Ireland themselves do not deny it) that some innocent bystanders have been struck and killed by baton rounds. However necessary it is to be conscious of this risk in considering tactical options, it does not by itself rule out the use of baton rounds. Other means of tackling disorder also contain risks, including the risk of causing fatalities.

No one disputes that the baton round is a dangerous weapon capable of inflicting serious injury or death. However, *any* forceful police intervention will be accompanied by some risks. To prescribe that the police should take no action unless it is free of risk is to prescribe total inaction. However, not even inaction is free from risk, for that would expose others to risk of injury and death at the hands of rioters. Prescribing tactics involves assessing risks. There is no simple conclusion to be drawn from the fact that some people have been killed by baton rounds, however tragic the circumstances of their deaths, and it is misleading to pretend, as do *They Shoot Children* and other similar publications, that there is.

The fact remains — and nothing in the critical literature contradicts it — that the baton round is a sub-lethal weapon. It can cause death, but the risk that it will do so are several thousand to one. Deployed appropriately, it is not only more effective than the traditional baton charge; it is a much more discriminating use of force.

### The baton gun: a design for disaster?

Small though the risks of death are, they should, of course, be minimized. Even more so, the risk of hitting innocent bystanders or others amongst the crowd who are not themselves committing serious criminal acts should be minimized. Unfortunately, those risks have *not* been minimized, for the L67 baton gun is both inaccurate and unreliable. It is nothing short of scandalous that such an unreliable weapon should be used for this purpose.

It is not possible to say whether inaccuracy and unreliability has been responsible for any of the deaths of, or injuries to, innocent bystanders, since the full facts of each case are not available. What can be said, is that the baton gun stocked by the police on the mainland of Britain is a wholly unsatisfactory and needlessly dangerous weapon.

The L67 baton gun is nothing more sophisticated than a signal pistol, used for firing flares, to which has been added a stock, so that it can be fired from the shoulder, and a 14-inch rifled barrel. Although baton gunners are instructed only to fire carefully aimed shots, the sights on the gun are hopelessly inadequate. It is simply impossible to obtain the kind of 'sight picture' which ensures accuracy with normal firearms. Gunners are instructed to sight the baton gun by aligning the fore sight with a white painted mark on the release catch at the rear of the weapon. If this did not make accurate marksmanship difficult enough, it is a fact that each baton gun varies in its ballistic characteristics. Under training, baton gunners find it necessary to expend several rounds simply in order to 'zero' the gun—that is, adjust for its idiosyncrasies. Finally, the baton round itself is apparently ballistically unstable, tending to topple in flight, and cannot be aimed accurately at a target twenty metres distant.

When the baton gun is fired, so much smoke is discharged that the gunner is unable to see what has happened. It is for this reason, amongst others, that he needs to be advised by his 'spotter'. Since the gun is also a single-shot weapon, the gunner must open the breach, eject the spent cartridge, and replace it with a live round. What would in any case be an unavoidably complicated exercise in manual dexterity (especially when wearing gloves) is handicapped by the absence of any ejection device on the gun itself. Occasionally, it is impossible to pull the spent cartridge from the breach because it has expanded upon firing and fits too tightly. At this point, in training, an instructor normally pokes a stick down the barrel to knock the spent cartridge out. It seems that the Metropolitan Police do not issue sticks for this purpose to gunners in operational circumstances!

The use of this weapon would be comical, if it were not so serious. In an operational situation, gunners are unlikely to have the opportunity to fire sufficient rounds to 'zero' the particular weapon with which they have been issued before its deployment at the scene of the riot. They will be expected to fire carefully aimed shots, using sights that offer little, if any, assistance, in conditions of chaos and high tension. Once they have fired the shot, they will be unable to determine its accuracy because of the cloud of dense smoke that obscures their vision. They will need to replace the spent cartridge with a live one and hope that attackers will not take advantage of their vulnerability as they struggle to do so. And, finally, if someone is struck by a baton round, the particular gunner will be held responsible in the criminal and civil courts for his action, if it is possible to identify him.

If this were the result of the unavoidable necessity quickly to develop and fabricate a suitable weapon, it might be defensible; but it is not. There exists, and has existed for some time, a far more sophisticated and reliable alternative weapon, produced by Royal Ordnance when still a nationalized company. It is the ARWEN 37 riot gun. In contrast to a

single-shot weapon, this gun carries five rounds in a
revolver-like cylinder. It is somewhat longer that the L67,
with properly calibrated rifle sights and twin pistol grips. In a
comparative demonstration against the L67 conducted in the
early 1980s, the ARWEN was able to fire all five rounds with
much greater speed and accuracy than its competitor. The
propellant used to discharge the projectile (a blank pistol
cartridge) creates much less smoke than that contained in
.the L5A4 baton round, thus allowing the gunner to evaluate
the accuracy of his shots. Moreover, the ARWEN, unlike the
L67, is capable of discharging more than just plastic baton
rounds. It can also fire CS gas canisters and smoke. The
projectile has a distinctive shape, with a heavy nose and 'tail'
to the rear which enhances its ballistic stability and hence its
accuracy. The projectile is lighter than the L5A4 baton round
and is fired with a higher velocity, with the result that it has
almost exactly the same impact energy as the baton round it
replaces, but is more accurate. One variant of this projectile
contains a sack of CS powder in the head which ruptures on
impact, thus doubly disabling the person hit by it. 'Low-
energy' versions of both these baton rounds enable this
weapon to be used at close quarters to disable dangerous
people who might now be shot with lethal weapons.

Why, then, have the authorities refused to authorize the
use of the ARWEN when it is clearly so superior to the L67?
The answer seems to lie in its appearance. The ARWEN 37
looks menacing: its large cylinder and twin pistol grips give it
the appearance of a machine-gun. In other words, the fact
that it is less likely to cause innocent bystanders to be struck
by PBRs because of its greater accuracy, as well as its
capacity to fire five rounds before reloading is required, have
both been relegated to concerns about its appearance. This is,
perversely, a triumph for those critics who refuse to accept
that in some situations the police should and must use
considerable force. The ARWEN 37 has been singled out by
such organizations as the misleadingly entitled 'Society for
Social Responsibility in Science' (BSSRS, 1985) for particular
condemnation, and the authorities have retreated in the face
of this criticism — to the detriment of rioters, who now risk
serious injury if the L67 is used against them, innocent

bystanders, who may be struck because of ballistic inaccuracy, and individual baton gunners, who will . be left to shoulder the responsibility for anything untoward that occurs.

A recent development of the ARWEN makes its use more politically acceptable. The five-shot revolver cylinder has been removed so that it becomes a single-shot weapon similar to the L67. However, it retains its advantages with regard to accuracy and interchangeability of projectiles. The ARWEN ACE, as this weapon is called, also has an ejection mechanism which both speeds reloading and allows easy confirmation of whether the weapon is loaded or not. However, the pursuit of the cosmetic acceptability of a single-shot weapon may well have unfortunate consequences. Baton gunners firing single-shot launchers, whether the L67 or ARWEN ACE, will be deployed in groups. In such a deployment it is more difficult both to control the gunners' actions and to ensure subsequent accountability. For example, once given the command to 'engage', more than one gunner may select the same individual as their target. This is not just possible, but quite likely, since gunners are required to fire at people who, by their actions, justify the use of such force to incapacitate them. As a result, an individual may well be struck almost simultaneously by more than one baton round, and severely injured or killed as a result. Such a situation is much less likely with one or two officers using a multi-shot weapon like the ARWEN 37.

Although the ARWEN was a leader in the field, the refusal of the Government to sanction procurement of this weapon meant that it only entered full production in 1988. Other manufacturers have also developed weapons for firing baton rounds or their equivalent. Some continue to use the L5A4 ammunition whilst others either use the ARWEN-type ammunition or specially developed alternatives. Therefore, there now exists the opportunity to replace the unsatisfactory L67 with a weapon properly designed for the purpose. The only responsible course of action is for the authorities to withdraw the L67 baton gun and replace it immediately with a weapon of the sophistication of the ARWEN riot gun. To do otherwise is reckless.

### Baton Rounds and Gas: Preferred Alternatives?

Once the police are properly equipped with a suitable baton gun, and CS gas launcher, how should these be employed? Is there not a danger of an escalating 'technological drift' in which the use of such a weapon will become increasingly common? Will police commanders not be inclined to climb the hierarchy of graduated force and use such a weapon in preference to traditional methods? The startling answer is that not only *might* they do so, but they *should* do so. Baton rounds and CS gas, far from being considered the last resort weapons of public-order policing, should occupy a lower position in the hierarchy of force than they do at the moment. In particular, they should be considered as preferred alternatives to the baton charge.

The disadvantages of the baton charge have been thoroughly discussed previously: it is inevitably indiscriminate; it is conducive to the use of excessive force by officers; it can be dangerous to the police; it is difficult to command; it suffers a confusion of purpose regarding whether to arrest, disperse, or incapacitate. By contrast, the use of either CS gas or baton rounds involves only as much force as is necessary to achieve its purpose. The difference is admirably summed up in the words of a senior officer, who commented, 'Well, at least a baton round won't chase you round the corner, kick in your front door, race upstairs and beat you to death in your bed'.

There can be little doubt that CS gas and baton rounds (as well as water cannon, if it was available) are tactically superior to the baton charge as a means of policing disorderly and violent crowds. It is, perhaps, worth noting that the Washington City Metropolitan Police, who suffer similar problems of controlling public protest, regard the use of gas as an early response to disorder. They regard the baton charge as a virtual last resort, because of the dangers to which it exposes members of the public, police officers, and the reputation of the police department.

## Coercive Technology and Minimum Force

The view that baton rounds and irritant agents are *less* dangerous than 'traditional methods' squarely contradicts the view of some commentators who believe that the developments in tactics, training, and equipment during the 1980s have already undermined the commitment of the police to 'minimum force', and who view the prospect of irritant agents and baton rounds with undisguised horror (Brewer *et al.*, 1988).

Perhaps the fear that lies behind the allegation that the possession of riot control equipment breaches the doctrine of 'minimum force' is that its availability will encourage its use. Brewer *et al.*, cite a number of incidents occurring during the late 1980s which, they claim, 'amount to a sea-change in the policing of disorder' (1988: 32), at least, in the post-Second World War context. The list includes the so-called 'battle of the beanfield' near Stonehenge, the eviction of CND supporters from land surrounding the Molesworth cruise missile base, the disorder outside Manchester University students' union, and the 1985 riots at Handsworth, Brixton, and Tottenham. It is fair to say that in some of these instances, notably the Stonehenge and Manchester incidents, complaints of excessive force were justified and subsequently endorsed by the Police Complaints Authority. It is equally relevant to note that in other incidents, such as the eviction of the 'Peace Convoy' from Stony Cross, Hampshire, in the year following the 'battle of the beanfield' (*The Times* 19 June 1986), the police operation was a model of restraint, not least because of effective tactics and deployment.

However, even if irritant agents or baton rounds are used these will amount to a *less extreme* level of force than such 'traditional methods' as charging a crowd with either officers on foot or horseback. Blair Peach was as much the victim of 'traditional methods' of policing civil disorder in Britain as he was the victim of the officer who struck him.

*Discarding a valuable tradition?*

It is sentimental indulgence to assume, as many commentators have assumed, that traditional methods of policing
public disorder are superior to either contemporary British or
colonial and Continental tactics. For example, Sir Robert
Mark (1978) seems to take pride in the fact that at the 1976
Notting Hill carnival the Metropolitan Police 'had no kind of
weaponry, defensive or offensive, no tear-gas, no riot-shields
or any other means of defence: just what ordinary police
would have, doing ordinary police duties'. However, if his
officers had been equipped with appropriate defensive and
offensive weaponry, not only might they have maintained
order at the 1976 carnival, but they might also not have
resorted to baton charging demonstrators three years later in
Southall with the resulting loss of Blair Peach's life.

Not only have traditional methods caused needless injury
to members of disorderly crowds, they have failed to contain
disorder effectively. Traditionally equipped officers were
unable to maintain order at Notting Hill in 1976, or at
Ladywood, Birmingham when rioting broke out after
members of the Anti-Nazi League tried forcibly to prevent a
march of the National Front in August 1977. Since those
occasions the police have responded to each escalation in the
violence used against them by providing better protective
equipment so as to enable the cordon to remain secure. Yet it
is clear that enhancement of traditional methods by affording
officers greater protection has not fared any better than
previous methods, for protected police have repeatedly been
defeated by rioters. In St Paul's, Bristol, in 1980, the police
were obliged to retreat, leaving the area unpoliced for several
hours; at Brixton, a year later, the rioting continued for three
days without an effective police response; in Toxteth, later
that year, the police were nearly overwhelmed; in Handsworth, in 1985, the police stood impotent as rioters sacked
Lozells Road, murdering two innocent people in the process;
and a few weeks later, at Broadwater Farm, a hail of missiles
and sporadic gunfire kept the police at bay, whilst a constable
was hacked to death by a mob.

There have been successes for the police, but these have
been principally during 'set-piece' confrontations, especially

in connection with industrial disputes. The miners' dispute which, after the violence at Ollerton, threatened to become another victory for mass flying pickets, saw the police succeed in preventing the forcible closure of premises. At the *Messenger* newspaper in Warrington and at the News International premises in Wapping, east London, mass picketing also failed in its objective of forcibly preventing the production and distribution of newspapers. Violent though these confrontations were, their occurrence was reasonably predictable, and order could be maintained by large numbers of police maintaining a physical barrier in the traditional manner. Missiles were thrown, there were baton charges, and mounted officers were deployed, but the scale of violence to which the police were subjected was significantly less than in the inner-city disturbances. Even so, the police have suffered from criticism of using excessive and indiscriminate violence against pickets through their use of such 'traditional' methods as the baton charge.[12]

In any case, *what* is the valuable tradition that we are in danger of losing? Certainly, the handling of a demonstration against the Sunday Trading Bill in 1855, and of another called to promote the extension of the franchise in 1866, which degenerated into serious disorder, were nothing to be proud of. The chaotic, ineffective, and ultimately violent police response on these occasions pale into insignificance, however, compared to the violent fiascos that occurred in and around Trafalgar Square on 8 February 1886 and on 13 November the following year in what came to be known as 'bloody Monday' and 'bloody Sunday' respectively (Critchley, 1970: 145–58). The violence that surrounded industrial disputes during the early years of the twentieth century reflect no better on 'traditional' methods of policing civil disorder, for contemporary accounts reveal the police using violence to a degree that would be wholly unacceptable today (Dunning *et al.*, 1987; Morgan, 1987). The inability of these traditional methods to effectively maintain order was demonstrated in 1911 at Liverpool, where troops were deployed and a police officer was kicked to death, just one of several violent confrontations between police and rioters in the period leading up to the First World War (Critchley 1970:

167–72). In the period between 1929 and 1931, the police baton charged strikers and hunger marchers on more than a hundred occasions (Bowden, 1978).

As radical police historians have been keen to remind us, 'traditional' methods of public-order policing have not been conspicuous for their display of discipline or impartiality. According to Scraton (1985), a mass protest in Birkenhead in support of the unemployed led to 'open conflict between the police and the marchers', and 'rioting had been persistent for almost a week' when police mounted a retaliatory mass raid on poor districts within the town (pp. 26–8). The apparent preference shown for Fascists who received police protection whilst marching provocatively through Jewish areas in the mid–1930s has been the object of widespread radical complaint (Bowden, 1978; Manwaring-White, 1983). It seems odd, to put it no more forcefully, that we are now enjoined to remain faithful to these very same traditions and not to seek alternatives.

*Importing an alien police tradition?*

This is not a view with which Northam (1985; 1986; 1988) would agree. He argues that not only do these methods abrogate valued policing traditions, but they represent the importation of colonial policing methods and the social attitudes that necessarily accompany them. The evidence for this contention is slender, to say the least. It relies upon the revelation that British police officers made visits to Hong Kong and other colonial police forces in the period following the Second World War. Moreover, the annual conference of ACPO in 1981, following the outbreak of rioting earlier that year, was addressed by a senior Hong Kong police officer on the public-order tactics employed in the colony. Together, these events are offered as an explanation of the similarity between contemporary British public-order policing and those used in the colony. This thesis gains credibility from the fact that its author was permitted unprecedented access to the ACPO *Tactical Options Manual*, substantial portions of which are reproduced in support of these allegations.

Unfortunately, there are several unexplained gaps in the

evidence. First, British police officers have regular and frequent contact with many police forces throughout the world, from whom some or all the tactics now in use may have been learned. This is because there is nothing peculiarly 'colonial' about paramilitary riot police or their tactics. Most European countries have police forces of this kind, and the USA has a 'third force' in the guise of the National Guard, which receives public-order training. Nearer home is the Royal Ulster Constabulary, with many years of experience in riot control, and from whom other authors believe the police on the mainland of Britain have learnt their public-order tactics (Hillyard, 1985; 1987; Ouseley, 1987). The only reason for emphasizing the 'Hong Kong connection' would seem to be to stigmatize contemporary police tactics as 'colonial'.

Second, Northam's account contains inconsistencies regarding the order of events. The crucial intervention, according to Northam, was at the 1981 ACPO conference, but this *followed* many of the innovations of which he is critical. The PSU was adapted as a public-order formation from its civil defence role in the early 1970s. The long shield was acquired in 1976 and first used at Lewisham in 1977. Protective helmets and overalls had already been acquired in the aftermath of the riots earlier in 1981, and tear gas had been used in Liverpool. Mounted officers have been a feature of public-order policing in Britain since the inception of the Metropolitan Police in 1829.

Third, many of the parallels drawn between British and colonial methods seem strained, if not simply spurious. The most glaring example is the view that the PSU comprising an inspector, two sergeants, and twenty constables is 'remarkably similar to the riot-control unit used for public order control throughout the British colonies' which apparently consists of an inspector, one NCO, and *eight* men. The use of short shields is by no means peculiar to colonial policing — it is, for example, characteristic of riot control throughout Western Europe — and the 'snatch squad' was familiar from Northern Ireland experience.

Fourth, and finally, Northam's equation between the riot control tactics of colonial police forces and a tendency towards forceful suppression of a dissident population is not supported. Similar riot control tactics are used by police operating under a wide range of regimes. They do not so much reflect an attitude towards the civil population as the tactical imperatives of riot control.

What is, however, undoubtedly true is that the changes in public-order policing introduced in the early 1980s have been kept a closely guarded secret. It is also true that central government has extended its influence over the police generally, but over the policing of public-order policing in particular. For example, the ACPO *Tactical Options Manual* has been read and approved by the Home Secretary (Northam, 1988). Not only has this manual and other aspects of public-order policing or the Home Office role gone without the explicit approval of Parliament, it is also the case that local police authorities, who are supposedly responsible for maintaining an effective and efficient police force in their respective areas, have been refused permission to see the contents of the manual, still less to approve them or otherwise. The secrecy, not to say furtiveness, surrounding recent developments in public-order policing have, not surprisingly, encouraged speculation that a paramilitary 'third force' (whether imported from Hong Kong or elsewhere) has been created by stealth in Britain.

## 'A Technological Fix'?

What many critics fear is that the acquisition of technology and weaponry, and tactical training in its use, sets Britain on a course of escalating social conflict. The mere possession of this technology might, it is feared, impel the police to use it, and, having used it, to acquire yet more offensive weaponry. These are the twin dangers of 'technological drift' and 'decision drift', respectively, perceived by some scientists and technologists who wish to halt the slide towards a greater reliance on technological solutions to problems of law and order.[13]

Is it true that a technologically sophisticated police are more repressive than their technologically impoverished counterparts of a previous era? This is not the conclusion to be reached from either orthodox or radical revisions of police history, which point to the brutality with which strikers and protesters were treated by the technologically unsophisticated forebears of today's riot-clad police officers (see pp. 212–13). In that mythical era when policing was 'by consent', if the police were in danger of being overwhelmed there was always the army ready to intervene, with even greater escalatory potential.

Contrary to the claimed correlation between the use of technology and an escalation in violence, there is good reason to believe that the acquisition of vehicles, radio communication, protective equipment, and so forth has been associated with a *reduction* in the use of force. Geary's (1985) analysis of the policing of industrial disputes suggests that it was *improvements* in tactics and intelligence which enabled police to make a more measured response to picketing.

More sophisticated tactics allow the police more options. If 'pushing and shoving' becomes too vigorous for the traditional cordon, the development of the 'chorus line' (see p. 317) enables the cordon to be maintained and avoids the need for a more forceful police response. If serious disorder erupts and dispersal becomes necessary, then the use of CS smoke, in preference to the baton charge, eliminates the possibility of people in the crowd being arbitrarily struck. If a street is ablaze, with burning barricades obstructing movement and a hail of missiles preventing police intervention (as occurred at Handsworth), then arsonists can be stopped from committing possibly murderous actions by an incapacitating baton round, instead of the use of lethal force — gunfire.

Not only do such tactics and the means of implementing them offer flexibility in the course of disorder, they also allow the police to negotiate mutually satisfactory arrangements with protesters and others in anticipation of some planned or continuing public order event. The capacity on the part of the police to control such a situation forcefully, if necessary, gives them something to negotiate with. For example, the Derbyshire police were able to police the miners' dispute in their area virtually without recourse to the use of riot equipment (Leonard, 1985), no doubt partly because both they and the local NUM knew that if no accommodation was reached, then forcible means could be used.

To argue that the possession of coercive technology can facilitate consensual policing contradicts much contemporary received wisdom. It is often claimed that the police unilaterally abandoned the consensual approach in favour of more coercive means. For example, Geary (1985) attributes the recent rise in picket-line violence to such a change of police policy. However, this is clearly a false interpretation. It was not the police who abandoned consent in favour of coercion. The acquisition of this technology has been, at every stage, a *reaction* to the violence with which the police have been faced. The tactic of mass flying picketing was designed to overwhelm the modest police presence that had traditionally maintained order on the picket-line, and was designed to achieve the pickets' goal by force. Violent political protest was intended to cause such disorder as to induce the Government to alter its policy for fear of the consequences. Ferocious counter-protest was not intended to voice opposition to the views of others but, illegally and forcibly, to prevent the expression of such views. Violent inner-city riots clearly had the purpose of inflicting as many serious injuries upon the police as the crowd could accomplish by recourse to missiles, petrol bombs, and, eventually, firearms.

The acquisition of the technology of coercion occurred in the *wake* of incidents of serious disorder in which traditional methods proved inadequate. The establishment of the National Reporting Centre and the changed role of PSUs was a response to the defeat of the Birmingham Police at Saltley coke depot in 1972; the acquisition of reinforced helmets and long shields followed the disorder at Notting Hill in 1976; the compilation of the ACPO manual was a result of the St Paul's riot in Bristol, during which police were obliged to withdraw from the area completely; the acquisition of protective helmets, shields, flame resistant overalls, and stocks of CS gas and baton rounds was a consequence of the 1981 inner-city riots; the further acquisition of long batons and ballistically protected vehicles was a repercussion of the use of firearms and savage violence directed towards the police at Broadwater Farm. Each step up the escalatory ladder of police preparedness has been a response to unacceptable levels of violence. To have acted otherwise would have been to abdicate from any attempt to maintain order against those who are prepared to resort to extreme violence to press their views or pursue their interests.

Would a police force capable of imposing its will by force feel any compulsion to negotiate an accommodation with protesters? The NCCL inquiry panel into the policing of the miners' strike complained that police in South Yorkshire had not negotiated amicable arrangements with the NUM and relied instead on more forceful tactics, in contrast to the West Yorkshire Police, where amicable arrangements were negotiated and conflict largely avoided (McCabe *et al.*, 1988). What this report fails fully to acknowledge, and what is made clear in the report of the Chief Constable of South Yorkshire (Wright, 1985: 93–4), is that the NUM in South Yorkshire *refused* to enter into any discussions designed to alleviate conflict and violence on the picket-line. Negotiated consent is necessarily limited by the willingness of all the parties to co-operate; when that willingness is absent, the duty of the police is clear: to maintain 'the peace', if necessary by force. Contrary to the worst imaginings of some critics, the police have no vested interest in suppressing disorder by force. Riot control is dangerous and financially costly. Thus, both parties have a vested interest in avoiding conflict and achieving accommodation.

What critics seem to fear is that, behind the repressive apparatus of a technologically equipped police, those in positions of social, political, and economic power (including the police themselves) have no incentive to negotiate with those whose only power is protest. As Rosenhead and Smith put it (1971: 376) in connection with riot control tactics in Northern Ireland: 'each technological escalation is likely to lead us further into a political blind-alley, in which the real grievances are untouched and become, in fact, more remote from solution.' A decade later, Rosenhead (1981: 212) criticizes the stocking of CS smoke and baton rounds by British police forces in essentially the same terms:

Injurious to the health of the public, they are likely to have a still more malign influence on that of the body-politic. There is no evidence that the economic and social injustices underlying the current wave of disorders can be handled by stamping on the symptoms.

In the view of these critics, investment in tactics, weaponry and other technology becomes a 'technological fix' — a vain search for technological solutions to far more fundamental problems. Instead of trying to resolve the social and economic problems that cause injustice which, in turn, lead to disorder, those in authority look for a simple, repressive solution in technology. Thus, effective computers used to process intelligence reports and televisual surveillance are not opposed by critics because they are likely to injure, but because they might make policing more effectively repressive.

However, this raises the argument above questions of technology and tactics and into the *political* realm, to which the next chapter will be devoted.

# 7

# The Politics of Explanation and Justification

## Introduction

The inner-city riots of the early 1980s produced a sea change in public-order policing. Once the missiles began to fly, the traditional bobby was replaced by the riot police, clad in protective clothing and protected by shields. In reserve there were now stocks of CS agent and plastic baton rounds. These developments in riot control tactics and technology are condemned by their critics as not only failing to address the 'real problems' but also obstructing the solution of these problems. Some police officers, local residents whose property has been destroyed by arson, and not a few observers of the riots might have thought that the missiles that have been thrown, and the arson, rape, and murder committed, *were* the 'real problem'. Not so, say the critics:[1] the 'real problems' are the social conditions that cause riots to occur in the first instance. These are left untouched by riot control technology.[2]

'Tooling up' by the police is not simply misdirected; it is, in this view, actually malign, for insofar as rioting is effectively suppressed, the underlying conditions will remain unresolved by those in social, political, and economic power. Worse still, developments in riot control techniques are not only an obstacle to social reform; they also threaten our democratic traditions by stifling dissent, portending a drift into authoritarianism. What is portrayed by the police as the 'maintenance and restoration of public order' is, from this perspective, 'policing political dissent'. Therefore, the growth in the tactics and technology of coercion is regarded as repressive.

What are the social conditions that go untouched by developments in riot control and require attention if rioting is to be avoided? They are summed up by the word 'injustice'

—the deprivation, dilapidation, discrimination, and decay—afflicting ethnic minorities. This is the conclusion of a variety of recent analyses of inner-city riots contained in an extensive literature emanating from various sources, including academic texts, official and semi-official reports,[3] investigative journalism,[4] and politically committed polemics.[5] These contributions to the literature overlap, sometimes being published together (see particularly Benyon, 1984*a*) and thus providing mutual support and apparent corroboration. In all these respects there is the distinct echo of the aftermath of the 'long hot summers' of the 1960s in the USA.[6] Indeed, comparisons are often drawn between the British and American experience (Harman, 1981), and especially between the Scarman inquiry (Scarman, 1981) and its American predecessor, the Kerner commission (Kerner, 1968).[7]

There are differences of emphasis and political allegiance amongst those who have contributed to this literature, but there is a clear consensual core. This core is the belief that inner-city riots were motivated by genuine grievances arising out of deprivation and discrimination generally, and especially police harassment. For convenience this view will be referred to throughout this chapter as the 'critical consensus', because it sets itself up in opposition to the Establishment–conservative view which describes the riots as, at best, an irrational and, at worst, a criminal outburst.

The critical consensus has become so widely and uncritically accepted in academic and related circles that it now occupies the position of a received wisdom. Sceptical scrutiny reveals that, on the one hand, the critical consensus is no more convincing an explanation of contemporary crowd violence than the Establishment–conservative view it seeks to replace. The importance of such a perspective lies less in its explanatory value than in its political significance. Before the perspective can be examined, it is first necessary to describe it.

## Popular Falsehoods

The literature prompted by the inner-city riots has been dominated by a desire to refute what are considered to be two popular falsehoods: first, that the riotous group is a mindless crowd, and second, that the riots of the recent period are unprecedented. It has become a commonplace for authors to point to the propagation of these falsehoods through the mass media and from the lips of politicians, police spokesmen, members of the judiciary and others in the Establishment.[8] However, dispassionate consideration of these two issues reveals a situation more complex than any of these commentators have so far acknowledged.

## Mindlessness or injustice?

Popular and official views of the causes of public disorder amount to an implicit endorsement of a particular theory of the causes of crowd violence. This theory is hotly disputed by the critical consensus, which regards it as demonstrably false, both theoretically and historically.

*The mindless mob*   The intellectual pedigree of the notion of the 'mindless mob' is normally traced back to Le Bon (1896), who pioneered scholarly research of crowd violence. For Le Bon, the crowd was to be understood as a decivilizing phenomenon, through which normal inhibitions were shed and its members returned to a state of irrational savagery. Le Bon contended that irrationality sweeps through a crowd by a form of emotional contagion, overwhelming restraint and liberating the passions. The crowd was an unstable entity which could be captured by the demagogue and used as his instrument. Because the crowd was an irrational manifestation, it was implicit that any claims made on its behalf could not be taken seriously. The crowd simply had to be controlled, not understood. If it were not controlled by the authorities, it would be vulnerable to control by agitators, infiltrators, and subversives, who will spread rumour and initiate violence.

The intellectual progeny of Le Bon is to be found in some contemporary social psychology of collective behaviour. This is rooted in various strands of social psychological research and theory.[9] Strains within the social system (Smelser, 1962), such as a gross disparity between expectations and achievement (Gurr, 1969; Davies, 1969), can induce feelings of frustration and aggression which find their expression in collective violence. The processes of group dynamics revealed in experimental studies explain the ferocity of the resulting crowd violence. Groups induce strong pressures to conform, especially when one group is in conflict with others. The anonymity of the crowd reduces feelings of individual responsibility, so that participants do not feel that they are inflicting harm on other individuals, but regard themselves as 'one of Us' attacking 'Them'.

This kind of theory is associated with a conservative point of view. It regards crowd violence as an 'eruption' or 'outburst', rather than a rational expression of grievances. Explanation is to be found, as it were, *within* the individuals who participate, rather than in the wider society of which they are members.

*'Politically motivated protest'*    The social-psychological explanation outlined above has been largely dismissed by those seeking explanations for inner-city riots. The critical consensus maintains that this view fails to comprehend the genuine grievances that promoted and directed violence. Inner-city riots have to be understood, it is contended, as political in nature—the rational expression of political grievances and aspirations by groups otherwise excluded from the political process. The riots did not simply erupt as some irrational outburst of rage, nor were they instigated or orchestrated by extremists manipulating rioters for their own malign purposes. The riots, it is insisted, were a rational attempt to make those in authority, who had hitherto been deaf to complaints of deprivation, discrimination, and harassment, listen and respond. In short, this alternative view disputes that crowd violence is 'caused' in the way that a volcanic eruption is caused—by forces acting upon it—and holds that it is the expression of a *'cause'*—a demand for socio-political change. As Bachrach and Baratz (1970) put it, riots are the ballot-box of the poor. Or, in the words of Kettle and Hodges (1982: 11): 'Riots, like other forms of violence, do not just "erupt". Riots have reasons and need to be understood as a specific popular activity.'

Accordingly, the vocabulary of 'riot' and 'civil disorder' is dismissed as inapplicable, and preference given instead to terms like 'protest', 'rebellion', or 'uprising'. Inner-city riots are seen as rational demands for change to rectify grievances (Macdonald, 1973; Harman, 1981; Gordon, 1985. Ethnic minorities are seen as powerless groups subject to disadvantage and injustice, the most obvious being racial discrimination. The circumstances which provoked or occasioned violence are not regarded as some momentary or isolated problem, but as merely the latest chapter in the persistent struggle against racial and class oppression in all its guises.[10] Their grievances, having gone unheard by those in authority, have been expressed in the only way left open to them.[11] Riots are not some mindless rampage; violence is not indiscriminate; arson and looting are selectively targeted at premises which are seen as sources and symbols of injustice (Quarantelli and Dynes, 1968; Fogelson, 1970; Reicher, 1984).

This view is both an expression of, and gains intellectual credibility from, the established sociological tradition of seeking empathetically to understand even the most apparently irrational behaviour. It has affinities with the broad study of social movements, in which an attempt has traditionally been made to understand the motivating beliefs that give rise to even the most irrational or objectionable social, political, religious, or moral campaigns (Turner and Killain, 1957; Smelser, 1962; Gusfield, 1970). What unites such highly diverse movements as millenarianism, anti-abortion, and the trade unions is that they are motivated by 'a cause'. Far from being irrational or mindless, they are expressions of genuinely felt grievances or ideals, even if the beliefs espoused are unpalatable to those who analyse them, such as British fascism in the 1930s (Thurlow, 1987) or 1950s McCarthyism (Trow, 1958).

## The riotous history of the British

Outbreaks of serious civil disorder have often been accompanied by the forebodings of politicians, judges, police chiefs, and newspapers editors who see in these events an unprecedented threat to the fabric of British society and its traditions. Implicitly and explicitly, such commentaries refer back to an idyllic past of peace and harmony which is now being rent asunder (Harman, 1981; Beynon, 1987; Dixon and Fishwick, 1984).

This too is a notion rejected by critical commentators, who argue that the recent disorders are not only political expressions of injustice but also a form of expression to which the powerless and under-privileged have persistently made recourse in Britain. These commentators ridicule the vision of the present and the past conveyed by references to 'unprecedented' recent disorders. They observe — correctly[12] — that British social history is littered with examples of periodic serious rioting. It was the depredations of the London mob which was one of the main incentives for introducing the 'New Police' in 1829. Throughout the remainder of that century and well into the present century the police, often accompanied by the military, fought Luddites, Chartists, and others seeking trade union rights and the extension of the franchise.

The conclusion seems clear: contemporary disorder is simply the most recent manifestation of a persistent historical process in which the disadvantaged express their grievances at social injustice and are confronted by the repressive apparatus of the State — the police.

Throughout British history, powerless people, feeling themselves oppressed and seeing no effective response to their grievances, have despaired of any improvement, formed themselves into crowds and physically challenged the world that seemed to deny them what they wanted. (Kettle and Hodges, 1982: 11)

The implication seems to be that, when the inner-city riots are viewed from a hundred years hence, the justice of the rioters' cause will be perceived as clearly as we now see the just demands of nineteenth-century rioters who sought the extension of the franchise and trade union rights.

### Prescriptions

The prescriptive implications for riot control are transparent: the injustices that provoke disorder will not be extinguished by repression. Indeed, some authors detect a connection between State repression and the likelihood of a violent response (Gurr, 1970). The attention being given to improved riot control equipment and training in its use is fundamentally misdirected (Hewitt, 1982; Clare, 1986). Mass protest represents a failure on the part of the political system to respond to social injustice and the grievances that such injustice arouses. To respond by increasing the repressive potential of the police simply allows the political system to remain unresponsive to its citizens, allowing injustice to persist and grievances to fester until even greater disorder occurs. It is for this reason that the growth of police technology is viewed with such alarm (Manwaring–White, 1983; BSSRS, 1983; Ackroyd *et al.*, 1977).

It was not bloody military and police control of the nineteenth-century mob which brought about the de-escalation of violence witnessed throughout this century. This was achieved through the incorporation of the working class into the legitimate institutions of economic and political life, allowing at least some of their grievances to be redressed (Reiner, 1985*a*; Geary, 1985). This capacity to incorporate social movements such as the Labour Movement into legitimate political channels has rightly been seen as the strength of democratic systems. What is now required, according to this view, is to incorporate and reincorporate excluded groups into legitimate political institutions (Lea and Young, 1982).

Without incorporation, it is feared that the forebodings which greeted the introduction of the New Police in 1829 (Emsley, 1983; Stead, 1985; Critchley, 1970) will actually be confirmed, the police having become, or revealed as being, the oppressive instrument of an unresponsive social, economic and political elite. For some commentators at least, this amounts to the abrogation of all that is valuable in the British police tradition (Alderson, 1985; Brewer *et al.*, 1988).

In rejecting the two popular falsehoods of the unprecedented mindlessness of contemporary collective violence, the two strands of the critical consensus converge upon a common basic explanation of recent disorders and upon agreed prescriptions for how to respond to them. It is maintained that both social research and history teach us that recent inner-city riots should not be seen as unprecedented and irrational outbursts, but as political demands expressed through the only means available to the deprived and under-privileged. It is to the critical appraisal of that view that we now turn.

## Selective Explanations

Much of what is claimed by the 'critical consensus' is correct: the decline in social, political, and industrial violence was the result of incorporating the working class into the political system; racial discrimination, inner-city deprivation and decay, and police harassment is all too common and should be eliminated; grievances and aspirations should be addressed through political channels where possible and not suppressed by force. These propositions are not at issue; what *is* at issue is whether the explanation so widely offered, and even more widely accepted, is an *accurate* account of disorder *per se*, and also whether the prescription of remedying grievances through political processes is universally applicable. Or does the explanation, and the prescription that follows from it, only apply to some crowds and to particular disorder? For if it does, the implications for criticisms of public order policing are significant.

When critically scrutinized, the explanation for recent episodes of civil disorder are seen to be highly selective. Some disorder is regarded as the 'political expression of injustice', whilst other episodes of disorder are not, without rational grounds being offered for inclusion or exclusion. It is to the exploration of this selectivity that this section will be devoted.

### Suffering injustice and voicing a grievance?

The basic contention of the 'critical consensus' is that the inner-city riots of the 1980s were the expression of grievances which originated in social injustice. However, this proposition raises more issues than it attempts to resolve.

It is indisputably the case that Black people actually suffer significant disadvantages and deprivations. Indeed, a great deal of the critical literature is devoted, not to the disorders themselves, but to the eloquent exposition of the injustices which, it is claimed, prompted the disorder. Clearly, the social disadvantage and discrimination suffered by ethnic minorities would give them ample reason to feel a sense of injustice. Well before rioting erupted in the inner-cities, representative pressure groups and some investigative journalists were complaining about police harassment of, and discrimination towards, Black people.[13] Moreover, there was plentiful evidence of widespread discrimination in all areas of social life. These complaints received limited official acknowledgement (Select Committee on Race Relations and Immigration, 1972), but little seemed to be done to remedy the situation. Far from being a spontaneous eruption, it is maintained, the inner-city riots were predictable and predicted.

The question is not whether those involved in civil disorders suffered injustices, but what *connection* there was between injustice and collective action.

*Injustice as an explanation*

It is one thing to observe that a disorderly or riotous group suffers certain injustices. It is quite another thing to assert that those injustices are perceived by members of the group in the way they are by the analyst, or indeed that they are perceived by members of the group at all. It is yet a further step to assert that it was perceived injustice that caused the disorder. The tendency of commentators to concentrate upon *post hoc* analysis of single instances of disorder considered in isolation means that, whilst it is possible to construct a plausible argument supporting such a chain of causation, the argument is unconvincing as a general explanation of civil disorder, for injustice does not arise nor dissipate as quickly as do riots. There are many examples of people suffering injustice in silence.[14]

For example, as Parry *et al.*'s (1987) comparative study of three urban areas of northern England shows, whilst all three suffered the same catalogue of deprivation normally credited with provoking disorder, rioting occurred only in one area. The authors were able to identify differences other than those of deprivation between the three areas, such as different policing policies, but this kind of *post hoc* analysis runs the risk that the retrospective search for causes is always likely to yield plausible contenders, given the myriad ways in which areas might differ. The fact remains that two of the three areas suffered those deprivations which reputedly caused their neighbours to riot, and yet they did not riot. Since people in the non-riot areas were as much the victims of injustice as those in the rioting area, this alone cannot *explain* why some people riot and others do not. Indeed, it is usually the case that explanations of disorder reveal long-standing injustices which the victims suffered without protest before their patience evaporated.

Nor does it seem that differences in that most popular of explanatory variables, the method of policing, explain why riots erupt where and when they do. Despite the fact that both the Kerner commission (1968) and Lord Scarman (1981) laid considerable responsibility on the police for creating the conditions in which disorder could easily be sparked, American experience does not endorse the view that 'heavy' policing is to blame.

Diverse approaches to policing the ghetto do not seem to have produced very different riot outcomes. The police in Newark were harsh; they thus provoked a riot. The police in Detroit were restrained; they permitted a riot to develop. (Horowitz, 1983: 194)

Indeed, Marx (1970: 34) notes: 'Ironically, indignation against the police has risen as police behaviour has improved.'

Thus, it would seem that those who elevate 'injustice' to the role of principal explanatory construct (Benyon and Solomos, 1987*b*) are left with a theory in which injustice causes rioting except when it does not!

These analytical problems were partially recognized in the aftermath of the 1981 riots. It was confidently expected that rioting would recur the following summer, since the grievances had not been remedied in the mean time. In fact, there were no riots comparable to those that had erupted a year previously. This left many commentators asking, 'Where did all the riots go?', and prompted some observers to move conceptually closer to the 'mindless mob' theory and suggest that rioting was 'fun' (Kettle, 1982; Rock, 1981).

### 'Precipitating incidents'

The more usual analytical solution to this problem is to regard injustice as creating a background of discontent (a necessary but not sufficient condition) and seeing other events sparking or precipitating the disorder (Smelser, 1962; Rainwater, 1967; D. Waddington *et al.*, 1987; 1989). However, similar problems of causal analysis arise from attempts to explain why the disorder erupted when it did. In a complex situation there is always likely to have been some incident which can plausibly serve the purpose of a 'flashpoint', particularly when such a precipitating event is retrospectively identified and defined in terms which allow otherwise trivial incidents to assume momentous significance.

Consider, for example, the incident widely credited as having sparked the Brixton riot of April 1981 (Scarman, 1981). Two plain-clothes police officers engaged on the ill-fated 'Swamp 81' operation saw a taxi-driver stuff something into his shoe, which they believed, erroneously, to have been drugs. They then tried to search the man and a crowd gathered. There was an altercation, which rapidly escalated into stone-throwing and thence to the full-blown riot. Now, in the sense that this incident was immediately followed by the rioting, it seems clearly to fit the description as the 'flashpoint'. Whilst we might be convinced that this episode, when viewed in isolation, *was* the spark which caused the conflagration, what remains unexplained is why *this* incident, rather than some other, sparked the disorder. During 'Swamp 81' many individuals were stopped and searched, and some were arrested, without provoking a riot. So why did this particular incident trigger disorder when possibly hundreds of comparable incidents did not? If the editors of the *Leveller* (1981: 3) are correct in saying: 'How the conflict actually started on the Friday night is almost academic now: it was the latest in a long line of incidents in which the youth of Brixton fight their daily battle with the police', why did this point in the 'line' break? If police harassment was a constant feature of life in Brixton prior to the riots, what was the variable that explains the occurrence of rioting on 10 April 1981?

Moreover, other supposed flash-points have not been nearly so proximate to the outbreak of rioting. The shooting of Mrs Groce sparked the 1985 Brixton riot some hours later; the death of Mrs Jarrett occurred over twenty-four hours before the Broadwater Farm riot. So we cannot rely even on the proximity of the incident to the onset of rioting to identify the 'flash-point'.

Theorists have been content to allow such issues to remain unanalysed; but the reason why some potentially disorderly situations erupt into disorder and others do not *has* been addressed by David Waddington and his colleagues (1987; 1989). They tried, in a responsible and scholarly manner, to identify and clearly to document the flash-points of disorder during demonstrations, pickets, and 'community disorder' during the miners' strike of 1984–5. They compared occasions where disorder was avoided with others where disorder broke out.

The fact that the authors display such scholarship serves only to demonstrate the inherent weakness of their principal explanatory concept, 'flash-points'. This concept is flawed in two respects. First, there is simply too much occurring on any occasion which *might* plausibly explain the presence or absence of disorder for an exhaustive account to be rendered. Different parties point to different features and incidents, defeating any attempt to disentangle cause and effect. No observer can isolate which amongst the welter of events caused or prevented the eruption of disorder. Moreover, there is the problem of determining the onset of disorder and who amongst the participants initiated it. When miners departing from a demonstration disrupted traffic by blocking the roadway and police decided forcibly to remove them, police intervention is treated, not as a *response* to an existing situation of disorder, but as the instigation of disorder.

Second, since the authors rightly insist that the significance of events lies in how participants interpret them, and since interpretation may vary widely, one can never be sure that any given event or incident was or was not interpreted in any particular way by any given party. This affords the concept tremendous explanatory elasticity, for any event, however trivial, can acquire the status of the provocative 'last straw' which explains disorder, or, by the same token, any incident, however provocative it might seem to an observer, can be overlooked if order is maintained. Thus, four rows of police supported by mounted officers obstructing the view of demonstrators does not qualify as 'provocative' at the 'Thatcher Unwelcoming' demonstration, presumably because no one was provoked. When police at Orgreave deployed a line of long shields after being stoned by pickets, this presumably provoked pickets, because it was followed by 'an even heavier bombardment'. The theory is, then, circular, if not tautological: if disorder occurred there must have been a flash-point; if disorder was averted, a flash-point could not have occurred. The interpretative licence afforded by the concept of flash-points results in the analyst's descriptions of events being no less contestable than any other.

## Perceiving injustice

Another problem that arises from the 'injustice' explanation is that all manner of people may plausibly be thought to suffer some injustice or another. It is not simply the fact that certain groups suffer deprivation and disadvantage that explains why they riot when they do, but also *how* those deprivations and disadvantages are perceived and understood by those afflicted by them. Beliefs intervene between the reality of injustice and the response of those who suffer from it (Smelser, 1962; Apter, 1964; Gusfield, 1970).

Because beliefs play such a crucial mediating role, they are worthy of scrutiny in their own right. If deprivation and disadvantage are understood from the perspective of, say, a millenarian belief system, the expression of collective action is likely to be very different from that which follows the perception of those same deprivations and disadvantages in terms of a secular ideology (Cohn, 1957). The relationship between the underlying social experience and the beliefs of those who take collective action is contingent. Mobilizing beliefs serves a psychological function: they lend comprehensibility to events and prescribe remedies. They gain credibility, not because they accurately diagnose the source of the problem, but often because they commandeer established cultural themes. The analyst's explanation of the bases of discontent will often be totally at variance with that proffered by the ideology (Wolfinger *et al.*, 1964; Janowitz, 1970; Trow, 1958; Thurlow, 1987). An agnostic approach by the analyst is facilitated when the beliefs themselves are absurdly irrational or morally degenerate, but the same stance can be, and has been, profitably taken towards more attractive social movements like the American humanitarian reform movement of the 1830s which, amongst other things, sought the abolition of slavery (Donald, 1970).

Apart from Cashmore and Troyna's analysis of Rastafarianism (1982), there has been a singular absence of research into the structure of the beliefs that mobilized the inner-city riots. Explanation tends to proceed directly from the description of deprivation, disadvantage, and discrimination suffered by Black people to the occurrence of rioting. Complaints made on behalf of young Black people are treated, not as beliefs which are grist for the analyst's mill, but as confirmation of the existence of injustice. Campaigners on behalf of the Black community, such as the Institute of Race Relations, the Runnymede Trust, and the publication *Race Today*, are treated as authoritative sources of information about the nature and scale of injustice. They are not regarded, as they might in a slightly different context be regarded, as 'moral entrepreneurs'. Complaints, allegations, and explanations offered on behalf of rioters are not treated with agnostic scepticism, but tend to be accepted uncritically.[15]

But what evidence is there that those who rioted were expressing anything at all? There is some limited data suggesting that many of those living in inner-city areas believed *subsequently* that the riots were justified (Field and Southgate, 1982). However, this does not establish the prior existence of these beliefs, for they may be an example of a 'post-riot ideology' (Tomlinson, 1968). The undoubted antipathy felt by young Blacks for the police[16] was probably shared by previous generations of working–class youth, who have always felt the brunt of the police's order maintenance function (Morris, 1957; Downes, 1966; Reiner, 1985*b*; Brogden, 1985; Brogden *et al.*, 1988). Although these same previous generations have also become involved in crowd disorders and confrontations with the police, their motivation for doing so was not seen, either at the time or since, as being the expression of a sense of grievance (Cohen, 1972).

The existence of pre-riot grievances is simply inferred retrospectively from the fact that actual injustices can be identified, that disorder occurred, and that rioters subsequently justify their actions as being a response to police harassment. Insisting that the riots must be 'understood' amounts to the uncritical acceptance of the justifications offered by rioters and their supporters for their actions. It *may* be the case that subsequent justifications accurately reflect the rioters' prior state of mind; equally, this may simply be a retrospective rationalization. We simply do not know, and are offered no means of discriminating between these equally plausible alternatives.

In contrast to the study of many forms of collective action, it is difficult to establish that inner-city rioters possessed *any* coherent set of felt grievances prior to the rioting. The existence of some comprehensible sense of grievance or ideals is readily—although not unproblematically (see Beckford, 1978) — established in the case of most social movements because their defining feature is that they are organized protest groups with clearly articulated ideologies. Indeed, Gusfield (1970: 2) explicitly distinguishes 'the study of social movements and collective action from the study of *elementary collective behaviour*' such as 'crowds, mobs, mass, public, and other phenomena representing sporadic and unstructured group behaviour'. The beliefs of structured and ideologically focused movements like the Campaign for Nuclear Disarmament or the British Union of Fascists can be identified unambiguously because they are propounded in ideological tracts, speeches, and so forth. The fact that people share these beliefs can be inferred from the fact that they join the movement (and even then there may be a myriad reasons why people become involved in such activity). On the other hand, the claim that Black people felt a sense of grievance is much more difficult to establish, given the unstructured nature of any pre-existing movement, even if one existed.

Faced with this kind of difficulty one response is simply to 'move the conceptual goalposts', by insisting that a social movement need not be organized or ideologically focused (Piven and Cloward, 1977). In the absence of these conceptual constraints, analysts are then able to contend that recent American history has witnessed the existence of a broad movement of 'poor people' of all races, including, but not restricted to, the Black civil-rights campaign. Such a movement is to be inferred from the existence of such disparate acts as, for example, sabotage or crimes like robbery, and which are conceived as legitimate protest activity. What gives 'poor people's movements' analytical unity is not what they do by way of protest or rebellion, but the victimization they all share. As Lewis (1970: 151) puts it, these disparate acts are 'expressions of the *same* discontent' whose common feature is 'to act beyond the constraints of institutionalized political process'.

The problem is that we do not know, and are given no means of determining, whether any given action of 'poor people' is an 'expression of the same discontent'. The only reason for believing that the American 'long hot summers' *were* ideologically motivated was their connection to the organized civil rights movement, which had campaigned against racism with increasing success and achieved some measure of unity under the charismatic leadership of Martin Luther King. Thus, despite the fact that diffuse protest activity had no 'corporate body' nor any 'monistic ideological core' (Lewis, 1970; 151), it can still credibly be linked to a wider movement of organized protest.

However, it is precisely in this respect that the British and American experience diverges, for although the events either side of the Atlantic invite comparison — especially in view of the similar analyses offered by the respective official inquiries

(Kerner, 1968; Scarman, 1981) — the inner-city riots of the 1980s, *unlike* their American counterparts, lacked any connection to an organized movement articulating any coherent ideology. As Lord Scarman (1981) put it, the Brixton riot was a 'spontaneous act of defiant aggression' and, if so, seems to have more in common with other forms of 'elementary collective behaviour' (Gusfield, 1970), such as soccer hooliganism.

Yet it is exactly this parallel with soccer hooliganism and other episodes of violence that many writers seek strenuously to deny. For example, Benyon (1987: 30) dismisses as a 'conservative . . . "riff-raff" explanation' the view that 'Rioting is seen as another manifestation of the football hooliganism syndrome'; and Murdoch (1984: 82) complains about the mass media's treatment of 'rioting . . . simply as an outbreak of adolescent "hooliganism", as ordinary gang behaviour on a mass scale, to be dealt with like any other wave of street crime'. Thus, it is maintained, inner-city disorder is not equivalent to the mayhem of the football terraces, or the confrontations between mods and rockers at seaside resorts. Unlike these forms of collective violence, inner-city riots are genuine expressions of grievances arising from social injustice. As such, they demand to be taken seriously.

But do inner-city rioters demand to be taken seriously *because* their actions are motivated by some shared sense of grievance, or is the reason their actions are believed to have been motivated by a shared grievance the *result* of their being taken seriously? For example, why is it assumed that inner-city rioters are expressing grievances and soccer hooligans are not? It is not absurd to suggest that soccer hooligans may indeed be motivated by a genuine sense of grievance. Ian Taylor (1971) has offered reasonably plausible grounds for believing that soccer hooligans do suffer grievances arising from the way in which the professional game has been divorced from its working-class roots — grievances which suddenly came to be taken seriously after the Hillsborough disaster. Yet there are few amongst the 'critical consensus' who would appear to welcome such a comparison: drawing similarities between inner-city rioters and football hooligans is the province only of 'conservatives', it seems.

Having pushed back the bounds of what is to count as 'protest activity' so as to include spontaneous rioting in the inner city, the critical consensus does not clearly relocate the boundaries of its explanatory framework. No clear and rational criteria are offered to allow us to distinguish between those episodes of violence that demand to be understood and be taken seriously and those that do not. The critical consensus is just as eager to dismiss soccer hooliganism as a mindless rampage as are those Establishment figures whose interpretation of the inner-city riots the former so hotly dispute. For example, football fans and 'lager louts' are excluded from D. Waddington, *et al.*'s (1989) analysis, whilst youths congregating in a shopping precinct and drunken young miners are included on the specious grounds that in the latter cases 'territory is at stake'.

Equally, those White people who participated in earlier race riots, such as those in Bristol in 1911, Liverpool in 1919, and Notting Hill in 1958, are summarily dismissed (Joshua and Wallace, 1983). Despite the fact that inter-war fascism was an organized ideological movement propounding both grievances and aspirations, there is not the slightest indication that the critical consensus would wish to understand it, still less to take it seriously. The Notting Hill race rioters of 1958 seemed to have had a clear, albeit wrong-headed, conception of the wrongs inflicted on them by mass immigration (Moore, 1988). Yet, however much those rioters may have believed they suffered injustice, their rioting is regarded, by the 'critical consensus', as no more than an eruption of racist sentiment that needs only to be condemned and suppressed.[17] At best, such beliefs and actions are regarded as a misguided 'backlash' rather than as a genuine cause (Skolnick, 1969; Janowitz, 1970).

There are, then, two types of collective violence tacitly acknowledged by the critical consensus: one, the political expression of genuine injustice, the other, an irrational backlash in response to an uncomprehended reality. The first type demands to be taken seriously, the second type can be dismissed as 'mindless' with impunity. However, there is no clear basis for distinguishing one from the other. It seems that the insistence that the inner-city riots must be understood and taken seriously is a presumption rather than a conclusion. It is this presumption which leads to the further selectivity in explanation.

### Incompatible theories of crowd violence?

Since the critical consensus tacitly acknowledges the existence of both 'politically protesting' and 'mindless' crowds, why are its adherents so anxious to dismiss psychological theories of crowd behaviour as a 'popular falsehood'? There would appear to be no logical inconsistency between what are almost invariably presented as two competing and contradictory theoretical frameworks. Each could be seen as having a different referent: psychological theories are concerned to explain the mindlessness of the irrational mob, whilst the critical consensus accounts for the political expression of injustice. Certainly, much of the research on mass society (Kornhauser, 1960), group conflict (Tajfel, 1981), the aggression–frustration syndrome (Dollard *et al.*, 1974), and 'de-individuation'(Zimbardo, 1970) were motivated by a desire to understand irrational behaviour of groups such as lynch mobs.

There seem no clear grounds for excluding the possibility that some crowds err towards the 'mindless mob' end of the spectrum, whilst others err towards the 'politically motivated' pole. Such a view would seem to offer the prospect of a more comprehensive explanation of crowd violence than either, supposedly competing, theory could achieve on its own. However, the purpose of analysis would seem not to be the objective explanation of the disorders *per se*, but rather to be an attempt to categorize *particular* groups as expressing grievances at social injustice, thus attributing to those groups a political status they would normally be denied a priori. Contributions to the debate often argue in the vein: 'Do not hastily dismiss this disorderly group as a "mindless mob", because if you look closely you will see that they are protesting about the genuine injustices they suffer' (Benyon, 1984*b*; Benyon and Solomos, 1987*b*; Kettle and Hodges, 1982).

*An absence of 'conspirators'?*

Whatever the cause of disorder may actually be, it is clear to the critical consensus that it is not the work of the 'extremist infiltrators' imagined by Establishment spokespeople (Dummett, 1980*a*; Benyon, 1984*b*; 1987; Murdock, 1984; Harris, 1985). Activists, holding views that might seem extreme to some observers, may become prominent during the course of an 'uprising', but they simply articulate the grievances of those on the streets and point to the injustices that have prompted violent action. Regarding activists as instigators of violence and the rioters as mere dupes is such a simplistic conspiracy theory that it does not merit, and rarely receives, serious consideration. Yet, once again, the argument is selectively applied. When the Establishment indulges in conspiracy theory, the latter is dismissed out of hand as naïve and simplistic, but when supporters of violent protesters indulge in the same kind of explanation, it is either ignored or actually cited as evidence by adherents of the critical consensus.

The Establishment has no monopoly of conspiracy theories. Others, too, attribute violence to the role of infiltrators, or see the malign hand of some surreptitious extremist organization manipulating events, but only when it suits their purpose. The occurrence of racially motivated attacks on ethnic minorities was attributed, at least in part, to the influence of extremist neo-fascist organizations which are believed to promote their ideologies amongst the supporters of certain football teams (Home Office, 1981; Select Committee on Home Affairs, 1986). Similarly, the holding of a concert in the predominantly Asian district of Southall by a rock music group known to attract 'skinheads' with extreme right-wing political views was seen as a deliberately provocative act designed to instigate the riot that actually erupted (*Sunday Times*, 4 July 1981). The arson attack on the Asian-owned supermarket which occurred during the height of the Broadwater Farm riot was attributed by Lord Gifford and his panel (Gifford, 1986) to unidentified White racists, who apparently disappeared as stealthily as they arrived.[18] More sinister still were persistent accusations voiced by supporters of striking miners that picket-line violence was sometimes instigated or encouraged by members of the police Special Branch who infiltrated pickets and demonstrations (Coulter *et al.*, 1984; Reed and Adamson, 1985; McIlroy, 1985. Of course, the miners' strike itself was seen by some commentators as deliberately orchestrated by the Government, which not only prepared itself for the confrontation by building up coal stocks and the means of transporting them but also deployed troops dressed as police to control the picket-lines (Coulter *et al.*, 1984; Lloyd, 1985).

### 'Unprecedented disorder'?

Similar problems arise in respect of the historical argument that contemporary disorders are not unprecedented. Whilst literally true, this argument fails to recognize the changes that have occurred during the past century. 'Peterloo' occurred in the context of agitation for parliamentary reform; nineteenth-century rioters were almost exclusively disenfranchised and denied (by law) effective trade union representation; the suffragettes were seeking the extension of the franchise to women; unemployed workers during the 1930s were protesting about the conditions of poverty which they suffered. Those conditions can hardly be said to persist today. Parliament is now a democratic institution, and channels exist for its further reform by democratic means; the franchise is universal, and political participation is possible for all citizens; the trade unions are no longer an outlawed institution; and the welfare state prevents mass hunger and poverty on anything approaching the scale of the 1930s. This is not to deny that further change may not be desirable, or that countervailing changes might have undermined the progress that has been achieved. Some sections of the population have been actually — if not formally — excluded from legitimate political expression. Nevertheless, if we are invited to place current events in their historical perspective, then that perspective must not be partial. The modern 'mob' is *not* the direct parallel of its historical predecessors.

Nor does antiquity confer normality: the fact that the British have a history of rioting does not mean that contemporary riots are unremarkable. If it did, then there would be nothing unremarkable about the forceful suppression of riots either, for this is the other side of Britain's tumultuous tradition. As Dunning *et al.* (1987), observe, police frequently and liberally used their batons to break up disorderly crowds in the past, leaving many rioters nursing broken heads (see also, Morgan, 1987). Even that measure of official force represented a significant reduction in the scale of violence, since the alternative was often the use of the military who could, and sometimes did, open fire with live ammunition (Geary, 1985; Morgan, 1987). To refer to Britain 'drifting into a law and order society' (Hall, 1979) is absurd when viewed in its historical perspective, since the contemporary means of suppressing disorder are comparatively restrained.

However, applying the same 'historical perspective' to both sides of the 'tumultuous past' reveals the distortion of that approach. What direct comparisons between contemporary and past disorders obscure is the intervening trend. As Dunning *et al.* (1987) also demonstrate, throughout this century there has been a secular decline in disorder, which has only recently shown signs of reversing (see also, Geary, 1985). There are plentiful reasons, therefore, for observers to lament the return to scenes which represent a reminder of an unpleasant and long-forgotten past. Riot and its forcible suppression may not be literally 'unprecedented' in Britain, but it has declined markedly throughout the twentieth-century. The reversal of a process of de-escalation on both sides is surely a matter for regret, not to say alarm.

*Should all demands be incorporated?*

Whilst the critical consensus ridicules, as historically false, the claim that recent riots are 'unprecedented', it does not propose that recent events should be regarded with equanimity. It prescribes the lesson of history: that violence will only decline when excluded groups are incorporated within the political process. Of course, differences exist within the 'critical consensus' as to the extent of socio-political change that would be necessary to accommodate the demands of excluded groups. The most radical versions see nothing short of revolutionary social and political change as being necessary to achieve this goal, whilst less radical versions regard change as possible within the established political framework. What is common to both, however, is the conviction that forceful suppression of popular protest is not the solution.

This is a valid argument, at least up to a point. As mentioned earlier, it is undoubtedly true that the relative absence of civil disorder in Britain, when compared to many other countries, can be attributed to the historical success of the political system in incorporating groups and issues, most notably the working class. The pride of the British police in being able to maintain public order without recourse to protective equipment, tear-gas, and water cannon, was misplaced. It was less of a *policing* success and more of a *political* success. The British police did not possess the paraphernalia of riot control because they did not need it.

Valid though the argument is, it is so only up to a point. For the lesson of history is not that *all* excluded groups have been accommodated within the political process: some groups were, and remain, excluded. Religious bigotry and racism have been, more or less, stubbornly resisted by the political élite. In the past thirty years, racist language and racial discrimination have been progressively outlawed, thus effectively excluding certain issues, at least as expressed in particular ways, from the political agenda. The critical consensus frequently complains that resistance to racism has been less than wholehearted, often insufficiently vigorous, and frequently fuelled by unscrupulous motives. The response of successive governments to popular demands for increasingly stringent restrictions on Black and Asian immigration and the coupling of anti-discrimination legislation with such increasingly severe restrictions have been regarded, not as an accommodation of the political system to mass opinion, but as, at best, capitulation to racist sentiment. In taking this view, however, adherents of the critical consensus testify to the inapplicability of their own prescription. They do not wish to see the political system incorporate *all* groups and issues, only selected groups and issues.

Nor does it seem that the critical consensus is averse to the forcible suppression of dissent, only to the forcible suppression of *some* dissent. If groups like racists and religious bigots are to be excluded, and should those excluded groups then express their sense of injustice by the only means open to them, it would be the task of the police to control any such protest. It is unlikely that under these conditions proponents of the critical consensus would complain about the forcible suppression of any violent protest that arose. Indeed, when similar circumstances have occurred in the past, the complaint is that the police have not taken stronger action. Thus the British police are criticized for failing in the past adequately to protect ethnic minorities from racist crowds (Joshua and Wallace, 1983) and also for protecting fascist marchers during the 1930s (Jacobs, 1973; Manwaring-White, 1983; but see Stevenson, 1980). However, had the police during the 1930s done as their critics now wish they had done and sought to prevent fascist marches through Jewish areas, and had those fascists violently resisted such a move, then the police would have been required to use force to achieve this desirable goal.

On the other hand, when the police have forcefully defended minority groups there has been a deafening absence of condemnation from the critical consensus. For example, when the 'Troops Out' movement marched through Glasgow in the summer of 1984 and met violent resistance from loyalist sympathizers, forceful police action against these particular counter-demonstrators went without condemnation (*The Times*, 9 September 1984). It is also instructive to note that the actions of the RUC in controlling the violent Loyalist protests against the Anglo-Irish Agreement, which included the use of plastic baton rounds resulting in the death of one protester, has not been the object of criticism by advocates of the critical consensus. Nor were the RUC condemned when they took forcible action to prevent loyalist marchers processing through the Catholic enclaves of Castlewellan and Portadown in 1985 (Ryder, 1989).

The situation in Northern Ireland exposes another flaw in the prescription that all groups and issues should be incorporated into the political process — its utopianism.

Governments are simply incapable of dealing with the multitude of often mutually contradictory demands that different citizens make. The British Government's attempt to provide some modest accommodation of the aspirations of the nationalist minority has led to violent protest from members of the loyalist majority. In Britain itself the Government faces demands from Islamic fundamentalists for the extention of the blasphemy laws and the banning of Salman Rushdie's *The Satanic Verses*—demands which are vigorously opposed by secular intellectuals who demand 'freedom of expression'.

It is clearly utopian to suppose that any political system would be able to accommodate *all* articulated demands. Short of utopia, there are going to be occasions when the police will be required forcibly to suppress violent political protest. The prescription that the political system should be more responsive to citizen demands is one that is selectively applied. It amounts to little more than saying that government should be more responsive to specific groups. The issue is: who specifies the groups?

In sum, as an explanation of why, when, where, and amongst whom rioting and disorder occur, the critical consensus seems no more convincing that the Establishment 'riff–raff' theory it seeks to replace.

## Explanation or Justification?

As an explanation of crowd violence and prescription of how to respond to it, the critical consensus is fatally flawed. Neither the explanatory framework nor the prescriptions are applied consistently. But perhaps explaining the riots is not what the critical consensus sets out to achieve. Despite its pretensions to the contrary, the critical consensus might better be seen as justifying or excusing the riots, and apportioning blame and responsibility to groups other than the rioters. In short, it might be regarded, not as analysis, but as advocacy.

Stan Taylor (1984) has observed that there are three popular explanations of disorder, which reflect fundamentally divergent political views. The conservative regards disorder as simply an irrational eruption, indistinguishable from plain criminality. The liberal view is that disorder arises from deprivation and injustice which, unless remedied, will continue to provoke further outbreaks of disorder. The radical sees disorder as proto-revolutionary activity, arising from the contradictions inherent in late capitalism and its imminent demise. Thus, it is not only the conventional wisdom of Establishment spokesmen that can be seen as reflecting a political viewpoint; so too does the critical consensus which spans Taylor's 'liberal' and 'radical' categories.

However, the division of explanatory frameworks into 'conservative', 'liberal', and 'radical' is limited, for whilst it fits the contemporary debate about the disorders of the 1980s quite well, it is not generalizable. Liberals and radicals do not perceive *all* crowd disorder as either prompted by deprivation or proto-revolutionary. As noted above, racist militants receive no such empathetic consideration. Nor do conservatives regard all disorder as equally mindless: protests by the citizens of what conservatives regard as morally bankrupt regimes, such as those held in the name of democracy in Eastern Europe and China, are regarded as expressions of a genuine cause. Like liberals and radicals, conservatives attribute political intent selectively to those with whom they sympathize. It is not the source of the explanation which determines the form it takes, but the relationship between the source and the object (the disorderly crowd). Where the source approves of, or sympathizes with, the members of the crowd, the explanation offered will take the form of a justification or excuse, but where the source disapproves or does not sympathize with the crowd the explanation will condemn. Put simply, it comes down to whether one is for or against the group in question.

Such naked partisanship is obscured by the selective application of what purport to be generally applicable explanations of crowd disorder, namely, that which conceives disorder as the 'political expression of injustice'. By the selective labelling of a riotous crowd as sufferers of injustice, the latter come to be accorded the status of victims rather than villains. Seen from this perspective, the selectivity of the critical consensus is readily explicable. The task is not analysis but advocacy — to convince the reader that the group in question are victims. The methods employed are those of polemic disguised as scholarly discourse.

What were earlier identified as flaws in explanation can be seen to arise from the need to justify riotous behaviour, not explain it. Hence the reason for passing directly from the documentation of injustice to the occurrence of disorder, without pausing to explain the origin and nature of mobilizing beliefs, is to gain sympathy for rioters by changing their moral status. By dint of insistence that injustice is suffered and that grievances are justified, rioters become 'more sinned against, than sinning'. As advocacy, the critical consensus does not maintain a stance of agnosticism towards the inner-city violence of the 1980s. The claim that young Black people in inner-city areas suffer disadvantage, discrimination, and police harassment is treated, not as a belief, but as a fact. The task of analysis, then, is not simply to show how the belief mobilizes collective action, but becomes instead a quest to reveal the injustices which substantiate the justifications for the riots.

Once a violent crowd have become defined as 'victims', explanation of the causes of their action and prescriptions as to how to remedy the problem can be selectively applied. Despite appearances to the contrary, the critical consensus does not maintain that members of a violent crowd, *per se*, 'have reasons and need to be understood'. In fact, a tacit and arbitrarily presumptive distinction is drawn between 'victim' and 'non-victim' crowd violence, selectively justifying the former, whilst ignoring or condemning the latter.

In order to maintain the status of victim, advocates must surmount the obstacle that members of the crowd are frequently the initiators of violence and, therefore, vulnerable to categorization as 'aggressors'. If it can be convincingly shown that the crowd was provoked, however, blame and responsibility can be deflected elsewhere. This, rather than any explanatory purpose, is the function of concepts like 'flash-points' or 'precipitating incidents'. Whether or not Reiner is correct in saying that 'The true function of the "police atrocity" incidents, which trigger riots, is to legitimate the crowd's violence *in its own mind*' (1985c: 150; emphasis added), it *does* have the effect of 'legitimating the crowd's violence' in the minds of others.

Like the notion that rioters are suffering from injustice, the concept that violence is sparked by some incident shifts responsibility for the riot from participants to 'society' or the police. In D. Waddington, *et al.*'s, account, disorder is not the wilful product of crowd behaviour but always a *reaction* to the provocation of the police who alone are credited with 'precipitating' action. Thus it is not the miners kicking at the door of a closed pub, or youths spitting on a passing shopper, or miners noisily disturbing the neighbours of a club that are responsible for disorder; it is the police responding to these incidents who are to blame. As a statement of fact, it may well be true that police intervention is met by resistance, but that pays no heed to the fact that the police have a duty to intervene, if necessary by force, to achieve their lawful purpose. Ignoring the role of police as 'monopolists of non-negotiable force' accords them the same status as that of football fans violently reacting to the taunts of their rivals. Not surprisingly, it is then the police who almost invariably emerge as the instigators of disorder.

Equally, the insistence that riots are not caused by psychological processes, such as 'aggression–frustration', is dictated by the need to safeguard the blameless status of 'victims', which might otherwise become compromised if they are seen as acting irrationally. Likewise, 'victims' must be seen as authentically expressing their own grievances and aspirations, not acting as dupes of malevolent subversives or extremists. On the other hand, acts that might discredit the rioters, such as the looting and burning of an Asian-owned supermarket, is eagerly attributed by advocates to outside infiltrators (Gifford, 1986). When it comes to conspiracy theories, there is a simple polemical rule: victims do not conspire, they are only conspired against.

Moreover, the violent response to injustice and provocation can be made to appear 'normal' if placed in the appropriate context — hence the appeal to history. Likening contemporary rioters to the disenfranchised, impoverished, and ununionized of a previous era is an invitation to consider today's rioters as merely the latest addition to history's gallery of 'victims'. The rioters of the past are selected as clear examples of those who now, in retrospect, receive sympathy. The fact that, in the past, riots were also occasioned by ethnic, racial, or religious intolerance (Critchley, 1970) is ignored, since those who stoned and looted for these motives are not regarded, even in retrospect, as victims'. Yet, they, no less than their more acceptable counterparts, were availing themselves of the traditional means of expressing their grievances in the only way open to them. By selectively comparing contemporary rioters to earlier generations of 'victims', the impression is conveyed that the judgement of posterity will vindicate today's rioters as it has, in retrospect, vindicated their historical counterparts. It is argued that, far from being 'unprecedented', rioting has historically been the normal response of victims of social injustice. This argument then appears to lend credence to the prescription of accommodating the demands of contemporary rioters, for it was by incorporating their predecessors into Society as a whole that violence and disorder were reduced.

What we are offered by way of explanation is not peculiar to riotous or disorderly behaviour. It is simply the collective expression of the 'techniques of neutralization' (Sykes and Matza, 1957) often resorted to by individual delinquents. Indeed, there is a striking similarity between the arguments of the critical consensus and the various 'techniques of neutralization' identified by Sykes and Matza. Individual delinquents deny responsibility by claiming that they were compelled to act as they did by the circumstances in which they live — the equivalent of blaming the riots on social injustice. Delinquents also 'deny the victim' by 'transforming him into a person deserving injury', just as a 'racist society' or 'racist police' are seen as 'deserving injury' inflicted by a rioting crowd. Like the delinquent, the critical consensus condemns the condemners, transforming the victim (society or the police) into the wrongdoer — the perpetrator of injustice.

Very few have proposed that riots are not invariably intended to convey sober meaning and political lessons. Very few have considered the possibility that some riots may be modelled on the carnival or Saturnalia, that they may be 'fun'.   (Rock, 1981: 3)

This is not only because in the wake of such an unaccustomed event those who 'attach weight to ideas, intentionality and thoughtfulness' seek to eliminate ambiguity by reaching for some 'simple pattern' (ibid) — even if all this is also true. The 'sober meanings and political lessons' are attributed to rioters (but only to *some* of them), to establish their credentials as 'victims'. Victims do not riot for fun — that is the preserve of lager louts and football hooligans.

## The politics of discreditability

The view that the argument is polemical rather than analytical is supported by the manner in which the debate about such issues is conducted. In contrast to other areas of scholarly debate, in which ideas and evidence may be vigorously challenged and defended, debate about the causes of disorder pays less attention to the ideas and evidence in contention and more to the status of those who propose them. To use a soccer analogy, it is the man that is played rather than the ball! The conservative or Establishment case can easily be dismissed without attention to the details of the argument on the grounds that 'they would say that, wouldn't they'. However, when scepticism is entertained by academic commentators with impeccable left-wing credentials (Lea and Young, 1984), this provokes a vitriolic campaign of denigration designed to discredit what is plainly seen as a secular heresy (Scraton, 1985; Sim *et al.*, 1987; Gilroy, 1987). Either way, it is clear from the content and tone of the debate regarding such matters that it is not scholarly discourse but an exercise in the politics of discreditability.

The clearest example of the 'politics of discreditability' is to be found, not in connection with the inner-city riots, but in relation to the miners' strike of 1984–5. Although the debate that surrounded the strike was in many respects different from the reaction that greeted the inner-city rioters, the reaction to heretical explanations was much the same. The National Council for Civil Liberties established an 'independent' inquiry into the policing of the strike under the chairmanship of Professor Peter Wallington. The committee's interim report, published whilst the strike was still in progress, contained the passage: 'freedom not to take part in

a strike is as much a fundamental right as the right to strike'
(McCabe *et al.*, 1988: 5). The response of the NCCL's AGM
was to reject the interim report because it had 'exceeded its
terms of reference in commenting on the conduct of striking
and working miners and setting out civil liberties principles
which did not directly relate to the role of the police' (ibid. 5–
6). The inquiry panel had naïvely followed its remit to be
'independent' too literally. Their impeccably argued logic
equating the rights of strikers and strike-breakers (ibid. ch.
2), failed authoritatively to place strikers in the position of
being victims. In terms of the politics of explanation, the
AGM was correct: the interim report *was* 'damaging to the
miners' cause' (ibid. 6).

The issue here is not whether any given explanation of
disorder and its antecedents is true or not, but whether it has
the capacity to convince significant political actors irrespect-
ive of its objective merits. What the critical consensus
presents us with, therefore, is not an explanation of recent
disorder but a morality play in which the normal roles are
reversed. The 'victim' is the rioter and the 'villain' is the
police, government, and society in general.

### Conclusions: Riot Control or Stifling Dissent?

As characters in this morality play, police engaged in riot
control have the part of the ogre — to use Reiner's imagery
(1985*a*), they have the 'Darth Vader' part. In this role, the
police achieve several theatrical aims. First, they are, through
their alleged harassment and discrimination, *a* cause, if not
*the* cause, of the problem. Second, they confirm the 'victim'
status of the rioters, because the latter are pitted against the
formidable power of the former. The contest is uneven, and
this evokes sympathy for the 'underdog'. Third, they
prevent a rational solution to the problem being found, for if
the police were not a formidable obstacle, the politicians
would be obliged to listen to the grievances being expressed
by the powerless and they would have to respond. If the
police can credibly be portrayed as 'tooling up' to suppress
dissent, then even groups, like the hippies who form the

'Peace Convoy', can be represented as the hapless victims of an oppressive style that threatens us all (National Council for Civil Liberties, 1986).

The objection that developments in police public-order tactics and technology fail to address the 'real' causes of riot and may obstruct grievances being remedied is not, however, as indiscriminate as it is often presented as being. It is not the possession or use of these tactics and technology *per se* to which critics object, but their use against specific groups. Football hooligans, lager louts, racists, and Ulster loyalists are fair game, but ethnic-minority rioters, strikers, and those voicing radical and liberal protests against a Conservative Government are not. It is only in the latter instances that police action becomes 'the authoritarian suppression of dissent'. In the event of widespread racist violence against ethnic minorities, there is no doubt that those who now complain about the policing of public order would be anxious to see the police take effective and, if necessary, forceful action, because now the police are not playing the part of oppressive ogres but are the equivalent of the 7th Cavalry.

What the critical consensus singularly refuses to acknowledge is that riot control technology and tactics are a *means*, not an end. These means could be used to stifle legitimate dissent, but they can also be used, and have been used, to protect vulnerable minorities. To deny the police or security forces the means of suppressing disorder for fear that it will be misdirected against those whom the critics favour will also prevent the police taking effective action to protect those same favoured groups.

Since the critical consensus does not ultimately deny that the police should use force against *some* violent crowds, it is surely better that when they do so it should be effective and with adherence to the principles of 'minimum force'. The need for effective public-order tactics and weapons, and training in their use, cannot be wished away because of the abhorrence that any civilized person feels for the necessity occasionally to resort to violent means.

# PART IV

# Conclusions

# 8

# The Politics of Force

## Imagery and Reality

The complaint of the 'critical consensus', amongst others, is
that there has been an escalation in the weaponry and tactics
of the police. The armed PT17 'blue berets' and riot-clad
members of PSUs have replaced the amiable face of
traditional policing. The reality is not nearly so simple: the
authorities compromise tactical necessity in the name of
'public acceptability' and apparent escalation involves sometimes a reduction in the potential for injury.

The Home Office has shrunk from authorizing ammunition which is likely to have the most effective 'stopping
power', because Magnum hollow-point, Glaser safety slugs,
or THV bullets all inflict 'unacceptable' injuries. The
Metropolitan Police has been reluctant to deploy armed-
response vehicles, or even to issue personal weapons to
armed officers, for fear of giving the impression of a
routinely armed police. In the public-order sphere, the police
continue to rely upon the traditional methods of cordons
supplemented with charging into crowds, because to em-
brace fully the logic of dispersal would involve the unacceptable use of methods of aggressive mobility and weapons such
as irritant agents, water cannon, and baton rounds. The Home
Office has justified its reluctance to authorize the purchase of
an accurate and tactically sensible weapon, the ARWEN 37,
on the grounds of its intimidating appearance.

But compromising tactical efficiency in the name of public
acceptability does not always mean that the police are
constrained to use less force than would otherwise be
prudent. The shotgun is regarded as an acceptable weapon,
despite the fact that it causes multiple serious wounds, but a
carbine like the Heckler and Koch MP5 is highly controversial, even though it fires only pistol ammunition. Likewise,

the baton charge is publicly acceptable, but the use of less arbitrary and injurious irritant agents and baton rounds are not.

Whatever the tactical, legal, and moral advantages of using non-traditional methods, *realpolitik* dictates that their use will remain politically hazardous. As one senior officer put it, when addressing a course for public-order commanders, 'The first person to order the use of baton rounds had better have his bags packed — he will be doing a speaking tour of Europe!' Politically speaking, it is the image, rather than the reality, that is often more important. The *image* which officers equipped with sub-machine-guns or attired in riot gear convey makes them unacceptable. They are not the amiable bobby, but an alien and alienating force.

## 'Public acceptability'

The image of the amiable bobby, who policed public disorder by traditional methods and with good humour, is and always was a fiction; but fictions are important, for they are often the basis of legitimacy. Whether it is founded on fact or myth, the British police have succeeded in convincing articulate public opinion of their non-aggressive reputation. This they have achieved mainly through concern for their *appearance*. From its inception, the British police force has pursued a policy of *concealing* weaponry. The truncheon (itself an acceptable description of what would otherwise be described — as the *Oxford English Dictionary* describes it — as a 'cosh' or 'cudgel') was always carried out of sight. That tradition continues with uniformed armed officers carrying hand-guns beneath their uniform. The overt use of protective equipment and acquisition of riot control weaponry brings that reputation into question. If the police were to adopt irritant agents for dispersal and baton rounds for incapacitation, the danger is that their non-aggressive reputation would be destroyed.

This threat to the traditional basis of police legitimacy is undoubtedly a major restraining influence upon the use of such weapons. Whether or not the British people cherish traditional methods of public-order policing, there is little doubt that newspaper editors, Members of Parliament, and campaigners do, or at least pretend to.

## Unpalatable decisions

The devotion to the image of the traditional bobby, armed with nothing more than the law, has the advantage that it avoids the confronting of unpalatable decisions about *how much* force is justifiable in any particular circumstances. No civilized person relishes the decision to inflict upon others the very serious injuries that would be caused by, say, hollow-point bullets. The rational contemplation of such a thing is repugnant even when injury would only be inflicted in the most extreme situation. The focus of concern is the injury that the police will inflict upon another human being, rather than the harm that that person might otherwise inflict upon others.

The careful and rational assessment of how much force to use may appear callous, even bloodthirsty. Rational issues become lost in the midst of emotional reaction, as was plainly illustrated by the outraged response of politicians to the suggestion that the police should be issued with hollow-point ammunition. The Conservative MP Ivor Stanbrook reacted by saying, 'The suggestion is totally out of the question', and his Labour colleague Robin Corbett was quoted as saying, 'It is a shocking and outrageous suggestion' (Daily Telegraph, 19 August 1988).

## The irrationalism of force

The repugnance at inflicting injury does not fully explain the reluctance to contemplate rationally the use of force by the police. If it did, there would be eager acceptance of those measures designed to *reduce* the amount of injury inflicted when police do use force. In fact, proposals to adopt alternative measures designed to inflict less injury are greeted with almost as much antipathy as those which advocate the opposite. It seems that to discuss the use of force *at all* is repugnant.

The explanation of this attitude lies at the very heart of

liberal rationalism which has dominated intellectual thought since the Enlightenment. Liberalism assumes that human beings are amenable to rational persuasion: the only force that is needed is the force of argument. Compliance is thus obtained freely, rather than being coerced, and human dignity is maintained. The use of force, on the other hand, is *anti-rational*, since it secures compliance without regard to the rational merits of either party's case. Indeed, it is a primitive means of achieving compliance in which might replaces right. Thus the only justifiable position is the total avoidance of force. To discuss even using reduced force is unjustified, for *any* measure of force is to be deplored.

It is an irony, to say the least, that the consequence of this attitude is to perpetuate rationally indefensible weaponry and tactics on those occasions when force *is* used. Since the use of force is not rationally considered, but rejected out of hand, weaponry and tactics continue to be used which are *incompatible* with the very principle of 'minimum force' which liberals seek to uphold. The Heckler and Koch MP5 carbine is not deployed as an alternative to the shotgun only because of the emotions evoked by its appearance. The same goes for public-order policing: baton charging may be more injurious to individuals than alternatives such as irritant agents, but to acknowledge and act upon that fact demands the rational assessment of forcible suppression.

Instead of confronting these issues, it is more comforting to imagine that recourse to force itself is unnecessary. The emphasis shifts from the competing merits of different types of firearm, or from alternative tactics of forcible dispersal, to how best to negotiate with adversaries so as to avoid recourse to force. Whilst negotiation may offer an alternative (and obviously a preferred alternative) to the use of force in any situation, it is not an alternative to the rational contemplation of forcible options. For if negotiation fails and force is required, it is surely better that it be employed effectively and yet with the minimum of injury to all concerned.

## The Threat of Force

The willingness to use force, and the acquisition of effective means of doing so, has a wider significance. It symbolizes the relationship between the State and the citizen. Whilst few are concerned about suppressing rampaging gunmen or racist thugs, the State's capacity to suppress must always be viewed with suspicion. The more a State acquires the capacity to coerce, the less it may seek to persuade. These liberal fears are clearly articulated by Uglow (1988), whose ignorance about the facts to which he refers and whose tendentious interpretation of events reflects not only the emotional repugnance with which the use of force is viewed but also how this taints the assessment of policing as a whole.

The fact that such weapons are associated with authoritarian regimes whose police enjoy a fearsome reputation in their use of them serves only to reinforce anxiety. When British police officers are attired in riot gear, the habitual comment is that they look like Continental or colonial paramilitary police. It is precisely this kind of analogy that Northam (1988) seeks to draw: the public-order tactics now used in Britain are similar to those previously employed in the colonies, and this portends an analogous relationship between government and people — namely, repression.

The irony is that the tactics and technology of riot control employed by colonial and Continental police forces, not to mention the RUC, are arguably *more* consistent with the principle of minimum force than the much vaunted 'traditional' methods of the British police. The oppressive agents of the apartheid State have traditionally used a sjambok,[1] which is designed to inflict only superficial injuries, whereas the guardians of British democracy use a more formidable weapon capable of inflicting serious, possibly even fatal, injury. Yet it is the latter who are regarded as custodians of the 'minimum-force' tradition and the former who represent its antithesis.

Perhaps there is more than simple irony in this. The South African police are condemned not only because they actually do resort to force readily and without restraint, but also because the political system they defend is itself reprehensible. It is not simply *how* they go about defending the State from violent disorder that is at issue, but the fact that they defend the State at all, even if they did so with the utmost restraint. South Africa is not simply, or even mainly, a policing problem, but a political problem. If it were not a racist State, but a multi racial democracy, then vigorous police action against anyone seeking its forcible overthrow would be regarded with equanimity. It is not only *what* the police do that makes their actions offensive, but also on *whose behalf* they do it.

In contradistinction to such oppressive regimes, the traditional acceptance of the British bobby may have been the result less of the way in which policing was conducted and more of the political system's ability to avoid tensions arising which could lead to bloody confrontation. The incorporation of the working class into constitutional politics meant that the police were not called upon to repress the expression of grievances by force. When clashes did occur, it was easier for the police to be presented as defending a state which was itself defensible. Perhaps during the last quarter of the twentieth century the State has come to be seen as less defensible, and in defending it by force the police have shed their 'good-guy' image.

The liberal fear is that those in positions of power can shelter behind an effectively repressive police apparatus, immune to popular discontent. This is indeed a genuine danger, for the very existence of a coercive force capable of suppressing disorder could provide a bulwark against dissent behind which a malign or simply an insensitive government could act to the detriment of significant sections of the public. If the public ultimately cannot, through overt signs of dissent, demonstrate to government or powerful private corporations that their policies are unacceptable, then there may be no effective obstacle to tyranny, even if it is an elective tyranny.

The insidious nature of this threat is that it requires no conspiracy, for radical dissent (which is not the province of 'radicals' alone) will often breach the peace that the police are charged with maintaining. The more effectively the police are able to maintain order, the less attention government or powerful private individuals need pay to popular demands. This fear is not restricted to liberal or radical opinion; it is shared by the Police Federation's spokesman, Tony Judge, who said, in connection with the policing of the miners' strike of 1984–5:

It's not simply a case of the employer saying 'Well, I won't go to court because it might make things worse'. Surely at the back of Mr. MacGregor's mind is the knowledge that these policemen are there, that the pits of Nottinghamshire have been kept open and that people have been able to go to work almost solely because of the presence of the police force. And so it looks to us as if there has been a deliberate decision to use the police as the way of keeping the coal industry producing some coal. (Quoted in McIlroy, 1985: 105.)

## Two Meanings of 'Minimum Force'

What emerges from this discussion is that there are two quite separate senses in which the notion of 'minimum force' is understood and which at times become confused. The first is to equate 'minimum force' with the *absence* of forceful means of achieving compliance. The benign, non-aggressive, traditional bobby does not and cannot use force, and must secure compliance 'by consent'. Confronting the armed robber in the film *The Blue Lamp*, George Dixon walks towards his youthful adversary with his hand outstretched, asking, 'Give me the gun, son'. 'Dirty Harry' — Dixon's *alter ego* — points a gun and says, 'Go ahead, punk. Make my day'. The fact that Dixon is shot and killed, whilst Dirty Harry lives, merely testifies to the vulnerability of the bobby as opposed to the invincibility of 'alien' police. When the public glimpse armed police, what they see is not benign non-aggression but a display of potentially lethal force; incompatible with the image of the traditional bobby and more in keeping with alien policing methods. Such a display associates the British police with styles of policing which are not restrained and which achieve compliance by veiled threat.

This first use of the term 'minimum force' is not so much a doctrine or principle, but a matter of general *style*—benign non-aggression and the inability to act forcibly. This differs from the doctrine or principle of minimum force, which is not concerned with the absence or presence of forceful means as such, but with the *relative justification* for the use of force. In this second sense, 'minimum force' simply means using no more force than is necessary to achieve a lawful purpose. As discussed on several occasions throughout this book, it is possible to justify the use of quite extreme force in these terms.

### Tradition versus a 'Brave New World'

A police without *force* avoids the threat of repression, but by the same token it cannot protect. So the problem remains of how much or how little force to allow the police to use. Even the amiable bobby carries a truncheon in his pocket that he might use to strike a fellow citizen. His colleagues might ride horses that can be, and have been, used to charge demonstrators, or might use dogs that bite. Why, then, are these methods publicly acceptable when CS gas or baton rounds are not? This may have something to do with the traditional British love of domestic animals. But this disparity is not restricted to animals alone; other means of using force are also publicly acceptable despite their potential to inflict serious injury. Not only is the police officer's truncheon acceptable, the fact that it is his only weapon is often treated as testimony to his non-aggressive reputation. Yet the police truncheon is a weapon capable of inflicting serious injury. Its replacement with something similar to Mace—an aerosol canister administering an irritant gas—would actually *reduce* the likelihood of serious injury being inflicted, but tends to be regarded nevertheless as an *escalation* in the use of force.

What dogs, horses, and truncheons share in common is an established place in traditional policing — they are familiar. None of this may be welcome, but we feel that we know the limits of these weapons because they have been tried and tested. The use of gas, baton rounds, and water cannon are alien, and to sanction their use is to enter an unfamiliar and unpredictable world. Better the devil one knows than the devil one does not, even if the latter is probably less evil. And it should be clearly acknowledged that, as 'devils' go, the use of traditional weapons by the British police compares very favourably with the use of alternative weapons by other police forces.

Technological alternatives offer the prospect of effectiveness combined with less injury, but it is these weapons' effectiveness that changes the relationship between the police and the public. Without these weapons and tactics the police need not be feared, because they lack the capacity effectively to instil fear. Batons in police officers' hands can injure those unfortunate enough to be struck by them, but their coercive potential is inherently restricted by the arm's length of the police. The coercive capacity of the police is greatly expanded by weapons like irritant agents and water cannon, for whilst they may be less injurious to individuals, they enable a few police to coerce a much larger number of fellow citizens. With these weapons and tactics the public will be obliged to *trust* the police not to use their capacity gratuitously or malignly. For whether the enhanced capacity to maintain or restore public order by force is used in the public interest or not will then become a matter of choice.

The enhanced capacity to use coercive force to achieve lawful purposes pose more, not fewer, dilemmas for the police policy-maker and commander. Simply because ends *can* be achieved, by force if necessary, does not mean that they *must* be achieved. Whereas previously, the policy-maker and commander knew that his ability to achieve an objective by force was limited by an insufficiency of resources, he must now take a calculated decision as to when and under what circumstances to use those resources to achieve his goal.

The case of the illegal Sri Lankan immigrant, Virag Mendes, who sought sanctuary in a Manchester church for two years before being arrested and expelled (*The Times*, 19 January 1989), is a case in point. One could plainly argue that the police objective was entirely lawful: it was to arrest Mendes and prevent a breach of the peace resulting from protests by sympathizers that might accompany his arrest. A dawn raid using equipment to gain access to the locked room in which he resided, by sufficient officers to ensure that once arrested the fugitive could not be released by sympathizers, was the option taken, and it proved successful. The cost was a widespread view, articulated in the news media, that an excessive amount of force had been used to crack a rather small nut. The police reply, albeit rather muted, was that the large force of officers had been necessary to prevent any breach of the peace consequent upon the arrest of Mendes. However, supposing such a force had not been used and a crowd had rescued Mendes, would that have been as damaging to the police reputation as reports of fifty or more police demolishing a church door with sledge-hammers? In effect, any police commander has now to take essentially *political* decisions regarding the desirability of competing options, when not only the achievement of the lawful purpose is at issue but also the legitimacy of the police institution.

The challenge that now faces the police lies in establishing a new basis of public acceptability and legitimacy. When using force, they must be seen to act not only with the competence which is characteristic of professionalism but also with the exemplary standards of conduct that are its hallmark. This can only be achieved through practice, for exemplary standards must be demonstrated, not just an-nounced. The mistaken shooting of Stephen Waldorf and Mrs Groce, the killing of Blair Peach, and acts of indiscipline witnessed during the course of serious disorder all severely undermine public trust.

### 'Incident-Driven' Policy-Making

Why, then, not simply stop the process and even return to a situation where the capacity of the police to coerce was significantly less than it is today? Whilst this is an appealing prospect when viewed from one perspective, it is not cost-free. When a gunman rampages around a quite rural town or rioters burn, loot, and kill, there is the demand that the police should 'do something'. The 'something' to be done, of course, is to use force to stop the gunman or rioter.

These episodic but intense demands for the police to 'do something' combined with the contrary pressure to maintain public acceptability so as to create *incident-driven* policy-making. This, in turn, means that police use of force tends to be ineffective, potentially dangerous, and more of a threat to liberal values than it might otherwise be. The *ad hoc* response to 'yesterday's battle' poses the danger not only that police will be ill-equipped to fight 'tomorrow's battle' but that incremental steps will be taken in the heat of the moment that would have been avoided following careful rational appraisal.

It was noted earlier that, far from the police initiating the acquisition of riot control equipment, developments in public-order tactics and equipment has been in response to a series of incidents in which the police conspicuously failed effectively to maintain or restore order. From Saltley gates to Broadwater Farm, serious public disorder has been followed by enhancement of the police capability to use force. The reason for this reactive approach is that in the aftermath of such failures, public attention focuses upon the often neglected consequences of failing to come to terms with the unpalatable. Thus, refusing to equip police officers with baton guns avoids the possibility of inflicting severe injuries upon rioters, but when the Lozells Road is blazing and two Asian sub-postmasters lie burned to death by arsonists, the potential injury to rioters is regarded, temporarily, in a new light.

Incident-driven policy-making means that the rioter, gunman, or terrorist 'states the case', by his actions, for using greater force. The emotional response is momentarily reversed, from concern about the injury that police may cause to outrage at what has happened, and public opinion is prepared to countenance resort to weapons and tactics necessary to prevent any recurrence of such an event. Prior to the Hungerford massacre, the disclosure that some police forces operated 'armed-response vehicles' was greeted with expressions of concern; afterwards, the widespread deployment of such vehicles was followed by a deafening silence — tacitly accepted as a regrettable necessity.

However, the grave disadvantage of reactive policy-making is that it allows rioters, gunmen, and terrorists to dictate the direction of policy. Policy formation becomes *ad hoc* and retrospective. Even a review as thorough as that conducted by the Metropolitan Police in the aftermath of the Brixton and Broadwater Farm riots of 1985 is directed to ensuring that past mistakes are not repeated. Whilst learning from experience is obviously necessary, it is also necessary to anticipate the future — in the terms used by some defence analysts, to 'think the unthinkable'. However, since rioters, gunmen, and terrorists have yet to realise the 'unthinkable' case by their 'unthinkable' actions, this kind of anticipation challenges public acceptability. As a result, the innocent are left, literally, as hostages to fortune.

Danger to the public does not only arise because the police are unable effectively to counter the threat of the gunman or rioter; there is also the threat posed by police inability to use force effectively. The 'endearing incompetence' (Greenwood, 1979) which the police traditionally displayed in their use of firearms and quelling public disorder also represented a threat to innocent people. Blair Peach and Stephen Waldorf were both victims of the less than endearing incompetence of traditional methods. In the aftermath of these respective disasters, the police took steps to correct their procedures, which inevitably involved increased professionalism. However, it was 'incident-driven' — it had to be, because rational appraisal of how to use force has to be avoided for fear of provoking an adverse public response.

Reacting to past events also contains the danger of 'over-correction', for only the most extreme incidents will present the window of opportunity in which change can be introduced. The very extremity of what has occurred — the Hungerford massacre or Broadwater Farm riot — allows an equally extreme response to go unquestioned. Thus, 'incident-driven' policy-making is dictated by extremes and may lead to a 'drift' towards extreme methods. Paradoxically, the desire to retain tradition and the reluctance to appraise change rationally conspires to undermine traditional methods.

## The Politics of Forcible Policing

How can the twin concerns of protection without oppression be reconciled? Hiding behind a wall of secrecy is counter-productive, for it only fuels anxiety, as the controversy surrounding the ACPO *Tactical Options Manual* illustrates. If there is to be public discussion of these issues and if anyone is to 'think the unthinkable' and take hard decisions regarding weaponry and tactics, the liberal position is that it should be the elected representatives of the citizens against some of whom those weapons and tactics may subsequently be used.

There seem to be two assumptions underlying this prescription: on the one hand, constitutional propriety and, on the other, the expectation that elected representatives would act with more restraint than unelected police policy-makers. From the perspective of constitutional propriety, it might be argued that 'policing by consent' entails that public agreement should be sought for policing policies via elected representatives, not imposed by unelected officials. One of the main planks in Northam's (1988) critique of the ACPO manual is that it has been published secretly.

On the other hand, political control over policy, weapons, and tactics could create the very conditions of authoritarian State oppression that liberal opinion wishes to avoid. An unpopular government could dictate that the police should use more aggressive tactics against those voicing dissent. It was alleged that this is exactly what the Thatcher Government did during the 1984–5 miners' strike (Fine and Millar, 1985). There seems no reason to suppose that a government that possessed the constitutional power to instruct the police overtly would retreat from doing so, any more than Mrs Thatcher's Government shrank from covertly using what power and influence it had. If dissidents were themselves an unpopular minority, repression might be endorsed by a majority of the electorate and the 'tyranny of the majority' could become tyrannical indeed. One lesson to be drawn from Northern Ireland is that prior to 1970 policing was both controlled by popularly elected representatives and repressive towards the nationalist minority (Ryder, 1989).

The belief that elected governments would show greater restraint seems demonstrably false: politicians in other liberal democracies do not show any disinclination to authorize extremely forceful weapons and tactics. These politically controlled police systems, which include paramilitary riot police and routinely armed officers, far from automatically springing to mind as exemplars of the use of minimum force, are often held up as a warning as to what may happen in Britain. Nor is there any reason to believe that Britain would be immune to what has occurred elsewhere. There seems precious little political capital in being seen as 'soft on crime'. Many of those who now prescribe the political control of the police also lament the 'law and order' campaign waged by the

Conservative Party as part of their successful 1979 general election manifesto.

Abuse of political power might be prevented by two frequently proffered constitutional mechanisms. First, elected representatives might be allowed only to decide upon the broad policy of weaponry and tactics, leaving the police to employ them in particular situations in accordance with the law. The use of firearms and public-order policing are, on the face of it, prime candidates for the political control of policy, for they are unusually policy-orientated. Unlike the vast majority of police work, these two areas are governed by detailed manuals of instruction and guidance which stipulate the range of suitable weaponry and permissible tactics. There *is* a policy on the use of firearms and public-order policing; what critics object to is that it is secretly made by unelected officials (Northam, 1988; Morgan, 1987). Elected representatives are constitutionally competent, it is argued, to decide upon the range of options which the police should be allowed, for they are the best arbiters of what is and is not 'publicly acceptable'. It would then be left to the police to decide upon the appropriateness of any particular option to employ in given circumstances. For example, elected representatives might decide that the police should or should not have tactics for combating gunmen firing upon them during the course of a riot. The operational police commander would still have the discretion to employ any of the tactics that had been approved if his officers came under fire.

Such a division of labour has distinct advantages for the police, for if tactics are ineffective, responsibility could be laid squarely where it belongs. For example, if police are denied the option of effectively neutralizing a sniper during a riot, their only alternative would be to withdraw and leave the area to the mercy of the rioters. There are also problems with this distinction between policy and operational implementation. The first has already been noted: an unpopular government could equip its police for repression and then insist that 'the peace' be maintained, thus circumventing constitutional constraints. The second is that a police force without self-imposed restraint might feel at greater liberty to use options approved by elected representatives to the full.

For example, if in these circumstances CS smoke is approved for use in public disorder, then officers might feel no hesitation in using it, whereas they now approach such an eventuality with trepidation. Either way, a possible consequence of granting elected representatives the right to determine policy might encourage a greater and more oppressive use of force by police, not the opposite.

A means of restraining such abuses of power, favoured by many who argue for greater political control, is through the law. A Bill of Rights entrenching the freedoms and liberties of the citizen might prevent the police being used in a repressive capacity even if they possessed coercive technology. The most conspicuous exemplar of such an approach does not inspire confidence that it would prove effective. The US Bill of Rights did not prevent the Chicago Police and National Guard from using excessive force upon demonstrators at the 1968 Democratic Party Convention, and being congratulated for doing so by Mayor Daley (Walker, 1968). Nor did the Constitution stop over 200 people being killed by law enforcement personnel during the 'long hot summers' of the 1960s (Kerner, 1968). Two hundred years after the 'fleeing-felon' justification was abandoned in Britain, it continues in only slightly modified form in America.[2]

## Judicial Review

The attraction of a Bill of Rights is that it offers independent public scrutiny of official actions. Its weakness is that it can only react to cases brought by citizens who feel a wrong has been done to them; it cannot easily *initiate* scrutiny of official actions. A more interventionist mechanism would seem appropriate if public confidence is to be restored and maintained. Perhaps such a mechanism is gradually evolving: the practice of automatically referring *all* shooting incidents to the Police Complaints Authority attempts to reassure the public that *any* use of firearms is justified without the need for wrongdoing to be alleged. By contrast, there is a hiatus following incidents of serious public disorder in which no authoritative response is made to public concern about police tactics. This hiatus is often filled by self-styled 'committees of inquiry' established by local authorities or by private campaigning organizations. Failing to secure the co-operation of the police and Home Office, these inquiries succeed only in providing a one-sided account which usually does further damage to the police reputation.

On the two occasions when judicial inquiries into incidents of serious public disorder have been held under the Police Act 1964, both chaired by Lord Scarman, this has provided reassurance either that police acted properly or, if they did not, that improprieties are remedied. Both the Red Lion Square inquiry of 1974 and the Brixton inquiry of 1981 allowed an informed, balanced, and authoritative version of events to be established. This was not only in the general public interest, but also to the advantage of the police, for, whilst the latter did not always appear in the best light, one-sided and tendentious accounts of what happened did not gain widespread acceptance. Thus, despite efforts to the contrary (Gilbert, 1975; Ward, 1987), the death of Kevin Gately at Red Lion Square did not come to symbolize 'police violence' as did the death of Blair Peach. The reason for this was simply that Scarman was able to interrogate the police evidence and authoritatively satisfy himself that Gately had not come into contact with police; whereas allegations made in the wake of the Southall disorders of 1979 went unanswered by the police and without independent adjudication. On the other hand, both inquiries identified errors of policy and its implementation, causing corrective action to be taken.

More valuable still would be the opportunity to hold the police *corporately* accountable to law. The reality of public-order policing and many armed operations is that the police act, not as individuals, but as a corporate entity. Often public anxieties are aroused less by the loss of control on the part of an individual officer and more by how that officer came to find himself in conditions in which he lost control. Nor are public anxieties limited to questions regarding the lawfulness of police conduct. What also causes concern is whether police action was prudent, competent, and restrained in the use of force. These are wider considerations that a judicial inquiry can examine. Perhaps legislation which might grant the police much-needed powers of dispersal should include provisions for an automatic inquiry each time such a power is used; if it were used repeatedly in a continuing situation, the inquiry could examine the whole policing operation.

## Clarity in the law

Judicial or quasi-judicial inquiries would usefully *supplement* the law, but they cannot replace the need to place necessary and proper police action clearly within the law. Credible allegations that the police have acted unlawfully, even when the individual wrongdoers cannot be identified, are bound to have the most damaging impact upon public acceptability. It is, therefore, particularly unfortunate that in using force the police seem to be placed within a legal grey area.

Since the police already impose more rigorous standards upon themselves when using firearms than the law seems to allow, there is every reason to incorporate those guidelines into law. The legal fog that surrounds the use of force to disperse violently disorderly crowds does neither the police nor the citizen any service, and it is clearly time to provide a statutory authority for crowd dispersal.

## The Ambivalent Force

The use of force goes to the very heart of policing. As 'monopolists of force in civil society' (Bittner, 1970), the police stand apart from their fellow citizens. On the one hand, they are protectors, empowered to defend individual liberty from being impaired by criminal behaviour. On the other, in using force, if necessary, to achieve this desirable end, they employ means which if used by anyone else would be unacceptable. Public attitudes are correspondingly ambivalent: we want the police to have sufficient force to protect us, but not to use it oppressively. When force is used, we want it to be used competently, but we distrust and fear those who are experts in its use.

Police use of force will remain inherently controversial, for, as Weber remarked, those who use power and force 'contract with diabolical powers' (Gerth and Mills, 1948).

# APPENDIX A

# Police Firearms: Policy, Training, and Weaponry

## Formal Policy: Containment not Confrontation

The media-inspired image of the policing of armed incidents seems to be that of police kicking down a door, yelling 'Freeze!', and exchanging shots with armed professional villains or terrorists. The reality, fortunately, is much more low-key than this image suggests. There will be occasions when armed officers *do* confront armed villains, but the emphasis is upon the avoidance of such a confrontation. The aim is to contain the armed suspect and seek his peaceful surrender. In this way the safety of the public, the police, and, last but by no means least, the armed suspect is maintained. Only if the safety of an innocent person or the overwhelming need to secure easily destroyed and vital evidence is likely to be jeopardized by containment will the police confront the armed person. For example, if there were good reason to believe that an innocent hostage was about to be seriously harmed, then police would be obliged to take forcible action to eliminate the threat.

The 'containment' of armed persons is achieved by establishing two cordons: an inner cordon, or 'cover group', of armed officers who may be needed to engage the armed person if he attempts to escape, and an outer cordon, or 'perimeter group', of usually unarmed officers who keep bystanders away from the scene. Officers arriving at the location do so by a prearranged route and assemble at a rendezvous out of range of the armed person.

Once the situation has been contained, officers will normally seek to make contact with the person, most often by telephoning the address or by hailing him. They will then endeavour to arrange his peaceful surrender. In extreme circumstances officers may storm the premises as a 'raid group'. If no contact is established and there is no sign of life for many hours, officers may enter and search the premises. This is usually a slow, quiet, and painstaking process, whereby a team of officers enters the building and, with each covering the other, search every room systematically. Devices such as mirrors fixed to extendable arms are used to peer into rooms and behind obstructions. This cautious and methodical approach is the very antithesis of media portrayals.

Confrontation is anticipated in two types of situation. First, 'forced entry' into a building in which a suspected armed person is located is the method of last resort. Except in the most unusual circumstances it is left to the élite specialist officers of the tactical firearms unit, PT17. This unit contains eighty-two officers, most of whom spend most of their time as firearms instructors, but who can be deployed in an operational role if the situation demands their expertise. The second situation in which a confrontation may occur is the interception of suspected armed criminals in the course of committing a crime, most commonly armed robbers. This will normally occur only when police have insufficient information or evidence to arrest at some other time and place. Under these circumstances, the police conceal themselves and await the arrival of the suspects, who are then confronted and challenged. Like 'forced entry', this type of operation places officers in the position of having to make 'shoot/no shoot' decisions. Depending upon the evaluation of the likely threat posed by the suspects, this task may be undertaken by either Level I or Level II officers from PT17, by one of the 'central squads' such as the Robbery Squad or Anti-Terrorist Squad (all of whom include officers authorized to carry firearms), or by divisional officers authorized to carry firearms.

In sum, the policy of the Metropolitan Police, reflecting that of the Home Office and the advice of the Association of Chief Police Officers, is one of systematic caution.

## The Organization of Armed Police

Since the review which accompanied the Report of the Home Office Working Party (1986), armed police in London have been organized into a three-tiered hierarchy: in ascending order of expertise, AFOs, Level II, and Level I.

The basic and broadest tier consists of Authorized Firearms Officers, or divisional AFOs, as they are widely known. They are the officers who are most commonly authorized to carry a gun, and provide the initial response to most armed incidents. The AFO will normally be a uniformed patrol officer working on division, and will be unarmed for much the greatest part of the time. In the event of an armed incident, for example, a suspected armed hostage-taking, this officer will receive authorization to draw a firearm by a senior officer of commander rank (or his deputy) and be deployed to the scene. The gun will be obtained from a station at which

'
weapons are held, and the AFO will only be allowed to draw the weapon for which he is currently authorized (that is, the weapon he has been trained to use and in the use of which he has been reclassified as proficient within the past three months). When the incident is over, he will return the gun to the station from which it came and continue with his routine police work.

Prior to the Home Office Working Party Report (1986) which followed the shooting of Mrs Groce, some divisional CID officers were also AFOs, but this has been discontinued. A few plain-clothes officers still remain AFOs, principally detectives working on central squads such as the Robbery Squad and Anti-Terrorist Squad, who, because of the nature of their work, are likely to encounter armed criminals. Various other specialist squads and departments also contain AFOs; sometimes being an AFO is a requirement for membership of such a squad. Perhaps the largest of these is the Royalty and Diplomatic Protection Department, whose members provide both uniformed protection of sensitive locations and plain-clothes bodyguards to high-risk royalty, diplomats, and ministers of the Crown. The Special Escort Group, who provide escorts for high-risk persons such as State dignitaries, terrorist prisoners, and high-risk consignments are also usually AFOs. Perhaps the most conspicuous armed officers are members of the Security Section at Heathrow airport, whose task it is to protect the travelling public from armed attack by terrorists. It is selected members of this group who carry the Heckler and Koch MP5 carbine; some also carry the Browning self-loading pistol. Those qualified to carry these more 'exotic' firearms receive additional training, and must requalify more frequently than other AFOs who are authorized only to carry revolvers.

A recent addition to the organizational structure has been to further strengthen the role of the Force Firearms Unit. This unit has always provided firearms instructors to act in an operational capacity when the situation demanded their specialist expertise. These instructors retain this role, but in addition another stratum of expertise has been introduced in the guise of Level II officers. These consist of three groups of six constables and a sergeant (a Level I instructor) who are based at the headquarters of the Force Firearms Unit and respond to incidents which demand greater expertise than that possessed by AFOs. Level II officers are more highly trained, practise regularly and work as a team in a way that officers committed to other duties find impossible. They will normally execute the slow search of premises and supervise the peaceful surrender of armed suspects. AFOs normally provide the initial response to an incident, and constitute the 'cover group', but Level

II officers will then take over. Level II will also take over the task of providing armed support for raids on premises. At the time Level II teams were introduced, it was intended that the plain-clothes central squads would have available two teams of officers trained to the Level II standard, but this policy was not implemented owing to manpower constraints. However, the success of the Level II teams seems likely to lead to their numbers being expanded and a team located on each of the force's eight territorial areas, thereby assuming many of the responsibilities still shouldered by divisional AFOs. In particular, it seems likely that they will provide the crews of armed-response vehicles which will in future provide an immediate mobile response to any armed incident. This will continue the trend, begun after the Waldorf shooting, of relying upon fewer, better-trained specialists in armed policing.

Level I teams deal with incidents the demands of which exceed the expertise of and equipment available to Level II officers. They are trained not only to use the more exotic firearms and equipment such as night-vision goggles but also to gain rapid entry to rescue hostages. Many of the tactics and much of their equipment is copied from the SAS and, indeed, when deployed in their operational cover-alls, wearing respirators, and carrying sub-machine-guns, they could easily be mistaken for SAS soldiers.

Aside from this hierarchy, there are 'force riflemen' who, like AFOs, undertake unarmed patrol duties for most of their time. If an incident or event occurs where it is thought necessary to provide long-range cover by the use of rifles with telescopic sights, then it is these officers who are called upon. It was they who featured prominently in the BBC TV documentary 'The Queen's Peace' (*Police*, November 1986).

In addition to the armed officers who contain a situation, there will often be 'negotiators' present at any hostage or barricade situation. These are officers, usually of fairly senior rank, who are normally engaged upon other duties. When a hostage-taking incident occurs, it is their function to establish contact with the hostage-takers and negotiate a peaceful conclusion to the episode. They will often spend long periods on the telephone patiently talking and listening to the hostage-taker and trying to persuade him to release his hostages. They are kept isolated from the rest of the officers engaged on the operation, so that they cannot be influenced by what others are doing, or, more importantly, inadvertently disclose what might be about to occur. Information flows to and fro from the negotiators' 'cell' to those in command, and negotiators will organize such things as the provision of refreshments or medicines, if it is thought necessary either to alleviate distress or to establish good faith. However, the basic principle is that the hostage-taker will receive no more than a sympathetic ear.

Another 'back-room' function performed at a hostage-taking or barricade situation is the maintenance of a minute-by-minute log of events. A firearms trained officer will seek first to make a plan of the building, or situation of the car, aircraft, or boat, depending on the circumstances. Remote from the danger of the immediate environs of the armed suspect, this officer must be able to construct his plan solely by radio communication. AFOs are instructed in how to do this using a common system of notation. The officer maintaining the log can then try to assemble the various reports of movement, noise, and so forth, so as to allow the commanding officer to form an assessment of the total situation. For example, it is obviously vital to know whether there is one or more (and if so how many) hostage-takers and hostages. The number of either hostage-takers or hostages may not be apparent to individual officers containing the situation, who only see part of the whole. Only by piecing together their respective observations is it possible to build a complete picture. In addition, inquiries may be made of neighbours and witnesses (including released hostages) which may yield important information about the number of people involved, their state of mind, the layout of the building, and so on. In the event that officers may have to enter the premises, it is obviously useful to have a clear idea of the interior plan of a building. Therefore, if the hostage situation has occurred in a row of houses all of which are alike, the raid or search group may visit another house to see what they are likely to encounter and decide how they will tackle it.

Last but by no means least is the officer in command of the operation. The rank of this officer may vary with the severity of the incident and at different stages of it. Initially, it may be an ordinary constable, who may then be replaced by officers of increasingly senior rank. Almost invariably, however, it will not be a specialist armed officer, such as a member of PT17. The latter provide a specialist service for either territorial divisions or squads. It is the senior officers of either the division or the squad who may have to take the most fateful decisions.

## Conclusion

Official policy and formal organization have developed over recent years in response to the need for more frequent armed operations.

The official policy (see Greenwood, 1979) emphasizes safety and caution. The aim is not to shoot it out with a suspected gunman, but to contain him and persuade him to surrender. The officers who are responsible for implementing this policy have become fewer and more highly specialized. They are now organized into a hierarchial structure in which AFOs are normally expected only to provide the initial response and containment. More demanding tasks are intended to be reserved for full-time armed officers of either Level I or Level II standard.

## Weaponry

Firearms for police use need to achieve a variety of goals: they must be easily carried for long periods; they must sometimes be kept concealed; they should be able to be used at a variety of ranges; and they must, of course, be reliable. Different types of weapon satisfy different needs: the hand-gun is easily carried and concealed, but is a relatively short-range weapon. Shotguns and carbines are intermediate-range weapons, but cannot be concealed. Rifles are long-range weapons unsuitable for many types of operation in congested urban areas.

### Revolvers

The basic weapon which AFOs are authorized to carry is the revolver. This is a readily concealed, easy to use, and versatile weapon for use at close range, appropriate for AFOs to carry when needed. The Home Office guidelines state that the revolver should be capable of firing .38-in. special + P ammunition which is of the 'semi-wadcutter, semi-jacketed' variety (that is, the bullet's nose is flattened, rather than dome-shaped, and only partially enclosed in a hard metal sheath designed to retain its integrity once it strikes the body). Individual forces are left free to decide which makes of weapon and ammunition to purchase. The Metropolitan Police, in company with most other forces, have adopted the Smith and Wesson Model 10 as their standard issue firearm. This revolver has a 4-in. heavy barrel and holds six rounds in the cylinder. Metropolitan Police officers engaged in regular plain-clothes duties are issued with the Smith and Wesson Model 64, which is a stainless-steel variant of the Model 10 with a 2-in. barrel.

In most instances, these guns are held in locked safes at police stations and issued to officers as and when necessary. Obviously, officers who carry a firearm regularly, for example, on protection duty, will normally be issued with the same weapon each time they report for work. However, only members of Level II teams and of a very few other specialist squads are issued with a revolver that they and they alone use.

### Self-loading pistols

Apart from revolvers, the other type of hand-gun is the self-loading pistol, sometimes misleadingly described as an 'automatic' or 'semi-automatic' pistol — misleadingly, because, whereas an 'automatic' weapon of any kind continues to fire repeatedly whilst the trigger is depressed, a self-loading weapon fires just one shot with each depression of the trigger. The confusion arises from the fact that self-loading and automatic weapons are both magazine-fed, that is, the rounds are held in a magazine attached to the weapon and fed into the breech mechanism one at a time.

In recent years the Metropolitan Police have used three makes of self-loading pistol, the Walther PP, the Browning Hi-Power, and, most recently, the Glock 17, all of which fire 9-mm ammunition. The Walther was discontinued after the attempted assassination of Princess Anne when the gun carried by her protection officer jammed (see p. 15). The Metropolitan Police had carried a small stock of Brownings since the mid–1960s to arm officers escorting extremely high-value loads, such as bullion, and in the mid–1970s the decision was taken also to arm officers of the Force Firearms Unit with this weapon in response to the growth of terrorist activity. It was felt that, whereas armed encounters with criminals tended to involve a limited exchange of fire, that between terrorists and police might entail a prolonged exchange. The Browning carries up to thirteen rounds in its magazine (hence the manu-facturer's description 'Hi-Power'), as compared to the seven rounds carried by the Walther, and six rounds carried by the Model 10 revolver; it therefore offers greater fire-power. Even greater fire-power is afforded by the newly introduced Glock 17, which carries a maximum of seventeen rounds in the magazine and one in the breech, and is currently issued only to Level I officers. Both the Browning and Glock fire 9-mm parabellum ammunition of either standard military, 108-grain, fully jacketed, round-nosed design or 95-grain, semi-wadcutter semi-jacketed design.

Self-loading pistols operate in the following way: rounds are stacked in a magazine under tension from a spring at the magazine's base. When a round is fired, the recoil is used to force the slide back, which causes the spent cartridge case to be ejected and pushes the hammer into the single-action position. As the slide returns to its initial position under the pressure of a spring, the round located at the top of the magazine is pushed up a ramp and into the breech ready to fire. Despite its evident complexity, this mechanism is operated with great speed and allows this type of weapon to be fired very rapidly — as fast as the trigger can be depressed.

*Holsters*

Except for officers at Heathrow airport, who carry the Heckler and Koch MP5 carbine overtly and are allowed also to display their hand-gun, all hand-guns issued to Metropolitan Police officers are carried covertly on the hip. Shoulder holsters are rarely used because, when drawing a gun from this type of holster, the gun is initially pointing to the rear, away from the target (and therefore contrary to one of the safety rules), and as the gun is then swung in an arc towards the target this has the disadvantage that either a premature or late shot will be fired at or about torso height, missing the target but endangering others. It is, in fact, difficult to swing a gun laterally onto a target for two reasons: first the width of the torso is less than its height so that if the gun remains in motion there is less opportunity to hit the target. Second, swinging the gun imparts lateral momentum which is difficult to arrest once the gun is pointing at the target.

Thus, police officers almost universally use a hip holster, so that when they are drawing and aiming their gun, it is always pointing either at the floor in front of the person aimed at or in his direction. If the person is missed, the shot will either strike the floor or fly over the person's head, rather than be fired at torso height (Greenwood, 1966). This is obviously less dangerous to innocent bystanders. It is also more difficult to overswing the gun when moving through a vertical as opposed to a horizontal arc. Moreover, since the torso is longer than its width, there is a greater likelihood that the shot fired will actually hit the person, if not the torso.

Like the guns that are used, holsters are officially issued and officers are not permitted to use any other. The basic holster does not have a flap covering the butt of the gun, which remains open and is secured by a 'thumb-break' strap. When the butt is held the thumb pushes against a press stud, which springs open, allowing the gun to be drawn rapidly. For those occasions where it is essential that guns should be carried as covertly as possible, there is a 'pancake' holster which is moulded to the curvature of the body and thus minimizes the bulge beneath clothing. The Glock is also supplied with a special plastic holster that fits onto a normal trouser belt and allows the weapon to be worn with normal civilian clothes. Officers who must carry a gun whilst in shirt-sleeves are issued with a holster that fits inside the trouser pocket, into which the gun is then placed.

*Sub-machine-guns and carbines*

Perhaps the most controversial weapon now supplied to police is the sub-machine-gun. The Stirling Mk.IV 9-mm L2A3 machine-gun has been carried covertly on board vehicles at Gatwick airport since the mid–1970s, and permission was granted for sub-machine-guns to be purchased for the use of the Force Firearms Unit in 1977. However, they came to public attention with the visit of President Reagan in 1984, when it was announced that twelve Heckler and Koch MP5K sub-machine-guns were to be purchased for protection officers. Then, in the wake of the terrorist attacks on Rome and Vienna airports in December 1985, it was decided to arm officers at Heathrow airport with the single-shot version of the Heckler and Koch MP5. Until 1989 these weapons were only carried with the express permission of the Home Secretary, from whom authorization had to be obtained each time the Heckler and Koch MP5 was carried for operational purposes; such authorization was granted on a monthly basis to officers carrying the Heckler and Koch MP5 at Heathrow airport.

Gradually the MP5 has become more widely and readily available. Certain officers on diplomatic, royalty, and ministerial protection duty now routinely carry it; so too do officers in the Special Escort Group, who previously were required to rely upon the overburdened Level I firearms teams to provide additional armed support when high-security prisoners had to be transported. Authorization has also been granted for all Level I and Level II teams to carry the weapon for operational purposes, and the monthly renewal of authority for officers at Heathrow is no longer necessary. Special authorization is still required for protection officers to carry the MP5K.

The Heckler and Koch MP5 fires a 9-mm parabellum round, identical to that fired by self-loading pistols. Essentially, the mechanism by which it operates is also the same as that of a self-loading pistol. However, there is a distinction between this and some other makes of weapon, in that the Heckler and Koch MP5 fires in a 'closed-bolt' not 'open-bolt' mode. This means that, when the Heckler and Koch MP5 is fired, the recoil mechanism ejects the spent cartridge, opens the firing mechanism, and places another round in the breech ready to fire. When the trigger is depressed, the firing-pin strikes the bullet and fires it. The open-bolt mechanism, by contrast, does not place a round into the breech until the trigger is depressed, whereupon the round is pushed into the breech and fired in a single movement. Instructors maintain that the open-bolt mechanism causes the weapon to move slightly, making it less accurate; a claim implicitly acknowledged by other manufacturers of sub-machine-guns, such as Stirling and Uzi, who have now developed 'closed-bolt' carbines for police use.

The Heckler and Koch MP5 is capable of automatic fire, but can also be fired in single-shot mode, and some models also have the option of three-round bursts. The advantage of using this weapon in single-shot mode is that it affords greater accuracy over longer distances than can be achieved with a revolver. Its shoulder stock and two-handed grip, together with its 8-in. barrel, means that it is accurate up to a hundred metres, compared to a maximum effective range of fifty metres for hand-guns (itself considered hopelessly optimistic by many). Its magazine of thirty rounds, with a second magazine carried in a separate holster on the hip, also offers considerable fire-power in a sustained gun-fight with terrorists. At the same time, it is relatively light to carry, on a strap which holds it high across the chest in what is called the 'high port' position. From this position the gun is easily and quickly aimed and fired from the shoulder.

It was in order to provide fire-power that the Heckler and Koch MP5K (that is, the shorter version with the twin pistol grips and no shoulder stock) was purchased for use by some protection officers. Like their colleagues at Heathrow, they are trained mainly to fire the gun in single-shot mode, but, unlike officers at Heathrow, they retain the option of automatic fire. Unlike the officers at Heathrow, they do not carry this weapon overtly. It is carried inside the jacket on a shoulder strap. If needed, the gun is held in both hands and pushed away from the body against the shoulder strap, thus giving it stability. The eighteen-round magazine is supplemented by a thirty-round back-up magazine.

It is sometimes thought that sub-machine-guns are designed to spray bullets rather than fire them accurately. This is not so, but it is true that the mechanism of automatic fire causes the weapon to ride upwards. Hence sub-machine-guns are intended to be fired in short bursts, and some of them can be set to fire just three rounds with each depression of the trigger. However, most instructors claim that automatic fire is rarely necessary, because it is possible to 'double-tap' (that is, fire a pair of shots in rapid succession) very rapidly and with great precision. Used in this single-shot mode, the Heckler and Koch MP5 is not a sub-machine-gun, but a carbine (that is, a short rifle). Perhaps the only appropriate use of automatic fire would be in conditions such as the SAS assault on the Iranian embassy in 1980. Automatic fire offers a greater prospect of immediate incapacitation of any adversary, who is likely to be struck by several bullets almost simultaneously. It has the disadvantage of expending bullets quite rapidly and thus requiring relatively frequent magazine changes.

It is important to distinguish the sub-machine-gun or carbine from other automatic weapons, such as the Kalashnikov AK47 or Armalite AR15 assault rifles, preferred by many terrorists. In contrast to sub-machine-guns, which fire 9-mm pistol ammunition, the AK47 is capable of firing 7.62-mm high velocity bullets and the AR15 fires .223-in. high-velocity rounds; either of these has a far more devastating effect on impact, travels a considerable distance, and is capable of penetrating solid obstacles. The Heckler and Koch MP5 should, by contrast, be considered as an intermediate weapon between the hand-gun and the high-velocity rifle.

*Shotguns*

Another intermediate-range weapon available to police is the shotgun. This weapon enables armed officers to engage armed suspects, if necessary, at greater range and with more stopping power than with a hand-gun.

Shotguns are smooth-bore weapons, that is, the interior of the barrel is *not* rifled so as to impart twist to the bullet as it travels along the barrel. The shotgun cartridge comprises a propellant, wadding, and the shot itself. The latter varies from 'birdshot', which consists of approximately 200 tiny lead pellets, through a series of progressively fewer but heavier pellets, to 'rifled slug' — a single hollow slug of lead which is rifled so that it spins and maintains accuracy after leaving the barrel. In addition, shotguns can discharge various specialist projectiles, for example CS gas cartridges (see p. 285).

In the Metropolitan Police, the Force Firearms Unit are responsible for the use of shotguns, and currently favour the Remington Model 870 12-bore pump-action with and without folding stock. The pump-action shotgun is a single-barrelled weapon which is fed by a tubular magazine lying parallel with and beneath the barrel. Cartridges are fed into the breech by drawing the forward grip towards the rear of the gun. This opens the breech and ejects the spent cartridge case. When the grip is pushed forward, a fresh cartridge is inserted into the breech and the weapon is ready to fire in single action. For use against persons, the Metropolitan Police use the cartridge commonly referred to by its sporting designation of 'SG' or 'small game'. This is a cartridge containing nine pellets, each of which strikes the target with roughly the ballistic effect of a .32-in. bullet and which together provide considerable stopping power. The use of the rifled slug is limited to killing crazed animals that have to be destroyed from a distance, such as bulls that escape *en route* to the abattoir. It is, however, worth mentioning that many American police forces, including the FBI, use rifled slugs against people, on the grounds that only this round has the accuracy and stopping power needed for police work.

It may be thought that the shotgun is an inappropriate weapon for police to use, and there was initial resistance to its proposed introduction in the 1960s (Greenwood, 1966). This view seems to rest upon the myth that the shotgun causes pellets to spread widely in flight, hitting an area much greater than the intended target. In fact, the SG cartridge gives a spread of shot of around eight to ten inches at fifteen metres, most of which would strike a person's torso if aimed in that direction. At the same time, the fact that shot does spread and some individual pellets might miss the armed person makes this an inappropriate weapon for use in crowded areas at ranges in excess of around fifteen metres. However, a recent report from the Sussex Police (Edwards and Menzies, 1986) suggests that some Continental forces are actively examining the feasibility of this weapon in precisely this context.

*Rifles*

For engaging targets at long distance, the police are equipped with high-velocity rifles. The Metropolitan Police use three types: the Steyr .308-in. bolt-action rifle firing a 147-grain bullet (which has replaced the 7.62-mm Enfield Enforcer), and the Heckler and Koch HK93 .223-in. and Ruger mini 14R .223-in. self-loading rifles, each of which fire a 55-grain bullet. All of these rifles are fitted with appropriate telescopic sights and image-intensifiers for use at night. The Steyr is used for long-range positions, whilst the Ruger and HK93 are designed for shorter ranges. The Ruger is issued to divisional riflemen, whilst the Heckler and Koch HK93 is issued to officers of the Force Firearms Unit instead of the Ruger. All three models fire fully jacketed, high–velocity ball ammunition, which is discussed more fully on pp. 90–2.

*Special weapons*

All the above are standard police or military weapons, but there are other specialist weapons issued to police. First is CS agent, which can either be delivered by a hand-thrown grenade or fired from a launcher. Two types of launcher are used, the purpose-made Webley/Schermuly 1.5-in. gas gun or shotguns used to deliver either the 'ferret' cartridge or 'RIP' (Round Irritant Personnel) round. The 'ferret' is a sack of CS liquid contained in a projectile which can penetrate a door or window before bursting and discharging its contents as an aerosol into the room beyond, and is designed for use against barricaded and armed persons. Specially modified shotguns also fire 'RIP' rounds, which comprise a slug of concentrated CS powder which is fired through a door or window at point-blank range.

Second, in effecting an entry the police have hitherto had to rely upon such methods as sledge-hammers, which obviously lack speed. Under certain circumstances they can now use the 'Hatton' round, a single slug of concentrated lead dust mixed with high melting-point wax, fired from a 12-bore shotgun at either the lock or the hinges of a door. Upon impact the slug disintegrates, but imparts sufficient energy to the door to dislodge the lock or hinges, thereby causing it to open. The danger is that a dislodged fitment may fly off and injure someone in the room, but since it is designed for use in 'forced entry' when someone's life is in danger, this might be thought to be a small risk to run. Also available is a hydraulic ram which locks against the door jamb and then demolishes the door. Third, in the event of a hostage rescue the police may need to use 'stun' or, more accurately, 'distraction' grenades. These are grenades which, when thrown, eject one or more capsules of explosive charge that explode with a bright flash and deafening bang of around 170 dB, startling and disorientating the person in the room for the few seconds it might take for officers to effect a safe entry. This device became famous after being used by the SAS at the Iranian embassy siege.

*Other equipment*

Apart from weapons designed for use against armed criminals and terrorists, police also have available a variety of defensive equipment to safeguard themselves from attack. The most commonly available is body armour, which is somewhat misleading described occasionally as the 'bullet-proof vest'. This is a garment of waistcoat design which can be worn under or over a jacket and is secured by velcro straps. It consists of sixteen to eighteen layers of the fabric Kevlar which was originally developed to provide the bracing for vehicle tyres. It will prevent penetration from .38-in. ammunition up to and including .375-in. magnum rounds and standard 9-mm. However, .44-in. magnum rounds will penetrate, albeit with much-reduced energy. Kevlar body armour is not 'bullet-proof' because it will not offer protection from armour-tipped or high-velocity ball ammunition.

Body armour takes two forms: lightweight and heavyweight. These do not differ in the number of layers of Kevlar nor in the protection offered from penetration. The difference lies in the fact that, whilst lightweight body armour may prevent a bullet from penetrating, the person wearing it will sustain quite severe internal injuries from the impact of the bullet. This so-called 'trauma effect' can be minimized by the addition of a 'trauma pad' of soft fabric which absorbs the impact energy of the bullet. The disadvantages of wearing heavyweight body armour are that it is less comfortable to wear, especially in warm weather, and it is bulky and cannot be worn covertly under other garments.

The protection afforded by body armour is greatly enhanced by the insertion of either a steel or ceramic plate into the front and/or back of the vest. This will offer protection even from 7.62-mm high-velocity ball ammunition. Ceramics are also used to provide protection to the head in the form of a helmet which can be worn by officers dealing with armed criminals or terrorists. The disadvantage with the helmet is its weight, which tends to impair movement, and so officers are disinclined to wear it.

In addition to basic body armour, other equipment can improve the protection offered to officers confronting armed criminals and terrorists. Kevlar blankets can provide easily transported and rapidly assembled screening and cover. Ceramic plate can be used externally as a portable shield, or what is called the 'ballistic clipboard' which, although quite small, is useful when approaching cars. Recently the Force Firearms Unit has acquired a number of glass-reinforced plastic shields which armed officers can carry and which were used operationally for the first time at the Plumstead abattoir incident in July 1987 (see p. 24). Larger shields are also available on wheels, which are designed to offer protective cover when moving towards the location of armed persons, perhaps in order to recover an injured victim.

Apart from armour that is worn, carried, or pushed, the police are equipped with armoured Land Rovers. These appear to be ordinary Land Rovers but are constructed from armour-plated steel, thus affording protection for passengers from most types of ammunition. However, their weight significantly reduces their speed and general performance. It was these vehicles, provided by the Metropolitan Police, which were used to evacuate casualties during the Hungerford massacre. Following the 1985 riot at Broadwater Farm, where firearms were used against police, the Metropolitan Police have now acquired twenty-four custom-built, armoured Land Rovers designed for use in public-order situations.

## Dogs

Specially trained police dogs are another resource available to armed officers. They may be used to search premises or vehicles for an armed person and/or to attack such a person. Special training is necessary for three reasons. The first is the need to ensure that the dog does not attack police officers holding guns. Secondly, because the dog-handler himself is not normally armed and should not be exposed to danger unnecessarily, the dog must perform its assigned task 'unsighted'. This means that, whereas normally a dog-handler will point directly at, say, the person whom the dog is to apprehend, in an armed operation the handler must instruct the dog without being able to see the suspect directly, for to do so would expose the handler to danger. Third, all this must be achieved with the minimum noise, so dogs must be trained not to bark except as a specific warning.

Dogs are particularly useful not only because they can search an area and bark in such a manner as to indicate the presence of an armed person, but because they can be used as a sub-lethal weapon in their own right. Thus, it has sometimes happened that an armed suspect has apparently surrendered, but failed to comply with police instructions, for example, refusing to stop when told or to lay down a weapon. In such a situation a dog could be sent to apprehend the suspect. This obviously exposes the dog to danger, but this is less than might at first appear, because a fast-running dog heading directly towards a gunman presents a small, rapidly moving target which is difficult to hit. For this reason, these dogs are known colloquially as 'furry Exocets'.

However, there are limits to the utility of dogs in these circumstances. Dogs are normally trained to 'stand off', circling and barking at a person who does not attempt to escape or offer violence. A person who calmly stands still whilst retaining possession of weapon would not be seized by such a dog. In the

1970s the Metropolitan Police experimented with a small number of specially trained 'anti-terrorist', (AT), dogs. They were trained to be more aggressive, seizing an adversary and dragging him down, even if he was not offering violence. This experiment was abandoned because these dogs were of little use in general police work, where such force could not so easily be justified. This does mean that, whilst dogs retain many of their uses in firearms operations, there is as yet nothing to fill the gap vacated by the AT dog that could be used to immobilize a passively non-compliant gunman.

## Training

Perhaps the clearest indication in the change of official attitude towards police use of firearms 'from amateurism to professionalism' is to be seen in the development of training. Training in the use of firearms in the Metropolitan Police occurs at several levels. AFOs receive a basic course, followed by regular refresher training; protection officers complete a special 'bodyguard' course; force riflemen also receive special training in the use of their weapons; Level II officers complete a four-week special course and train regularly; and Level I officers complete a six-week instructor's course, followed by a three-week advanced team training course, after which they follow a cycle of instructing others, team training, and operational readiness.

### The basic firearms course

Basic firearms training has been gradually extended since it was first introduced on a systematic basis in 1966. It now lasts two weeks, at the end of which trainees are given a written and practical test before acquiring their authorization to carry a revolver. Roughly half the time is spent on the practice range, acquiring shooting and handling skills. The other half is spent in the classroom being taught aspects of law and procedure or engaging in various practical exercises (see, *International Law Enforcement*, 1984).

On the range, trainees fire at a man-sized target portraying a man wearing sunglasses holding a gun at waist-height which is pointed towards the officer. The torso is marked by an oval, and shots inside this area score two points, whereas shots hitting the target outside the torso score one point. The targets swivel on their axis from the edge facing the trainee to the full face of the target being presented. The duration of the exposure of the target is varied for different tests. All shots are fired from the 'isosceles' position, that is, the officer faces the target squarely holding the gun in both hands with the arms fully extended. This is in contrast to the so-called 'Weaver' stance, favoured by the FBI, in which the officer adopts a stance similar to that of a boxer with one foot forward of the other. In this stance, the gun is held in both hands, but only the strong arm is fully extended, whilst the weak arm is bent, exerting a backward pressure. The officer looks along the length of the extended arm as he may do along a rifle. There is considerable controversy regarding the advantages and disadvantages of these competing methods. The Metropolitan Police are currently committed to the 'isosceles' position, and this is taught without equivocation.

Officers are taught the two basic methods of double-handed shooting — 'sense-of-direction' and aimed. 'Sense-of-direction' shooting is designed for responding to surprise encounters at close range. At seven metres the officer is taught to punch the gun directly towards the target, whilst continuing to look at the target with both eyes. The punching action locks the arms, and the parallax effect of keeping both eyes focused on the target whilst bringing the gun into the field of view causes the shape of the gun to be superimposed upon that of the target when it is correctly aligned. The officer then momentarily pauses before firing a pair of shots towards the target as rapidly as possible. The aim is to hit the torso of the target with both shots. This skill is tested in two examined 'shoots' of ten rounds each: in the first the officer must fire three pairs of shots, reload, and fire the remaining two pairs at a static target within twenty-five seconds; in the second he must fire a pair of shots at a turning target which is exposed for two seconds each time.

Aimed shooting occurs under circumstances when the officer has time to sight the gun, usually from a distance of at least fifteen metres, and fire a single shot. Unlike 'sense-of-direction', the attention of the officer is focused on the sights of the gun as he attempts to obtain and maintain a good 'sight picture'. This mode of shooting is tested at fifteen and, for officers authorized to carry the Model 10, twenty-five metres. At fifteen metres the officer is presented with a target that turns and remains exposed for three seconds, during which time he must bring his gun into the aim, align the sights, and fire at the torso. At twenty-five metres, it is envisaged that the officer will be behind protective cover which can also be used to support the gun. In one test the officer must fire two rounds freestanding, two rounds standing using the support of the barricade, two rounds kneeling, two rounds sitting, and, finally, two rounds lying down. Until recently this included firing two rounds with the weak hand (for example, a right-handed officer would fire using his left hand). This was based on the view that an officer could keep more of his body behind protective cover if he were obliged to fire from the right-hand side. However, weak-hand shooting is usually of a poor standard, and officers tend not to adopt it operationally, so it has now been discontinued.

Also discontinued is the single-action mode of shooting (see p. 97). Instead of the 'single-action shoot', officers now complete a 'walk-down shoot'. That is, starting at twenty-five metres, officers walk line abreast down the range towards the targets. When the targets turn they must fire an aimed shot. When they reach ten metres, they stop and fire a pair of shots at each turning target.

All classification shoots during the basic course require only that officers begin from the 'drawn-weapons position', that is, the gun is drawn from the holster and held at waist height pointing towards the target. From this position it is brought to the aim and fired. This rests on the assumption that officers are unlikely to be surprised and need to draw their weapon rapidly from the holster and fire it. The basic course does include instruction on how to draw from the holster, but it is not until the officer begins refresher training that he will need to show proficiency in this mode of shooting.

An officer is required to obtain a total score of 70 per cent to receive authorization, and in no individual test should he obtain less than 50 per cent. A score of 90 per cent earns the appellation of 'marksman'. However, authorization does not depend solely upon how well a person can shoot, although minimal competence is the *sine qua non* for passing the course. Throughout the course, instructors assess each trainee to determine whether he has the necessary aptitude for authorization. It is in a variety of theoretical and practical exercises that this aptitude is gauged.

Away from the practice range, students are taught the law and internal police regulations governing the use of firearms. They are reminded not only of section 3 of the Criminal Law Act 1967 but also the 'strict reminder' in the Home Office guidelines:

A firearm is to be used only as a last resort. Other methods must have been tried and failed, or must — because of the circumstances — be unlikely to succeed if tried. For example, a firearm may be fired when it is apparent that the police cannot achieve the lawful purpose of preventing the loss, or further loss, of life, by any other means. If it is reasonable to do so, an oral warning is to be given before opening fire.

And officers are forcefully reminded by those guidelines that: 'The responsibility for use of a firearm rests with the individual officer and he is answerable to the courts, both criminal and civil.' Both the seriousness of the task and the responsibility of the officer discharging his duty are repeatedly affirmed by instructors, who use anecdotes to reinforce the dilemmas that officers might face.

Apart from the general law and regulations governing the use of firearms, trainees are also taught tactics to employ in various situations. For example, they are taught that, in dealing with armed persons in buildings or other premises, the procedure is first to contain the situation, plan further action, organize personnel, and then activate the plan. In containing the situation, they are told that it is important to protect the public and other police officers by placing an outer cordon around the scene and preventing entry, and taking steps to evacuate if necessary. Planning not only involves the possibility of a sudden raid, but includes subterfuge and, most important of all, direct contact by the use of the telephone or shouted conversation. If all this sounds only common sense, the course includes video and slide presentations of actual events in which common sense did not prevail and where people were actually killed as a result.

Tactical exercises in each of the major types of incident are staged, and also videotaped and replayed to trainees showing them the mistakes they have made. As instructors acknowledge, this does no more than caution trainees against over-hasty action, rather than establish their competence in actually dealing with complex situations.

Also emphasized is the level of threat posed by firearms, especially shotguns. Slides of scenes where shotguns have been used and the mortuary photographs of victims demonstrate the lethality of this and other weapons. Trainees are taken onto the range, where an instructor demonstrates how little protection is afforded against shotgun pellets by doors and similar barriers. A two-gallon plastic container full of water is used to simulate the effect on a person's head of being shot with a cartridge containing SG pellets. It is ripped apart by the impact, and its contents explode, showering those standing several metres away.

Throughout training the emphasis is upon avoiding direct confrontation unless it is absolutely necessary. Officers are told of the dangers of trying to burst in and catch a wanted person off his guard. The most often cited cautionary tale concerned the wanted gunman, Toni Baldessare, who fortified his flat and had intended to kill as many police officers as possible when they stormed in to arrest him. Fortunately, he was frustrated by the caution shown by the arresting officers, who laid siege to his flat for two days before he shot and killed himself (see Gould and Waldren, 1986: 195–6).

The dangers of such confrontations extend not only to the police officer but also to innocent people who may inadvertently become involved. The case of Cherry Groce, mistakenly shot during an early-morning raid in 1985 by officers searching for her son, is pointed to as tragic evidence of the dangers inherent in this type of operation. This lesson is reinforced by a session on a specially constructed range, where photographs and videos are projected onto a screen and the trainee must decide whether or not to shoot, and when. This is used to reinforce the lesson that it is very easy to misinterpret an innocuous action as threatening, and to shoot where there was no just cause.

A good example of the importance of taking a cautious approach can be found in how officers are taught to take the surrender of an armed person. The great danger in such a situation is that officers will relax, thinking the whole episode is finished and the threat eliminated. Trainees are shown news film showing an actual surrender where the attention of surrounding officers quite clearly diminishes dramatically. It is emphasized that, even if it is believed that, say, only one person is involved and he has surrendered, officers can never be sure that premises or vehicles are safe until they have been properly searched and their safety verified. Thus, a surrender is not taken in full view of premises or vehicles that have not been searched. Instead, the person is taken to a safe location where he can be searched without the operation being overlooked.

When it comes to searching the person, trainees are again shown the importance of caution and being thorough. If a person is carrying a gun when he emerges, they are shown how he should be directed to hold it so that it cannot quickly be turned on them and fired. The speed with which this can be done is demonstrated, and trainees are reminded to remain behind protective cover. Armed persons should not be told to drop their gun, in the manner so often seen on the screen, because this can be sufficient to cause it to discharge; again, this is demonstrated. The person is instructed to place the gun carefully on the ground at an appointed place, well away from the premises or vehicle from which he has emerged and away from where he will be eventually searched.

If possible, the person is made to lie face down with arms and legs spreadeagled, and to look in the opposite direction to that from which the searching officer will approach him. Before approaching, the officer will instruct the person to interlace his fingers behind his back and pull his hands as far up his back as possible. The officer then takes hold of the interlaced fingers; this prevents the person letting go, and slight pressure can cause sufficient pain to inhibit any threatening move. Handcuffs are then applied and the person's entire body thoroughly searched for hidden weapons. During exercises involving the surrender of armed persons, weapons are deliberately hidden in the most unlikely places to test the thoroughness with which trainees search the person. Then the person is assisted to his feet in a particular manner, so that control can be retained over his movements. In demonstrations, instructors show the danger that can arise from sudden and unexpected actions on the part of a person who has apparently surrendered. The emphasis is upon guarding against the unanticipated danger: 'What if . . . ?'

This same caution is paramount in dealing with each of the tactical situations with which officers are taught to deal — the armed criminal barricaded in a building, armed persons in vehicles, and armed robbers at the scene of a robbery.

*Barricaded armed person in a building*  The most common type of armed operation is that involving a person who has barricaded himself within a building and has possibly taken a hostage. Typically, the person or persons concerned may be criminals who have been disturbed and sought refuge in a building, or a party to a violent 'domestic' quarrel who is holding other members of the family hostage. In any event, the task of the police is to contain the building and seek to negotiate the surrender of the person concerned. During training, officers are required to deal with simulated situations of this kind, during which instructors entice them into making premature attempts to rescue hostages or otherwise expose themselves to danger. The lesson is that officers must be patient and not take precipitate action. Once the person has surrendered and any hostages have been liberated, the premises must be searched. This is undertaken by a team of officers who methodically and cautiously search each room in turn, maintaining as much silence as possible. Only when each room, including cupboards and lofts or cellars, has been searched and declared safe can others be allowed in, for example, to search for evidence.

*Armed persons in vehicles*  Another common armed operation is to stop and arrest suspected armed persons in a vehicle. Since the vehicle is likely to be on the public highway, officers are instructed in how to bring it to a halt without exposing members of the public to unnecessary danger. Once halted, the occupants of the vehicle must alight in an orderly manner whilst officers maintain as much cover as possible. To this end, officers are shown how to position their own vehicle so as to afford maximum protection, and how to instruct occupants to behave so as to minimize danger to all concerned. Thus, occupants will be instructed to display both hands and to leave the doors open as each of them alights, at the command of the police, in turn. The last occupant will be instructed to open the boot of the car before joining his colleagues lying face down in the road. Then officers will visually inspect the car from behind cover to ensure that no one remains within it, before the occupants are approached, searched, and arrested.

*Intercepting armed robbers* Perhaps the most dangerous type of armed operation that an AFO will be called upon to undertake is the interception of armed robbers at the scene of a robbery. Before such an interception (or 'ambush' as it is more colloquially known) can occur, senior officers must assure themselves that it is based on sound intelligence, and the Force Firearms Unit must be consulted. If the assessment of the likely threat is that it will be high, then the operation will be taken over by members of PT17. Usually, one or more AFOs will accompany members of the Robbery Squad, or other specialist squad, who are responsible for the investigation. At the critical moment when the robbers move in to attack the victim, the police will intercept and capture them. It is the task of the AFO to confront, contain, and, if possible, take the surrender of any armed members of the gang. The operation will have been planned in advance, but, as officers under training are made aware, operations rarely go entirely according to plan. In the rapidly unfolding circumstances of the operation, in which innocent people are almost inevitably involved, the officer is bound to make split-second decisions, particularly concerning whether to open fire or not.

AFOs are unlikely to deal with any of these situations except in a secondary role, but it is considered important that they understand fully what is happening.

Basic training has been dealt with at length because this is both the foundation for all further training and also the full extent of initial training received by most AFOs, who make up the majority of officers authorized to carry firearms.

## Reclassification

Four times annually, AFOs and all other authorized officers must satisfy the standards of marksmanship required to maintain authorization. Officers attend at a variety of ranges situated throughout the Metropolitan Police District, where they spend some time in practice and the remainder being tested on their marksmanship. Where changes have been introduced, either in procedures or training, these are explained to officers and discussed with them. Officers also receive additional training to improve techniques in conformity to changing standards.

Following this period of instruction and training, officers are then tested. The tests do not follow a standard pattern, but are designed to present to officers previously unencountered situations for them to cope with, the aim being to test how well officers adapt. One such test consisted of a total of forty rounds fired in three shoots. The first required officers to be seated and then to stand and fire a pair of shots 'sense-of-direction' at a turning seven-metre target exposed for three seconds. The second involved the fifteen-metre target being exposed briefly (a 'flash exposure'), whereupon officers were required to draw their gun and shout a warning. When the target reappeared for a total of four seconds, they were to fire a pair of aimed shots. Both of these first two shoots were each of ten rounds, thus requiring officers to reload with four rounds having expended the first six. The final test involved firing four rounds standing, four kneeling, four sitting, four kneeling, and four standing at a target twenty-five metres distant in two minutes. Between each set of four shots the expended rounds were to be discarded and the gun topped up with live rounds.

### Annual refresher training

Each year AFOs must attend a one-day refresher training course at the firearms training establishment at Lippitts Hill. Officers must demonstrate that they are still physically fit by completing a short assault course, then carrying a dummy weighing eleven stones and holding a gun steady in the aim for one minute. This is a repetition of what is now required for the basic course, but not all AFOs had previously to satisfy this requirement, and an annual retest was only introduced at the beginning of 1987.

The remainder of the day is given over to improving skills on the practice range and, more importantly, refreshing and improving tactical knowledge through exercises similar to those completed as part of the basic course.

### *Training of officers using special weapons*

Before AFOs can be authorized to carry either the Browning 9-mm or the Heckler and Koch MP5, they must complete additional training. They also attend reclassification tests once a month, and are required to satisfy more demanding examinations of their marksmanship. For example, officers authorized to carry Brownings must engage more than one target, sometimes positioned at different distances, which in aimed shooting requires some refocusing of the eye. Those on the Heckler and Koch MP5 reclassification engage in exercises such as requiring them to walk around as they might in a terminal building and then fire at a target which turns; or to be seated behind a check-in desk and have to shoot one of six targets as nominated by the instructor; or to fend off another person whilst firing single-handed. They must also learn what action to take if their weapon jams, which involves discarding the Heckler and Koch MP5 and drawing and firing their back-up side arm.

### Training protection officers

Officers from the Royalty and Diplomatic Protection Department and Special Branch, responsible for protecting embassies and VIPs, receive an additional three-week course designed to teach them the skills and knowledge needed in their role. These include higher standards of marksmanship, involving shooting with one hand whilst protecting the 'principal' (the person they are protecting) with the other, or blocking an attack with one arm and firing with the other hand. Some highly selected officers also learn how to fire the Heckler and Koch MP5K.

Again, equal attention is paid to tactical considerations. Thus, officers are shown how to deploy themselves around a 'principal' and what to do should an attack take place. There are staged exercises in which attempts are made on the life of a 'principal', for example, as the party arrive at a location by car. Officers are taught how to get the 'principal' out of the line of fire and return fire, if necessary. The assessment of situations and liaison with other divisions within the Metropolitan Police or other police forces also commands considerable attention.

### Level II training

Level II officers are selected from AFOs who have applied for training and shown themselves specially competent in the use of firearms. They complete a gruelling three-week residential course designed to develop the basic techniques taught to AFOs to a much higher level of competence.

In addition to initial training, Level II officers are supposed to train whilst not on operational duties, the aim being to maintain a highly skilled cadre of officers who can relieve AFOs of the more dangerous and difficult tasks such as house-searching, taking the surrender of armed persons, and 'ambushes' where the threat level is judged to be moderate. They will normally be called in once AFOs have contained an armed person, and are often called to undertake planned arrests of suspected armed offenders, where a slow search of the premises is likely to prove necessary.

*Level I training*

Not only must Level I officers provide the response to incidents requiring special weapons and tactics, but they must also train all other officers in the force authorized to carry any particular weapon. Hence their training requires them to qualify at the highest standard on all the weapons used by police. Their training is divided into an instructor's course lasting six weeks and a three-week advanced team training course. The former concentrates on developing their own tactical and firearm abilities, as well as acquiring instructional skills.

The team training course is a relatively recent innovation. Previously, new members of PT17 who joined singly when vacancies arose were trained by other members of the team to which they were assigned. However, this takes some considerable time and reduces the operational effectiveness of the new officer. In 1988 a new course was introduced to provide an intensive and standardized introduction to the principle skills needed by Level I officers. The task which they, and they alone, perform is hostage rescue. That is, they must be able to force an entry, engage hostile suspects, and rescue hostages. They must acquire skills in abseiling down the outside of buildings, as did the SAS at the Iranian embassy siege, so as to obtain access to the building at points that have been left insecure. It is also necessary to learn how to use ladders to climb through windows (not an easy task when wearing body armour, radios, gun-belts, and a respirator, and carrying a gun at the same time). Most important of all is learning how to enter a room and engage hostile suspects without endangering innocent hostages. This, of course, relies on skills that must practised repeatedly, not only on buildings but also coaches, trains, and aircraft. It demands rapid and accurate shooting in all kinds of conditions, and also an ability to use Hatton rounds and distraction grenades.

Forced entry is also required when essential, and easily destroyed evidence must be seized. With the growth of organized drug-pushing, there has been a commensurate growth in the frequency with which premises are raided where occupants are believed to be armed. Because the purpose of the raid is to secure evidence, and because drugs are easily disposed of, it is essential that officers gain rapid access to the premises. Consequently, officers must burst in and possibly confront suspected armed persons who are intent on delaying them, at least.

Level I officers follow a five-week cycle: four weeks of instructional duty at either Lippitts Hill or one of the ranges in and around London is followed by a week's team training and operational stand-by. In addition, Level I officers liaise with other police forces and the SAS, and engage in occasional joint exercises in preparation for an incident such as the Iranian embassy seige, in which both police and SAS were involved.

## Conclusions

Training in the use of firearms by the police is now taken more seriously than at any time in the history of the Metropolitan Police. All officers who are authorized to carry firearms are trained in marksmanship skills and tactical awareness. Those who are given more onerous operational responsibilities receive additional training.

# APPENDIX B

# Public-Order Policing: Equipment, Tactics, and Training

## Introduction

Recent years have witnessed a qualitative change in the equipment and tactics used to control serious public disorder, a function for which officers must now be specially trained. It is important to note that here we are concerned only with the control of the most serious public disorder; most public-order events pass without there being recourse to any of the matters discussed here.

## Protective Equipment

*Ordinary uniform*

Even normally dressed police officers are provided with limited protective equipment. As noted earlier, since 1976 the traditional police helmet as been subtly redesigned to afford increased head protection. This has been achieved by inserting at first a cork and, later, a plastic reinforced interior, and by adding velcro chin-straps. This means that the helmet can resist fairly substantial blows, and is much less likely to fall off than was its predecessor. When officers believe that they might become involved in violence, they can quickly lift the helmet, shake the chin-straps down and fasten the helmet firmly to the head. Female officers are issued with a public-order 'bowler' hat which is similarly reinforced.

The other principal item of protective equipment normally carried is, of course, the truncheon. This is a twelve-inch length of hardwood, with a finger grip at one end and a leather thong. It is carried in a concealed pocket down the thigh and is drawn ready for use by inserting the thumb into the thong (normally kept tucked out of sight) in such a way that, when held, the thong stretches across the back of the hand, thus preventing it from easily being snatched by an adversary. The truncheon is used principally, though not exclusively, to strike a violent opponent on the arms or legs. Officers are officially warned never to strike an opponent across the head, but in the heat of combat anyone, police officer or not, is likely to strike downwards. Whether such a measure of force is legally justified would, of course, depend upon its reasonable necessity.

It should also be recognized that almost all officers carry handcuffs which can be used to subdue violent persons, and also usually have a radio which can be used to summon help. They should also be reasonably physically fit and have the use of arms and legs which can be used to strike, grasp, or trip opponents. Recruits are instructed in rudimentary self-defence, but few possess any knowledge or skills beyond those acquired in the school playground (Policy Studies Institute, 1983c).

### Head protection

Once the level of violence escalates beyond that for which the ordinary uniform offers protection, special items of clothing and equipment will be deployed. One of the first items of protective equipment issued is the plastic eye-shield, which safeguards the eyes from missiles such as coins which are not infrequently thrown at police by football hooligans and some pickets and demonstrators.

If violence continues to escalate, a special protective helmet with a visor will be worn. This is little more than a motorcycle crash helmet, secured to the head by a chin-cup strap. The visor is made of polycarbonate, and to prevent corrosive or flammable liquid from seeping down the helmet and onto the face, the visor is sealed to the helmet by a strip of rubber. The latest visors are designed to protect the face fully by covering the small gap which the earlier visors had left at the side. The latest helmets incorporate flexible neck protection in the form of a leather pad protruding from beneath the rear of the helmet.

The problems that have been encountered with the riot helmet concern ventilation and hearing. Sufficiently encasing the head in a helmet which must be impervious even to corrosive chemicals tends to militate against effective ventilation: the visor often mists up, thus inhibiting vision — a major problem when it comes to the identification of offenders either for the purpose of arrest or, later, for giving evidence in court. Since the side of the head, around the ears, must be protected as much, if not more, than the rest of the head, it means that auditory communication is impeded.

*Shields*

If protective helmets are worn, shields will almost certainly be also carried, because officers have no alternative means of body protection. There are two types of shield, long and short.

The long shield was developed by the Metropolitan Police in the immediate aftermath of the disturbances at Notting Hill in 1976, and is marketed as the 'Met' shield by manufacturers. It is constructed from 4-mm polycarbonate transparent plastic which is flame-resistant and capable of absorbing heavy impacts. There are slight variations, particularly in height. The traditional shield is 5 ft. 6 in. tall, but some others may be as high as 6 ft. They are all approximately 2 ft. wide. The bottom part has tapered flanges to the sides to give it greater rigidity, whilst the top 9-in. section is inclined forwards in order to deflect missiles downwards. To the rear of the shield is a metal plate bolted to the face of the shield, with foam sandwiched between the two to absorb the shock of missile impact. On the metal plate are three handles in the form of inverted U-shaped loops. In the normal mode of carriage, the left hand grasps the upper right handle and the left forearm is inserted beneath the left handle so that the shield rests on the left forearm. The right hand then grasps the lower right handle to give the shield rigidity. This tends to inhibit rapid movement, and so, for some manoeuvres, the so-called 'open grip' is used: the left forearm is released and the left hand grasps the left handle. Both hands are needed to hold the shield in front of the officer, both because it is heavy—16 lb. in weight—and because it has the properties of a sail and so tends to be easily caught by the wind. It was designed to offer full-length body protection to an otherwise unprotected officer, and is essentially defensive in conception.

With escalating levels of violence being experienced during the 1980s, it became obvious that the long shield prevented the kind of rapid movement that might be necessary to arrest or disperse rioters. As a result, a short shield was introduced, also made from 4-mm polycarbonate plastic. Some of the earlier shields were simply shorter versions of the long shield, but gradually a round shield has come to be almost universally adopted. This shield is designed to be carried on one arm: the weak arm is inserted through a loop at the elbow and the hand grasps a handle on the opposite side of the rear of the shield. Apart from leaving the strong hand free to hold a truncheon or grasp a prisoner, the weak hand can also release the shield, allowing the shield to swing freely so that both hands can be employed. Initially black in colour, the most recent shields are transparent and a little larger. They are shaped rather like an enlarged 'frisbee', with the lip around the edge providing rigidity. Since officers who carry short shields lack full body protection, many forces equip them with shin pads and knee protection. However, this is not yet standard practice in the Metropolitan Police.

*Protection from fire*

The helmet and shield are designed to offer protection from missiles, but the increased use of fire bombs, or 'Molotov cocktails', as they are sometimes known, has meant that officers also need special flame-retardant overalls. The normal uniform jacket and trousers has a considerable measure of flame resistance, but being in two pieces with a low neckline, it can expose officers to burning. Thus, officers are equipped with a one-piece, zip-fastened overall which encloses the body from the ankle to the neck — colloquially known as a 'baby-gro'. Sleeves and trouser bottoms are buttoned down over gloves and boots respectively, so that, should burning chemicals splash onto the overall, they will drain away without coming into contact with the skin. The overall is secured at the waist by a separate leather belt. Because of the fear of fire, some officers are also equipped with halogen fire-extinguishers. In the Metropolitan Police these are carried in a satchel on the back, and are designed to be used not so much by the officers carrying them as by those behind. Being halogen gas, the contents of the extinguisher are non-toxic, and it is designed for use on people.

Mounted officers present a particular problem of personal protection: since they need at least one hand, and preferably two, to control their horse, they cannot be encumbered with a shield. They are equipped with the same protective helmet and flame-retardant overall as their colleagues on foot, but also wear various items of body armour to offer some protection to the torso, arms, and legs against missiles. Although horses are relatively impervious to pain, they too receive protection for their most vulnerable parts, the eyes and nose.

Another group of officers requiring special protection are women, who, since the Sex Discrimination Act, have been increasingly exposed to the full range of police duties, including public order. The police have experimented with specially designed torso body armour to be worn beneath the flame-retardant overall, but this is still under evaluation and no decision has yet been taken as to its adoption.

*Vehicles*

Not only individuals but also vehicles must be protected from fire and missiles. In the aftermath of the 1984–5 miners' strike, during which police were conveyed in a motley assortment of vehicles, including privately hired mini-buses without any protection at all, the Association of Chief Police Officers agreed on a common standard for Police Support Unit transportation. The vehicle which has now been almost universally adopted is based on the Austin Rover 3-litre Sherpa van with an elevated roof-line. Windscreens are either made of specially toughened glass and/or protected by mesh grills that can quickly be affixed. Side windows are usually made of polycarbonate plastic and/or protected by exterior polycarbonate windows or mesh grills. Headlamps and radiator grills are also protected by wire mesh. Of course, fire-extinguishers are readily accessible. Some earlier vehicles were also equipped with wire mesh 'wings' attached to the side of the vehicle by hinges which allowed them to be opened and thus afford protection to officers on foot walking beside the vehicle. Unfortunately, the 'wings' had a tendency to become unlocked, flying open and causing damage, and they have since been removed.

A hazard that often confronts officers in quelling serious disorder is the erection of barricades, which are frequently ignited. These barriers can easily halt the advance of police cordons, and provide a strong vantage-point from which rioters can attack police with missiles. To counter this threat, the police have invested in two specialized vehicles: a fork-lift truck and a JCB, both of which are equipped with additional protection from missile attack.

Missiles thrown by rioters are not, unfortunately, the only — or even potentially the most injurious — threat that rioters can pose for police. The use of vehicles driven at police lines has become an increasing common feature of serious disorder. During the Brixton riot of April 1981, a hijacked bus was aimed, driverless, at the police; in Toxteth, later that year, at least one milk float was employed in much the same way; and during the miners' dispute of 1984–5 a variety of vehicles, such as caravans used by road construction companies, were propelled at the police. To cope with this threat, the police will deploy vehicles, such as Range Rovers, driven by highly skilled traffic officers, to intercept these vehicles.

*Animals*

So far, this examination of 'equipment' has been concerned with inanimate and entirely defensive items; but dogs and horses have formed part of the police public-order armoury for a very long time, providing an aggressive capability if required. Although dogs are of limited use in a public-order situation, they can be used effectively for the guarding of fixed locations, and are frequently used at railway stations and similar places in connection with the control of football supporters.

Horses play a much greater role in public-order situations. In non-violent situations, the elevated position of the rider allows for a clear overview of the crowd. When it comes to 'pushing and shoving', the weight and strength of the horse enables a few officers to control a substantial crowd of people. In more aggressive situations, horses can be used to disperse violent crowds by being ridden at a trot or canter towards those creating trouble. If necessary, mounted officers can also use their long or short batons to subdue violent people, although riders prefer to use both hands to retain control of the horse. As mentioned previously, riders need to be specially protected from missile attack in these more aggressive circumstances, because they are unable to protect themselves with shields.

## Weaponry

### Truncheons

The weapon traditionally used by police against members of violent crowds is the truncheon or baton. 'Baton charging' such a crowd was a tactic devised during the infancy of the Metropolitan Police, and has been used periodically ever since by all British police forces. What *has* changed over this period is the type of baton. In the past, the normal-issue truncheon was longer and much heavier than that carried today. At night, some officers, especially sergeants, would carry a much longer truncheon called a night-stick. The degree of injury that either of these formerly available weapons could inflict was significantly greater than that of the modern truncheon.

The truncheon available for use in public-order situations is the same as that normally carried. The Public Order Review of 1986 did lead to the acquisition of a number of long truncheons especially for use in conditions of severe disorder. These truncheons would only be issued on the authority of a commander or officer of more senior rank. The long truncheon issued to the Metropolitan Police measures 27 in. and is made of wood, although some other forces have opted for synthetic composite materials.

Like the ordinary baton, the long truncheon should only be used to strike the arms and legs.

There were always significant reservations about the use of this type of weapon amongst not only senior officers but also some shield instructors. The extended length meant that the potential for inflicting serious injury was considerable. The Metropolitan Police have decided to abandon the use of this weapon, and many other forces seem likely to follow suit (see pp. 178–81). Moreover, the *baton* charge has now been discontinued as a tactic available to Metropolitan Police officers. It is still envisaged that officers will charge into violent crowds, but the use of the baton other than for self-defence has now been dropped. (For further discussion see pp. 181–2.)

## Baton rounds and 'Gas'

If dispersal tactics using foot or mounted officers fail to achieve their objective, and serious violence continues or escalates, then the next step in the hierarchy of force is the use of CS gas or plastic baton rounds. Both projectiles are launched from a type of firearm. The CS gas launcher uses an electrical charge, whilst the baton round is propelled from a cartridge.

'CS gas' is something of a misnomer, since it is not a gas which carries the CS irritant, but smoke. Once inhaled, the CS agent causes the recipient's eyes to sting and shed tears uncontrollably; the person also coughs, becomes nauseous, and generally suffers such unpleasant symptoms that he will feel compelled to escape. Because of the disabling effect of CS, police officers themselves need protection, in the form of respirators which restrict mobility and create other practical problems. What inhibits police from using CS smoke, however, is not tactical considerations so much as its symbolic significance as an alien instrument used freely by more oppressive regimes. (For further discussion see pp. 189–91)

Baton rounds are, if anything, even more symbolically sensitive, perhaps because of their association with Northern Ireland, and the deaths that have resulted from their use. The baton round itself is a 4-oz. cylinder of plastic, 4.5 in. long and 1.5 in. in diameter. It is fired from the L67 launcher, and travels at a speed of approximately 120 m.p.h. from a distance of between 20 and 30 m. It is designed to hit and incapacitate identified members of the crowd committing serious acts of violence, such as throwing fire bombs or other missiles. It is likely to inflict serious injury upon those who are hit, causing severe bruising and internal bleeding and possibly breaking limbs. For this reason, 'baton gunners' are taught to aim low, to hit the lower portion of the torso. However, unlike the wooden baton round used by the Hong Kong Police or the predecessor of the plastic baton round, made of rubber, the baton round is not designed to be deliberately ricocheted off the ground. (For further discussion see pp. 196–210)

*Firearms*

The final stage in the hierarchy of force is the use of lethal firearms. These are envisaged as being employed against members of the crowd using firearms against the police, as was the case at Broadwater Farm in 1985. Officers from the tactical firearms unit would be responsible for providing armed support and using whichever weapons were appropriate in the circumstances. Unlike the practice in other countries, it is *not* envisaged that shotguns or other lethal firearms will be used upon those who are simply engaged in rioting. Their use would be restricted to countering the use of lethal force against police.

It is envisaged that the scale of violence would have escalated to a pitch that would possibly threaten the safety of baton gunners, and so the Metropolitan Police have taken possession of twenty-four ballistically protected Land Rovers. These vehicles replaced a similar number of armoured personnel carriers borrowed from the army and painted in police livery. They offer their occupants full protection from incendiary attack and even from high-velocity rifle ammunition. Baton rounds, or live ammunition in the most extreme situations, are fired from small portholes located on the side.

*Excluded equipment*

Although the hierarchy of force might appear impressive, there are some weapons and other equipment commonly used in other countries which are not available to police in Britain. One has already been mentioned, the shotgun. Shotguns are, of course, available as part of the police armoury, but not for use in riot situations as they are in South Africa, the USA, and many other countries.

More obvious perhaps is the unavailability of water cannon. These vehicles, containing several hundred gallons of water (the amount varying with the size of the vehicle) which can be used to dowse a crowd, extinguish fires, or knock people down by using water pressure, are commonly used in Europe. Two such vehicles were specially constructed for evaluation, but the Home Office eventually decided against their use. (For further discussion see pp. 191–3.)

Apart from metal barriers, which need to be defended by officers, the police also lack sufficient means of creating a physical barrier between the crowd and, say, a building. The Americans have developed a variety of chemicals, such as 'banana-skin pavement', designed to be spread across the road surface making it too slippery to stand on. This would have obvious advantages for protecting a static defensive operation, such as a violent picket line like that at Orgreave or at the *Warrington Messenger* or *Times* newspapers, where the normal tactics based on movement do not apply. However, it seems that this and other forms of barrier have yet to be evaluated.

*Conclusion*

It is clear that, in authorizing equipment, considerable attention is paid to perceived public acceptability rather than simple tactical effectiveness. This can produce somewhat bizarre results: wooden batons used to strike people are acceptable, but Mace and 'sting sticks' are not; horses, which can knock people down and trample on them, are acceptable, but the water cannon is not. However, as argued in the main text, the control of public disorder is as much a political-symbolic process as it is a tactical one.

## Organization

Traditionally, public-order situations have been policed by *ad hoc* collections of ordinary uniformed officers. It has become increasingly common in recent years to deploy officers for public-order duties as Police Support Units (PSUs). Since this term has, whether wilfully or not, been the source of some confusion, it will be explained in full. Because some genuine confusion has arisen from the similarity of this term with that of the District Support Units (DSUs), which until 1986 were a unique feature of the Metropolitan Police and which have now been superseded by Territorial Support Groups (TSGs), the distinctions between these forms of police deployment will need to be explained.

After some initial divergence between the Metropolitan Police and provincial police forces, it is now standard practice for a PSU to comprise twenty constables, two sergeants, and one inspector.

They can be subdivided into two separate 'serials' comprising a sergeant and ten constables, although on some occasions an inspector will be placed in charge of each serial. The PSU is a public-order formation raised from amongst the *ordinary uniformed officers* working from police stations throughout the force area. Officers must normally have completed their probationary period and not exceed a maximum age limit (which varies from one force to another) in order to be eligible for PSU duty. Each division will be obliged to provide a number of PSUs corresponding to its manpower levels.

Although officers assigned to PSUs should be trained at least to the minimal agreed standard, they are not specialists in public-order policing, and PSUs themselves are not dedicated public-order units. Most of the time, these officers will be engaged in normal police duties. However, if personnel are needed to police a public-order event or if spontaneous disorder breaks out, these officers will form up into their respective PSUs and be deployed as such.

District Support Units (DSUs) and Territorial Support Groups (TSGs) were or are peculiar to the Metropolitan Police. DSUs were, until their replacement by TSGs, composed of specially trained officers with a primarily, but not exclusively, public-order role. They have their counterparts in most forces, known by a variety of names, including 'Operational Support Group' and 'Tactical Aid Group'. The principal difference between DSUs and TSGs is that, whereas the former was organized at district level, the latter come under the responsibility of the newly created eight areas into which the Metropolitan Police is now divided. Unlike PSUs, members of TSGs work together on a regular basis, and these units do not therefore have to be raised from amongst the officers engaged on routine duties. Their task is to provide the immediate response to incidents of spontaneous public disorder or to provide specialist support for preplanned events. In the event that disorder broke out, a limited number of TSGs who are designated as being on immediate stand-by would attend, if requested. Their task would be to effect an early resolution of the disorder, if possible. Other TSGs, employed on tasks which allow them to respond reasonably swiftly to disorder, but not immediately, would begin to mobilize in case they were needed. Once the TSGs have been committed, PSUs would begin to be mobilized and deployed as the second wave of the force 'mobilization plan', about which more will be written shortly.

In a preplanned event which is likely to be accompanied by disorder, such as a mass picket or the Notting Hill carnival (which has a history of disorder), PSUs will be mobilized in advance to deal with routine crowd control. TSGs are more likely to be held in reserve, perhaps in protective clothing, to be deployed in the event of serious trouble. A limited number of TSG officers are trained in the use of baton guns should they be needed.

## PT18

Instructors who train other officers in the use of shields and public-order manœuvres provide an élite operational capability equivalent to that provided by PT17 in relation to armed incidents. These officers would be deployed to the most sensitive tasks, especially in preplanned operations or where specialized skills were necessary. For example, although a proportion of TSG officers are authorized to use baton guns if necessary, it is most likely that, if such weapons were ever used, it would be by PT17. They have the opportunity regularly to practise special skills and also to operate as a team.

A specialist capability that has been used fairly frequently in recent years is that of rapid entry into barricaded premises. For example, if it is suspected that drugs are being supplied from particular premises, PT18 officers have the skills of smashing reinforced doors down and overcoming unarmed but violent resistance. They have also learned, often from bitter experience, how best to subdue aggressive dogs used by some drug-dealers as protection.

## Specialist officers

PT18 is only one group of specialists amongst many available to the Metropolitan Police for deployment in public-order situations. Some of these will be discussed in greater detail later. Three specialist roles demand attention at this stage: evidence-gathering teams, arrest squads, and medical teams.

*Evidence-gathering teams.* Although the essence of civil disorder is collective action, the criminal law insists that the individual should be held culpable only for those actions that he has individually committed. So despite the fact that the sheer presence of large numbers of people allows, and perhaps even encourages, some individuals to commit serious offences, the law acknowledges no culpability in simply being present at the scene. Therefore, the police have had to devise means of identifying individual offenders amongst the crowd, and proving beyond a reasonable doubt that they committed specific offences.

Since this task requires a set of priorities contradictory to those of the officers trying to restore order, it has been given to specialist officers with different skills and facilities. Detectives have only recently been recognized as having a role in the policing of civil disorder. Their task is not to attend to the restoration of order, but to observe and obtain evidence that can later be used to arrest and prosecute individuals. They witness offences as they are committed and describe offenders. They can also gather identification evidence from officers behind shields, particularly from local officers who might recognize particular individuals within the crowd. In the aftermath of disorder, detectives can gather material evidence and arrange for its forensic examination. They can also take statements from officers and others present at the scene, eliciting information from a variety of sources which provides the necessary proof against a particular individual. They can also interview those arrested during the course of the disorder, to obtain incriminating information regarding not only the suspect in custody but also others who have yet to be arrested.

In addition to the role of the detective, increasing emphasis has been placed upon the contemporaneous acquisition of photographic and videotaped evidence. In the Metropolitan Police there is a corps of photographers whose task it is to accompany the most forward cordons and to photograph members of the crowd as they commit offences. Although they are civilian employees, not police officers, they wear protective clothing when necessary and expose themselves to considerable personal risk. Using sophisticated cameras with powerful flash-guns for use at night, they move amongst shield serials taking enormous quantities of photographs. Motor-driven shutters enable a succession of photographs to reveal the successive stages of a particular act. Each photograph is automatically imprinted with the date and time it was taken to establish veracity. Subsequent enlargement of portions of the photograph can be used to provide identification of distinctive items of clothing or physical characteristics. However, impressive though the photographic evidence collected by these means undoubtedly is, it is only corroborative evidence, and must be accompanied by other evidence of criminal conduct.

Despite motor-driven shutters, the still camera cannot capture movement nearly so well as can video equipment. Many professional soccer grounds — the source of most incidents of serious disorder in recent years — have now installed video cameras to monitor the behaviour of crowds and gather evidence of wrong-doing. Equally, it is possible to erect television surveillance equipment for preplanned public-order events, like the Notting Hill carnival. From remote-control rooms, the cameras can be manipulated and scenes taped to provide evidence later in court. A development of this evidence gathering capacity is the so-called 'Hoolivan'. This is a vehicle equipped with video cameras in a turret-like pod on the roof which can be directed by an operator inside the van. This has the advantage that it can provide videotaped evidence of mobile crowds, but is too vulnerable to attack to be used on occasions of serious disorder.

*Arrest squads.* In all public-order situations, one task will be to arrest those committing offences. This is a responsibility that all police officers share, but in some situations the opportunity to gather the necessary evidence and actually accomplish a successful arrest will be absent. The sheer volume of people and the presence of potentially hostile bystanders may prevent officers from making satisfactory arrests. Thus, special arrest squads are sometimes formed. They may comprise ordinary uniformed police officers diverted from other public-order functions, who seek to observe those committing offences and arrest them by quickly moving into the crowd and 'snatching' the suspect.

At the Notting Hill carnival, which for some time has been plagued by offenders using the dense crowds to avoid capture, squads of CID officers, temporarily wearing uniform, have been formed to follow and apprehend suspects. Using information gained from remote-camera surveillance (about which more will be explained shortly) and other sources, they seek to identify those committing offences such as 'steaming'. Once the suspect is identified, these officers move into the crowd, arrest the suspect, and remove him to a 'sterile area' (in which only the police and other emergency service personnel are permitted), where he is searched before being taken to a holding centre for interview and charge. Because of the potentially dangerous nature of this task, these arrest squad officers are equipped with body armour, and when they are about to make an arrest, nearby serials of officers in ordinary uniform are alerted in case assistance is required.

*Medical teams.* In cases of serious disorder, it has become apparent that immediate medical assistance cannot easily be provided. All police officers receive rudimentary training in first aid, but the kinds of injury which might be sustained during a riot could easily exceed the training normally provided. Shield serials are instructed in manœuvres designed to protect and remove officers who are injured, especially those who collapse. What is now provided are additional officers, specially trained in more advanced first-aid techniques, who can render immediate attention. They are equipped with a lightweight pouch containing dressings and other equipment, and they too are provided with protective clothing.

## Mobilization

One of the major problems in past incidents has been to deploy this manpower effectively. All too often, officers have rushed, or been rushed, to the scene of disorder as they became available. The Metropolitan Police aim in future to mobilize officers in a regulated manner in accordance with the severity of the incident. This is the 'force mobilization plan'.

The plan envisages five levels or 'phases' in the severity of disorder:

*Green*: This is a normal policing environment in which some initial incident has occurred and receives an initial response — for example, a fight at a pub.

*Amber*: At this stage the incident cannot be dealt with by the initial response and additional officers must be deployed from locally available manpower.

*Blue*: The disorder now exceeds the capacity of local officers to contain.

*Red*: Serious disorder.

*Black*: Major disorder. In either of the last two stages the Metropolitan Police as a whole would be mobilized.

Although the disorder may grow progressively in its severity, so that what began as a fight outside a public house becomes a major riot (much as the raid on the 'Black and White' cafe in St Paul's, Bristol, became a major riot), it is perfectly possible for disorder to be designated at any level from the outset. Once a situation has passed the Green phase, a series of prepared messages are relayed to stations by the central command complex. The colour-coded phase and the division affected are identified, and the message then stipulates what action has to be taken. For example, at the Amber phase, duty officers are to be informed and station officers should study the divisional contingency plan.

According to the severity of the disorder, the Metropolitan Police can commit officers in up to five 'waves', although their deployment need not necessarily correspond to the five levels of severity of disorder. The first wave can be drawn from between two and six TSG units available on 'Commissioner's Reserve'. These are officers who are on immediate stand-by to respond to disorder anywhere in the Metropolitan Police District. They could be deployed in Green or Amber phases, depending upon the nature of the disorder. It would not normally be until the Blue phase that the second wave, comprising ten TSG units who are not on immediate stand-by but who can be activated in a reasonably short time, would be deployed. If deployed, they would cease whatever they were doing (for example, a surveillance operation), don their equipment, and go to a rendezvous point. The third wave consists of eight PSUs, one from each of the force's areas. The fourth wave envisages a further eight PSUs; and the fifth wave will involve indefinite demands on areas to provide personnel in order to supplement or relieve officers who were deployed earlier.

It is hoped by this means to ensure that the appropriate personnel are deployed in the right numbers at the scene of the disorder. One difficulty is that the 'third wave' might well arrive before the 'second wave', because it is often easier to redeploy ordinary patrol officers than it is to redeploy members of the TSG who might be engaged on a plain-clothes assignment. However, given that the police cannot place large numbers of officers on permanent stand-by, but must instead redeploy officers as best they can in reaction to some unanticipated outbreak of disorder, it is unlikely that an unplanned mobilization will ever be implemented smoothly.

In the event that disorder exceeds the capacity of the Metropolitan Police to contain, then it, like all other police forces, will seek aid from neighbouring forces under mutual aid arrangements. All police forces throughout Britain have standing arrangements to provide each other with PSUs up to predetermined levels. By these means the Metropolitan Police could receive a maximum of 1,104 fully equipped and trained officers, if the situation were to demand it. If the situation exceeded even the capacity of such a supplemented force to cope with, then *ad hoc* arrangements would be made, and the National Reporting Centre would by then have probably been activated.

## Tactics

*Public-order manual*

The tactics approved for use in public-order situations are contained in the infamous *Tactical Options Manual* published by the Association of Chief Police Officers and made available only, save in the most exceptional circumstances, to officers of ACPO rank (chief, deputy chief and assistant chief constables in the provinces, and ranks of and above commander in the Metropolitan Police).

The infamy of this document has probably more to do with its secrecy than with its contents. The first edition was little more than a compilation of experience amassed after the St Paul's riot in 1980, when it became clear that there was no standardization in how police in different areas dealt with public disorder. Some 200 tactical options were listed along with their advantages and disadvantages. The more recent edition has fewer options listed and pays more attention to the wider context, including intelligence assessment, community conciliation, and Press relations. It is for the officer in command, usually guided by force policy, to select which tactics he will use in what circumstances. Since it is difficult to prescribe tactics for all occasions, he has the discretion to amend tactics contained in the manual as he thinks fit. In other words, the manual is advisory rather than prescriptive, sharing experience acquired in practice.

Why, then, the secrecy that surrounds it? This has fuelled suspicions that it contains tactics of dubious legality and extreme force. The selective disclosure during the course of the Orgreave riot trial of certain passages during the course of Orgreave riot trial which referred to the use of batons for 'incapacitating' ringleaders, which defence lawyers claimed amounted to an incitement to illegal violence, appeared to give some credibility to these suspicions. The issues raised in the course of that trial are considered in the main text, but it is unlikely, even if the manual did contain tactics employing extreme force, that these would justify its being kept secret, since ultimately lethal force can be and has been used in the past if rioting is severe enough. Probably nearer to the truth is a remark attributed to Christopher Paine, former Chief Constable of Cleveland and then chairman of the ACPO public-order commit- tee. He was quoted as saying that it would be foolish for a commander to disclose his battle plans to an enemy (Northam, 1985; 1986; 1988). This unfortunate imagery was taken as evidence of a paramilitaristic approach to public-order, more in keeping with Continental or colonial styles of policing than that tradition- ally practised in Britain. The comment can be interpreted differ- ently when it is appreciated that some tactics employ a measure of bluff and subterfuge in order to be effective. If a crowd were to be aware that a particular manœuvre was meant to deceive, not only would they be wise to the deception and so not prompted to act as desired by the police, but that awareness could actually prove dangerous to the police, whose weakness (rather than strength) might be detected. Either way, the failure of tactics of deception could lead to an escalation of violence, since bluff would be replaced by force. For these reasons, no detailed illustrations of such tactics will be given here.

A handbook containing so many possible options is simply too complex for all but a few specialists to comprehend. Moreover, some tactics might be rejected as inappropriate or unsuitable by any particular police force. The tactics that are actually taught to Metropolitan Police officers represent a selection from those contained in the manual. Some tactics have been omitted on purely technical grounds; others have been omitted because of wider considerations. An example of wider considerations influencing policy is that of the use of dogs in public-order situations. Dogs are commonly used and accepted as appropriate in dealing with football supporters, but the symbolic association of dogs with racial oppression in the southern US States during the civil-rights marches of the early 1960s, and more recently in South Africa, has meant that dogs are not seen as a viable option in the racially sensitive inner-city areas of London. Areas outside London which do not face the problem of racial sensitivity may well decide to retain the use of dogs as a public-order tactic.

### 'Taking the ground' and 'early resolution'

The basic tactic that police employ is the traditional one of 'taking the ground'. The aim of this tactic is for police to arrive at the scene of some public-order event well in advance of the crowd. As the crowd begins to arrive, the police will have already demarcated those areas in which the crowd can gather and march, as opposed to those areas where they may not go: police will, for example, allow protesters to gather on one side of a street, but not the other, in order to permit the free passage of pedestrians. By arriving first, the police are, simply by their deployment, often able to reinforce the 'rules of the game', which most crowds passively accept. Frequently, the ground rules are negotiated between police and organizers of demonstrations and rallies, or other gatherings. Sometimes a series of repeated demonstrations leads to the emergence of ground rules even though none have been explicitly negotiated. Thus, at various pits in the Derbyshire coalfield, during the miners' strike of 1984–5, police had imposed certain ground rules upon reluctant pickets which the latter had come gradually to accept and comply with. By the middle of the strike, pickets were assembling, unbidden, in their allocated locations. The Public Order Act, 1986 has made prior notification of marches mandatory, and allows the police to impose conditions on both processions and static demonstrations, thus formalizing the tactic of 'taking the ground' (Smith, 1987).

If the 'ground' is not effectively 'taken', then it might need to be fought for. This is often the situation in spontaneous public disorder, where the police must react to a disorderly crowd who have already assembled. Sometimes the police may anticipate disorder, as they did at Broadwater Farm following the death of Mrs Jarrett. However, 'taking the ground' in that situation, by occupying the walkways and stair-wells of the estate, might have been perceived by the residents as oppressive and provoked the disorder the police wished to avoid (Richards, 1986). Perhaps the most conspicuous example of the police failing to 'take the ground', and subsequently having to fight for it, was at the Manchester University students' union, where the Police Complaints Authority concluded that some officers had used excessive force. It is obviously to the advantage of all that violence should be avoided and the 'ground' be 'taken' well in advance.

Where, because of the unpredictable eruption of disorder, the 'ground' cannot be 'taken' in anticipation, the policy currently is to seek an early resolution of the disorder before it spreads. This requires determined action to disperse a crowd before too many other people join it. This is the task envisaged for the first wave of TSG officers deployed to a scene of disorder. The intention is to avoid repetition of past events, in which a slow build-up of officers and a relatively static containment of the situation led to the crowd being allowed to gather and throw missiles at shield units. No longer are the Metropolitan Police prepared to allow their officers to be Aunt Sallies. However, it is recognized that early resolution, which envisages using quite forcible means at an early stage of disorder, may be seen on some occasions as an unjustified use of force.

*Cordons*

The basic tactic of public-order policing is the sheer presence of the police, which in this context normally takes the form of a cordon — typified by a number of officers standing in line. The cordon is the means by which the police 'take the ground'. As disorder escalates, so the 'line' is defined with progressive rigour.

However, it is worth noting that the most commonly used cordon is inanimate. Fluorescent tape used to demarcate areas or metal crush barriers are frequently used for crowd control, and most people comply. Metal barriers can be linked together or left free-standing to allow people to pass through.

Sometimes the symbolic authority of tape, signs, and barriers needs to be reinforced by the physical presence of police officers, but, again, it is commonly the case that their impact is symbolic rather than either physically restraining or coercive. Normally, the physical presence of police takes the form of an 'open cordon' — officers simply standing in line without making physical contact with each other, and possibly spaced out too thinly to make physical contact even if they wished to do so. For example, in escorting football supporters from railway station to stadium, officers will stand across an entrance to a side street to signal those areas into which the fans are not allowed to go. The less a crowd is thought to respect the symbolic authority of the police, the more police will be in the line and the nearer they will be spaced.

Such a cordon can also be used as a 'filter cordon' through which people are allowed to pass in a regulated manner. Thus, officers standing across the entrance to a side street will allow residents and others wishing to gain *bona fide* access, but exclude football supporters. In other circumstances, a filter cordon will be used to regulate the rate of flow into an area so that it does not become hazardously crowded. In yet other circumstances, a filter cordon may be used to identify, question, and arrest suspects leaving an area in which offences have been committed.

A cordon becomes 'absolute' when police physically block access to an area, usually by holding each other to create a human barrier. Traditionally, officers have simply linked arms and faced a crowd or turned their backs and pushed against a crowd who are pushing against the police line. The disadvantage of this so-called 'butcher's grip' cordon is that, if officers use both arms and hands in holding onto their colleagues, they are vulnerable to attack and have no means of defending themselves. Also, presenting the front or rear of the body to the crowd leaves areas such as genitals or kidneys vulnerable to injury. Because of experience of assaults on officers in this type of cordon, an alternative has been developed — the 'chorus line' as it is colloquially known. Instead of either facing or turning their back to the crowd, officers in the cordon stand at right angles to the crowd and grasp the belt of the officer either immediately in front of them ('single-belt cordon') or immediately in front of the officer immediately in front of them ('double-belt cordon'). This allows the officer to keep one hand free to defend himself in the eventuality of attack and/or to arrest offenders, who can either be passed along the line from hand to hand or pulled through it and handed to arresting officers located to the rear. It also has the merit of not leaving the genitals and abdomen vulnerable to attack. With one foot forward, the formation is also more resilient against pushing. The main disadvantage is that it has a more aggressive appearance.

Cordons can be reinforced by the use of mounted officers, who can employ the weight of the horse to hold back a crowd and the height of the rider to command a view of the crowd. In order to deploy horses, officers have to learn how to split a cordon so as to allow the horses out without letting the crowd push through the lines, whilst at the same time avoid being trampled themselves. Also, senior officers must be aware of when to introduce horses into a cordon and when also to withdraw them.

Another means of reinforcing a cordon is to use vehicles as barriers. These can be deployed either side-on or facing the crowd, either with gaps between them to allow people to pass through or close together to form a complete barrier. Since the vehicles cannot protect themselves, they must be protected by officers and have drivers in position ready to remove them if violence should erupt.

Even when violence erupts and police can no longer safely maintain close physical proximity to a crowd, it is important to recognize that the cordon remains the basic tactic. Even officers behind shields form a cordon, and, indeed, this is what such a formation is called. Since this marks a qualitative change in tactics, however, perhaps it is better treated as a separate category.

### 'Trudging and wedging'

Although normally conceived of as static, cordons can move, progressively forcing a crowd back either by the symbolic authority of an advancing line of police or by sheer physical force. This is the traditional method of 'pushing and shoving', but one which has gradually been polished into more effective methods of crowd control. It has been found that the disciplined and concerted movement of a police cordon, especially the 'chorus line', can move a crowd of far superior numbers. This is known as 'trudging': a series of short side-steps directed into the crowd, co-ordinated so that the moment of advance is simultaneous. When used in combination with a wedge formation, it can be very effective in splitting a crowd, gaining access to offenders in the centre of the crowd or moving a section of the crowd.

The wedge is a chevron formation in which the point of the chevron is driven into the crowd as officers trudge forward, slowly but irresistibly. Like the 'chorus line' cordon, the wedge gains its strength from officers each holding the belt of their immediate or next-to-immediate neighbour. A wedge is formed behind a cordon which opens progressively as the wedge passes through. Once driven into the crowd, the wedge can open, hinged at the centre so as to form a new cordon, with officers from the previous cordon coming from the rear to assist. Or it can open at the centre to split a crowd into two halves. Sometimes wedges used in combination, entering the crowd from different locations, can isolate sections of the crowd and push them to some other position. Wedges may comprise a single line of officers or as many additional lines as are necessary to drive into a resisting mass of people.

Apart from its tactical effectiveness in being able to drive the crowd back, the wedge has other advantages. The first is that it allows a high degree of supervision, for the sergeant or inspector in charge of the group of officers forming the wedge will normally be positioned at the centre of the chevron, with ease of supervision and command. In addition, arresting officers can also be positioned in the centre of the chevron to take prisoners handed through the lines. However, it is an aggressive manœuvre, albeit one of low intensity, and one which may escalate tension and possibly lead to violence. Some police officers believe that when violence has reached levels which would justify the use of the wedge, that manœuvre is no longer tactically viable.

*Shield cordons*

The deployment of shields is not a departure from the principle of establishing a cordon: the aim continues to be one of demarcating areas of police control. However, it clearly differs from the ordinary cordon in two respects:

Shield cordons are not, or should not be, in direct physical contact with members of the crowd. The violence is such that officers should maintain a distance between themselves and the crowd for their own protection.

Shield cordons do not form a continuous line, but take the form of groups of officers spaced at intervals across a road or other open space.

Shield cordons comprise several 'shield units', each of which has three officers at the front, holding long shields which are locked together. The design of the long shield is such that, when placed side by side and slid together, the edge of one shield locks behind the metal plate of its neighbour on which the handles are located. Thus, the two shields on either side of the centre shield lock into the centre and form a resilient wall. A further two officers then crouch behind the three officers holding the shields with their arms around the latter's waists, holding them together in much the same way as a rugby scrum is held. Since holding a shield in this crouched position is physically tiring, the front and back rows of a shield unit are instructed to interchange periodically to prevent exhaustion.

A PSU or TSG can form four such shield units. Each sergeant takes responsibility for two of them, and the inspector has responsibility for the deployment of the whole unit. Although operating as four shield units, the PSU should, except in exceptional circumstances, continue to act as a single entity. A gap is maintained between shield units so as not to provide a single target. If officers formed a continuous line, then missiles thrown in their direction would be unlikely to miss. Presenting missile throwers with several discrete, but relatively small, moving targets has been found to encourage indecision and reduce the number of accurate hits.

The spaces between shield units also allows for flexibility and movement. If a PSU is in a narrow street, only two or three shield units may be able to space themselves across the width of the road. The others will fall behind, but covering the gaps in the front line. These rear units can then quickly move into any gaps that arise, for example, as the PSU advances around a corner and into a wider space. Also, should officers in the front line of shields be injured and need to be removed, shield units to the rear can quickly replace them in the line. Finally, if rioters attack the line itself, the officers in the second row of each of the shield units are able to run from behind the shields, through the gaps between shield units, make arrests, and return with prisoners behind the shields.

Although in some instances it is necessary or appropriate for the shield cordon to be static, for example, when protecting a fire engine or ambulance, it is normally expected that shield cordons will advance, forcing the crowd to retreat and thereby extending the area of police control. Given the crouching stance made necessary by the height of the shield and the 'rugby scrum' formation, advances tend to be slow. The tactic is to present the crowd with an inexorable police advance which progressively pushes it back, denying it territory.

It is essential that the crowd be kept to the front of the advancing police, for the officers are most vulnerable to attack from the sides and rear. Therefore, each shield unit must maintain its 'dressing' with others and not advance too far ahead. This becomes problematic when reaching road junctions. At its simplest, it means that as shield units turn a corner they must do so like an imaginary door hinged at the inside corner. However, if advancing into, say, a crossroads where rioters occupy all three exit roads, the manœuvre becomes much more complex. Three or four PSUs must assemble in the secured road and then move swiftly into the entrances of all three roads simultaneously — obviously a manœuvre that calls for considerable co-ordination.

Another manœuvre calling for co-ordination is that which allows mounted officers to pass through a shield cordon. This is, in principle, not dissimilar to the manœuvre in which mounted officers pass through a normal cordon. The cordon must swing open and close behind the mounted officers. The difference is that officers in the shield cordon have to manœuvre their shields and move quickly as a five-man unit. Speed becomes essential, since horses deployed in such circumstances would advance at a canter, not a walk.

The obvious limitation of the long-shield formation is that of speed. Whilst it is possible for officers to learn to move short distances at a run, for example, when turning corners, the need to keep shields locked together and maintain the integrity of the five-man unit necessarily inhibits speed. Unavoidably, then, the use of long shields is a primarily defensive tactic, even when advancing, for only 'volunteers' amongst the crowd are going to come close enough to the shield cordon to be vulnerable to arrest. Moreover, unless the crowd retreats, the shield cordon will find it difficult to advance. Apart from the fact that it is a line of police who possess legitimate authority, the cordon presents little threat, since most officers will literally have both hands occupied holding their shields. In fact, long-shield cordons can easily become Aunt Sallies to be bombarded by the crowd with missiles from a safe distance. The slow advance allows members of the crowd the opportunity to pick up missiles and time to throw them.

Recent innovations have been made to increase the speed at which shield units can advance. The first is the three-man shield unit, which dispenses with the two rear officers and relies simply on the three officers carrying the shields to hold themselves and their shields together. This avoids the problem of the front and rear officers tripping over each others' feet. The difficulty with this manœuvre is retaining the integrity of the shield wall, particularly when moving at speed. The second and third variants progressively reduce the numbers of officers carrying shields. Either two officers can form a unit, or just a single officer acting alone. This last alternative has long been included in the *Tactical Options Manual* as the 'free-running line', but has hitherto been rejected by the Metropolitan Police. It was feared that, if officers carrying shields with both hands came into close contact with the crowd, they could be vulnerable to attack. What is now envisaged is that officers with long shields, in whatever formation, would always be deployed with other officers carrying short shields close behind. The long shields provide cover for the short shields, but the short shields also protect the long shields, if necessary.

*Short shields*

This brings us to the second type of shield deployment, officers carrying the short, round shield on their weak arm. This type of shield allows a measure of speed, manœuvrability, and self-protection that the long cumbersome shield could never match. Short-shield officers run through the gaps in the long-shield cordon, towards the crowd, either to disperse or to effect arrests. For example, a four-man arrest squad contains two officers carrying short shields, followed by two others who are otherwise unprotected. Having identified an offender prior to their man-œuvre, they run from behind the long-shield cordon into the crowd. The leading short-shield officers push into the crowd whilst the other two officers arrest the offender and then, protected by their two short-shield colleagues, retreat behind the line of long shields. Alternatively, short-shield officers, all of whom carry shields, will advance quickly upon a crowd, causing them to flee for fear of being arrested. In either manœuvre, the long-shield cordon also advances to provide protection for the short-shield officers when they retreat.

Increasing emphasis is being laid upon the combination of short and long shields, with TSGs, in particular, but also PSUs being organized in 'mix and match' formations. These are two long-shield units of five men each, with the remainder of the TSG/PSU being deployed with short shields. By the use of these formations it is hoped to increase the speed with which the shield cordons can move, thus preventing rioters from re-forming and re-arming.

*Special Shield Manœuvres*

Apart from their use in advancing upon missile-throwing crowds, long shields can also be used to protect officers, say, gaining access to buildings or other locations where they might be vulnerable to attack from overhead. If the means of access is open, then three officers will combine, with two shields locked into the upright position and the third locked above their heads. They move swiftly up to and into the opening. If the opening is closed, for example, by a locked door, then officers must form a protective shell of long shields under which they can work to demolish the obstruction whilst remaining protected from overhead attack.

Once into a building, officers may need to advance up stairways whilst being bombarded by those above. Officers are shown how to use the shield both to protect themselves and to cause attackers to retreat by using the base of the shield as a weapon jabbed at the ankles and feet of attackers. Equally, officers might need to enter a room or other small area occupied by a person armed with a knife or continuing to throw missiles. With three shields locked together, if possible, they steer the attacker into a corner and overpower him by their combined pressure, until he can be pulled to the floor and arrested.

*Vehicle tactics*

Protected vehicles offer speed and shelter from missiles for their occupants, and are increasingly being used as cordons. With lights and beacons on, and klaxon sounding, such vehicles deployed in combination can make a formidable appearance and possibly dissuade a crowd from further violence. They can also provide protection for baton gunners engaging a crowd with plastic baton rounds.

The use of vehicles in close proximity to a crowd requires effective means of 'debussing', that is, vacating the bus in an orderly and speedy manner when possibly under attack. Officers are taught to 'debuss' in a disciplined manner, with the front row of long-shield officers providing protection for the rear pair and then moving away, to allow the second shield unit to 'debuss' before moving forward to protect the front seat passengers (normally including a sergeant) as they 'debuss'.

A further development in vehicle tactics arose in response to the miners' strike, when protesting miners began blocking motorways by driving very slowly across all three lanes. Police have devised a tactic for escorting the procession of traffic until the demonstrators can be stopped and the obstructed vehicles diverted around them.

## Training

Training for public-order duties in the Metropolitan Police is conducted at the Public-Order Training Centre in Hounslow, west London. This is a 9-acre complex, unique in Britain, comprising a number of streets of varying layouts and frontages, from shops to residential housing, from streets with vehicular carriageways to narrow, pedestrian-only passages; the aim is to present officers with a variety of situations and obstacles they are likely to confront. For example, a shield cordon should stretch across the entire street from building line to building line, but street furniture, such as lamp-posts or permanent pedestrian barriers, obstruct the use of the footpaths. Officers carrying shields need practice in how to negotiate these obstacles.

In these conditions, officers can be instructed in various public-order tactics and experience having missiles and fire bombs thrown at them. Wooden blocks are used instead of house-bricks in order to minimize serious injury; however, the possibility of being struck by such a missile provides ample incentive for officers to perfect their shield tactics. Fire bombs are usually thrown at shield serials only under controlled conditions; but this is sufficient to convey the experience of coming under such an attack and provide officers with confidence in their training and equipment. Indeed, whilst the fire-bomb exercise is carefully controlled, the fire bombs are thrown so as to present the greatest danger to the shield serials, for it is done so as to maximize the likelihood that the burning petrol will seep beneath the shields if the appropriate shield tactics are not properly employed. For obvious reasons, the precise means of presenting this danger to shield serials will not be explained here. Senior officers also have the opportunity to practice deploying serials in rapidly changing circumstances.

Training is at three levels:

1. *Basic familiarization.* As part of their initial training, recruits spend two days at the centre learning basic cordon and shield tactics. The purpose is only to familiarize recruits with basic tactics, and they are not deemed to be 'shield-trained' upon completion of the course.

2. *'Broadway serials'.* PSU officers, traditionally known in the Metropolitan Police as 'Broadway serials', are trained for two days twice a year. Most emphasis is laid upon basic long-shield tactics, but these officers are introduced to short-shield manœuvres, even though it is unlikely that they would be asked to use them.

3. *TSGs* Territorial Support Group officers both provide the first response to spontaneous civil disorder and have responsibility for more aggressive or complicated tactics in situations where PSUs are deployed. Therefore they train more frequently (one day per month) and are required to achieve a higher level of competence. They receive more training in short-shield tactics. They also concentrate upon such manœuvres as gaining entry to premises and climbing stairways whilst under attack.

4. *Baton gunners.* As mentioned previously, a minority of TSG officers are trained to fire baton rounds, and they are required to demonstrate their proficiency four times each year. This takes place in a special building, about the size of a small aircraft hangar, so that there is no danger of the baton rounds flying beyond the

confines of the centre. The targets are rubber tyres, stacked around pylons to enable them to survive the battering they inevitably receive from baton rounds repeatedly fired at them. The bottom half of the target is painted white, corresponding to the lower half of the torso at which gunners are instructed to aim. Scattered amongst these targets are ordinary firearms practice targets, which represent innocent members of the crowd. The task, of course, is to hit the target whilst avoiding other people. However, this is made much easier under training, since neither the targets nor the 'innocents' move.

A recent innovation has been designed to increase the verisimilitude of training. A screen is placed in the hangar, and onto it are displayed videotaped scenes of actual riots. Scattered around are burned-out cars and other debris, as well as street furniture. Baton gunners are trained to take advantage of the available cover and fire at the screen if a situation presents itself. It is hoped shortly to install a device similar to that used by armed officers, where the noise of the baton gun being fired causes the video to stop and the accuracy of the shot assessed.

Usually, the morning is spent training and practising tactics. During the afternoon, the gunners are given a series of tests of marksmanship. For example, one test involves gunners running approximately 150 metres into the hangar, where they engage targets at 40, 30, and 20 metres.

5. *Commanders.* Apart from the training of PSUs, TSGs, and baton gunners, courses are also held periodically for senior officers who form a cadre of specially trained public-order commanders on each of the eight areas within the Metropolitan Police District. In the event of large-scale or serious disorder, these officers would take command of PSUs dealing with the disorder. They receive five days' training in all aspects of public-order strategy and tactics. This includes practising some shield tactics, so that they can appreciate the demands made upon officers engaged in riot control as well as be aware of what such officers are capable of doing effectively. These senior officers are officially encouraged to attend refresher training along with PSUs and TSGs from their respective areas, but other demands upon their time obviously limit the opportunities for them to do so.

## Command and Control

Attention has concentrated so far on the most obvious aspects of public-order policing — those related to the point of conflict between police and rioters. Equally significant, however, are developments away from the immediate area of conflict. Officers have to be mobilized, deployed, and equipped effectively. They must also be relieved and refreshed from time to time. Liaison must be maintained with various official and unofficial bodies and organizations. Intelligence must be gathered, analysed, and acted upon. In short, the officers on the street must be effectively commanded and controlled if they, in turn, are to achieve their purpose of restoring peace and order.

It is in this respect, perhaps more than any other, that recent events have revealed a major weakness. In some riots, officers have been on duty, engaged in riot control, for many hours without relief or refreshment. At the same time, large numbers of officers have been mobilized but not deployed. The result has been that exhausted officers have suffered prolonged exposure to the physically demanding and dangerous rigours of riot control, whilst others have grown frustrated by their inability to play any constructive part. Another problem was illustrated during the Broadwater Farm riot, when DSUs (as they were then known), responding to calls for assistance, all approached the area along Mount Pleasant Road. The results were, first, traffic congestion caused by the personnel carriers left abandoned at the scene and, second, a concentration of officers at the locations of disorder adjoining Mount Pleasant Road, but insufficient officers in Gloucester Road, where PC Blakelock was eventually murdered.

These failures do not stem from incompetence, and still less from the wilful disregard of the welfare of officers. They arise from the fact that, once disorder breaks out, events occur with such rapidity that commanders find themselves facing a situation of kaleidoscopic unpredictability. So many decisions must be taken immediately that there is little opportunity to stand back and consider less immediate, but no less important, issues such as the relief and refreshment of officers engaged in controlling the riot.

### The chain of command

The Public Order Review of 1986 addressed this issue directly, and drew a distinction between 'slow-time' and 'quick-time' decisions. Slow-time decisions concern the strategy to be employed, the logistics of mobilization, deployment, relief and refreshment of officers, as well as intelligence and logistics. Quick-time decisions are tactical decisions regarding which PSUs/TSGs should do what. This distinction has become embodied in a three-level structure of command that has been adopted nationally.

*Gold control.*   Gold control is responsible for slow-time decisions and is remote from the area of disorder itself. In the Gold control room, the availability and status of various PSUs/TSGs is monitored. Liaison is maintained with other relevant police and public services — for example, there will often be representatives of the traffic division, British Transport Police, London Fire Brigade, and ambulance services. There will also be an 'intelligence cell', about which more will be said shortly./

Gold control is under the command of the Gold commander, who is responsible for the strategy and overall conduct of the event. In large-scale, but orderly, public-order situations, Gold control will command the whole scene, ensuring that officers are regularly relieved and receive refreshment. The Gold controller under these circumstances will be responsible for deciding when and how many PSUs should be dismissed at the end of their tour of duty.

*Silver control.*   Once disorder breaks out and tactical decisions must be made rapidly, a Silver control room will be established under the direction of a Silver commander. Silver control will be much smaller than Gold control, because it needs only to attend to the immediate situation. Gold will be responsible for suggesting that certain PSUs/TSGs should be relieved, refreshed, or dismissed. The Silver commander simply has to concentrate upon dealing with the disorder. Thus, he will decide how many PSUs/TSGs to deploy at any given location and what their purpose should be. For example, he might decide to form a cordon at a particular junction whilst asking PSUs/TSGs elsewhere to push the crowd in a given direction. The hope is that this measure of tactical command will help avoid the recurrence of a situation like that which occurred in Red Lion Square, when a cordon of officers on foot and a cordon of mounted officers pushed the same crowd in contradictory directions, due to a failure of co-ordination (see Scarman, 1975).

Silver control should not be too distant from the scene of disorder itself. It may be housed in premises, but to provide mobility the Metropolitan Police have adapted a vehicle to serve as Silver control. This will allow officers in command of PSUs/TSGs to meet and discuss tactics with the Silver commander if necessary.

*Bronze control.*   Whilst Silver control might determine that a crowd should be moved in a particular direction, how that is to be achieved will be the responsibility of the Bronze commander at the scene and directly in command of his officers. In large-scale or widely dispersed disorder, it may be necessary to deploy a number

of Bronze commanders, each responsible for several PSUs/TSGs.
They will decide whether to advance using long shields, short-
shield baton charges, vehicles, or mounted officers. Gold, Silver,
and Bronze levels of command are conceived as roles, and are not
intended to correspond to any particular rank. In a relatively small-
scale public-order event, the functions of Gold might be taken by a
chief inspector, whereas in a major event or serious incident it may
be the task of a deputy assistant commissioner, or even the
commissioner himself. However, it is assumed that Gold, Silver,
and Bronze will correspond to a hierarchy of relative rank relations.
It is hardly conceivable that a junior officer would set the strategy
to be implemented by his superior who acted as Silver.

*Communications*

A ubiquitous source of complaint throughout the modern police
service is radio communication. Considering the technical advances
made during the past twenty years, when personal radios have been
transformed from a futuristic dream to an indispensable item of
equipment, this complaint may sound churlish. However, adequate communication is essential to public-order policing, since
without it there can be no effective command and control, and thus
no co-ordinated action. Some may wonder what happened in the
past, before the invention of personal radios. The answer is that
events were often chaotic, as on the occasion of the Hyde Park riot
of 1855 when, through want of adequate information and channels
of communication, rioting occurred unabated (Critchley, 1970:
146–7).

The problems of communication occur at each level, from the
officer on the street to the commander at headquarters. The
Metropolitan Police, like all police forces in Britain, is chronically
short of radio channels. Under normal circumstances, officers must
at times compete for access to the airways. This chronic problem
becomes acute during public disorder, when information and
commands must be received and relayed to large numbers of
personnel.

At present, radio communication is partitioned between 'command' and 'support' frequencies. That is, Bronze commanders
communicate with Silver control or with each other on one
frequency, and with their inspectors and sergeants in charge of
PSUs/TSGs on another. This is in an attempt to prevent
overloading each channel, and also to insulate PSUs/TSGs from
information that does not concern them. For example, if a Silver

commander were to refuse a request for additional officers made by one of his Bronze commanders, and this was overheard by the PSUs/TSGs under that Bronze commander's direction, it could adversely affect morale. The problem is that, except in unusual circumstances, all Bronze commanders will share the same radio frequency. This means that they must compete with each other for air-time, and in a rapidly changing situation this can mean that necessary action is delayed or not taken at all. It would seem essential for each Bronze commander to have his own channel through which to direct the officers under his command; at present, however, the channels are simply not available.

Moreover, despite attempts to segregate channels and the information they carry, the limited number of channels means that information which should only be disseminated to a limited number of personnel is universally available. In an attempt to overcome this and other difficulties, the police have begun to take advantage of cellular telephones, which enable selected officers (usually senior officers and those engaged as intelligence teams) to communicate privately.

Public-order policing is one of the very few situations in which officers are operationally deployed without each of them possessing a personal radio. This is for two reasons: first, there are simply too few radios available to supply all the officers concerned; and, second, if every officer had a radio there would be the likelihood, if not the certainty, that the channels would become jammed. The second problem is not at all insuperable, for some radios can be configured so that they only receive and cannot transmit. This has the advantage that officers can be directly and privately instructed, but cannot clog the transmission network. However, this encounters a major obstacle — money. There would be considerable advantages to having radios — all radios — issued as items of personal equipment for which particular officers were individually responsible. If these radios could be switched from 'receive only' to 'receive and transmit', they could be used in all forms of police work. Unfortunately, the required capital expenditure for such a policy is regarded as prohibitive.

If it is not possible for all officers to be equipped with personal radios, some other form of communication is necessary. The difficulty is that the noise often accompanying crowds, which increases enormously in the event of civil disorder, is so great that any form of shouted or broadcast instruction might easily go unheard by the officers to whom it was addressed. Moreover, the crowd (or at least some members of it) are likely to be as informed about police intentions as are the officers who are supposed to carry them out. A system of hand signals has been devised (much of it borrowed from the military) in order to convey coded instructions to officers. However, in serious disorder the use of hand signals is limited because it exposes the signaller — usually a senior officer — to danger of attack.

At each point along the chain of command, therefore, the communications system is fragile. This inevitably jeopardizes effective command and control.

*Liaison and information*

It has been noted above that liaison with other public services and community leaders may be necessary during the course of any public-order event or incident. Public transport has to be diverted away from areas of disorder and/or danger, and the police wish to know of the movements of large numbers of people towards or away from the scene. The traffic department of the police needs also to establish diversions of ordinary motor vehicles to prevent them straying into an area of disorder, at the same time minimizing disruption and delay to the travelling public. Hospitals might need to be informed about the likelihood of casualties (indeed, when disasters such as train or aeroplane crashes occur, the police usually act as the principal conduit for such information). Occasions of violent disorder also require that police casualties should be treated at different hospitals from those treating members of the crowd. There have been occasions in the past where fighting has flared up between police and crowd casualties and/or their respective visitors, and this is best avoided in future. When police casualties do occur, members of their families must be informed, and in serious cases they might require welfare support. Scotland Yard houses an information centre which monitors the number and identity of casualties and to which officers' families might refer if worried. Indeed, there are myriad considerations of this kind which must be addressed by those behind the scenes.

# Intelligence

No topic is more controversial than intelligence-gathering in the context of public disorder. The term 'intelligence' conjures up images of the murky world of undercover agents and telephone tapping. Its association with the 'thought police' of totalitarian societies is seen as a threat to the democratic freedom of expression and right of dissent. However, as with so much else to do with the policing of public order, intelligence-gathering is mostly mundane and unexceptionable.

Since public-order policing is concerned with collective rather than individual action, a great deal of information will be publicly available. If a protest march, meeting, or picket is to be held, then potential supporters have to be informed and even encouraged to attend. Intelligence-gathering in this context may consist of little more than reading the posters, handbills, and other advertising that is addressed to supporters. Of course, some protest groups may have very restricted inner groups amongst whom such material is designed to circulate. The police may have to take special measures to obtain copies of 'underground' publications not available at high street bookstalls. (It is suggested by some cynical police officers that if it were not for the patronage of the Special Branch, many left-wing bookshops would go out of business.) It certainly appears to be the case that the most avid readers of the radical press are the Special Branch. It was through such means that they were able to prepare for the action of anarchists to 'Stop the City' (the financial centre of London) and 'Bash the Rich' (at the Henley regatta), because these events had been promoted by the newspaper *Class War*.

In addition to such explicit advertising, the police try to be sensitive to rumour. During the confrontations between mods and rockers at seaside resorts during the late 1960s, the forthcoming locations for such battles became known amongst young people frequenting clubs and similar establishments. In so far as the police could tap into the 'grapevine' by keeping their eyes and ears open, and reporting back what they heard, officers could be mobilized accordingly and pre-emptive action taken. Informants, who turn out less often to be paid people posing as genuine members of a group and more often to take the form of individuals to whom the police routinely talk (including 'community leaders') or those whom they arrest, directly advise or warn the police of forthcoming threats to public order, from anticipated gang-fights to flying pickets. As often as not this information is volunteered, not from any expectation of reward, but in the form of bragging or threatening.

In addition to such direct information, the police can monitor indirect signs of trouble — so-called 'tension indicators'. The pattern of non-co-operation with, abuse towards, and assaults upon police officers is taken as indicative of fluctuating levels of tension in a community which, if it becomes high enough, can explode into 'spontaneous' disorder. In those districts where the threat of disorder is chronically high, senior officers will often review the 'tension indicators' on a regular basis and deploy their officers accordingly. Of course, major events and incidents will signal an increase in tension. Thus, the shooting of Mrs Groce and the death of Mrs Jarrett were both interpreted by police as likely to increase tension dramatically, and officers were placed on stand-by accordingly.

Other signs of impending disorder may be less opaque. Thus, the movement of large numbers of people by public transport or in vehicles can, and has been, monitored. Public authorities like British Rail may be asked to supply information about the provision of special trains, and traffic patrols may be asked to report on the movement of motor vehicles.

All the above provide information, but intelligence comes from the interpretation of that information so as to draw valid conclusions. The most obvious necessity is to place information in its appropriate context. The action of one group, say, in assembling at a particular location can have quite a different significance to that of the same action taken by another group. Knowing that a large group gathering at the rendezvous point for a fox–hunt are supporters of the hunt has quite a different significance to the assembly at the same point of hunt saboteurs. Probably the best example of this function is the routine operation conducted at Scotland Yard by the Soccer Intelligence Unit (now taken over by the National Football Intelligence Unit), who collect and evaluate information regarding the relative troublesomeness of the fans of different clubs. They evaluate the likelihood of trouble erupting at each of the matches that occur nation-wide on any given day and advise the local police accordingly, who in turn deploy officers in appropriate numbers.

Apart from anticipatory intelligence, the assessment of the situation as it develops is equally important. Reports back to Gold control from Bronze commanders enables a coherent overview to be maintained in what can otherwise be perceived as chaotic flux. Simple matters such as the progress of a march along its route and its expected time of arrival at its destination may rely upon the collation of individual items of information received from various officers at the scene. The pattern of offending can also provide valuable intelligence to commanders regarding the deployment of officers and the success or failure of the police operation. More immediate intelligence may take the form of anticipating an outbreak of disorder amongst a large crowd. For example, the detection of rival football supporters on the same unsegregated terraces portends the likelihood of fighting, which can be prevented by removing fans who have infiltrated their rivals' enclosure.

Because officers at the scene may have other concerns, or might simply not pay sufficient attention to the events occurring around them, a recent development has been the formation of 'intelligence teams'. These were introduced at the Notting Hill carnival in 1988. Each team consists normally of a sergeant and four constables (although the size of the team depends on the circumstances), all of whom wear uniform, and whose only responsibility is to report what is happening. They can identify signs of potential trouble, or of reduction in tension, which might be missed by officers responsible for police serials. Also, because they are free to roam freely, they are more readily able to piece together features of the situation which would otherwise remain fragmented.

This and other information is monitored, collated, and interpreted by members of the 'intelligence cell': a small group of officers attached to the Gold control room. Using micro-computers and other technical aids, they attempt to assemble available information into meaningful patterns. For example, during recurring public order events, such as the Notting Hill carnival, the scale and pattern of offending in any one year can be compared with previous years to allow the detection of any noticeable changes, or the identification of particular locations where offences are being committed so that officers might be posted there or asked to be attentive to particular problems, such as groups of youths 'steaming'. They are also able to carry out routine monitoring of the location of sound systems or speakers' platforms. Increasingly, tactical advisers from specialist units, such as the Force Firearms Unit and the shield training instructors (who provide specialist support at major events where serious disorder is likely), are attached to the intelligence cell to provide advice, if it becomes necessary.

Finally, the availability of valid intelligence can enable those in command of a police operation to convey an accurate account of an outbreak of disorder to the authorities or to the public in its immediate aftermath. Not only is this important for accountability, but it can prevent false rumours from perpetuating tension.

### Evidence-Gathering

Closely allied to intelligence-gathering is obtaining evidence necessary for subsequent prosecution. Where these functions differ is in the purpose for which the information is gathered and the standards of proof required. Valid intelligence may well prevent offences being committed at all, thus obviating the need for evidence to be presented in court. Intelligence may be valid, although it may not meet the standard of proof required by a court—'beyond reasonable doubt'—with respect to any given individual. On the other hand, evidence gathered pursuant to the arrest and trial of suspects can contribute to the assessment of a situation.

The principal difficulty facing evidence-gatherers goes to the heart of the difference between public-order and other criminal offences. The social harm created by disorder lies not only in the aggregate level of crimes committed by individuals but in the demonstration that collective action confers immunity upon those who participate. This represents a challenge to the rule of law itself. Thus, the first priority of the police is simply to restore order and that requires addressing the crowd as an entity, rather than identifying individual acts of criminality. Tactics tend to reflect that goal, so that dispersal of the whole crowd is often preferable to arrest of given individuals.

Moreover, the detection and successful prosecution of individuals committing offences during the course of disorder is notoriously difficult. In part this has been because of the way in which serious public-order offences have been defined. For example, the St Paul's, Bristol, riot trial foundered on the question of whether those arrested had the 'common purpose' required by the offence of riot as defined at common law (Joshua and Wallace, 1983). However, a much more substantial obstacle to the successful prosecution of offenders is provided by the circumstances of disorder itself. The relative immunity to arrest afforded by membership of a large crowd, the anonymity of participants, and the concurrent commission of offences by large numbers of individuals makes both arrest and the acquisition of proof to be submitted later in court difficult. It is in order to overcome these difficulties as much as possible that increasing attention has been given to adequate evidence-gathering, by photographic and video surveillance.

## Conclusion

There can be little doubt that policing methods have changed considerably in response to the growth of serious public disorder that has been witnessed during the past twenty years. In the eyes of many people, these changes represent an abrogation of the traditions of British policing and the adoption of an alien style of paramilitary policing. These are the issues addressed in the main body of the text.

# NOTES

## Chapter 1

1 In the interest of simplicity I will use the masculine form throughout.
2 Ashworth, 1975; Harlow, 1974; Asmal, 1985; Kitchin, 1988; Stobart, 1989; Brownlee, 1989.

## Chapter 2

1 The Special Patrol Group (SPG) was established in the mid-1960s as a strategic reserve of officers under direct control of Scotland Yard and trained in specialist duties such as the use of firearms and public-order tactics.
2 The instrument used to strike Peach was never identified, and itself became the object of concern, particularly after unauthorized weapons, including a lead-weighted cosh, were found amongst the possessions of the officers apparently involved. However, the explanation favoured at the inquest was that Peach had been struck by a police radio (*The Times*, 7 June 1979; Dummett, 1980).
3 For a general analysis of the strike, see *Sunday Times* Insight Team, 1985.

## Chapter 3

1 See Greater London Council, 1984; Blom-Cooper in Home Office, 1986*a*; Benn and Worpole, 1986.
2 For another example see Yardley and Eliot, 1986*c*.
3 See Greenwood, 1979: ch. 2 for a general discussion of the legal position of police using deadly force.
4 Incidentally, the situation is no different for soldiers acting in aid of the civil power, as in Northern Ireland. This too has been criticized for undermining military discipline, and it has been proposed that soldiers should have a defence of obeying an order that was not manifestly unlawful (Brownlee, 1989).
5 See Harding, 1970; 1975; Harding and Fahey, 1973; Kobler, 1975; Abraham *et al.*, 1981; Chappell and Graham, 1985.

## Chapter 4

1 It is an irony that the application of the Hague Conventions on military ammunition might encourage soldiers to fire a fusillade of shots in

almost any event. Because full-metal jacketed bullets create little cavitation and over-penetrate, the amount of injury inflicted upon the adversary cannot be guaranteed to incapacitate. To compensate for the inadequate stopping power of military ammunition, soldiers may feel obliged to fire a fusillade of shots.

## Chapter 5

1 Rollo, 1979; Bunyan and Kettle, 1980; Kettle and Hodges, 1982: Manwaring-White, 1983: Coulter, *et al.*, 1984; Lea and Young, 1984; Scraton, 1985; Fine and Millar, 1985; McCabe *et al.*, 1988; Northam, 1985; 1986; 1988.
2 See Bowden, 1977; 1978; Roach and Thomaneck, 1985; Brewer *et al.*, 1988.
3 In more recent times, soldiers acting in aid of the civil power have found themselves in a situation increasingly analogous with that of the police officer, especially when using force. A general discussion of these issues is to be found in Bennett and Ryan, 1985. See also Whelan, 1985.
4 For further details, see pp. 177–8.
5 The massacre of Vietnamese women and children by US troops commanded by Lt. William Calley in the village of that name.
6 For details, see Appendix B.

## Chapter 6

1 See Rollo, 1979; State Research, 1981; Manwaring-White, 1983; Benyon, 1984*b*; 1987; BSSRS, 1985; Cousin *et al.*, 1985; Gordon, 1985; Lloyd, 1985; Scraton, 1985; Clare 1984; 1987; Brewer *et al.*, 1988; McCabe *et al.*, 1988; Northam, 1988.
2 See Appendix B for details.
3 See Appendix B for details.
4 'Serious' here means causing bruising to the arms, legs, and torso, which if committed illegally would amount to the offence of 'assault occasioning actual bodily harm'; if struck on the head, a person might expect to suffer at least a split scalp, which if committed illegally would constitute a 'wounding'—both offences within the meaning of the Offences Against the Person Act, 1861, s. 47 and 20 respectively. Of the truncheon, the Council for Science and Society wrote, 'Easily misused, in which event there may be serious injury including *irreversible brain damage*' (1978: 51; emphasis added).
5 See Marx, 1970, for a discussion of this phenomenon in the American context and, for a police officer's account, see 'A Met PC' (*Police Review*, 24 May 1985).
6 Note that in 1989 the South African Government announced the withdrawal of the sjambok because of its repressive associations. It is

ironic that the Government felt able to retain more injurious weaponry like batons, not to mention shotguns.

7 Manwaring-White, 1983; Northam, 1988; Nally, 1984; Kettle and Hodges, 1982.

8 For details, see Himsworth report, 1969*b*; Ballantyne *et al.*, 1973; Ballantyne and Swanston, 1974; Ballantyne *et al.*, 1975; Ballantyne *et al.*, 1976; Ballantyne, 1977; Sanford, 1976.

9 Himsworth Report, 1969*a*; and see n. 8 above.

10 Rosenhead and Smith, 1971; Rosenhead, 1973; 1976; 1981; Rosenhead and Shallice, 1978; Shallice, 1981; Manwaring-White, 1983; BSSRS, 1985; Information on Ireland, 1987; Northam, 1988.

11 Scarman, 1981; Kettle and Hodges, 1982; Benyon, 1984*b*; Nally, 1984; Clare, 1986.

12 Coulter *et al.*, 1984; Reed and Adamson, 1985; Fine and Millar, 1985; McCabe, *et al.*, 1988. See also *Police Review*, 23 Feb. 1990.

13 Council for Science and Society, 1978; Rosenhead and Smith, 1971; Sieghart, 1978; Rosenhead and Shallice, 1978; Rosenhead, 1981.


*Chapter 7*

1 The principal contributions to the critical literature that will be the focus of this chapter are: Baxter and Koffman, 1985; Benyon, 1984*a*; Benyon and Solomos, 1987*a*; Benyon, 1986; Bowden, 1978; Brewer *et al.*, 1988; Clare, 1986; Cowell *et al.*, 1982; Fine and Millar, 1985; Greater London Council, 1986; Gordon, 1985; Hain *et al.*, 1980; Hall, 1979; 1981; Joshua and Wallace, 1983; Kinsey and Young, 1982; Lloyd, 1985; McCabe *et al.*, 1988; Northam, 1988; Reiner, 1985*a*; 1985*b*; Scraton, 1985; 1987; State Research, 1981. Additional refrences will be restricted only to texts which make a specific contribution.

2 Manwaring-White, 1983; BSSRS, 1985; Ackroyd *et al.*, 1977.

3 Scarman, 1981; Hytner, 1981; Greater Manchester Council Independent Inquiry Panel, 1985; Silverman, 1986; Gifford, 1986; Ward, 1986; London Strategic Policy Unit, 1987.

4 See Kettle and Hodges, 1982; *Sunday Times* Insight Team, 1985; Harris, 1985.

5 Howe, 1980*a*; 1980*b*; 1981; Rodrigues, 1981.

6 Skolnick, 1969; Stark, 1972; McLaughlin, 1969; Masotti and Bowen, 1968; Allen and Adair, 1969; Walker, 1968; National Commission on the Causes and Prevention of Violence, 1969; Fogelson, 1970; Feagin and Hahn, 1973.

7 For a review of the literature, see Field and Southgate, 1982.

8 See e.g. Platt, 1979; Gilroy, 1987.

9 For a summary see Field and Southgate, 1982; Taylor, 1984; Gaskell and Benewick, 1987.

10 See e.g. Howe, 1973; 1980; 1981; 1982; Hall, 1981; Rodrigues, 1981; Sivanandan, 1982; Gordon, 1983.

11 See e.g. Kirsch, 1981; Chatwin, 1981.

12 Rudé, 1964; Hobsbawn and Rudé, 1970; Tilly, 1969; Roberts, 1969; Critchley, 1978; Geary, 1985; Morgan, 1987.

13 Humphry, 1972; Hiro, 1973; Mullard, 1973; Affor, 1978; Institute of Race Relations, 1979.

14 See Fogelson, 1970, for an attempt to explain why American Blacks rioted in the 1960s, whereas other comparably deprived and discriminated against groups had not done so previously.

15 Benyon, 1984*b*; Benyon and Solomos, 1987*b*; Kettle and Hodges, 1982; Joshua and Wallace, 1983.

16 Humphry, 1972; Hall *et al.*, 1978; Reiner, 1981; Gaskell, 1983; 1985; Gaskell and Smith, 1981*a*; 1981*b*; 1981*c*; 1985; Policy Studies Institute, 1983; Field, 1984.

17 Jacobs, 1973; Home Office, 1981; Home Affairs Committee, 1986; Carey, 1986.

18 However, Lord Gifford did not explain the cause of the harassment of the supermarket owners by Black and White youths on the estate (Platt, 1985), nor why a gang of Black rioters felt it necessary to attack the firemen, who were seeking only to extinguish the blaze, and the police protecting them.


*Chapter 8*

1 The withdrawal of the sjambok by the South African Government in 1989 testifies to the power of imagery, for this weapon was withdrawn not because it is notably injurious (since the South African Police retain far more injurious weapons) but because of its association with the traditional 'rhino whip' used by slave-owners – a symbolism which the de Klerk Government could ill afford as it sought a *reapproachment* with its black population.

2 Even then these modifications have only recently been introduced (see *Tennessee vs. Garner*, U.S. 36 CrL 3233).

# BIBLIOGRAPHY

Abraham, J. D., Field, J. C., Harding, R. W., and Skurka, S. (1981). 'Police Use of Lethal Force: A Toronto Perspective', *Osgoode Hall Law Journal*, 19/2.

Ackroyd, C., Rosenhead, J., and Shallice, T. (1977). *The Technology of Political Control*. Harmondsworth, Middx.: Penguin.

Adams, J., Morgan, R., and Bambridge, A. (1989). *Ambush: The War Between the SAS and the IRA*. London: Pan.

Affor (1978). *Talking Blues: The Black Community Speaks About its Relationship with the Police*. Birmingham: Affor.

Alderson, J. C. (1979). *Policing Freedom*. Plymouth: MacDonald and Evans.

—— (1985). 'Police and the Social Order', in Roach and Thomaneck, (eds.) 1985.

Allen, R. F., and Adair, C. H. (1969). *Violence and Riots in Urban America*. Worthington, Oh: Charles A. Jones.

Anderton, J. (1981). 'Statement of James Anderton, Chief Constable of Greater Manchester Police, to the Greater Manchester Police Committee'. Unpublished statement, Manchester.

Apter, D. (ed.) (1964). *Ideology and Discontent*. New York: Wiley.

Ashworth, A. J. (1975). 'Self Defence and the Right to Life', *Criminal Law Review*.

Asmal, K. (1985). *Shoot to Kill: International Lawyer's Inquiry into the Lethal Use of Firearms by the Security Forces in Northern Ireland*. Dublin: Mercier Press.

Ayoob, M. (1984). *Stressfire*. M. and D. Ayoob, available from Police Bookshelf, Concord, NH.

Bachrach, P., and Baratz, M. (1970). *Power and Poverty*. New York: Oxford Univ. Press.

Ballantyne, B. (1977). 'Riot Control Agents: Biomedical and Health Aspects of the Use of Chemicals in Civil Disturbances', in R. B. Scott and J. Fraser (eds.), *Medical Annual*. Bristol: Wright.

—— Beswick, F. W., and Price Thomas, D. (1973). 'The Presentation and Management of Individuals Contaminated with Solutions of Dibenzoxaepine (CR)', *Medicine, Science and the Law*, 13.

—— Gall, D., and Robson, D. C. (1976). 'Effects on Man of Drenching with Dilute Solutions of 0-Chlorobenzylidene Malononitrile (CS) and Dibenz (b.f)−1:4−oxazepine (CR)', *Medicine, Science and the Law*, 16.

—— Gazzard, M. F., Swanston, D. W., and Williams, P. (1975). 'The Comparative Ophthalmic Toxicology of 1-Chloroacetophenone (CN) and Dibenz (b.f)−1:4−oxazepine', *Arch. Toxicol.*, 34.

—— and Swanston, D. W. (1974). 'The Irritant Effects of Dilute Solutions of Dibenzoxazepine (CR) on the Eye and Tongue', *Acta Pharmacologica et Toxicologica*, 35.

Banton, M. (1964). *The Policeman in the Community*. London: Tavistock.
Baxter, J., and Koffman, L. (eds.) (1985). *Police: The Constitution and the Community*. Abingdon, Oxon: Professional Books.
Beckford, J. A. (1978). 'Accounting for Conversion', *British Journal of Sociology*, 29/2.
Benn, M., and Worpole, K. (1986). *Death in the City*. London: Canary Press.
Bennett, G. J., and Ryan, C. L. (1985). 'Armed Forces, Public Disorder and the Law in the United Kingdom', in R. Rowe and C. J. Whelan (eds.), *Military Intervention in Democratic Societies*. London: Croom Helm.
Benyon, J. (ed.) (1984a). *Scarman and After*. Oxford: Pergamon.
—— (1984b). 'Scarman and After', in Benyon 1984a.
—— (1984c). 'The Policing Issues', in Benyon, 1984a.
——(1984d). 'The Riots: Perceptions and Distortions', in Benyon, 1984a.
—— (1987a). 'Interpretations of Civil Disorders', in Benyon and Solomos, 1987b.
—— and Solomos, J. (eds.) (1987b). *The Roots of Urban Unrest*. Oxford: Pergamon.
—— —— (1987c). 'The Roots of Urban Unrest', in Benyon and Solomos, 1987a.
Bittner, E. (1970). *The Functions of the Police in a Modern Society*. Washington, DC: US Govt. Printing Office.
—— (1975). 'A Theory of the Police', in H. Jacob (ed.), *Potential for Reform of Criminal Justice*. Beverly Hills, Calif.: Sage.
Blom–Cooper, L. (1988). 'Justifications for Homicide', *Independent*, 1 Sept.
Bowden, T. (1977). *Beyond the Limits of the Law*. Harmondsworth, Middx.: Penguin.
Brewer, J. D., Guelke, A., Hume, I., Moxon-Browne, E., and Wilford, R. (1988). *The Police, Public Order and the State*. London: Macmillan.
Brittan, Rt. Hon. Leon, MP (1985). Letter to Rt. Hon. David Owen, MP. Unpublished, House of Commons, 25 June.
Brogden, M. (1985). 'Stopping the People: Crime Control versus Social Control', in Baxter and Koffman, 1985.
——Jefferson, T., and Walklate, S. (1988). *Introducing Police Work*. London: Unwin Hyman.
Brownlee, I. D. (1989). 'Superior Orders: Time for a New Realism?', *Criminal Law Review*.
BSSRS (British Society for Social Responsibility in Science) (1983). *Technocop*. London: Free Association.
Bunyan, T., and Kettle, M. (1980). 'The Police Force of the Future is Now Here', *New Society*, 21 Aug.
Carey, S. (1986). 'Anatomy of Racial Violence', *New Society*, 11 Apr.
Cashmore, E., and Troyna, B. (1982). 'Growing up in Babylon', in E. Cashmore and B. Troyna (eds.), *Black Youth in Crisis*. London: Allen & Unwin.
Chappell, D., and Graham, L. P. (1985). *Police Use of Deadly Force: Canadian Perspectives*. Centre of Criminology, Univ. of Toronto.

Chatwin, R. (1981). 'Brixton and After', *Marxism Today*, Sept.

Clare, J. (1984). 'Eyewitness in Brixton', in Benyon, 1984.

—— (1987). 'The Rachet Advances Another Turn', in Benyon and Solomos, 1987.

Clutterbuck, R. (1980). *Britain in Agony*. Rev. edn., Harmondsworth, Middx: Penguin.

Cohen, S. (1972). *Folk Devils and Moral Panics*. Oxford: Martin Robertson.

Cohn, N. (1957). *The Pursuit of the Millennium*. London: Secker & Warburg.

Condon, R. J. (1985). *Police Use of Deadly Force in New York State: A Report to Governor Mario M. Cuomo*. Albany, NY: Division of Criminal Justice Services.

Coulter, J., Miller, S., and Walker, M. (1984). *State of Siege: Miners' Strike 1984*. London: Canary Press.

Council for Science and Society (1978). *'Harmless Weapons'*. London: Barry Rose.

Cousin, G., Fine, B., and Millar, R. (1985). 'Conclusion: The Politics of Policing', in Fine and Millar, 1985.

Cowell, D., Jones, T., and Young, J. (eds.) (1982). *Policing the Riots*. London: Junction Books.

Critchley, T. A. (1967). *A History of Police in England and Wales*. London: Constable.

—— (1970). *The Conquest of Violence*. London: Constable.

Dahrendorf, R. (1985). *Law and Order*. Hamlyn Lectures, 37th ser. London: Stevens.

Davies: J. C. (1969). 'The J-Curve of Rising and Declining Satisfactions as a Cause of some Great Revolutions and a Contained Rebellion', in National Commission on the Causes and Prevention of Violence, 1969.

Dawkins, K. (1989). 'Police Weapons (I): Soft-Nose Bullets', *New Zealand Law Journal*, Feb.

Dear, G. J. (1986). *Report of the Chief Constable West Midlands Police, Handsworth/Lozells—September 1985*. Birmingham: West Midlands Police.

Desborough Committee (1920). *Report of the Committee on the Police Service*. Cmnd. 574 and Cmnd. 874, London: HMSO.

Dixon, D., and Fishwick, E. (1984). 'The Law and Order Debate in Historical Perspective', in P. Norton (ed.), *Law and Order in British Politics*. Aldershot, Hants: Gower.

Dollard, J., Doob, L., Miller, N., Mowrer, O., and Sears, D. (1974). *Frustration and Aggression*. New Haven, Conn: Yale Univ. Press.

Donald, D. (1970). 'Toward a Reconsideration of Abolitionists', in Gusfield, 1970.

Downes, D. (1966). *The Delinquent Solution*. London: Routledge.

Dummett, M. (1980a). *Southall 23 April 1979*. London: NCCL.

—— (1980b). *The Death of Blair Peach*. London: NCCL.

Dunning, E., Murphy, P., Newburn, T., and Waddington, I. (1987). 'Violent Disorders in Twentieth-Century Britain', in G. Gaskell and R. Benewick (eds.), *The Crowd in Contemporary Britain*. London: Sage.

Edwards, C. (1988). 'Was Hungerford "a basic failure of the police"?', *Listener* 14 Jan.

Edwards, G. S., and Menzies, K. (1986). 'Visits to Leonardo Da Vinci Airport, Rome, and Schwechat Airport, Vienna, following Terrorist Attacks on 27th Dec., 1985'. Unpublished report, Gatwick Airport: Sussex Police.

Emsley, C. (1983). *Policing and its Context*. London: Macmillan.

Feagin, J. R., and Hahn, H. (1973). *Ghetto Revolts: The Politics of Violence in American Cities*. New York: Macmillan.

Field, S. (1984). *The Attitudes of Ethnic Minorities*. Home Office Research Study No. 80, London: HMSO.

—— and Southgate, P. (1982). *Public Disorder: A Review of Research and a Study in One Inner City Area*. Home Office Research Study No. 72, London: HMSO.

Fine, B., and Millar, R. (eds.) (1985). *Policing the Miners' Strike*. London: Lawrence & Wishart.

Fogelson, R. M. (1970). 'Violence and Grievances: Reflections of the 1960s Riots', *Journal of Social Issues*, 26/1.

Gaskell, G. (1983). 'The Young, the Black and the Police', *New Society*, 24 Nov.

—— and Benewick, R. (1987). 'The Crowd in Context', in G. Gaskell and R. Benewick (eds.), *The Crowd in Contemporary Britain*. London: Sage.

—— and Smith, P. (1981*a*). 'Are Young blacks Really Alienated?', *New Society*, 14 May.

—— —— ( 1981*b*). Alienated Black Youth: An Investigation of Conventional Widsom Explanations', *New Community*, 11/2.

—— —— (1981*c*). 'Young Blacks' Hostility to the Police: An Investigation into its Causes', *New Community*, 12/1.

—— —— (1985). 'How Young Blacks See the Police', *New Society*, 23 Aug.

Gaskell, R. (1986). 'Police and Black Youth', *Policing*, 2/1.

Geary, R. (1985). *Policing Industrial Disputes: 1893 to 1985*. Cambridge: Cambridge Univ. Press.

Gerth, H. H., and Mills, C. W. (1948). *From Max Weber*. London: Routledge & Kegan Paul.

Gifford, Lord (1986). *Report of the Independent Inquiry into Disturbances of October 1985 at the Broadwater Farm Estate, Tottenham*. London: Broadwater Farm Inquiry.

Gilbert, T. (1975). *Only One Died: An Account of the Scarman Inquiry into the Events of 15 June 1974 in Red Lion Square, when Kevin Gately Died Opposing Racism and Fascism*. London: Kay Beauchamp.

Gilroy, P. (1987). 'The Myth of Black Criminality', in Scraton, 1987.

Gordon, P. (1983). *White Law*. London: Pluto Press.

—— (1985). ' "If they come in the morning. . .": The Police, the Miners and Black People', in Fine and Millar, 1985.

Gorer, G. (1955). *Exploring English Character*. London: Cresset.

Gould, R. W., and Waldren, M. J. (1986). *London's Armed Police*. London Arms & Armour.

Greater London Council (1984). *Proposed Inquiry into the Issuance and Use of Firearms by Police in London*. London: GLC.
—— (1986). *The Control of Protest*. London: GLC.
Greenwood, C. (1966). *Police Firearms Training*. London: Forensic Science Society.
—— (1979). *Police Tactics in Armed Operations*. Paladin, Colo.: Paladin Press.
—— (1986). 'Where Gun Training Fails', *Police Review*, 10 Oct.
Gregory, F. E. C. (1985). 'The British Police System: With Special Reference to Public Order Problems', in Roach and Thomaneck, 1985.
—— (1987). *Policing the Democratic State: How Much Force?* Conflict Studies 194, London: Institute for the Study of Conflict.
Gurr, T. R. (1969). 'A Comparative Study of Civil Strife', in National Commission on the Causes and Prevention of Violence, 1969.
—— (1970). *Why Men Rebel*. Princeton, NJ: Princeton Univ. Press.
Gusfield, J. R. (ed.) (1970). *Protest, Reform, and Revolt*. New York: Wiley.
Hain, P., Kettle, M., Campbell D., and Rollo J. (1979). *Policing the Police*. London: John Calder.
Hall, S. (1979). *Drifting into a Law and Order Society*. London: Cobden Trust.
—— (1981). 'Summer in the City', *New Socialist*, 1.
—— Critcher, C., Jefferson, T., Clarke, J., and Roberts, B. (1978). *Policing the Crisis*. London: Macmillan.
Hanley, D., and Kerr, P. (eds.) (1989). *May '68: Coming of Age*. London: Macmillan.
Harding, R. W. (1970). *Police Killings in Australia*. Sydney: Penguin.
—— (1975). 'Changing Patterns of the Use of Lethal Force by Police in Australia', *Australian and New Zealand Journal of Criminology*, 8/2.
—— and Fahey R. P. (1973). 'Killings by Chicago Police, 1967–70: An Empirical Study', *Southern California Law Review*, 46.
Harlow, C. (1974), 'Self-Defence: Public Right or Private Privilege', *Criminal Law Review*.
Harman, C. (1981). 'The Summer of 1981: A Post-Riot Analysis', *International Socialism*, 14.
Harold, M. C. D. (1974). 'Armaments for Police Officers on Protection', *Police Journal*, Oct.
Harris, M. (1985). 'Looking Back on the Riot', *New Society*, 4 Oct.
Hewitt, P. (1982). *The Abuse of Power: Civil Liberties in the UK*. Oxford: Martin Robertson.
Hillyard, P. (1985). 'Lessons from Ireland', in Fine and Millar, 1985.
—— (1987). 'The Normalization of Special Powers: From Northern Ireland to Britain', in Scraton, 1987.
Himsworth Report (1969a). *Report of the Enquiry into the Medical and Toxicological Aspects of CS (Orthochlorobenzilidene Malononitrile)*, pt. 1. Cmnd 4173, London: HMSO.
—— (1969b). *Report of the Enquiry into the Medical and Toxicological Aspects of CS (Orthochlorobenzilidene Malononitrile)*, pt. ii. Cmnd. 4775, London: HMSO.

Hiro, D. (1973). *Black British, White British*. Harmondsworth, Middx.: Penguin.

Hoare, M. (1980). 'The Pattern of Experience in the Use of Firearms by Criminals and the Police Response'. Unpublished M.Sc. thesis, Cranfield Institute of Technology.

Hobsbawm, E. J., and Rudé, G. (1970). *Captain Swing*. Harmondsworth, Middx.: Penguin.

Home Affairs Select Committee (1986). *Racial Attacks and Harassment*. London: HMSO.

Home Office (1972). *Firearms for Police Use in Peacetime*. Scientific Advisory Branch Information Note No. 1/72, unpublished report.

—— (1980). *Review of the Public Order Act 1936 and Related Legislation*. White Paper. Cmnd. 7891, London: HMSO.

—— (1981). *Racial Attacks: Report of a Home Office Study*. London: Home Office.

—— (1986a). *Report by the Home Office Working Group on the Police Use of Firearms*. Unpublished report.

—— (1986b). *Criminal Statistics for England and Wales*. London: Home Office.

Horowitz, D. L. (1983). 'Racial Violence in the United States', in N. Glazer and K. Young (eds.), *Ethnic Pluralism and Public Policy*. Lexington, Mass.: D. C. Heath.

Howe, D. (1973). 'Fighting Back: West Indian Youth and the Police in Notting Hill', *Race Today*, Dec.

—— (1980a). 'From Bobby to Babylon', *Race Today*, May/June.

—— (1980b). 'From Bobby to Babylon', pt. ii, *Race Today*.

—— (1981). 'From Bobby to Babylon: Blacks and the British Police', pt. iii, *Race Today*, Feb.

Humphry, D. (1972). *Police Power and Black People*. London: Panther.

Hytner, B. A., QC (1981). *Report of the Moss Side Enquiry Panel to the Leader of the Greater Manchester Council*. Manchester: Greater Manchester Council.

Information on Ireland (1987). *They Shoot Children*. London: Information on Ireland.

Institute of Race Relations (1979). *Police Against Black People*. Race and Class, No. 6, London: Institute of Race Relations.

*International Law Enforcement* (1984). 'Police Firearms Training in the United Kingdom', pts. i and ii, vols. 1 and 2.

Jackson, B. (1986), with Wardle, T. *The Battle for Orgreave*. Brighton, Sussex: Vanson, Wardle.

Jacobs, J. (1973). 'The Police and the Fascists: East London 1932–36', *Race Today*, Dec.

Jacobs, J. and Sanders, A., (1986). 'Should Police Be Armed?', *New Society*, 11 July.

Janowitz, M. (1970). *Political Conflict: Essays in Political Sociology*. Chicago: Quadrangle Books.

Jeffery, K., and Hennessy, P. (1983). *States of Emergency*. London: Routledge & Kegan Paul.

Joshua, H., and Wallace, T., with the assistance of Booth, H. (1983). *To Ride the Storm*. London: Heinemann.

Kerner, O. (1968). *The Report of the National Advisory Commission on Civil Disorders*. Washington, DC: US Govt. Printing Office.

Kettle, M. (1982). 'Where Did All the Riots Go?', *New Society*, 61/1034.

——(1985). 'The National Reporting Centre and the 1984 Miners' Strike', in Fine and Millar, 1985.

—— and Hodges, L. (1982). *Uprising*. London: Pan.

Kilroy-Silk, R. (1987). 'Why are the White Rioters Being Ignored?', *Police Review*, 9 Oct.

Kinsey, R., and Young, J. (1982). 'Police Autonomy and the Politics of Discretion', in Cowell *et al.*, 1982.

Kirsch, B. (1981). 'Brixton and After', *Marxism Today*, July.

Kitchin, H. (1988). *The Gibraltar Report: Inquest into the Deaths of Mairead Farrell, Daniel McCann and Sean Savage, Gibraltar, September 1988*. London: National Council for Civil Liberties.

Klockars, C. B. (1985). *The Idea of Police*. Beverly Hills, Calif.: Sage.

Kobler, A. L. (1975). 'Police Homicide in a Democracy', *Journal of Social Issues*, 31/1.

Kornhauser, W. (1960). *The Politics of Mass Society*. London: Routledge & Kegan Paul.

Le Bon, G. (1896). *The Crowd*. English translation, New York: Viking, 1960.

Lea, J., and Young, J. (1982). 'The Riots in Britain 1981: Urban Violence and Political Marginalisation', in Cowell *et al.*, 1982.

—— (1984), *What Is to Be Done about Law and Order?* Harmondsworth, Middx.: Penguin.

Leonard, T. (1985). 'Policing the Miners', *Policing*, 1/2.

*Leveller, The* (1981). Editorial: 'Rebellion in Brixton', No. 54, 17 Apr.

Lewis, M. (1970). 'The Negro Protest in Urban America', in Gusfield, 1970.

Lloyd, C. (1985). 'A National Riot Police: Britain's "Third Force"?', in Fine and Millar, 1985.

London Strategic Policy Unit (1987). *Policing Wapping: An Account of the Dispute 1986/7*. Briefing Paper No. 3, London: LSPU.

Loveday, B. (1986). 'Central Coordination, Police Authorities and the Miners' Strike', *Political Quarterly*, Jan-Mar.

McCabe, S., and Wallington, P., with Alderson, J., Gostin, L., and Mason, C. (1988). *The Police, Public Order and Civil Liberties: Legacies of the Miners' Strike*. London: Routledge & Kegan Paul.

Macdonald, I. (1973). 'The Creation of the British Police', *Race Today*, Dec.

McIlroy, J. (1985). '"The law struck dumb"? Labour Law and the Miners' Strike', in Fine and Millar, 1985.

McLaulin, B. (ed.) (1969). *Studies in Social Movement*. New York: Free Press.

McLaughlin, C. (1988). *The Hungerford Incident*. Unpublished report.

Manchester City Council, Independent Inquiry Panel (1985). *Leon Brittan's Visit to Manchester University Students' Union*. Manchester: MCC.

Manolias, M., and Hyatt-Williams, A. (1988). *Post-Shooting Experiences in Firearms Officers*. London: Joint Working Party on Organisational Health and Welfare.

Manwaring-White, S. (1983). *The Policing Revolution*. Brighton, Sussex: Harvester.

Masotti, L. H., and Bowen, D. R. (1968). *Civil Violence in the Urban Community*. Beverly Hills, Calif.: Sage.

Mark, R. (1978). *In the Office of Constable*. London: Collins.

Marx, G. (1970). 'Civil Disorder and the Agents of Social Control', *Journal of Social Issues*, 26/1.

Metropolitan Police (n.d.). *Mass Demonstrations*. Unpublished Department Handbook for Management of Mass Demonstrations. Washington, DC: Metropolitan Police.

Miller, W. R. (1977). *Cops and Bobbies: Police Authority in New York and London, 1830–1870*. Chicago: Univ. of Chicago Press.

Milton, C. H., Halleck, J. W., Lardner, J., and Abrecht, G. L. (1977). *Police Use of Deadly Force*. Washington, DC: Police Foundation.

Moore, T. (1988). 'A Riot of Colour', *Police Review*, 26 Aug.

Morgan, J. (1987). *Conflict and Order*. Oxford: Clarendon Press.

Morris, T. (1957). *The Criminal Area*. London: Routledge & Kegan Paul.

—— (1985). 'The Case for a Riot Squad', *New Society*, 29 Nov.

Mullard, C. (1973). *Black Britain*. London: Allen & Unwin.

Murdock, G. (1984). 'Reporting the Riots: Images and Impact', in Benyon, 1984a.

Nally, M. (1984). 'Eyewitness in Moss Side', in Benyon, 1984a.

National Commission on the Causes and Prevention of Violence (1969). *Violence in America*. New York: Signet.

National Council for Civil Liberties (1986). *Stonehenge*. London: NCCL.

Northam, G. (1985). "People May Be Violent . . . They Are Not Enemies to be Destroyed", *The Listener*, 31 Oct.

—— (1986). 'Plastic Bullets: A Shot in the Dark which Could Prove Fatal', *Listener*, 17 July.

—— (1988). *Shooting in the Dark*. London: Faber & Faber.

Ouseley, H. (1987). 'The Way Forward: Proposals and Prospects', in Benyon and Solomos, 1987b.

Oxford, K. G. (1981). *Public Disorder on Merseyside, July–August 1981: Report to the Merseyside, Police Committee*. Liverpool: Merseyside Police.

Palmer, S. H. (1988). *Police and Protest in England and Ireland, 1780–1850*. Cambridge: Cambridge Univ. Press.

Parry, G., Moyser, G., and Wagstaff, M. (1985). 'The Crowd and the Community: Context, Content and Aftermath', in G. Gaskell and R. Benewick (eds.), *The Crowd in Contemporary Britain*. London: Sage.

Piven, F. F., and Cloward, R. A. (1977). *Poor People's Movements*. New York: Random House.

Platt, A. (ed.) (1971). *The Politics of Riot Commissions 1917–1970*. New York: Macmillan.

Platt, S. (1985). 'The Innocents of Broadwater Estate', *New Society*, 11 Oct.

Policy Studies Institute (1983*a*). *Police and People in London*, vol. 1: *A Survey of Londoners*, by D. J. Smith, London: PSI.
—— (1983*b*). *Police and People in London*, vol. ii: *A Group of Young Black People*, by S. Small. London: PSI.
—— (1983*c*). *Police and People in London*, vol. iv: *The Police in Action*, by D. J. Smith and J. Gray. London: PSI.
Power, P. (1988). 'Control on the Move', *Police Review*, 18 Mar.
Quarantelli, E. L., and Dynes, R. (1968). 'Looting in Civil Disorders: An Index of Social Change', in Masotti and Bowen, 1968.
Rae, A. (1987). 'The Medals of the Met.', *Police Review*, 30 Jan.
Rainwater, L. (1967). 'Open Letter on White Justice and the Riots', *Transaction*, Sept.
Reed, D., and Adamson, O. (1985). *Miners' Strike 1984–1985: People Versus State*. London: Larkin.
Reicher, S. D. (1984). 'The St. Paul's Riot: An Explanation of the Limits of Crowd Action in Terms of a Social Identity Model', *European Journal of Social Psychology*, 14.
Reiner, R. (1981). 'Black and Blue: Race and the Police', *New Society*, 17 Sept.
—— (1984). 'Is Britain Turning into a Police State?', *New Society*, 2 Aug.
—— (1985*a*). *Politics of the Police*. Brighton, Sussex: Wheatsheaf.
—— (1985*b*). 'Police and Race Relations', in Baxter and Koffman, 1985.
—— (1985*c*). 'Retrospect on the Riots', *New Society*, 25 Oct.
Richards, M. D. (1986). *Public Disorder in Tottenham, 6th October 1985*. London: Metropolitan Police.
Roach, J. (1985). 'The French Police', in Roach and Thomaneck, 1985.
Roach, J., and Thomaneck, J. (eds.) (1985). *Police and Public Order in Europe*. London: Croom Helm.
Roberts, B. R. (1973). 'Arms for the Police', *Police College Magazine*, 12/4.
Rock, P. (1981). 'Rioting', *London Review of Books*, 17–30 Sept.
Rodrigues, R. (1981). 'The Riots of 81', *Marxism Today*, Oct.
Rogaly, J. (1977). *Grunwick*. Harmondsworth, Middx.: Penguin.
Rollo, J. (1979). 'The Special Patrol Group', in Hain *et al.*, 1979.
Rosenhead, J. (1973). 'Rubber Bullets and Riot Control', *New Scientist*, 14 June.
—— (1976). 'A New Look at "Less Lethal" Weapons', *New Scientist*, 16 Dec.
—— (1981). 'The Technology of Riot Control', *New Scientist*, 91.
—— and Shallice, T. (1978). 'A Blunt Weapon', *New Scientist*, 88.
—— and Smith, P. J. (1971). 'Ulster Riot Control: A Warning', *New Scientist and Science Journal*, 81.
*Royal Commission on Police Powers* (1929). Cmnd. 3297, London: HMSO.
Rubenstein, J. (1973). *City Police*. New York: Farrar, Strauss & Giroux.
Rudé, G. (1964). *The Crowd in History*. New York: Wiley.
Ryder, C. (1989). *The RUC: A Force Under Fire*. London: Methuen.
Sanford, J. P. (1976). 'Medical Aspects of Riot Control (Harrassing) Agents', *Annual Review of Medicine*, 27.

Scarman, Rt. Hon. the Lord (1975). *The Red Lion Square Disorders of 15 June 1974*. Cmnd. 5915, London: HMSO.

—— (1981). *The Brixton Disorders 10–12 April 1981: Report of an Inquiry by the Rt. Hon. The Lord Scarman, O.B.E.* Cmnd. 8427, London: HMSO.

Scraton, P. (1985). *The State of the Police*. London: Pluto Press.

—— (ed.) (1987). *Law, Order and the Authoritarian State*. Milton Keynes: Open Univ. Press.

Select Committee on Home Affairs (1986). *Racial Attacks and Harassment*. London: HMSO.

Select Committee on Race Relations and Immigration (1972). *Police Immigrant Relations*. London: HMSO.

Shallice, T. (1981). 'The Harmless Bullet that Kills', *New Statesman*, 14 Aug.

Sieghart, P. (1978). 'Harmless Weapons: A Threat to Liberty?', *New Scientist*, 88.

Silverman, J. (1986). *Independent Inquiry into the Handsworth Disturbances, September 1985*. Birmingham: City of Birmingham District Council.

Sim, J., Scraton, P., and Gordon, P. (1987). 'Introduction: Crime, the State and Critical Analysis', in Scraton, 1987.

Silvanandan, A. (1982). 'From Resistance to Rebellion: Asian and Afro-Caribbean Struggles in Britain', *Race and Class*, 23/2–3.

Skolnick, J. H. (1969). *The Politics of Protest: A Task Force Report to the National Commission on the Causes and Prevention of Violence*. New York: Simon & Schuster.

Smelser, N. J. (1962). Theory of Collective Behaviour. London: Routledge & Kegan Paul.

Smith, A. T. H. (1987). *Offences Against Public Order*. London: Sweet & Maxwell.

Snyder, S. H. (1986). *Drugs and the Brain*. New York: Scientific American.

Spencer, S. (1985). 'The Eclipse of the Police Authority', in Fine and Millar, 1985.

Stark, R. (1972). *Police Riots: Collective Violence and Law Enforcement*. Belmont, Calif.: Wadsworth Press.

State Research (1981). *Policing the Eighties: The Iron Fist*. State Research Pamphlet No. 2, London: Independent Research Publications.

Stead, P. J. (1977). 'The New Police', in D. H. Bayley (ed.), *Police and Society*. Beverly Hills, Calif.: Sage.

—— (1983). *The Police of France*. New York: Macmillan.

—— (1985). *The Police of Britain*. New York: Macmillan.

Stevenson, J. (1980). 'The BUF, the Metropolitan Police and Public Order', in K. Lunn and R. C. Thurlow (eds.), *British Fascism*. London: Croom Helm.

Stobart, R. (1989). 'Gunning for Justice', *Police Review*, 6 Jan.

Storch, R. (1975). 'The Plague of Blue Locusts: Police Reform and Popular Resistance in Northern England 1840–57', *International Review of Social History*, 20.

*Sunday Times* Insight Team (1985). *Strike*. London: Coronet.

Sykes, G., and Matza, D. (1957). 'Techniques of Neutralization: A Theory of Delinquency', *American Sociological Review*, 22.

Tajfel, H. (1981). *Human Groups and Social Categories*. Cambridge: Cambridge Univ. Press.

Taylor, I. (1971). 'Soccer Consciousness and Soccer Hooliganism', in S. Cohen (ed.), *Images of Deviance*. Harmondsworth, Middx.: Penguin.

Taylor, S. (1984). 'The Scarman Report and Explanations of Riots', in Benyon, 1984*a*.

Thurlow, R. (1987). *Fascism in Britain*. Oxford: Blackwell.

Tilly, C. (1969). 'Collective Violence in European Perspective', in National Commission on the Causes and Prevention of Violence, 1969.

Tomlinson, T. M. (1968). 'Riot Ideology among Urban Negroes', in Masotti and Bowen, 1968.

Trow, M. J. (1958). 'Small Businessmen, Political Tolerance, and Support for McCarthy', *American Journal of Sociology*, 64.

Turner, R. H., and Killain, L. M. (1957). *Collective Behaviour*. Englewood Cliffs, NJ: Prentice Hall.

Uglow, S. (1988). *Policing Liberal Society*. Oxford: Oxford Univ. Press.

Waddington, D., Jones, K., and Critcher, C. (1987). 'Flashpoints of Public Disorder', in G. Gaskell and R. Benewick (eds.), *The Crowd in Contemporary Britain*. London: Sage.

—— —— (1989). *Flashpoints: Studies in Public Disorder*. London: Routledge.

Waddington, P. A. J. (1985). *The Effects of Manpower Depletion During the NUM Strike, 1984–85*. London: Police Foundation.

—— (1988). 'The Unacceptable Price of a Routinely Armed Police', *Independent*, 7 Jan.

—— (1989). 'Beware the Shot in the Dark', *Police*, 21/6.

Walker, D. (1968). *Rights in Conflict: The Violent Confrontation of Demonstrators and Police during the Week of the Democratic National Convention*. New York: Bantam.

Ward, T. (1986). *Death and Disorder: Three Case Studies of Public Order Policing in London*. London: Inquest.

Whelan, C. J. (1985). 'Military Intervention in Democratic Societies: The Role of Law', in R. Rowe and C. J. Whelan (eds.), *Military Intervention in Democratic Societies*. London: Croom Helm.

Wolfinger, R. E., Wolfinger, B. K., Prewitt, K., and Rosenhack, S. (1964). 'America's Radical Right: Politics and Ideology', in Apter, 1964.

Wright, P. (1985). *Policing the Coal Industry Dispute in South Yorkshire*. Sheffield: South Yorkshire Police.

Wright, S. (1977). 'An Assessment of the New Technologies of Repression', in M. Hoefnagels (ed.), *Repression and Repressive Violence*. The Hague, Swets & Zeitlinger.

—— (1978). 'New Police Technologies: An Exploration of the Social Implications and Unforeseen Impacts of Some Recent Developments', *Journal of Peace Research*, 15/4.

Yardley, M. (1986). 'Wrong', *Police*, 18/6.

—— and Eliot, P. (1986*a*). 'Is Police Firearms Training Good Enough?, *Police*, 18/9.

—— —— (1986*b*). 'The Case for Special Units', *Police*, 18/10.

—— —— (1986*c*). 'Wanted: A National Firearms School', *Police*, 18/11.

Yardley, M., and Eliot, P. (1986c). 'Wanted: A National Firearms School', *Police*, 18/11.

Zimbardo, P. G. (1970). 'The Human Choice: Individuation, Reason, and Order versus Deindividuation, Impulse and Chaos', in W. J. Arnold and D. Levine (eds.), *Nebraska Symposium on Motivation*, vol. xvii. Lincoln, Nebr.: Univ. of Nebraska.

# INDEX